For M. Francis Abraham

my first colleague

THIRD WORLD MEDICINE AND SOCIAL CHANGE

A Reader in
Social Science
and Medicine

Edited by

John H. Morgan

UNIVERSITY
PRESS OF
AMERICA

LANHAM • NEW YORK • LONDON

Copyright © 1983 by

University Press of America,™ Inc.

4720 Boston Way
Lanham, MD 20706

3 Henrietta Street
London WC2E 8LU England

Printed in the United States of America

ISBN (Perfect): 0-8191-3420-1
ISBN   (Cloth): 0-8191-3419-8

Library of Congress Catalog Card Number : 83-12542

ACKNOWLEDGEMENTS

There are numerous individuals to whom expressions of thanks must be stated. First, to my wife, Linda, and my three daughters, Kendra, Bethany, and Kyna, who endured the hours of typing and the weeks of bombardment with Third World medicine tabletalk and telephone interruptions. While the book was in final form, the farm was buzzing with activity—the sows were farrowing, the turkeys and chickens arrived from the hatchery, the rabbits had litters every one, the calves broke into the orchard, and the ponies went unridden. For my family's tolerance, indeed, support during the editing process, I am most grateful.

To Father Robley Edward Whitson and Prof. Bhabagrahi Misra, my anthropology teachers, I express gratitude for stimulating my interest in the Third World. To George Davy who encouraged me to think of pharmacology from a broader perspective than the textbook and to the community of Notre Dame for countless aid in time, money, and understanding.

Finally, to Gregory Peploe soon to be at Purdue University who served as my copy editor for his care in reading and his tolerance of my impatience, I am most appreciative.

TABLE OF CONTENTS

PREFACE

Amidst the acceleration of a converging world, the inequities and dispari-
ties become strikingly evident. Whether in terms of educational opportunities, scientific and industrial technologies, communications networks
or agricultural development, the gap of quality and accessibility which
exists between world societies constitutes one of the major crises facing
the human community. Nowhere is this gap broader and more complicated
than in the field of health care.

The nature and quality of health care and its delivery varies profoundly
from culture to culture and society to society. Those socio-cultural
and politico-economic factors which contribute to this disparity constitute
a formidable force in the deterrence of quality health care delivery to
many peoples of the world. In scientifically developed societies of the
world, advancement in medical technology and in the mechanisms for
the delivery of quality health care to most of its people is normative,
perceived by some governments and societies as more than a privilege,
rather as a right of citizens. Not so, however, in much of the world.

The study of the social and cultural dimensions of medicine and health
care is a central activity of the social sciences. The nature and function
of folk medicine, the social impact western medicine has on traditional
societies, the cultural aspects of the healing process in Third World countries, the complexities or absence of health delivery institutions in developing societies all come within the pail of social scientific study of medicine
and health care.

In the following collection of previously unpublished essays, a concerted
effort has been put forth to provide the reader with a sense of the breadth
of issues in the field of Third World medicine and social change as well
as to acquaint the reader with a serious understanding of several specific
instances of applied social science in the study of health care--the first
chapter is illustrative of the sophistication of the application of the
science in our own society and is included to assist the student's perception
of the depth of present-day research applied in our own medical system
of delivery.

There has been the intentional absence of a pre-determined ideology or
standarized methodology to which each contributor must conform. On
the contrary, the following collection of recently conducted research
(predominantly data-base field studies in developing societies), represents
a broad spectrum of theoretical options and methodological alternatives
in the study of medicine and social change in the Third World.

John H. Morgan   Notre Dame, Indiana

CHAPTER I

HOSPITALS AND PHYSICIANS: A SOCIAL NETWORK ANALYSIS
OF PHYSICIANS' ADOPTION OF A MEDICAL INNOVATION

James G. Anderson

with Stephen J. Jay, Pamela A. Gray-Toft, and Frank P. Lloyd

abstract

Theory and research suggest that the diffusion of innovation is highly dependent upon the social network that links members of a reference group. Diffusion of new procedures and techniques generally takes place in two steps. First, individuals who have contacts outside of the local group learn of the new approach and adopt it. Subsequently, other group members who come into contact with these innovators adopt the innovation. The process is also influenced by characteristics of the innovation itself. This model was tested with data from 24 physicians who belong to a private group practice. It was hypothesized that use of a computerized hospital medical information system by these physicians would be low due to the functional nature of such a system. Second, it was hypothesized that utilization would be related to the physician's location in the professional network linking him to his colleagues. Third, it was hypothesized that physicians involved in professional and administrative roles outside of the group would be more likely to use the system. Findings of the study confirm all three hypotheses. The information system was utilized extensively by only six of the 24 physicians five years after the system's installation at the hospital. The two factors found to be significant predictors of utilization werre the physician's location in the professional network and degree of involvement in professional/administrative activities. The implications of these findings for efforts to introduce new medical technology or to change established practices among physicians are discussed.

* * *

INTRODUCTION

Studies of the diffusion of medical innovations have, for the most part, focused on organizational adoption rather than physician utilization. There is evidence that the two decisions are somewhat independent. For example, Cromwell et al. (1975) found utilization rates of expensive capital equipment in Boston hospitals to be only 50-60 percent of capacity. Moreover, wide and unexplained variations in utilization of routine established practices as well as new procedures exist even within institutions and organized group practices. Freeborn's et al. (1972) study

1

of physicians in a prepaid group practice found wide-spread variation in the use of laboratory services. Anderson et al. (1981) found that only 20 percent of a hospital's medical staff utilized a computerized medical information system for direct order entry five years after the system's implementation. Walker (1980) reported a similar experience with the Exeter System in Scotland. After four years, only two practices involving 11 physicians utilized an on-line medical information system. A recent extensive review of the research on the adoption and utilization of medical technology (Greer, 1981: 141) concluded that "Clearly the social and psychological variables that may intervene in decisions to use a particular procedure or technology are still not understood."

Theory and research suggest several factors that may affect the diffusion of medical innovations. A large number of studies have demonstrated the importance of an individual's location in the social network that links him/her to a reference group (Rogers, 1962; Rogers and Shoemaker, 1971). In general, individuals centrally located in the communication network are more likely to be early adopters of innovations; whereas, marginal individuals may not adopt the innovation at all. Location appears to affect adoption by providing individuals with information about new approaches as well as by exposing them to the influence and support of others who have adopted the innovation. The adoption process involves much more than exposure to technical information concerning the availability of new equipment, drugs, and/or procedures. Rather peers who have adopted an innovation are the most important source of information concerning costs, effectiveness, risks, and professional acceptance of the new approach (Becker, 1970a, b).

A second set of factors influencing adoption has to do with characteristics of the individual. Early adopters generally are individuals who participate in and identify with professional organizations and other professionals outside of their own institution and community. These "cosmopolitans," who tend to be younger, better educated, more mobile, and to have more outside sources of information, usually are the first to become aware of the availability of new approaches and to adopt them. In most instances, they are located at the center of the communication network. These "opinion leaders" are respected by their peers for their technical competence, are viewed as generally conforming to the group's standards and as contributing to the group's interests (Greer, 1977). Coleman's et al. (1966) study of the adoption of new drugs by physicians not only found that early adopters fit this profile, but that other physicians did not adopt the new drug unless they were directly involved in professional contacts with physicians who had.

Attributes of the innovation itself comprise a third important set of factors that influence adoption (Greer, 19771, 1981). Fliegel and Kivlin (1966) found that agricultural innovations perceived as most rewarding, most compatible with existing practices, and least risky were most rapidly adopted. Becker's (1970a, b) study of local health departments found that young cosmopolitan public health officers were the first to adopt

2

an innovation rated as practical, easily communicated, and as generally compatible with existing practices and community interest. In contrast, early adopters of an innovation rated much lower on these attributes were older, more oriented to the local community, and not viewed generally as innovative by their peers. Beckere suggests that this latter group may be responding more to local interests in adopting such innovations.

Another important attribute affecting the rate of diffusion of a medical innovation has to do with its function. The National Academy of Sciences (1979) classified equipment-embodied health care technology as serving clinical, ancillary, or coordinative functions. They concluded that coordinative technology, such as emergency medical services and medical information systems, perceived as not directly associated with patient care and which must be implemented across the departments, suffers from major barriers to its adoption and utilization. In contrast, clinical and ancillary technology is subject to strong pressures for adoption and use.

OBJECTIVES

The purpose of this study was to determine the degree to which the factors reviewed above account for differential utilization of a medical innovation by physicians belonging to the same group practice. The innovation selected by study was a compterized hospital medical information system. This system combines the patient's financial and medical data into a common computer data file which is then available to all departments of the hospital for purposes of patient care, business management, administration, research, and education (Anderson and Jay, 1982). The system was designed to facilitate direct medical order entry through video terminals located on the hospital units. It allows physicians to create, store, and retrieve personal order sets tailored for their own patients (Traska, 1978).

It was hypothesized that physician utilization of the medical information system would be generally low. This is based on the fact that both the initial implementation and subsequent changes in the system require coordination and integration across services and departments of the hospital. Moreover the overall benefits of coordinative technology systems for the hospital and patient generally outweigh the benefits perceived as accruing to the individual physician (National Academy of Sciences, 1979).

It was also hypothesized that the extent to which individual physicians used the medical information system for direct order entry would be related to their location in the professional network linking them to their colleagues. It was predicted that physicians who were the heaviest users of the medical information system would be located closer to the center of the network and would have more frequent professional contracts

3

with one another than with other members of the group practice. At the same time, it was anticipated that non-users of the system would be located on the periphery of the network reflecting their more limited professional relations with colleagues.

Finally, it was hypothesized that physicians who were involved in professional and administrative roles would be more likely to utilize the medical information system than their colleagues who were more exclusively concerned with their own individual patients. This former group of "cosmopolitans" generally uses outside sources to obtain information about the relative advantages and disadvantages of a new approach such as a medical information system. They are also more likely to consider the overall advantages of its adoption rather than focusing entirely on its individual advantages.

METHODS

Subjects

The study was carried out among 24 physicians who comprise a private group practice in a large midwestern city. The group included a number of subspecialties of internal medicine such as cardiology, oncology, neurology, gastroenterology, and infectious diseases. Most of the group's patients who require hospitalization are admitted to a large private, gneral hospital located near the group's office building.

Data Collection

Each physician was interviewed and asked to indicate how many times during the past six weeks he/she had:
(1) Referred a patient to
(2) Consulted about a patient with
(3) Discussed professional matters with
(4) Taken calls for
each of the other physicians in the group. From this data, the matrix shown in **Table 1** was constructed. It indicated the number of different types of professional contact between two physicians during the period of study. A zero indicates no professional contact during the six weeks; a four indicates all four types of professional relations occurred between the two physicians.

Physicians were also asked about their perceptions of the relative advantages of using the medical information system. Actual utilizatin of the computer terminals for direct order entry was obtained from the computer system file. The overall proportion of medical orders entered directly through a terminal on six days was computed for each physician. Additional information concerning the physician's age, specialty, number of patients admitted to the hospital over a six month period and the number of house staff assigned to him for educational purposes were

4

TABLE 1

Professional Relations Among Physicians

Initiating Physician	Responding Physician																							
	A	B	C	D	E	F	G	H	I	J	K	L	M	N	O	P	Q	R	S	T	U	V	W	X
A	-	0	0	1	3	1	3	1	3	1	2	1	0	1	2	0	3	1	0	0	1	1	3	2
B	1	-	0	0	0	1	1	0	2	1	0	1	2	0	0	1	1	0	1	0	0	0	0	1
C	3	0	-	1	0	3	0	3	3	2	0	2	2	1	0	2	1	4	1	1	2	1	0	2
D	3	3	0	-	0	2	0	0	3	2	0	3	3	0	0	0	0	3	1	3	3	2	0	0
E	4	3	1	1	-	3	1	3	3	1	3	1	3	1	1	3	2	1	3	1	1	1	2	1
F	0	0	2	1	1	-	0	0	1	1	1	1	1	1	0	0	1	2	1	2	2	0	0	2
G	2	3	0	0	0	2	-	0	3	0	1	0	1	0	0	1	0	1	1	0	1	0	1	3
H	0	1	1	2	0	0	0	-	2	2	2	1	1	3	0	1	0	0	0	0	1	0	0	0
I	2	0	2	0	0	3	0	1	-	2	2	1	1	1	0	0	2	1	1	2	0	0	1	2
J	3	3	3	1	1	2	1	3	4	-	4	3	3	1	1	3	2	1	3	1	2	1	2	2
K	1	0	0	0	1	1	0	1	2	1	-	1	0	1	0	0	2	2	0	0	0	0	2	0
L	2	3	3	2	2	3	1	3	3	2	1	-	3	3	0	2	2	2	3	3	3	4	0	2
M	1	2	1	1	1	1	2	2	2	2	0	2	-	2	1	2	2	1	2	2	0	3	2	2
N	3	1	3	1	3	3	2	4	4	3	4	3	3	-	0	3	3	1	2	1	3	3	3	2
O	1	0	0	0	1	0	0	0	1	0	0	0	0	0	-	0	1	0	1	1	0	0	1	1
P	0	3	0	0	0	1	2	0	1	1	1	0	1	1	0	-	1	1	1	1	2	1	1	0
Q	3	1	1	1	3	1	1	2	1	2	1	1	1	2	2	2	-	1	2	1	1	1	3	1
R	0	1	2	0	2	3	1	3	3	0	3	1	2	0	0	2	1	-	0	1	2	1	0	2
S	1	2	1	1	1	2	2	1	2	2	2	2	2	1	3	2	2	2	-	1	2	2	2	3
T	0	0	1	1	0	2	1	0	2	0	2	0	2	0	0	2	0	0	0	-	0	0	0	4
U	3	1	2	2	2	3	1	3	3	2	3	4	2	1	1	3	2	2	3	3	-	2	3	3
V	1	1	0	2	0	2	0	0	1	0	1	2	1	0	0	0	1	1	0	0	2	-	1	0
W	2	1	1	0	1	2	0	0	2	0	2	0	2	0	0	2	1	0	2	0	0	0	-	2
X	1	3	1	0	0	2	2	0	1	1	1	1	2	0	1	1	1	1	0	3	1	1	0	-

obtained from hospital records. The physician's professional involvement was coded into three categories: (0) for no professional or administrative activities; (1) for participation on routine hospital committees; (2) for involvement as president of the medical staff, chairman of an important hospital committee, or a leadership position in an outside professional association such as the American Cancer Society.

Social Network Analysis

Smallest space analysis, a form of multidimensional scaling, was used to analyze the structure of the network of professional relations among members of the group practice (Guttman, 1968; Kruskal and Wish, 1978; McFarland and Brown, 1973). The matrix shown in **Table 1**, which indicates the strength of the professional relationship between each pair of physicians, was used as input to the KYST multidimensional scaling program (Kruskal et al., 1973). The analysis results in a spatial representation of the network in two or more dimensions where each point represents a physician. The program attempts to preserve the rank-order of the distances between physicians while, at the same time, arranging them in a space with as few dimensions as possible. Thus, the Euclidean distances among the physicians are a monotonic function of the strength of their original ties. For example, the weaker the professional relationship between two physicians, the farther apart they should be in the spatial configuration. A measure of how well the spatial configuration fits the original data is provided. This measure termed **Stress** ranges from 0 to 1. The larger the stress value, the worse the fit to the original data (Kruskal and Wish, 1978).

The structure of the social network has been examined by identifying how physicians at opposite ends of each dimension systematically differ from one another. This was done by regressing each of a number of physician characteristics on their spatial coordinates (Kruskal and Wish, 1978).

Finally, the relative effect of the physician's location in the professional network on his/her utilization of the computerized medical information system was examined. This analysis involved regressing utilization rates on a distance measure and a number of physician characteristics.

FINDINGS

Results from the multidimensional scaling program indicate that the physician network shown in **Table 1** can be represented by three dimensions. The stress index, which measures goodness of fit, was 0.28 as compared to 0.33 for two dimensions and 0.52 for one dimension. **Figure 1** shows the location of the 24 physicians in the space defined by the three dimensions.

The second step in the analysis was to interpret the three dimensions. This was done by regressing several physician characteristics on the cartesian coordinates that indicate the physician's position in the professional network. The results are shown in **Table 2.**

The x-dimension appears to separate high and low users of the hospital medical information system. The regression co-efficient for this dimension is significant (p < 0.10). Physicians who utilize the system most often for direct medical order entry generally are concentrated in the region around the negative x-axis (Physicians A, B, L, Q, R, U).

FIGURE 1

Three Dimensional Representation of the
Professional Relations Network Among 24 Physicians

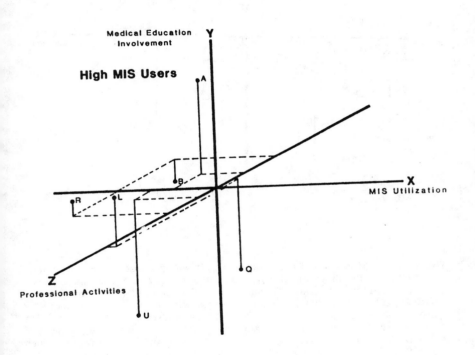

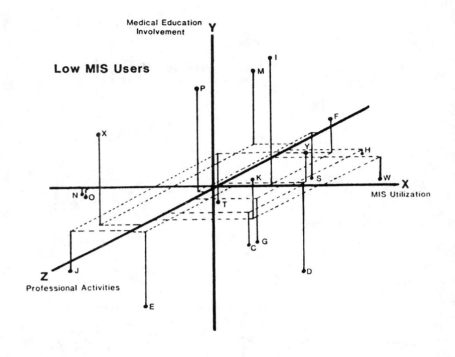

This result confirms the first hypothesis. It was predicted that physicians who utilized the medical information system to enter the majority of their medical orders would be more centrally located in the professinal network and would have frequent contacts with other high users of the system. These contacts serve to provide individual physicians with information concerning new and/or more effective ways of using the system. They also expose the physician to the influence of colleagues who actively use the medical information system in their practice.

Moreover, non-users of the system, as predicted, are generally located on the periphery of the professional network. Physicians N, O, P, and V have never applied for computer codes. Their position in the three dimensional space shown in **Fugure 1** indicates that these physicians have more limited professional contacts with their colleagues. This result is similar to Coleman's et al. (1966) finding that physicians did not adopt a new drug unless they had some professional contact with a colleague who had.

TABLE 2

Multiple Regression of Physician Characteristics on Professional Relations Dimensions

Physician Characteristic	Regression Coefficient			Multiple Correlation Coefficient
	Dimension X	Dimension Y	Dimension Z	
Age	-0.69	-1.85	5.24	0.31
Professional/ Administrative Activities	0.04	-1.13	0.48**	0.38
Medical Education	-0.55	2.78*	-1.01	0.34
Admissions	20.50	-4.60	0.67	0.25
Utilization of MIS	-0.19**	-0.08	0.06	0.39
Attitude Toward MIS	0.20	-0.10	0.22	0.18

* $p < 0.15$ ** $p < 0.10$

The second dimension that differentiates physicians is their degree of involvement in graduate medical education. Physicians with the greatest number of residents assigned to them for clinical training generally cluster in the region around the positive y-axis. This suggests that physicians who are engaged in training house staff have more frequent professional contacts with one another than with their colleagues who are generally not involved in graduate medical education.

The third dimension appears to reflect physician involvement in professional or administrative activities. Physicians located along the positive z-axis are generally involved in professional medical associations or have assumed administrative responsibilities in the hospital. Their relative proximity to one another in the network suggests that these physicians have more frequent professional contacts with one another than with their colleagues who have little or no professional involvement

9

outside of their own private practice. This latter group of physicians, for the most part, is located around the negative end of the z-axis.

On the basis of the findings of other studies of the diffusion of innovation, it was hypothesized that physicians who were involved in professional and and administrative roles outside of their own private practice would be more likely to utilize the medical information system. This hypothesis was tested by regressing computer utilization rates on the index created to measure the physician's professional involvement outside of his/her own practice. Location in the professional network as measured by the x-coordinate, a second factor hypothesized to be related to computer utilization, was introduced into the equation as were the physician's age, subspecialty, degree of involvement in medical education, and perceptions of the benefits of using the medical information system. The results are presented in **Table 3.**

TABLE 3

Regression Analysis Factors Affecting MIS Utilization

Variable	Regression Coefficient	Standard Error	Probability Level
Professional Relations	-0.31	0.12	0.01
Administrative/ Professional Activities	0.18	0.09	0.05
Constant	-0.04	0.13	0.76

R = 0.64

Only two factors were found to be significant predictors of the physician's rate of utilization of the medical information system. These were: location in the network of professional relations and degree of involvement in professional and/or administrative activities. Together these two factors explain 41 percent of the variation in computer utilization rates. The two factors appear to have largely independent effects. Location accounts for 23 percent of the variance explained, while professional administrative activities account for 14 percent. Only 4 percent of the variation in utilization rates is explained by the joint effect of the two variables.

10

The third hypothesis has to do with the effect of characteristics of the innovation on the extent of its utilization. Since medical information systems are a type of coordinative technology where the collective advantages to the hospital staff and patients outweigh the individual advantages perceived by individual physicians, a relatively low level of utilization by physicians was anticipated. Data from the study support this hypothesis. Only six of the 24 physicians comprising the group practice utilized the medical information system to directly enter more than 60 percent of their medical orders. Four physicians had not even applied for a computer code. The remaining 14 physicians utilized the system for order entry less than three percent of the time.

CONCLUSION

The findings of this investigation are important because of the limited number of empirical studies that have dealt with the diffusion of medical technology among physicians. Greer (1977: 529) concludes her extensive review of the literature on the diffusion of innovation in health care organizations by stating that "Available theory depends almost exclusively upon studies which analyze the diffusion of procedures and programs among health organizations." She cites problems of access as a major factor in limiting the number of empirical studies involving physicians as decision makers.

Results of this study confirm the importance of social networks in accounting for differential adoption of medical innovations by physicians. An extensive body of literature suggests a two-step process where by certain individuals first learn about and try a new approach and then influence others to adopt it (Katz et al., 1963; Rogers, 1962; Rogers and Shoemaker, 1971). These innovators are generally individuals who are involved with other professionals outside their local group or community.

In the present study, physicians who heavily utilized the medical information system were more likely to be involved in professional organizations or to have assumed positions of leadership on the hospital's medical staff. Such professional involvement outside of the physician's own private practice may be a critical factor in the adoption of coordinative technology such as a computerized medical information system. In general, there are significant barriers to the diffusion of this type of medical technology (National Academy of Sciences, 1979). Adoption requires cooperation across hospital departments and medical specialties. Also the advantages to the individual physician are not as apparent as are the advantages to the hospital as a whole. Consequently, physicians who are more broadly concerned with the institutiion's well being and its ability to offer high quality patient care may well be the first to adopt new medical technology that promises to further institutional goals. At the same time, adoption of such innovations may increase their own status within the institution and among professional colleagues.

11

The second step in the diffusion process involves interpersonal relations among adopters. Close professional ties to a physician who has adopted some new innovation subjects the other physician to information about the approach, to influence concerning its perceived efficacy, and to support in initial attempts to try the new technique or procedure (Becker, 1970a, b; Coleman et al., 1966).

Results from this study confirm the importance of the physician's location in the professional network in accounting for differential utilization of a medical innovation such as the medical information system. Heavy users of the system were found to have more frequent professional contacts with one another than with colleagues who used the information system to a more limited extent. Moreover, physicians who were without a computer code at all, in general, were located on the periphery of the network indicating limited professional contacts with their colleagues.

The findings of this study have important practical implications as well. Mayer' (1979) review concludes that efforts to change physician behavior by providing information concerning peer behavior have been generally ineffective. His review indicated greater success where personal consultation was involved. Goran (1979) reached the same conclusion in citing the relative lack of success of Professional Standards Review Organizations in correcting problems that were detected. Eisenberg (1977a, 1977b) reported that an educational program that attempted to modify laboratory use by house staff was unsuccessful in bringing about lasting changes in practice.

This study suggests the importance of peer influence both in introducing new approaches and attempting to change established practices. The adoption of medical innovations by physicians might be enhanced by identifying individuals who are most frequently consulted in providing patient care and in discussing professional affairs as was done in this study. These opinion leaders might be encouraged to participate in professional meetings, short courses, and continuing education programs at which new medical technology is discussed, demonstrated, and evaluated. Once these individuals adopt the new approach, diffusion could be facilitated by ensuring that the innovators communicate their experience with and appraisal of the innovation to other physicians. The use of physicians who are part of the professional network to provide information, answer questions, and to overcome difficulties concerning the use of the new techniques or procedure would appear to be preferable to bringing in outside consultants and speakers for the purpose.

REFERENCES

ANDERSON, J.G., P.A. GRAY-TOFT, F.P. LLOYD, and S.J. JAY (1981) "Factors Affecting Physician Utilization of a Computerized Hospital Medical Information System: A Social Network Analysis," pp. 791-796 in PROCEEDINGS OF THE FIFTH ANNUAL SYMPOSIUM ON COMPUTER APPLICATIONS IN MEDICAL CARE. Los Angeles, CA: IEEE Computer Society.

ANDERSON, J.G. and S.J. Jay (1982) "Computerized Hospital Information Systems: Their Future Role in Medicine," JOURNAL OF THE ROYAL SOCIETY OF MEDICINE, 75 (in press).

BAKER, S.R. (1979) "The Diffusion of High Technology Medical Innovations: The Computed Tomography Scanner Example," SOCIAL SCIENCE AND MEDICINE, 130: 155-162.

BECKER, M.H. (1970) "Factors Affecting Diffusion of Innovations Among Health Professionals," AMERICAN JOURNAL OF PUBLIC HEALTH, 60(2): 294-304.

BECKER, M.H. (1970), "Sociometric Location and innovativeness: Reformulation and Extension of the Diffusion Model," AMERICAN SOCIOLOGICAL REVIEW, 35(2): 267-282.

COLEMAN, J.S., E. KATZ, and H. MENZEL (1966) MEDICAL INNOVATION: A DIFFUSION STUDY. Indianapolis, IN: Bobbs-Merrill Company.

CROMWELL, J., P. GENSBERG, D. HAMILTON, and M. SUMMER (1975) "Incentives and Decisions Underlying Hospitals' Adoption of a Major Capital Equipment." Report for NCHSR Contract No. HSM-110-73-513. Cambridge, MA: abt Associates.

EISENBERG, J.M., S.V. WILLIAMS, L. GARNER, R. VIATE, and H. SMITH (1977) "Computer-Based Audit to Direct and Correct Overutilization of Laboratory Tests" MEDICAL CARE 15: 915-921.

EISENBERG, J.M. (1977) "An Educational Program to Modify Laboratory Use By House Staff," JOURNAL OF MEDICAL EDUCATION, 52: 578-581.

FLIEGEL, F.C. and J.E. KIVLIN (1966) "Attributes of Innovations as Factors in Diffusion," AMERICAN JOURNAL OF SOCIOLOGY, 72: 235-248.

FREEBORN, D.K., et al. (1972) "Determinants of Medical Care Utilization: Physicians' ;Use of Laboratory Services," AMERICAN JOURNAL OF PUBLIC HEALTH, 62: 846-853.

GORAN, M.J. (1979) "The Evolution of the PSRO Hospital Review System," MEDICAL CARE, 17(5) (Supplement).

GORDON, G. and G.L. GISHER (1975) THE DIFFUSION OF MEDICAL TECHNOLOGY. Cambridge, MA: Ballinger Publishing Company.

GREER, A.L. (1977) "Advances in the Study of Diffusion of Innovation in Health Care Organization," HEALTH AND SOCIETY/MILBANK MEMORIAL FUND QUARTERLY, 55(4): 505-632.

Greer, A.L. (1981) "Medical Technology Assessment, Diffusion, and Utilization," JOURNAL OF MEDICAL SYSTEMS, 5(1/2): 129-145.

GUTTMAN, L. (1968) "A General Nonmetric Technique for Finding the Smallest Coordinate Space for a Configuration of Points, PSYCHOMETRIKA, 33: 369-506.

KATZ, E., M.L. LEVIN and H. HAMILTON (1963) "Traditions of Research on the Diffusion of Innovation," AMERICAN SOCILOGICAL REVIEW, 28: 237-252.

KRUSKAL, J.B. and M. WISH (1978) MULTIDIMENSIONAL SCALING. Beverly Hills, CA: Sage Publications.

KRUSKAL, J.B., F.W. YOUNG, and J.B. SEERY (1973) "How to Use KYST, a Very Flexible Program to Do Multidimensional Scaling and Unfolding," Murray Hill, NJ: Bell Laboratories.

McFARLAND, D. and D. BROWN (1973) "Social Distance as a Metric: A Systematic Analysis," pp. 213-253 in E.O. Laumann, BONDS OF PLURALISM: THE FORM AND SUBSTANCE OF URBAN SOCIAL NETWORKS. NY: Wiley Interscience.

MAYERS, A. (1979) "Doing Unto Others as Others Do: Inducing Change in Physician Behavior by Citing Peer-Based Norms." Paper presented at the Urban Research Center. University of Wisconsin-Milwaukee.

NATIONAL ACADEMY OF SCIENCES, Committee on Technology and Health Care (1979). MEDICAL TECHNOLOGY AND THE HEALTH CARE SYSTEM: A STUDY OF THE DIFFUSION OF EQUIPMENT-EMBODIED TECHNOLOGY. Washington, DC.

ROBERS, E.M. (1962) DIFFUSION OF INNOVATIONS. New York: The Free Press.

ROGERS, E.M. and F.F. SHOEMAKER (1971) COMMUNICATION OF INNOVATIONS: A CROSS-CULTURAL APPROACH NY: Free Press.

RUSSELL, L.B. (1979) TECHNOLOGY IN HOSPITALS: MEDICAL ADVANCES AND THEIR DIFFUSION. Washington, D.C.: The Brookings

Institution.

TRASKA, M.R. (1978) "Methodist of Indiana Tailors Patient Computer System to Hospital Routine," MODERN HEALTHCARE, 8(10): 34-39.

WALKER, C.H.M. (1980) "Batch or 'On-Line' for Child Health-A Review," BRITISH MEDICAL JOURNAL, 281: 90-92.

CHAPTER 2

AN AMERICAN CONTRIBUTION TO THIRD WORLD MEDICINE: SPINAL MANIPULATIVE THERAPY

Robert T. Anderson

INTRODUCTION

For well over a decade, the American medical community has shown more than a mere scholarly interest in the traditional medical systems of Asia. At various medical centers in the Unted States today one encounters scientists attempting to evaluate old treatment techniques as well as physicians who are incorporating them into their practice (American Herbal, 1946; Siegel, 1979). Most impressive in this new openness to ancient forms of medicine is the widespread acceptance of Chinese acupuncture for the control of pain (American Acupuncture, 1976). Medical investigators looking to South Asia have also borrowed heavily in the realm of meditational techniques. Herbert Benson, M.D., Associate Professor of Medicine at the Harvard Medical School and Director of the Hypertension Section of Boston's Beth Israel Hospital, exemplifies this clinical interest. He adapted the meditational techniques of Maharishi Mahesh Yogi for use in the treatment of essential hypertension (Benson and Klipper, 1973).

Although Western medicine has utilized or adapted ancient practices from Asia, borrowing in the opposite direction has almost completely failed to take place. Indeed, it is not generally realized that the West has traditional medical practices to offer. Homeopathy, widely practiced in India, is only an apparent exception, since it emerged in the early nineteenth century as a divergent approach within medicine. Its founder, Samuel Hahnemann, was a German physician, and early homeopaths were all medical doctors (Coulter, 1970).

The West, however, does have a traditional form of health care that is now widely practiced in Europe and America. At a workshop held at the National Institutes of Health in Washington, D.C., it was agreed that the generic name for this approach should be spinal manipulative therapy [SMT] (Goldstein, 1975). Primarily an American development, it rivals the age of many Asian practices to the extent that it has roots in the ancient European folk practice of bone-setting (Schiotz and Cyriax, 1975).

SMT first emerged as an elaborated system of health care in the 1870's when Andrew Taylor Still created the field of osteopathy (Northup, 1966). The first institution to train practitioners of osteopathy was opened in 1892 in Kirksville, Missouri, where graduates were given the degree of Doctor of Osteopathy (D.O.). Three years later, the second major school of spinal manipulative therapy appeared on the scene in another midwestern town when Daniel David Palmer, a self-educated frontiersman, began to practice what was eventually termed chiropractic. Schools were founded offering the degree of Doctor of Chiropractic (D.C.) (Gibbons, 1981). Eventually the approach of SMT was adopted by a small number of medical doctors who refer to their work as manipulative medicine, manual medicine, or orthopedic medicine (Schiotz and Cyriax, 1975). Even more recently, SMT emerged as a speciality of certain physical therapists who identify themselves as orthopedic manipulative therapists.

DEFINITION OF THE FIELD

Osteopaths, chiropractors, practitioners of manual medicine and orthopedic manipulative therapists insist that they differ to some degree in what they do. Indeed, even within any one of these disciplines, factions divide advocates into differing and sometimes hostile camps. Yet they are alike to this extent: all aproach the treatment of musculo-skeletal lesions (Tyle M disorders) by identifying disfuction in the vertebral architecture that can be corrected through the application of carefully calculated vectors of forces administered by the hands of the clinician.

The purpose in administering an adjustive or manipulative thrust is to move the vertebra, sacrum, innominate or occiput in a way that will break fixations of the apophyseal, sacro-iliac, atlanto-occipital, unco-vertebral or other joints, including those composed of intervertebral discs. Relief from pain, tenderness, paresthesia, contraction, spasm, and limited range of motion frequently follows. These techniques appear to be most effective in the treatment of musculo-skeletal symptoms deriving from mechanical disfunctions that evince either in the spine as such (i.e., simple backache), or in closely associated areas (e.g., headache, torticollis, brachialgia, lumbago, or sciatica). This belief that SMT is effective in the treatment of Type M disorders is based primarily upon clinical experience, however. The amount of research completed at this time is still small, and while it tends to support the claims of SMT, it is far from conclusive (Anderson, 1980).

Osteopathy and chiropractic orginated as self-contained healing systems in which it was claimed that the effectiveness of SMT went beyond the cure of Type M disorders. The central nervous system, housed in the cranium and the neural canal of the vertebral column, was considered so essential to proper health, and so vulnerable to lesions in its osseous encasement, that all disease was thought to originate from the failure of these structures. Hence it followed in traditional thought that healing would take place if the integrity of the system could be restored through repositioning misaligned vertebrae. Doctors of osteopathy and doctors of chiropractic claimed a high success rate in treating high blood pressure, peptic ulcers, sinusitis, asthma, diabetes and other disorders with

18

substantial autonomic nervous system or psychogenic components. Thus, osteopaths and chiropractors set themselves up as general practitioners who treated all types of organic or visceral disease (Type O disorders) as well as musculo-skeletal problems.

These claims for success in the treatment of Type O disorders brought chiropractors and osteopaths into disrepute within the medical community. The Commission of Inquiry (1979: 42, 56) established by the governor-general of New Zealand to evaluate the efficacy of chiropractic, while concluding that SMT worked well in Type M disorders, rejected these broader claims. "It is the chiropractors' claims of success in treatment of the Type O category which principally strains the credulity of medical practitioners, and in their minds invalidates the whole chiropractic system." Most chiropractors and osteopaths today admit that their methods are either ineffective for Type O disorders or, where beneficial, are unpredictable. They continue to claim success in Type M disorders, however, where most critics are also willing to admit that they probably can be effective, and advance only limited claims in the treatment of Type O disorders.

THE POTENTIAL FOR DEVELOPING NATIONS

Osteopathy and chiropractic grew to early success in the American midwest at a time when the ecnomy was land based, and farmers frequently suffered from Type M disorders (McCorkle, 1961). Osteopaths and chiropractors offered quick relief from this type of pain and incapacity without the need for expensive drugs and facilities. All they required was their hands, and a bench upon which to place the patient.

In developing nations, conditions resemle those of the nineteenth century American frontier. Hard manual labor characterizes populations who work close to the soil. People frequently suffer from Type M disorders.

This became clear in February, 1982, when I participated in a public health survey carried out in an agricultural community in the Tanahu District of Nepal. Led by Drs. Carl Taylor, Henry Taylor and Melvyn Thorne of Johns Hopkins University and the Woodlands Institute, and by Drs. Mathura Shresta and Dev Khota of the Institute of Medicine, a survey of 213 households revealed that in slightly over half (53.5%), at least one member had some form of active orthopedic problem at the time of inquiry. In just under half of the 213 households (47.9%), these orthopedic problems could be localized to the neck or spine, precisely the kind of Type M disorder for which SMT is indicated. Other surveys in Nepal report similar findings (Taylor-Ide, et al, n.d.; Voorhees and Taylor-Ide, n.d.).

Traditional forms of medicine, whether Asian or American, clearly made claims in the past that went far beyond a demonstrated capacity to produce cures, yet they were effective in some ways. In the West, the search

19

for effectiveness in certain old Asian techniques has led to new applications in modern hospitals. In the East, borrowing western traditional practices has scarcely begun. It would seem, however, that a most promising place to begin might well be to apply the techniques of osteopathy and chiropractic to the treatment of Type M disorders. The high incidence of back and neck pain uncovered in surveys in Nepal would, at the very least, justify further exploration of this possibility.

THE COMPATIBILITY OF MEDICAL THEORIES

In advocating the potentiality of SMT for inclusion in Third World Medicine, one must ask if the medical theory that is used to "explain" SMT is compatible with the medical theory that sanctions other health practices in Third World nations. Since the various approaches to SMT differ somewhat, we will confine our attention to chiropractic, which is the most widely practied version of these variants. Additionally, since each society has its own history and theory of medicine, this question is also best approached by confining our study to a specific nation. We shall explore chiropractic as it might acculturate to health care in the People's Republic of China (PRC).

In recent months, the opportunity to carry out that assessment occurred when an outstanding Chinese specialist was brought to San Francisco for six months under the joint sponsorship of the Pacific Medical Center and of the United States-China Educational Institute, wherein I serve as a member of the Board of Advisors.

The specialist is Xie Zhu-fan, M.D., who is trained in both Western and traditional Chinese medicine. An internist, Dr. Xie is an associate professor in the Department of Internal Medicine at Beijing Medical College. Fully trained in traditional Chinese medicine as well, Dr. Xie simultaneously holds the post of Head of the Department of Traditional Chinese Medicine in the same institution. Conversant in both medical systems, he plays a leading role in China's efforts to integrate the two systems.

Based upon recent encounters with Dr. Xie, one can speculate upon the kind of reception chiropractic might expect if it were to be advocated in contemporary China. The conclusion can be stated at the outset. From all that can be known at this time, chiropractic would probably earn itself a very positive response.

This finding that chiropractic might well fit in with other health practices in China is based upon the observation that traditional Chinese medicine and chiropractic are remarkably alike in their underlying theories. This is evident, for example, in a shared devotion to technologically simple approaches to health care.

Chiropractic can be practiced by the use of the doctor's hands alone.

20

Tables, heat-sensing devices and X-ray setups may be used to extend the competence of the practitioner; but, in the final analysis, a chiropractor needs only his or her hands for palpating and adjusting patients. This very simplicity, in fact, is one of the most impressive advantages of bringing SMT to any underdeveloped nation where budgets for health care are necessarily small.

Traditional Chinese medicine, too, is a low-technology system. Acupuncture may be enhanced with adjunctive devices such as electrical stimulation and infrared heat. It can, however, be practiced with only a set of long, sharp needles. Ultimately, by direct pressure of the fingers upon selected acupoints, it may be practiced with the hands alone in the system known as acupressure.

In comparing these Chinese and American systems, other similarities also are found. Through the use of message, Chinese practitioners manipulate soft tissue rather than the bones and joints to which chiropractors address themselves. It is striking, however, that the theory behind Chinese massage includes the chiropractic principle that the specific effect may take place at some distance from the area touched by the practitioner's hands (Huard and Wong, 1972: 52-53). The same principle is also articulated for acupuncture. Through deep massage at the occiput, for example, Chinese practitioners find that they can bring down high blood pressure, a practice analogous to that of chiropractors.

Chinese medicine even includes an acknowledgment of the spine "...as a canal linking the cerebral cavities with the genitalia," a point of view found widely throughout South Asia and the Far East (Huard and Wong, 1972: 54). The key importance of the spine, of course, is a central tenet of chiropractic theory.

It is especially striking that, in its deepest, most general form, the theory of disease causation is essentially identical for both systems. At times, both intervene directly to resolve musculoskeletal problems--Type M disorders. Chiropractors do this by adjusting subluxated vertebrae. Acupuncturists, in a comparable manner, often insert their needles for the palliative effect they may exert upon musculoskeletal pain.

Chiropractors, however, may also treat organic lesions, the Type O disorders. In cases of this nature, they do not speak of direct intervention. Rather, according to chiropractic theory, the goal is to remove neurological stress that results from minor derangements of vertebral alignment, the well-known spinal subluxations. In this manner, they enhance the functioning of all systems of the body so that natural defense mechanisms can clear out athogens and restore health. As chiropractic philosophers have put it, by removing nerve interference caused by vertebral subluxations, the innatge intelligence of the body is freed to fight off disease. Thus, chiropractors do not concern themselves with specific countermeasures against microbes and the symptoms that they

21

produce. Rather, they concern themselves with the body as a holistic system which, when in good adjustment, can fight off infection and degeneration.

Chinese doctors also treat Type O disorders. A master acupuncturist in San Francisco, for example, advertises, "Treatment of: Skin Problems, Chronic Coughing, Urinary System, Nerve and Muscular System, Digestive System, Nervousness and Mental Problems, Joint Pain, Back Problems and Other Disorders." Dr. Xie speaks more conservatively, on the basis of clinical trials, of partial success in the treatment of influenza, hepatitis and glomerulonephritis.

At issue here is not the scope and success of traditional practice. Rather, it is the medical theory upon which such practice is based, and that theory shows remarkable parrallels to the theory of chiropractic. Thus, Dr. Xie argues that a pathogenic factor, as as <u>Mycobacterium</u> <u>tuberculosis</u>, does not cause sickness. Many are exposed to these disease-producing microbes, yet only some get sick. Clearly, the pathogenic factor itself is not enough to cause disease.

This, of course, was also the position taken by Robert Koch, the German microbiologist who first identified disease-producing microorganisms. When Dr. Koch identified the tubercle bacillus in 1882, he referred to it as the necessary cause of tuberculosis, but not the sufficient cause. That principle is congenial to both chiropractors and Chinese traditional doctors.

The Chinese equivalent to the chiropractic concept of innate intelligence is the concept of q̲i̲, which can be translated as "vital energy." While many are exposed to tuberculosis, only those who have an insufficiency of vital energy will succumb. To fight off disease, then, the microorganism is not the focus of the doctor's efforts. Rather, the goal of therapy is to strengthen body resistance. In the words of Dr. Xie, "We treat the patient, not the disease." A chiropractic doctor would say the same.

Both systems are based upon this fundamental and scientifically indisputable principle that doctors do not cure disease; they merely prepare the patient's body so that it can resist or eliminate lesions. Chiropractors are distinguished by their skills in correcting maladjusted vertebrae. Chinese traditional doctors, in contrast, rely primarily upon herbal medications and acupuncture. (Both schools, of course, may invoke other modalities as well.) This fundamental sameness in medical theory, combined with thoroughly different modes of therapy, is precisely what gives so much promise to the effort to integrate chiropractic into Chinese health care practices. Chiropractic theory is understandable and meaningful to the Chinese, while chiropractic skills offer otherwise unknown techniques for achieving the goals of good health care.

THE PRECEDENT OF ACCEPTANCE

One issue of medical theory remains as we contemplate the potential for chiropractic in the PRC. Is Chinese medical theory open enough to permit the incorporation of some form of SMT into their present system of practice?

That the answer is affirmative is suggested by findings in Chinese societies in which SMT is already part of the medical mix available to patients. In 1979, I visited every chiropractor and osteopath in Hong Kong. The one osteopath in Hong Kong has abandoned his practice because of licensing problems, but seven chiropractors were intereviewed and observed in their work.

The overwhelming majority of the patients of these practitioners were found to be Chinese in culture. Of course, the Chinese of Hong Kong are greatly westernized in comparison with the population of mainland China, so perhaps they are more receptive to a western form of treatment. To the extent, however, that their health attitudes remain culturally Chinese, the success of these chiropractors provides a model for success on a much bigger scale if chiropractice were to be made available to the one billion residents of the People's Republic of China.

The addition of this American system of traditional medicine did not appear to conflict with indigenous forms of practice. On the contrary, health practices in Hong Kong are highly eclectic. Health care is provided by a variety of practitioners: some highly specialized; others practicing a variety of modalities. These include ocularists, aurists, bonesetters, acupuncturists, herbal doctors, herbal pharmacists, native dentists, cuppers, barber-masseurs, street-pavement practitioners, monk healers and lama doctors as well as Western doctors, dentists and optometrists.

According to Dr. Marjorie Topley (1975: 252), patients are not troubled by this diversity of medical theory and pratice. "People in Hong Kong may wander in and out of these idea systems or sub-systems, using different specialists and techniques for handling problems of health." Expanding the number of systems to include chiropractic thus requires no sharp break with Chinese medical culture.

ORGANIZATIONAL ISSUES IN ACCULTURATION

The international, urban-industrial world of Hong Kong includes the organizational principle of making health care available through private practice with an entrepreneurial focus upon the doctor's office. The PRC is totally different organizationally. To explore the potential role of SMT in the health care system of contemporary China, I spent three weeks in the PRC in 1979, focusing the efforts of that short visit upon health care facilities.

The PRC resembles other Third World Nations in its continuing reliance upon traditional forms of therapy. Of course, western (allopathic) medicine is widely practiced. In certain specialties, it is even quite innovative. This is particularly true for the management of severe burns, for the reduction of fractures and rapair of ruptured ligaments, for the re-attatchment of severed limbs, and for acupuncture analgesia in controlling surgical pain (Horn, 1971: 78-80, 110, 117).

The practice of allopathic medicine is severely limited, however, by an insufficient number of trained personnel, by inadequate facilites, and by the prohibitive expense of acquiring and distributing pharmaceutical materials. Quite aside, then, from the widespread belief that traditional forms of therapy are efficacious, and perhaps even superior for certain purposes, the nation continues to rely upon older practices for sound practical reasons. Particularly for non-infectious, chronic complaints, useful treatment can be offered under the economic and technological limitations which prevail by supporting and expanding traditional medicine.

In site visits to primary care centers in two communes and two workers' residential areas I found traditional Chinese medical procedures the preferred treatment for most patients. Even more impressive in my experience, however, is the Railroad Workers' Hosital in Hangzhow, a 225 bed facility for the practice of traditional medicine. Therapeutic procedures in this facility contrast sharply with those of allopathic hospitals in China, where medical doctors and their procedures dominate. In this hospital, little if any allopathic medicine is practiced. Rather, doctors and staff rely upon acupuncture, herbal infusions, medicinal baths, heat, light, diet and exercise.

According to the chief of staff, most patients are admitted for chronic illness, many on an out-patient basis. Problems of infectious disease, acute injury and those requiring surgery are referred to allopathic facilities located elsewhere. Among the most common conditions treated in this hospital, we were told, are hypertension, gastrointestinal malfunction, persistent and severe headache, arthritis, dyspnea, insomnia, musculoskeletal problems, and malaise.

It is recognized that psychiatric difficulties complicate, if indeed they do not initiate, many of these illnesses. Psychotherapy is therefore practiced consciously as part of a basically holistic approach to disease. It is quite different from western practice, where the therapeutic interview tends to dominate treatment. In Hangzhow the peace and quiet along with good weather, a lovely lake and restful pathways are believed in themselves to have therapeutic value (See Sidel and Sidel, 1974: 162-165). Because the hospital was created, in 1953, for the benefit of railroad workers, the staff and facilities are specialized for the management of the musculoskeletal injuries and strains that are the frequent consequences of railroad labor, including prolonged standing or sitting as well as accidents.

It is in the area of primary care centers and hospitals for the practice of traditional medicine such as in this hospital in Hangzhow that an American contribution to the medical armamentarium of China especially suggests itself. In the West, as indicated above, studies and clinical experiences indicate that chiropractic can be effective in the treatment of injuries and diseases resulting from physical labor, specifically as concerns sprains and strains of the neck, shoulders and back (Kane et al, 1974). It is also believed, although precise documentation is lacking, that chiropractic sometimes benefits many if not all of the Type O disorders customarily treated in the Railroad Workers' Hospital, not excluding psychosomatic illness (Sato, 1980). Thus, chiropractic would appear promising as an innovation that might function well organizationally within the framework of traditional medicine as it is now set up in the PRC.

CONCLUSION

Spinal maniuplative therapy, with roots in European bonesetting, emerged in late nineteenth century America as osteopathy and chiropractic. Although beneficial at times in the treatment of visceral-organic disorders, these disciplines have particularly demonstrated their usefulness in muscuoskeletal disorders. Third World nations must cope with a wide range of health problems. Orthopedic disorders are clearly among them, as demonstrated in the survey we recently undertook in Nepal.

To explore the potential reception for SMT in a developing nation, this paper focused upon the PRC and chiropractic. Based upon interviews with a Chinese internist involved in testing the medical value of traditional Chinese medicine,, we conclude that the medical theory of China and that of chiropractic are highly congenial. From field studies carried out among chiropractors in Hong Kong, we find that the openness of Chinese medicine would allow room for the addition of chiropractic. Finally, from site visits in the PRC, it is concluded that the organization of health care could accommodate chiropractic within existing facilities for the practice of traditional medicine.

In every country, whether in Asia, Africa, Latin America, or elsewhere, it will be necessary to examine indigenous forms of medical theory, openness to foreign practices, and the organizational framework of health care. The PRC is not a model for most nations, since theory, openness, practice, and organization can be highly variable. Our investigation of the Chinese potential for adopting chiropractic, however, does suggest that in our time, when the West is very willing to borrowing traditional medical practices from Third World nations, perhaps the Third World might want to accept in exchange the introduction of SMT as a return payment in kind.

REFERENCES

THE AMERICAN ACUPUNCTURE ANESTHESIA STUDY GROUP (1976). ACUPUNCTURE ANESTHESIA IN THE PEOPLE'S REPUBLIC OF CHINA. Washington, DC: National Academy of Sciences.

THE AMERICAN HERBAL PHARMACOLOGY DELEGATION (1976). HERBAN PHARMACOLOGY IN THE PEOPLE'S REPUBLIC OF CHINA. Washington, DC: National Academy of Sciences.

ANDERSON, ROBERT T. (1980) "Chiropractice: Recognized but Unproved," NEW ENGLAND JOURNAL OF MEDICINE 302 (6): 354.

BENSON, HERBERT and MIRIAM Z. KLIPPER (1975) THE RELAXATION RESPONSE. N.Y.: William Morrow and Co., Inc.

COMMISSION OF INQUIRY (1979) CHIROPRACTIC IN NEW ZEALAND. Wellington, N.Z.: P. D. Hasselberg, Government Printer.

COULTER, HARRIS L. (1970) "Homeopathy Revisited," SCOPE (Boston University Medical Center Magazine), Sept./Oct.: 16-21.

GIBBONS, RUSSELL W. (1981) "Physician-Chiropractors: Medical Presence in the Evolution of Chiropractic," BULLETIN OF THE HISTORY OF MEDICINE 55(2): 233-245.

GOLDSTEIN, MURRAY, ed. (1975) THE RESEARCH STATUS OF SPINAL MANIPULATIVE THERAPY. NINCDS MONOGRAPH NO. 15. Bethesda, MD: U.S. Department of Health, Education and Welfare.

HORN, JOSHUA S. (1971) AWAY WITH ALL PESTS. N.Y.: Modern Reader Paperback.

HUARD, PIERRE and MING WONG (1972) CHINESE MEDICINE. N.Y.: McGraw-Hill.

KANE, ROBERT L. et al. (1974) "Manipulating the Patient, A Comparison of the Effectiveness of Physician and Chiropractor Care," THE LANCET, June 29: 1333-1336.

McCORKLE, THOMAS (1961) "Chiropractic: A Deviant Theory of Disease and Treatment in Contemporary Western Culture," HUMAN ORGANIZATION 20(1): 20-22.

NORTHUP, GEORGE W. (1966) OSTEOPATHIC MEDICINE: AN AMERICAN REFORMATION. Chicago: American Osteopathic Association.

SATO, AKIO (1980) "Physiological Studies of the Somatoautonomic Reflexes," in Scott Haldeman, ed., MODERN DEVELOPMENTS IN THE PRINCIPLES AND PRACTICE OF CHIROPRACTIC. N.Y.: Appleton-Century--Crofts, pp. 93-105.

SCHIOTZ, EILER H. and JAMES CYRIAX (1975) MANIPULATION, PAST AND PRESENT. London: William Heinemann Medical Books, Ltd.

SIDEL, VICTOR W. and RUTH SIDEL (1974) SERVE THE PEOPLE: OBSERVATIONS ON MEDICINE IN THE PEOPLE'S REPUBLIC OF CHINA. Boston: Beacon Press.

SIEGEL, RONALD K. (1979) "Ginseng Abuse Syndrome: Problems with the Panacea," JOURNAL OF THE AMERICAN MEDICAL ASSOCIATION 241(15): 1614-1615.

TAYLOR-IDE, DANIEL and ROBERT QERTLEY, et al. (n.d.) "Health Observations from Northern Humla," JOURNAL OF THE INSTITUTE OF MEDICINE 1(1): 135-144.

TOPLEY, MARJORIE (1975) "Chinese Traditional Etiology and Methods of Cure in Hong Kong," in Charles Leslie, ed., ASIAN MEDICAL SYSTEMS: A COMPARATIVE STUDY. Berkeley: University of California Press.

VOORHEES, RONALD E. and DANIEL TAYLOR-IDE (n.d.) "A Report on Health Conditions in the Manang Valley, Manang District, Nepal," JOURNAL OF THE INSTITUTE OF MEDICINE 2(1): 37-48.

CHAPTER 3

MOTHERS AS RESOURCES FOR COMMUNITY HEALTH
IN THE THIRD WORLD: A BOLIVIAN EXAMPLE

Deborah E. Bender and Carolyn R. Cantlay

INTRODUCTION

The particular skills and talents of women often go unrecognized. In most cultures, the protection, support, and nurturing they provide in their traditional roles of homemaking and childrearing are not as highly valued as the political and productive functions men usually perform, although they are of equally central importance to the community (Kitzinger, 1978; Huston, 1979). In the developed nations, women have attained greater access to the political and productive sectors of society, due at least in part to the convenience revolution of modern technology. In the developing countries of the Third World, however, life and work are largely unaided by technology; routine household tasks, including marketing, preparation of meals, and childcare, still require considerable portions of each woman's day.

Development activities in Third World areas have been ongoing since World War II, but only in the past decade has their impact on women been of concern. In 1975, the World Conference of the International Woman's Year was held in Mexico City (Buvinic, 1976), affirming the importance of women in society and bringing to light their needs in the development context. This was a critical first step toward integrating women into development. Now the next step is being taken, that of recognizing not only their needs, but their potential.

THE BOLIVIAN SITUATION

Parallel situations exist in many countries of the world. In this chapter the present situation as it exists in Bolivia, South America, will be examined as a case example because of one author's experience in that country with a rural health project. Because of the activities in which they alone engage, in Bolivia and much of the developing world, viz., food handling, housekeeping, childrearing, women as mothers play an unquestionably major role in the health of their families. It has been an objective of the Bolivian government for many years to encourage healthful mothering. Since 1955, it has provided supplementary foods through community-based mothers' clubs, **clubs de madres,** in an effort to imporve the nutritutional status of low-income women of childbearing age and their young children

29

(DIVISION NACIONAL DE NUTRICION, 1982). However, the provision of food supplments alone does not make full use of the potential vehicle these mothers' clubs provide for the promotion of health. In rural Bolivia, where basic health services are not readily available to the vast majority of the population, mothers are providers of care by default, and the passive recipients of such stop-gap measures as food supplements. Instead, mothers should be recognized as the care providers by choice in developing regions. Expanding the role of the existing mothers' clubs would be a culturally and politically acceptable means of implementing this important policy alternative.

The Altiplano is a high plain over a hundred miles long and as much as forty miles wide which lies between two spines of the Andes cordillera running through western Bolivia. The mountains reach peaks of 20,000 feet; the plain itself is at an elevation of 12-14,000 feet. The altiplano region, which borders Lake Titicaca, is predominantly settled by two indigenous Indian groups, the Aymara and the Quechua. These Indian groups number about seven hundred thousand and one million, respectively. They made their homes in the mountains and valleys of the Andes long before those lands came to be called by their present country names, Bolivia and Peru. In Bolivia, the Indians comprise the majority of the population. The total population of the country breaks down into three broad categories: Indians, 65%; white (of Spanish descent), 10-15%; and mestizo (mixed), 2-25%. Indians are the ethnic majority, but their political and economic power in no way equals their numbers. The government is controlled by those of Spanish descent and the typical rural Indian **campesino** (peasant) continues to eke out a life that is barely above the subsistence level.

The Aymara are generally acknowledged to be the oldest of the Indian groups of Bolivia, pre-dating the Incas. Their culture has survived two distinct periods of conquest, by the Incas in the mid-15th century, and by the Spanish in the mid-16th century. Aymara culture is perhaps facing a conqueror it will not outlast, in the guise of "modernizatin;" nevertheless, they remain for the present a culturally distinct people within the nation of Bolivia. An early observer of the Aymara described them as "anxious, hostile, irresponsible, submissive, disorderly, and utilitarian" (ethnographer Harry Tschopik, quoted in Carter, 1971: 89), and this perception has a basis in fact. However, it also has an explanation in their history and environment: "If they are anxious, it is because of a hostile natural and human environment. If they are hostile, it is because the Spaniard has done his best to pilfer them of all their goods. If they are irresponsible, it is because the white man has divested them of any real responsibility. If they are submissive, it is because, after various uprisings, they have become reconciled to the inevitable technological superiority of the enemy. And, if they are utilitarian, it is because, in a spare environment, this is the only way they have to be able to meet their material needs (Carter, 1971: 90).

The Aymara continue to make their living by subsistence farming and by herding alpacas and llamas under harsh conditions on the Altiplano.

Their traditional social structure is centered on the nuclear family, and strongly values responsibility for one's self and one's immediate neighbors. These characteristics of self-sufficiency and localism have kept the Aymara isolated, not integrated into the Bolivian national economic and social systems. Although the changes in Bolivia since the revolution in 1952, which brought land reform and universal suffrage, have begun to lessen the political isolation of the Aymara **campesinos,** within Aymara communities the traditional values predominate. Women are clearly subordinate to men; for example, educational opportunities are not valued for young women as they are for men. Dissatisfaction with such aspects of rural society has led to the formation of women's clubs, and even, in 1973, to the first National Seminar on the Problems of Peasant Women (Weil et al., 1974: 123). **Campesinas** have proved their eagerness and their ability to take an active part in improving their lives. Because literacy is especially low among women, there is a tendency among government officials and professionals to assume that the women of the Altiplano cannot learn, or do, very much. A more important indicator of their potential to effect positive change than their level of literacy is the nature and magnitude of the problems with which they cope. Aymara mothers **are** in the position to promote better health.

The health status of the Bolivian population is among the lowest in Latin America. In 1971, the average life expectancy at birth was 46 years (US—AID, 1975: 65), with the majority of sickness and death attributable to communicable and parasitic diseases such as tuberculosis, pneumonia, whooping cough, measles and infant diarrhea. Malnutrition and complications of pregnancy are important contributing causes of morbidity and mortality. The infant mortality rate, that is, deaths in the first year of life per live births, is 154/1,000 in the country as a whole; in the rural regions, where sixty to eighty per cent of the population live, the infant mortality rate is believed to be at least 250/1,000 (US-AID, 1975: 65). Again, respiratory and diarrheal diseases are the major causes of death. These data are not exact and probably are underestimated due to poor reporting, but they are instructive. In the United States, the comparable figure for infant mortality is 14.1/1,000 (US-DHHS, 1980). Although treatment for the major causes of death are well-known and relatively simple to administer, in Bolivia and other developing countries such primary care services are not available to the entire population.

Standard but diligent public health measures are the necessary means to combat disease conditions in countries at this stage in the national development whose populations suffer more from infectious diseases than from the chronic, degenerative diseases of developed nations such as our own (Omran, 1977). Such public health practices include provision of clean water supply and sanitation systems, improvements in housing, vaccination against infectious diseases of childhood, maternal and child health services, and health education programs. Although prevention of the major health problems of the people could be managed by trained, auxiliary, personnel in the rural areas where they occur, the Bolivian health system has concentrated its resources on curative medicine, provided by physicians, in urban areas.

PROMOTING HEALTH AND COMMUNITY DEVELOPMENT

For twenty-five years, the Division of Nutrition of the Bolivian Ministry of Health has used mothers' clubs as the means of monthly distribution of six supplementary foods, including powdered milk, cooking oil, and grains. Now government health officials are interested in providing education in nutrition and health through these clubs. In order to assess the feasibility of such a program, field research was conducted by Deborah Bender. Aymara communities with mothers' clubs were identified and visited. A number of topics broadly related to health were discussed with members of the clubs, including the mothers' clubs themselves, feeding practices in the family, interaction with health care delivery systems, care of children under five, pregnancy and lactation, and sanitation and water supply within the community. Additionally, some demographic data was obtained, such as name, age, occupation of self and husband, age of living children and age of deceased children at their death. In exchange, each mother was given an instant color photo of herself and her family. Most chose to dress in their festival best clothes, for color photographs were infrequent in the rural area.

The purpose of discussing those topics is to understand and subsequently to incorporate the practices of the Aymara people as fully as possible into any proposed health education and delivery system. The goal is to identify and build onto any working system of care, not to replace it. By analogy, the process resembles grafting more than transplanting or planting anew. As such, cultural grafting involves more than simply cultural sensitivity; in applying the concept it is essential to recognize and use the practices of the indigenous group as a baseline and to intervene with other practices, notably those of Western practitioners, only when necessary. This is not to say that every practice of every indigenous system of medical care is good; rather, it is to stress that before a wholly new solution is proposed, one must assess whether a practice already exists in the community that can be used as the basis for improving health, or curing disease, or solving other of the community's problems. Only by making full use of the material, intellectual and cultural resources available in the community can one hope to close the gap between needs and resources in a scarce resource environment.

It was noted above that some health professionals hold the perception that the illiterate women of the Altiplano are incapable of learning very much. This perception by those with advanced education of those lacking book learning is common, ungrounded, and only serves to widen the communication gap between the Spanish descendent and the Indian. Field research, including living in the community, revealed refined levels of knowledge and an eagerness to learn among the illiterate women. Despite their lack of formal education, these women have a substantial and differential knowledge of herbal medicines. For example, seven distinct dried grasses are collected for one medicinal **mate,** a tea of boiled water and herbs; fevers are controlled by linaya seeds and lemon boiled in water; slices from the sank'aya cactus are used to decrease the swelling associated with mumps. These few examples make clear that a body of knowledge exists and is in use, that discrete categories are distinguished; and that each generation of women learns the plants and their uses from the one before. It is also clear that these women are able to learn new material. It is incumbent upon the "teachers" to present material which enhances present knowledge, builds on long-held cultural practices and therefore, is relevant to the potential users. Pictures, drawings, role plays, skits and case examples are teaching methods which do not rely primarily on the written word.

Another assumption that is held concerning these women and their communities' health is that people receive a great deal of care from traditional healers, **curanderos,** or herbalists. In fact, self-care seems to be a far more prevalent source of care than traditional curers, and women, for the most part, provide it. Exceptions mentioned to the reliance on self-treatment include the immunization of children, the occasional purchase of medicines, infrequent reference to actual use of a **curandero,** and rare reference to use of a hospital. Most often when women are asked, "Who cares for you and your family when you are ill?", the answer is, "We do." The following responses to that question are illustrative:

"We are the best. We never take our children to a **curandero** or a **medico** (doctor). The doctor said, 'Don't bring the children when they are very sick; it's too late'." "The **curandero** doesn't know too much. We know the same as he does about herbs." "Only we ourselves can cure the children. I don't take them to the **curandero** (even though he lives quite nearby) because I have to pay, and sometimes it doesn't work." "I treat myself. Sometimes I ask the **curandero** (in this case, the woman's father) to get rid of a cold-spirit."

These comments were made so frequently that any listener could surmise that reliance on family members and individuals in the community will not be easily replaced by practitioners of Western medicine who are unconnected to the community and whose healing practices are based on premises unfamiliar to the Aymara **campesinos.**

A third common assumption is that the **compesinos** are somehow, somewhat, inured to the sickness and death that claim their children at such high rates. Because so many children die as infants or under five years of age, there is a vague sense that the people expect some of their children to die and do little to prevent it; indeed are little disturbed by it. In fact, interviewed women cried as they told of their children's deaths and were able to tell the age at death in days as well as months and years. Their concern and their sorrow are real; what is different may be a cultural perception on their part that they are a part of, rather than in control of, the larger world.

An organizational strategy has been developed for identifying and enhancing the special skills of women as health collaborators or colaboradoras. The initiative's goals are to provide greater knowledge of health related issues, increased ability to use natural helping skills, and an appreciation of the role the women themselves can play in improving health and nutrition in their communities. The program for training one or two women in each community in basic curative and preventive medicine and for developing helping skills will be grafted onto the existing mothers' clubs. Recognized natural helpers will receive this training. Natural helpers are individuals whose interest in others and natural empathy combine so that they are often sought out as helpers or advisors by extended family members, neighbors, or others in the community (Service and Salber, 1977). The identification of role models and organization of the resources they offer encourages the community to recognize and utilize the strengths of its members.

The training of women for service in their communities involves three phases of effort and three concomitant levels of impact: (1) increased education in health and training in helping skills; (2) community organization; (3) community-based resource development. Each phase builds on the successes of the previous activity, and requires greater commitments of time, personnel and community responsibility. This is a realistic, graduated approach toward community development, which tries to take into account Bolivia's long history of economic crises and political instability. The ultimate goal is community self-support; organic, if slow, growth of community-based institutions will insure the sustained accomplishment of that goal more surely than "all or nothing" programs of radical change.

The first phase of efforts at developing mothers' clubs is the provision of education and training in nutrition and health, and some basic training in helping skills. These last are also known as counseling skills: careful listening, reflection of feelings, focusing, understanding and empathizing, summarizing and action or decision planning (Bender and Bean, 1982). The training is to be offered in monthly sessions in the city of La Paz at the times the women already come to the city to pick up their food supplements. After the careful establishment of a mutual problem-solving relationship between the training staff and the Aymara mothers, the classes will focus on content that stems from discussion of community needs and that can easily be applied, by the **colaboradoras** transferring their knowledge to others in the community.

It is important to remember that the training must seek to enhance skills and practices already present in the community, whenever possible, not to supply new solutions. For example, if diarrhea were recognized as a problem, the training content might be conceptualized as follows: **First,** diarrhea is a problem; **Second,** the Aymara solution is to give a **mate** with herbs, two spoonfuls at a time, three times a day. **Third,** the culturally appropriate intervention might be formulated in this way: "Add a handful of sugar and a pinch of salt to the **mate** you have already made. Continue to give it to your child at meal times, but also give it to him once or twice between meals. (Note hours are not used, few of the women have watches.) Let the child have as much as he wants.

34

More is better than less. Remember he is not eating other foods, and you know that it takes more liquid than solid food to fill you up."

This process encourages the growth of a new shoot, i.e., making oral rehydration solution, on an already strong stem, i.e., indigenous practices for treating infant diarrhea (WHO, 1980). Training of this kind is responsive to both the felt needs of the **colaboradas** and their needs as perceived by the outside health agency. The topics presented in this first stage of development of the mothers' clubs are important, but even more important is the fostering of the women's self-help skills. This is the ultimate objective of the trianing; every lesson, every activity should be evaluated before it is presented, to determine its potential contribution toward helping women help themselves and others through their clubs.

The second phase of mothers' club efforts, community organization, must take place in the community. This strategy requires **colaboradoras,** working through the mothers' clubs, to help the women of the community to determine what additional knowledge and skills they would like, what their goals for improved health and nutrition are, and what activities they would choose to engage in cooperatively to raise funds to assist their community in reaching their goals. The mobilization of mothers' clubs within the community setting offers a potentially greater benefit to the women enrolled in the clubs. Organization within the community may result in a group decision to purchase a needed resource with the funds saved from the monthly contribution for supplementary food. This decision might be to purchase a sewing nachine for the women to use, to secure a plot of land on which to plant a vegetable crop or build a mothers' club meeting house, to barter for several sheep with which to start a wool-producing flock. Through such community organizations, each member benefits, and each family is the potential beneficiary of pooled resources, energies, and skills.

The third phase of activity, that of community resource development, is more sophisticated than community organization. Community organization is suggested as a strategy for increasing resources for use within the community; resource development involves organization for the production of resources to be sold for use outside the community. Members of individual mothers' clubs may form themselves into an association or cooperative. It is the final step in the process of community development. The community has come full-circle, back to important, indeed sustaining, relationships with outsiders. But at this point, the community is not dependent on outsiders, it interacts productively with them. Funds received through any resource development scheme should be used to enrich the community. The choice of how the money is spent is the community's. It could be spent to purchase foods to broaden the base of the diet, to obtain necessary medical services, or to acquire equipment and materials needed to increase production.

At all times every member of the community should benefit equally from the decision. This may be only theoretically possible, but there is merit in establishing an ideal toward which the community can strive. Even the community's poorest and least powerful members are often divided among themselves (Werner and Bower, 1982: 6-11); in setting out the ideal of equal benefit, it is made clear that all who participate in the community's effort share its profits. The community begins to work together to help itself.

THEORETICAL PERSPECTIVES

The development of mothers' clubs in Bolivia to serve community health and development ends is "work in progress" at this writing. The vicissitudes of political and economic life in a developing country will no doubt have an impact on the process; delays and setbacks, even abandonments, are common to these programs. Nevertheless, there are truths underlying the concept elucidated here, and they deserve mention. These truths are of two kinds, fundamental and programmatic.

Promoting better health and preventing disease through mothers' clubs presupposes an understanding of a perception of health which is fundamental to the community, yet may bear little resemblance to the Western scientific model of health and illness. The latter is based on the germ theory of disease and is the dominant perspective in clinical training programs. Despite this dominance, even in scientific circles there is no agreement on the one, best definition of health. In the developing world, definitions of health and the values ascribed to it are more broad and more varied. In 1947, the World Health Organization defined health as "a state of complete mental, physical and social well-being, and not merely the absence of disease or infirmity." The intent is to digress from a negative definition of health (such as health is the absence of disease and infirmity) and to incorporate the range of values ascribed to health in each society or culture. Biological, cultural, psychological and societal components may be a part of every society's perception of health, but the combination and the relative emphasis given each component influences how people think about health and what they do to achieve or maintain it (cf. Coe, 1970; Mechanic, 1978).

For instance, among the Aymara, infant diarrhea is not considered an illness. Rather, it occurs in conjunction with early developmental stages. It is considered normal for a child to have diarrhea when she learns to sit, to crawl, to stand, and to walk. Since the condition is a normal one within the Aymara system of beliefs about health and illness, no treatment is deemed necessary. Unfortunately, in infants and small children, diarrhea leads quickly to dehydration and possibly death if not treated. On the other hand, it is recognized that trauma (i.e., broken bones, and lacerations or cuts) are best treated by Western practitioners in hospitals or health posts. These injuries are readily brought for treatment, transportation and expense not withstanding.

Neither the traditional Aymara definition nor the Western scientific one has a monopoly or truth; each is appropriate to its cultural and techno-logical milieu. What would be inappropriate would be to try to address both perspectives with the same system of care. The point that bears repeating is that any programmatic effort must be compatible with the perception of health held by the community it is intended to serve. It is fundamental to problem solving that the problem must be defined in such a way that it is soluble; a program to improve community health must **approach** community health from the community's perspective, or it will fail.

Likewise, the introduction of scientific medicine without consideration of its interface with the system of medical care already operative in the culture reasserts the sense of "doing-for" rather than "doing-with." It is this latter attitude which is critical to the improvement of self-esteem and self-worth necessary to self-help. If a program intends to help people help themselves, then "doing-with" is a concept which must undergird the effort from its incepient stages. This may imply doing more with less, but ultimately it is the only reasonable way to assure that the members of a particular community are able to sustain fundamental improvements in their own health once the interim programmatic resources are expended.

In its many phases, the mothers' clubs community health and development scheme addresses these two important concerns: the fundamental concept of different health perspectives requiring different delivery systems, and the programmatic goal of a self-sustaining, community-determined approach to health and development. Aymara mothers, through mothers' clubs, within communities, are resources for health promotion, community organization, and resource development; they cannot continue unrecognized, while the effective implementation of the concepts of primary health care goes unfulfilled (cf. UNDP, 1980: 41). What keeps them from realizing their potential as community resources is not that they lack interest, ability, or leadership, but rather that they lack the skills for organization to actualize the opportunities before them. With adequate support and direction, these women can and will serve and strengthen their communities.

REFERENCES

BENDER, DEBORAH E. and CYDNE BEAN, eds. (1982) COUNSELING SKILLS IN FAMILY PLANNING. Chapel Hill, NC: Carolina Population Center.

BUVINIC, MAYRA (1976) WOMEN AND WORLD DEVELOPMENT: AN ANNOTATED BIBLIOGRAPHY. Washington, DC: Overseas Development Council.

CARTER, WILLIAM E. (1971) BOLIVIA, A PROFILE. NY: Praeger.

COE, RODNEY M. (1970) SOCIOLOGY OF MEDICINE. NY: McGraw-Hill.

DIVISION NACIONAL DE NUTRICION (1982) PROGRAMAS DE LA DIVISION NACIONAL DE NUTRICION, 1982-1983: ALIMENTACION COMPLIMENTARIA. La Paz, Bolivia: Division Nacional de Nutricion, Ministerio de Prevision Social y. Salud Publica.

HUSTON, PERDIATA (1979) THIRD WORLD WOMEN SPEAK OUT. NY: Praeger.

KITZINGER, SHEILA (1978) WOMEN AS MOTHERS. NY: Random House.

MECHANIC, DAVID (1978) MEDICAL SOCIOLOGY. 2nd Edition. NY: The Free Press.

OMRAN, ABDEL (1977) "Epidemiologic Transition," POPULATION REFERENCE BUREAU BULLETIN 32(2): 1-42.

RODMAN, ANNE (1981) "A Nonformal In-Service Training Program for Auxiliary Nurses in Bolivia," In NATIONAL COUNCIL FOR INTERNATIONAL HEALTH, THE TRAINING AND SUPPORT OF PRIMARY HEALTH CARE WORKERS. Washington, DC: National Council for International Health.

SERVICE, CONNIE and EVA J. SALBER (1977) COMMUNITY HEALTH EDUCATION: THE LAY ADVISOR APPROACH. Durham, NC: Community Health Educatin Program, Duke University Medical Center.

UNITED NATIONS DEVELOPMENT PROGRAMME (1980) RURAL WOMEN'S PARTICIPATION IN DEVELOPMENT. NY: UNDP Evaluation Study No. 3.

U.S. AGENCY FOR INTERNATIONAL DEVELOPMENT (1975) BOLIVIA: HEALTH SECTOR ASSESSMENT. Washington, DC: USAID.

U.S. DEPARTMENT OF HEALTH AND HUMAN SERVICES (1980) HEALTH

UNITED STATES. Hyattsville, MD: DHHS.

WEIL, THOMAS E., et al. AREA HANDBOOK FOR BOLIVIA. Washington, DC: Foreign Area Studies, American University.

WERNER, DAVID and BILL BOWER (1982) HELPING HEALTH WORKERS LEARN. Palo Alto, CA: The Hesperian Foundation.

WORLD HEALTH ORGANIZATION (1980) GUIDELINES FOR THE PRODUCTION OF ORAL REHYDRATION SALTS. Geneva: WHO Programme for Control of Diarrhoeal Diseases, Series No. 80.3.

SOUTH AMERICA

CHAPTER 4

THE CHANGING ROLE OF THE INDIAN MEDICINE MAN:
THREE CASE STUDIES

Gene E. Carnicom

INTRODUCTION

This paper illustrates some changes in the role of the medicine man in three Indian cultures: the Brule Sioux of Rosebud, South Dakota; the Oglala Sioux of Pine Ridge, South Dakota; and the Omaha Tribe of Macy, Nebraska. An individual identified as a medicine man was the subject of a case study in each of these cultures. It was discovered that the role of the medicine man has vanished from the Omaha. The role of the medicine man, at least in two of the cases studied, has been modified among the Brule and Oglala Sioux. The loss of the Omaha medicine man coincides with a general decline of the traditional Omaha culture as its members have become assimilated into the majority culture. The medicine man of the Oglala has integrated Christianity into his traditional belief system, while the beliefs of the Brule medicine man remain traditional.

Once persecuted by educators, government officials, and missionaries, the medicine man has gained increased acceptance by physicians and mental health professionals in recent years. There is little integration of traditional and Western medicine on the three reserversations studied. At Rosebud, however, Sinte Gleska College in a cooperative venture with the local organization of traditional healers, Medicine Men and Associates, does work with medicine men on a consultation basis in the field of mental health.

This paper will note several factors which can enhance the survivability of traditional Indian medicine in the future. A proposal for the formation of an association of medicine men is explored and endorsed.

PURPOSE OF THE STUDY

By the time sociology had established itself as a science, the great assault on Indian cultures by "civilized" Europeans had long been underway. The story of this process of cultural destruction is described in such varied works as Dee Brown's popular book, BURY MY HEART AT WOUNDED KNEE (1970), Peter Farb's anthropological study, MAN'S RISE TO CIVILIZATION: THE CULTURAL ASCENT OF THE INDIANS OF NORTH AMERICA (1978), and Vine Deloria, Jr.'s CUSTER DIED FOR YOUR

SINS (1970). History records the deliberate process of cultural annihilation undertaken by many of the settlers of the New World against the native populations of the Americas. In spite of efforts by some to protect Indians, other settlers, politicians, missionaries, and soldiers of fortune used ancient tactics in an attempt to destroy Indian cultures—through genocide; through religious conversion, especially of the young; and through destruction of cultural artifacts including those of the great Indian civilizations of Central and South America.

To a great extent, this cultural destruction was successful. Many groups of Indians, however, managed to maintain their cultural identities. Today, one can still observe "Sun Dances" and other Indian ceremonies across the continent. Recent books, magazine articles, and motion pictures like A MAN CALLED HORSE demonstrate a current interest in Indian cultures. It can be seriously questioned, however, whether ceremonies such as the Sun Dance, the wearing of braided hair, or the proliferation of Indian ethnic bumper stickers are evidence that Indians have arrested the process of losing their cultures. It is reasonable to assume that the process of assimilation of Indians into the majority culture has been accelerated by technological change, such as the introduction of the automobile and the television on the reservation.

Sociologists, anthropologists, and others interested in the study of cultures have the opportunity today not only to observe the process of social change in Indian societies, but also to study, record, and maintain for posterity those aspects of Indian culture which may soon fade into history. One such area of interest is the traditional form of health care practiced by those Indians known commonly as "medicine men," and it is this aspect of the Indian culture which is the focus of this study.

REVIEW OF RELATED LITERATURE

A number of computer searches were completed to reviewing the literature related to the changing role of the medicine man. Systems accessed included MEDLARS, MEDLINE, NIHM, MESH, PSYCHOLOGICAL AB-STRACTS, INDEX MEDICUS, the National Library of Medicine, and the White Cloud Center. In addition, a special computer run was done by the Burea of the Census on data from the three reservations in the study.

A review of related literature revealed a relatively large number of studies on Indian culture, traditional Indian medicine, and medicine men. It is apparent from the literature that Indian societies developed individual health care delivery systems, but these systems were consistent with generic Indian values. Indian health statistics, while still greatly inferior to those of Americans in general, have greatly improved over the last 25 years. Traditional medicine remains popular because it meets the emotional needs of patients. Traditional Indian medicine and Indian religion are inseparable. Cures are effected with the assistance of the supernatural and are usually public occurrences which reinforce Indian societies. Indian pharmacology is effective in dealing with some physiological complaints, and Indian spiritual healing is in some cases superior to Western medicine in dealing with culture-specific psychophysiologic disorders. While some writers have noted a decline in the role of the medicine man, or even his disappearance, the majority of recent researchers report survival of the role and in some Indian cultures an increase in its acceptance.

While in the past medicine men were an institution under attack by the government, there is increasing acknowledgement by physicians of the medicine man today as a prospective member of the health care team. Recent government policy has recognized traditional Indian medicine, and further policy changes favoring the medicine man are anticipated.

METHODOLOGY

Three medicine men were the subjects of this study. Each subject was drawn from a different tribal group, one each from the Oglala Sioux, the Brule Sioux, and the Omaha. The method selected for gathering research data was the "case study/focused interview" approach. The interview guide used in the research was liberally adapted from the outline for cross-cultural analysis in health care given by Brownlee (1978). In addition to the interviews, some information was gathered from local agencies (such as the Burea of Indian Affairs and the U.S. Public Health Service offices on the reservations studied) and other informants at the sites of the interviews.

CONCLUSIONS

The conclusions from this study are drawn from the interviews with the three subjects as well as information supplied from health care professionals who work with the three tribes studied and a review of related literature. These conclusions apply specifically to the cultures and individuals which were the focus of this research, but the findings may provide guidance for future research in this area. The conclusions may be briefly stated as follows.

First, the concept of **traditional Indian medicine** covers a broad area of health care beliefs and practices, although there appears to be a generic core of Indian values and beliefs toward health and illness.

Second, unlike some other tribes, the Brule, Oglala, and Omaha have no institutionalized relationship between their medicine men and their Western medical hospitals.

Third, the role of the medicine man survives among the Brule and Oglala, but is absent in Omaha culture.

Fourth, changes in the role of the medicine men studied include loss of political influence and social status as well as the appearance of deviant behavior by some other unidentified Oglala and Rosebud medicine men; this deviant behavior includes the use of alcohol by the medicine men during rituals as well as the use of the position of medicine man to personal advantage.

Fifth, many Indians have turned to alternative methods for satisfaction of their spiritual and communal needs; some of these methods, such as substance abuse, have resulted in great social problems.

Sixth, efforts are being made to preserve traditional Indian medicine and to interface it with Western medicine.

Seventh, there are several factors which could tend to strengthen the role of the medicine man in the future, or at least contribute to its survivability.

The objective of this study was to illustrate some changes in the traditional role of the Indian medicine man. This was to be accomplished by way of the case studies of three medicine men and their three separate tribal cultures. The cultures selected provided a good reason to avoid making generalizations about "Indian culture" or "Indian medicine." At opposite ends of the spectrum of culture retention were Rosebud, which is actively attempting to maintain the old ways, and Omaha, which has nearly lost its, with Pine Ridge lying somewhere between these extremes.

From the reports of the three subjects, as well as from reports by health professionals and other informants on the three reservations, none of the three cultures studied seem to have integrated the two medical systems (Western and traditional) to the extent that the Navajo have (see Adair and Deuschle, 1970). In none of the three is found a formalized relationship between medicine men and their Indian Health Service hospitals, although Rosebud has had experience with this in the past and is moving toward establishing it again. Judging from lifestyle, values, and other aspects of culture, the Indians of Pine Ridge and Rosebud appear to be approximately equal in assimilation, having adopted many of the ways of the whites while still in degree preserving some of the old cultural traits such as language, ceremony, and traditional medicine. The Omaha have exchanged more of the old for the new, much to the dismay of their elders.

While Western medical care on all three reservations involves nearly all of their populations, the role of traditional medicine at Pine Ridge and Rosebud has not been destroyed. The loss of the medicine man role in the Omaha is but one aspect of this culture which has been assimilated to a greater extent than the other two into mainstream American society.

According to physicians and the subjects of the study, physician referrals to medicine men appear to be minimal at Pine Ridge and Rosebud. Inform-al interviews with physicians at Pine Ridge tend to confirm the findings of Attneave (1974): overworked physicians have little time to tend to the emotional needs of their patients beyond genuine efforts at providing words of encouragement and support to allay fears, and so forth. At least one physician at Pine Ridge, however, has made a serious attempt at working with the medicine men over the past two years. Dr. Ron Forgey has established close relationships with several Oglala Sioux medicine men. However, the two practicing medicine men in this study reported little or no utilization of their services by Indian Health Service physicians.

Tradition is being kept alive at Rosebud and Pine Ridge by ritual observance of both Yuwipi and Sun Dance. These ceremonies still draw great numbers of Indian participants for the two tribal cultures, as well as many outsiders including researchers, tourists, and other interested parties. Some whites participate in the Sun Dance, even subjecting theimselves to piercing. One of the dancers at a Sun Dance held in Pine Ridge in the summer of 1981 was reportedly the star of the movie Billy Jack. At the same Sun Dance was a participant who had previously done research among the Oglala at Pine Ridge, and a white caseworker from the local social service agency who has obligated himself to participate in future Sun Dances.

Even though the role of the medicine man has survived at Pine Ridge and Rosebud, there have been major changes in it. The "purity" of some of the medicine men on both reservations was questioned by all three subjects in the study. In addition, conversations with residents of Pine Ridge and Rosebud generated anecdotal information regarding inappropriate behavior of some medicine men, such as consuming alcohol at Sun Dances or using their positions to gain sexual favors from patients. The medicine men no longer wield political power as in the past. They are not consulted by the tribal councils for opinions, although the Medicine Men and Associates group at Rosebud does have influence with its tribal health board. If asked whether they know any medicine men, most residents would probably respond that they do and that they know someone who has gone to a medicine man for healing, but they are not willing to openly discuss with an outsider any possible use of traditional healing by themselves.

According to health professionals and other informants, those that use the services of medicine men at Pine Ridge and Rosebud tend to be the more traditional Sioux. Many of the younger generation fall into this category as there has been recently a reawakening of interest in tribal lore among many young adults, especially among the more activist-oriented. Overall, however, the researcher got the impression that these individuals comprise a relatively small proportion of the reservation populations.

According to the subjects, other informants, and the literature, those that have given up the old ways often attempt to have spiritual and communal needs fulfilled through various methods such as: group use of alcohol or drugs in an almost ritualistic manner; Catholicism and other Western religions; and peyotism and the Native American Church. The popularity of these social forms among the Brule and Oglala could be perceived as attempts by the Sioux to maintain a sense of tribal unity as well as to seek spiritual fulfillment. The use of alcohol, however, has contributed to major social and health problems on all three reservations including alcoholism, motor vehicle accidents, violent behavior in and outside the family, alcohol-related illness, suicide, and instability of Indian families.

The future of the role of the medicine man on all three reservations would seem to be related to several factors. Present government policy, while not deleterious to the medicine man, does not aggressively support traditional medicine whereas changes in policy could be supportive of the role. If medicine men do in fact organize themselves into an association with some system of certification of their membership, they might present a united front in dealings with the governmental and medical establishments. There is, however, resistance to this type of organization from some medicine men including one of the subjects of this study. An increase in cultural awareness and cultural pride by Indians in general has generated increased interest in the traditional healing systems. This may motivate more young Oglala, Brule, and Omaha to consider traditional medicine as a vocation. Finally, if the medical, social, and behavioral sciences were to increase their study of traditional Indian medicine, a determination of the efficacy of medicine men could be made. If this finding were positive, it might lead to a determination of which areas of traditional medicine can be incorporated into Western medicine, as well as provide a rationale for the inclusion of medicine men as associate therapists in the delivery of health care to Indians.

All of these factors could possibly provide support for the role of the medicine man in the future, and therefore this researcher remains cautiously optimistic about the survival of the medicine man role in Indian society. Further changes in this role may occur if traditional Indian medicine becomes organized into an association or if it becomes more interfaced with Western medicine.

RECOMMENDATIONS

There are five areas of recommendations that appear to be warranted by the conclusions of this study: further research; planning and policy making; preservation of traditional culture; holistic health care; and political organization of medicine men.

Even though the Indian is one of the most researched ethnic groups in history (the saying that every Indian has his own personal anthropologist may sometimes seem to the Indian to be not far from the truth), there remains much fertile ground for medical, behavioral, and social science research with this population. In the area of traditional medicine, further

46

research needs to be undertaken to determine the effectiveness of medicine men in dealing with various types of physical, psychological, and psychophysiological disorders. There is at present insufficient information available to enable health care providers to determine which aspects of Indian medicine should be integrated into Western medicine provided to Indian populations. Such research is needed if there is to be increased utilization of traditional healers as consultants or physician extenders.

Indian Health Service officials, recognizing the failure of alcoholism rehabilitation, alcoholism prevent, and other similar medical and social programs might consider whether traditional medicine has some components which can be effective in solving some of the problems of the Indians. Although health care has greatly improved for the Indian, social problems have greatly worsened, and the level of Indian health is still far below that of the American population in general. If the Indian Health Service discovers effectiveness in traditional medicine, it could provide increased support to traditional Indian healers. This support could include facilitating the payment of medicine men for services rendered.

The experience of the Omaha should be noted by other Indian trabies as an example of how a culture can lose one of its major traditional social institutions. All Indians who examine the role of their medicine men in their history, culture, and future and who decides that it is a valued role may need to take affirmative actions to preserve this role. These actions might include giving increased public recognition to medicine men and providing political support to them. Indians might also consider whether the schools which educate their children are doing an adequate job of teaching the young the old ways, including the spiritual and medical beliefs and practices of their forefathers.

There are perhaps things physicians who work with Indian populations can learn from the traditional healer. The medicine man's system of health care is truly holistic and deals with all the causes and effects of people's illness. Physicians who work in Indian health care could attempt to learn their patients' cultures, specifically cultural beliefs concerning health and illness. They might seek out traditional healers, and then decide for themselves what kind of professional relationship they need to establish with them to provide the best, most comprehensive, and effective medical and spiritual care possible.

Finally, medicine men might consider formal organization and certification as a viable political option. While this may not be the old way, for some it may be not too different from the medicine society of the past. Medicine men have a tradition of cooperation, sharing, and helping. To increase the survivability of the role of the medicine man, these traits are needed now more than ever.

SUMMARY

This study attempted to illustrate changes in the role of the medicine man in three Indian tribes, the Oglala Sioux, the Brule Sioux, and the Omaha. It was accomplished by case studies of an individual from each of these cultures who was identified as a practicing medicine man as well as information from physicians, other health care providers, and informants, and a review of related literature.

Among the Omaha, the medicine man is no longer to be found. This loss can be related to a general decline in the keeping of the old ways by the Omaha as they were assimilated into the majority culture. The two Sioux tribes still have several practicing medicine men each, and ritual ceremonies are still an important part of reservation life. The Christian religion has been integrated into the belief system of some of the medicine men. The medicine men no longer have the social or political influence they once had. Some young Indians have demonstrated a desire to select Indian medicine as a vocation.

The traditional Indian medicine, once subject to repression from government, church, and educators, has recently been viewed more positively. Some researchers have determined that, for certain types of health problems, traditional medicine is as effective, or more so, than Western medicine. There have been attempts at integrating Western and traditional medicine, including the collaboration between Sinte Gleska College and Medicine Men and Associates in Rosebud.

There still remin valid areas of traditional Indian medicine to be researched by behavioral and social scientists. Indians who feel the medicine man is a valued role in their society should determine if the medicine man institution is in any danger of disappearing.

Physicians who work with Indians can learn much from traditional Indian medicine in terms of relationship with their patients and the spiritual needs of Indians. It may be beneficial, therefore, for physicians to seek out medicine men in their communities. Finally, the time may be right for medicine men to organize themselves into a formal association to gain political influence. There is room for increased support of traditional Indian medicine by the Indian Health Service. The IHS could determine if traditional medicine holds promise for combating some of the social and health problems facing the Indian today. This study closes with an old Omaha saying:

Young people who think first
of themselves
and forget the old
will never prosper.

Nothing will go straight for them.

REFERENCES

ADAIR, J., and DEUSCHLE, K.W. (1970) THE PEOPLE'S HEALTH: ANTHROPOLOGY AND MEDICINE IN A NAVAJO COMMUNITY. N.Y.: Appleton-Century-Crofts.

ATTNEAVE, C.L. (1974) "Medicine Men and Psychiatrists in the Indian Health Service," PSYCHIATRIC ANNALS 4(9): 49, 53-55.

BROWN, D. (1970) BURY MY HEART AT WOUNDED KNEE N.Y.: Holt, Rinehart, and Winston.

BROWNLEE, A.T. (1978) COMMUNITY, CULTURE, AND CARE: A CROSS--CULTURAL GUIDE FOR HEALTH WORKERS. St. Louis: C.V. Mosby.

DELORIA, V., JR. (1970) CUSTER DIED FOR YOUR SINS: AN INDIAN MANIFESTO. N.Y.: Avon Books.

FARB, P. (1978) MAN'S RISE TO CIVILIZATION: THE CULTURAL ASCENT OF THE INDIANS OF NORTH AMERICA (2nd ed.) N.Y.: E.P. Dutton.

SUGGESTED READINGS

Oglala Sioux

MAYNARD, E. and TWISS, G. THAT THESE PEOPLE MAY LIVE (1970) (DHEW Publ. No. HSM 720508). Washington, D.C.: U.S. Government Printing Office.

SCHWEIGMAN, W.H. (1978) In Crazy Horse School, PUTE TIYOSPAYE [Lip's Camp]: THE HISTORY AND CULTURE OF A SIOUX INDIAN VILLAGE. Albuquerque, N.M.: Sloves-Burnell, Inc.

Omaha Tribe

FLETCHER, A.C. and LaFLESCHE, F. (1905) THE OMAHA TRIBE (2 volumes). Washington, D.C.: U.S. Government Printing Office.

LEITCH, B.A. (1979) A CONCISE DICTIONARY OF INDIAN TRIBES OF NORTH AMERICA. Algonac, MI.: Reference Publications, Inc.

Brule Sioux

CASH, J.H. (1971) THE SIOUX PEOPLE. Phoenix, AZ.: Indian Tribal Series.

NURGE, E. (ed.) (1970) THE MODERN SIOUX. Omaha, NB.: University of Nebraska Press.

Indian Medicine

BROWN, J.E. (ed.) (1953) THE SACRED PIPE: BLACK ELK'S ACCOUNT OF THE SEVEN RITES OF THE OGLALA SIOUX. Norman, OK.: University of Oklahoma Press.

JORGENSEN, J.G. (1972) THE SUN DANCE RELIGION: POWER FOR THE POWERELESS. Chicago: University of Chicago Press.

LAME DEER, J. (Fire) and ERDOES, R. (1976) LAME DEER, SEEKER OF VISIONS. N.Y.: Pocket Books.

MAILS, T.E. (1979) FOOLS CROW. N.Y.: Doubleday.

NEWCOMB, F.J. (1964) HOSTEEN KLAH: NAVAJO MEDICINE MAN AND SAND PAINTER. Norman, OK.: University of Oklahoma Press.

STORM, H. (1972) SEVEN ARROWS. N.Y.: Ballantine Books.

VOGEL, V. (197) AMERICAN INDIAN MEDICINE. Norman, OK.: University of Oklahoma Press.

CHAPTER 5

DEMOGRAPHIC EVIDENCE OF RESISTANCE TO CHANGING HEALTH PRACTICES IN SOUTH AMERICA

Charles E. Cipolla

abstract

Examination of cause-of-dath statistics from South American nations reveals that the great reductions in mortality have resulted from decreases in deaths due to conditions amenable to public health measures requiring little or no individual effort. There has been no corresponding reduction in deaths due to conditions that require individual efforts for prevention or therapy. This observation reconciles demongraphers' claims of great decreases leading to exceedingly low mortality levels with behavioral scientists' claims of resistance to the adoption of modern health practices in developing countries. The apparent contradictions resulted from the use of initial mortality levels that were too low.

INTRODUCTION

An assessment of the literature pertaining to the current health situation in South America reveals two conflicting sets of evidence and conclusions. Demographers are claiming that there have been exceedingly rapid declines in the mortality levels of these countries following the importation of advanced methods of public health, preventive medicine, and therapeutic medicine. It is not unusual to set claims that the mortality levels of these countries approximate those of the developed nations.

In turn, behavioral scientists have presented numberous observations attesting to the fact that there is great resistance to the adoption of new cultural practices that are not readily integrated into the previously existing culture. Medical sociologists and anthropologists have reported numerous examples of resistance to the adoption of new health practices in Latin America.

Until this time, the two sets of apparently contradictory claims have been allowed to exist in the literature with no efforts or investigations that would examine their validity. The respective claimants have not found any substantial evidence that is acceptable both to persons utilizing the field-study approach and to those using the demographic approach. The demographer has not been influenced by the isolated case studies and theoretical claims made by behavioral scientists working at the applied health level. In turn, these persons have not been overly impressed by the supposed evidence of the demographers' model life tables which indicate great improvements in health conditions since these changes are to visible at the level of local villages.

This study examines the respective claims and the available deomgraphic data to determine the validity of the respective observations and conclusions. Which of the two should be accepted? Or, is there the possibility that these seemingly contradictory observations can be reconciled?

NEW HEALTH PRACTICES: CONSIDERATIONS AND ACCEPTANCE

Resistance to the adoption of Western medical and public health practices has been exhibited by the people of South America for a variety of reasons. In many cases, this resistance has been compounded by the change agent's lack of understanding of the host culture.

Western medical culture has failed to consider the merits of the existing, indigenous explanations and methods of treatment of disease. Present knowledge of the nature of culture indicates that there is a degree of integration that exists among the "parts" of a culture. In other words, the methods of coping with diseases that exist within a given culture have specific meaning to that culture. Polgar (1963) states in his treatment of the "fallacy of the empty vessels" that we attempt to pour out the "new wine" of information only to see it spill upon the ground unused. We have failed to regard the fact that the indigenous peoples already have explanations and practices for coping with disease.

Also, little consideration has been given to the existing levels of understanding concerning environmental sanitation and the germ theory of disease, both critical to the nature of public health as we know it. Foster (1953) points to these as reasons for the failure of the "pit privy" program in Latin American villages. In addition, Erasmus (1954) states that a basic lack of understanding of modern concepts of the etiology of disease is responsible for the failure to adopt modern methods of prevention. Microbes are credited with causative powers, but many tradition diseases have not been linked to them (Erasmus, 1952). Consequently, when there is conflict between folk and scientific medicine, the physician frequently comes off second best (Foster, 1953).

Our ethnocentric point of view combined with our fine technical training has led us to believe that the best way to accomplish the goal of assisting South American and other developing nations is to duplicate Western medical programs and projects (Foster, 1962). We exported health centers, designed according to Western concepts, that "offered maternal and child health services, laboratory analyses, dental care, home visits by public health nurses, environmental sanitation control exercised by sanitarians, and vital statistics analysis" (Foster, 1969). The problem these newly exported health centers faced was to convince people to reject their old customs and ideas about health and to substitute new ones which lay outside their conceptual world; i.e., to convince the people that modern medicine and hygenic living are forms of personal health insurance that will keep them in better health, make them live longer, make them able to work more efficiently, and allow them to enjoy life more fully (Foster, 1953).

In order to accept these basic assumptions and embrace Western medicine, South Americans would be forced to reject integral parts of their culture; namely, their traditional medical beliefs and practices. Explanations of illness and appropriate means for dealing with it are deeply rooted in the basic assumptions of a culture (Simmons, 1960). Western health teams have tended to ignore the problems of integration of modern medical practices into Latin American cultures.

The degree of "goodness of fit" has a bearing on whether or not the host culture accepts "alien" health practices. Since diffusion of culture traits is not a passive process, it is only logical to assume that the host culture will modify, interpret or possibly reject new ideas depending upon whether or not these ideas are culturally compatible (Roney, 1954). The process of reinterpretation of new ideas in order to insure proper cultural "fit," allows for the retention of the original function of the practice and the conformity to the patterns of meaning of the "host" culture (Foster, 1962). Western medical agents have attempted to modify or eliminate beliefs which are in conflict with the teachings of modern medicine, rather than utilizing those beliefs that **are** or **can be made** consonant with these teachings (Foster, 1953). There is a good case to be made for "resistance to change" on the grounds that Western health agents have not been sufficiently flexible to allow for some degree of reinterpretation of function to occur. This flexibility aids in the integration of modern medical practices to a greater extent than does the outright denial of existing popular medical practices.

In some cases, flexibility is almost precluded by virtue of the magnitude of the differences between the underlying philosophies concerning health and illness. To Latin Americans, health consists of feeling well, and illness is largely a matter of fate, luck, or carelessness in personal habits (Foster, 1953). Luck and fate are incorporated into Western medical philosophy to the extent that we can be exposed to a germ or virus, or inherit a tendency toward illness but, for the most part, Westerners believe that they can control the direction of their health through individual responsibility in keeping fit (Gonzalez, 1966). The Latin American fatalistic orientation toward the question of health and illness is more easily understood if consideration is given to their conception of the causation of disease.

In addition to the causes of disease which correspond to modern medical etiology, Latin Americans also give credence to magical and supernatural causes that are not verifiable or understandable in terms of their knowledge (Forster, 1953). In the case of magical causation, Foster points to **mal de ojo** (evil eye) as a widespread "illness" in Latin America. He also indicates psychological causes as being important and cites **susto** (fright) which results from a shock that separates the spirit from the body (Foster, 1953). Illnesses of supernatural, magical, and psychological etiology are in the domain of folk medicine and, therefore, are inaccesible to the ministrations of modern medicine (Simmons, 1960). Therefore, due to differing conceptions of health, illness, and etiology on the part of modern medicine as opposed to the popular medical beliefs, strong resistance to changes in health practices can be expected and are well documented.

On the basis of the existing cultural resistance to modern public health and medical practices, it would seem that those practices that have been most successful involve little individual action on the part of South Americans. In other words, chlorination of drinking water, spraying D.D.T. for malaria reduction, innoculation for smallpox, etc., have been critical in the eradiction of disease vectors, but the sense of individual responsibility in hygiene and public health is lacking.

DEMOGRAPHIC CLAIMS OF GREAT IMPROVEMENTS IN HEALTH

The most obvious examples of available demographic materials upon which claims of greatly reduced mortality are based may be found in any of the DEMOGRAPHIC YEARBOOKS published by the United Nations during the past decade. The reported death rates for the nations of South America approximate, and in some cases are even lower than the rates reported for the most highly developed countries. These examples tend to be reinforced by a report on mortality levels using model life tables found in the UNITED NATIONS DEPARTMENT OF SOCIAL AND ECO- NOMIC AFFAIRS POPULATION BULLETIN.

Because the mortality statistics for the nations of South America are incomplete and/or of a highly dubious quality, most demographers have tended to rely heavily upon the construction of life tables from which the average expectations of life and mortality rates can be derived. All of the claims pertaining to the levels of mortality and the decreases in these levels are based on (or substantiated by) life table values.

Using this type of data, Stolnitz (1955; 1956) was able to trace the historical trends to the reduction of mortality in both the presently developed portions of the world as well as those areas that are presently considered to be developing. He notes that a relatively unrecognized factor in the reduction of mortality in the presently developed countries was that of innovations in public health and sanitation. Therefore, it should not be surprising that the importation of this factor into developing nations has also resulted in substantial declines in mortality (Stolnitz, 1965).

Davis (1956), who initially approaches declines in mortality from an eco- nomic perspective, is also quick to state that the drastic decreases in the mortality rates of developing areas are the result of new public health and medical programs rather than economic development. Using improved life tables, Arriaga and Davis (1969) again document the rapid declines in mortality in Latin America and predict that this trend will continue. The present interpretations of the demographic data tend to agree that (1) there have been drastic decreases in the mortality levels of the countries of South America; (2) the most substantial part of the decrease has taken place since the 1930's; and, (3) the present mortality levels approximate those of the developed nations.

There can be little controversy about the first two conclusions. By applying the same techniques to the demographic data for different time periods, it becomes obvious that a decrease in mortality has taken place in these countries. Futhermore, it is apparent that most of the decline has taken place since the 1930's. The question that remains unanswered is, "Given the known resistance to changing health practices, how could these very low levels of mortality have been achieved?" Actually the phrasing of the preceding question results in the dilemma of trying to reconcile the two contradictory sets of claims made by behavioral scientists and demographers, respectively.

The question only becomes answerable if it is broken into two components:

1. What types of deaths have been reduced sufficiently so as to result in the downward trend of the death rate? and
2. How accurate are the claims about the present levels of mortality?

ANALYSIS OF CAUSE-OF-DEATH STATISTICS

Although cause-of-death statistics ostensibly provide only data about the number of persons succumbing to the various underlying causes of death, this approach largely limits the usefulness of these materials to clinical studies and evaluations of specific programs. Furthermore, the information can be used for these purposes only when there is a relatively high degree of accuracy in the diagnoses and certification of the causes of death. Thus, an analysis of the ranking of the importance of specific causes of death in the various nations of South America would be of little value.

However, cause-of-death statistics can be used as a source of basic data for two types of analyses of health and illness in populations. First, they can provide a good index of the level of public health problems of a population. The proportion that conditions amenable to public health measures (i.e., infective and parasitic diseases [B1-B17], certain diseases of the digestive syistem [B33-B37], and certain diseases of early infancy [B42-B44] are of all deaths can be used as such a yardstick. (**Note:** The numbers in brackets refer to the classification in **List B** of the Sixth and Seventh Revisions of the International and Statistical Classification of Diseases, Injuries and Causes of Death, 1955, 1957). The degenerative diseases (such as malignant neoplasms [B18], vascular lesions of the central

55

nervous system [B22], and certain diseases of the circulatory system [B24-B29] which are not readily influenced by known public health measures may be considered as complementary to those that respond to public health programs. (**Note:** Although statistics are available that are four to six years more recent than those presented here, we are particularly interested in the period of the early 1960's which was selected as a benchmark since it approximates the time of extensive field observations by one of the authors [Linden]. We are unaware of any drastic changes in health conditions that have taken place since that time.)

A second type of analysis utilizing cause-of-death statistics is the measurement of the level of medical attention available to a population. Accurate diagnoses are essential in order for apropriate and effective therapeutic measures to be applied successfully. The level of medical resources is reflected in the adequacy of diagnoses and the utilization of therapy to prevent death from those conditions that can be controlled by modern medical techniques.

CONDITIONS AMENABLE TO PUBLIC HEALTH MEASURES

The prevention of diseases that can lead to death is the primary objective of public health programs. Immunization, the control of insect and animal vectors of disease, quarantine, and sanitation are basic public health techniques that have been used with great success to reduce mortality in the economically and socially developed countries throughout the world. These techniques function by breaking the chain of transmission of the disease and are effective primarily against the infective and parasitic diseases.

Although most diseases having infective or parasitic etiologies were included in the category of infective and parasitic diseases [B1-B17], there were important exclusions. The gastro-enteric diseases were included in the infective and parasitic category only when the etiological organism had been specifically diagnosed and certified. Unless there had been this precise diagnosis, the death was classified to gastritis, duodenitis, enteritis, and colitis [B36]. Similarly, most infections of infants were attributed to infections of the newborn [B43] or other diseases peculiar to early infancy [B44] unless there was a diagnosis of the specific etiological organism.

In order to combine the deaths due to gastro-enteric diseases and the infections of infants with the other infective and parasitic diseases, it is necessary also to include deaths from certain diseases that are classified similarly, but that are not of infective or parasitic origin. The error that is introduced by this procedure is comparatively small, and it becomes insignificant when consideration is given to the problem of distinguishing between these infective and noninfective conditions when the symptomology may be similar and only the results of laboratory tests can supply the correct answer. (See **Table 1**)

56

TABLE 1

NUMBER AND PERCENTAGES OF DEATHS DUE TO DISEASES AMENABLE TO
PUBLIC HEALTH MEASURES IN THE NATIONS OF SOUTH AMERICA,
SELECTED YEARS IN THE PERIOD 1954-1964

Country and year	Total number of deaths	Deaths due to diseases amenable to public health measures*	
		Number	Per cent of total deaths
Argentina			
1955 (P)	167,178	25,110	15.0
1960	170,195	23,462	13.8
Bolivia			
1954	36,812	14,411	31.0
Brazil			
d/ 1954	32,339	10,173	31.4
a/ 1961	162,710	48,298	29.7
Chile			
1955	87,843	25,520	29.0
1964	94,058	29,864	31.6
Colombia			
e/ 1955	161,863	50,893	31.4
1964 (P)	175,349	59,245	33.8
Ecuador			
1955	57,226	25,146	43.9
1964	58,989	21,531	39.9
Paraguay			
f/ 1955	9,129	2,311	25.3
1962	9,311	2,091	22.4
Peru			
c,g/ 1955	36,310	15,006	41.3
b/ 1963	56,276	21,416	38.0
Uruguay			
1955	20,611	2,322	11.3
1961	21,954	3,272	14.9

TABLE 1 --Continued

Country and year	Total number of deaths	Deaths due to diseases amenable to public health measures*	
		Number	Per cent of total deaths
Venezuela			
a/ 1955	52,294	15,400	29.4
c/ 1963	58,269	14,859	25.5

*Includes infective and parasitic diseases (B1-B17), certain diseases of the digestive system (B33-B37), and certain diseases of early infancy (B42-B44).

(P)   Provisional or preliminary.

a/   Statistics only for the State of Sao Paulo and the Cities of Recife and Rio de Janeiro.

b/   Comprises only those deaths with medical certification and excludes deaths due to accident, suicide, and homicide.

c/   Excludes Indian jungle population.

d/   Statistics only for the Federal District, which is now the State of Guanabara.

e/   Data are burial permits.

f/   Data are for an area covered by 44 Health Units and 76 Health Posts, which is not representative of Paraguay.

g/   Data are medically certified deaths only.

Sources: Compiled and computed from data in the United Nations, Demographic Yearbook, 1961 (New York: United Nations Statistical Office, 1961); United Nations, Demographic Yearbook, 1957 (New York: United Nations Statistical Office, 1957); and Inter American Statistical Institute, American en Cifras, 1965, Situacion Demografica: Estado y Movimiento de la Poblacion (Washington, D.C.: Pan American Union, 1966).

58

No nation in South America has achieved the same low proportion of deaths due to diseases amenable to public health measures as may be found in most of the countries of Europe and in the United States of America and Australia. In most of these countries, less than 10 percent of the deaths are attributed to these causes. Only Argentina and Uruguay approach this level. (See **Table 4** for comparative statistics. Differences between the Sixth and Seventh Revisions of the Internation Classification of Diseases are ignored since only insignificant changes would result in any but the most detailed categories [Faust and Dolman, 1958; 1965]). The other nations of that continent have two to four times this relative number of preventable deaths.

DISEASES REFLECTING LEVELS OF AVAILABLE MEDICAL CARE

When adequate measures for the prevention of infective and parasitic diseases are lacking, it does not necessarily follow that deaths from these causes will be numerous. Modern medicine has a large arsenal of weapons for the cure of infective and parasitic diseases. Thes range from direct antibiotic therapy to general supportive therapy and symptomatic treatment of the illness. However, where reliance is placed upon the medical treatment of illness rather than the prevention of disease, the level of mortality from infective and parasitic diseases will be slightly higher. This is because some ill persons will die despite adequate therapy when they would not have even become ill had there been effective prevention.

The level of medical care is inversely related to the proportion of deaths occurring with lack of precise diagnoses of the illnesses, as well as deaths from causes due to diseases amenable to public health measures where effective therapy is known to exist. Statistics for deaths amenable to public health measures; deaths that are inaccurately diagnosed or certified and are classified to senility, ill-defined, and unknown causes (B45) and all other causes (B46); and deaths due to certain diseases of the respiratory system (B30-B32) are combined and presented in **Table 2.** The diseases of the respiratory system are included because even when there may not be a specific antibiotic therapy available for a particular disease, a high level of general supportive and symptomatic therapy will markedly reduce mortality from these diseases.

Only Uruguay compares favorably with the countries of the world known to have high levels of medical care. In the other nations of South America, deaths due to diseases that reflect a low level of available medical care number 50 to 75 per cent of the total deaths. This compares with the approximately 25 per cent that these causes are of all causes of death in the United States of America, Denmark, England, Wales, and Australia.

TABLE 2

NUMBER AND PERCENTAGES OF DEATHS DUE TO DISEASES WHICH
REFLECT THE LEVEL OF AVAILABLE MEDICAL CARE IN THE
NATIONS OF SOUTH AMERICA, SELECTED YEARS IN THE
PERIOD 1954-1964

Country and year		Total number of deaths	Deaths due to diseases which reflect the level of available medical care	
			Number	Per cent of total deaths
Argentina				
	1955 (P)	167,178	83,339	49.8
	1960	170,195	97,131	57.1
Bolivia				
	1954	36,812	25,242	68.6
Brazil				
d/	1954	32,339	16,500	51.0
a/	1961	162,710	94,398	58.0
Chile				
	1955	87,843	61,498	70.0
	1964	94,058	55,579	59.1
Colombia				
e/	1955	161,863	121,476	75.0
	1964 (P)	175,349	110,601	63.1
Ecuador				
	1955	57,226	50,104	87.6
	1964	58,989	46,364	78.6
Paraguay				
f/	1955	9,129	7,038	77.1
	1962	9,311	5,336	57.3
Peru				
c,g/	1955	36,310	26,123	71.9
	1963	56,276	45,731	81.3
Uruguay				
	1955	20,611	6,922	33.6
	1961	21,954	6,254	29.7

TABLE 2 --Continued

Country and year	Total number of deaths	Deaths due to diseases which reflect the level of available medical care	
		Number	Per cent of total deaths
Venezuela			
a/ 1955	52,294	38,953	74.5
c/ 1963	58,269	38,015	65.2

*Includes infective and parasitic diseases (B1-B17); certain diseases of the respiratory system (B30-B32); certain diseases of the digestive system (B33-B37); certain diseases of early infancy (B42-B44); senility, ill-defined, and unknown causes (B45); and all other diseases (B46).

(P)· Provisional or preliminary.

a/ Statistics only for the State of Sao Paulo and the Cities of Recife and Rio de Janeiro.

b/ Comprises only those deaths with medical certification and excludes deaths due to accident, suicide, and homicide.

c/ Excludes Indian jungle population.

d/ Statistics only for the Federal District, which is now the State of Guanabara.

e/ Data are burial permits.

f/ Data are for an area covered by 44 Health Units and 76 Health Posts, which is not representative of Paraguay.

g/ Data are medically certified deaths only.

Sources: Compiled and computed from data in the United Nations, Demographic Yearbook, 1961 (New York: United Nations Statistical Office, 1961); United Nations, Demographic Yearbook, 1957 (New York: United Nations Statistical Office, 1957); and Inter American Statistical Institute, America en Cifras, 1965, Situacion Demografica: Estado y Movimiento de la Poblacion (Washington, D.C.: Pan American Union, 1966).

TABLE 3

NUMBER AND PERCENTAGES OF DEATHS DUE TO DEGENERATIVE DISEASES
IN THE NATIONS OF SOUTH AMERICA, SELECTED YEARS
IN THE PERIOD 1954-1964

Country and year	Total number of deaths	Deaths due to degenerative diseases*	
		Number	Per cent of total deaths
Argentina			
1955(P)	167,178	65,677	39.3
1960	170,195	53,472	31.4
Bolivia			
1954	36,812	1,678	4.6
Brazil			
d/ 1954			
a/ 1961	162,710	50,030	30.7
Chile			
1955	87,843	17,074	19.4
1964	94,058	23,137	24.6
Colombia			
e/ 1955	161,863	18,418	11.4
1964 (P)	175,349	26,461	15.1
Ecuador			
1955	57,226	3,147	5.5
1964	58,989	4,124	7.0
Paraguay			
f/ 1955	9,126	1,140	12.5
1962	9,311	1,455	15.6
Peru			
c,a/ 1955	36,210	5,690	15.7
1963	56,276	7,115	12.6
Uruguay			
1955	20,611	10,064	48.8
1961	21,954	11,657	53.1

TABLE 3 --Continued

Country and year	Total number of deaths	Deaths due to degenerative diseases*	
		Number	Per cent of total deaths
Venezuela			
g/ 1955	52,294	8,091	15.5
c/ 1963	58,269	12,182	20.9

*Includes malignant neoplasms (B18), vascular lesions of the central nervous system (B22), and certain diseases of the circulatory system (B24-B29).

(P)   Provisional or preliminary.

a/   Statistics only for the State of Sao Paulo and the Cities of Recife and Rio de Janeiro.

b/   Comprises only those deaths with medical certification and excludes deaths due to accident, suicide, and homicide.

c/   Excludes Indian jungle population.

d/   Statistics only for the Federal District, which is now the State of Guanabara.

e/   Data are burial permits.

f/   Data are for an area covered by 44 Health Units and 76 Health Posts, which is not representative of Paraguay.

g/   Data are medically certified deaths only.

Sources: Compiled and computed from data in the United Nations, Demographic Yearbook, 1961 (New York: United Nations Statistical Office, 1961); United Nations, Demographic Yearbook, 1957 (New York: United Nations Statistical Office, 1957); and Inter American Statistical Institute, America en Cifras, 1965, Situacion Demografica: Estado y Movimiento de la Poblacion (Washington, D.C.: Pan American Union, 1966).

The degenerative diseases, malignant neoplasms (B18), vascular lesions of the central nervous system (B22), and certain diseases of the circulatory system (B24-B29), are causes of death for which modern medicine lacks cures and can only delay the time of death. Despite their association with the aging process of humans, these diseases can be important causes of death even in the younger ages when mortality from other causes of death are reduced to comparatively low levels (cf. NATIONAL CENTER FOR HEALTH STATISTICS, Series 3, No. 1). In this sense they are complementary to the diseases that reflect the level of medical care.

In all of South America, only in Uruguay does the proportion of deaths due to degenerative diseases compare to those found in countries known to have high levels of medical care. In these countries over 50 to almost 70 per cent of all deaths are attributed to these diseases. In comparison less than one-third of all deaths are so classified in the other nations of South America.

CONCLUSIONS

Deaths due to diseases amenable to public health measures still constitute a sizable proportion of the total deaths in most countries of South America. However, analysis of detailed cause of death statistics reveals that no longer do scourges such as yellow fever, malaria, smallpox, cholera, etc., continue to run rampant. They have essentially been eliminated by public health methods requiring little or no individual participation. When deaths due to causes that require modern medicine or individual actions, such as personal hygiene, are considered, it may be seen that these still constitute an exceedingly high percentage of all deaths. This pattern is in contrast to the causes of death found in the developed countries of the world.

Therefore, on the basis of the analysis presented here, it can be concluded that there have been substantial reductions in the death rates of the nations of South America since the 1930's. Almost all of this reduction must have taken place among the diseases that do not require individual effort in order to be amenable to public health measures. With regard to the accuracy of the low levels of mortality that are claimed, we can find very little validity for such statements. Low levels of mortality and great proportions of deaths from causes that reflect the level of medical care cannot and do not co-exist in any place for which we have accurate mortality statistics.

It is necessary to conclude that demographers, in developing their trend lines, **have utilized an original level of mortality that is too low.** The observed trend is compatible with present levels of mortality, indicated by causes of death, only if the original levels were approximately 20 per thousand higher than those commonly mentioned. The apparent contradiction that prompted this investigation is the result of the apparent inability of demographers to accept the possibility that the developing countries might have had mortality levels far above any known today. For this reason it was easier for demographers to ignore the observations of applied behavioral scientists than to question the accuracy of the data produced by theoretical life-table models.

The author, Dr. Charles E. Cipolla, wishes to express gratitude to the first author of this essay, Dr. Leonard L. Linden (deceased), formerly Associate Professor of Sociology at the University of Georgia.

TABLE 4

PERCENTAGES SELECTED CAUSES OF DEATH ARE OF ALL REPORTED DEATHS IN SELECTED NATIONS
KNOWN TO HAVE MORTALITY STATISTICS OF HIGH QUALITY

Cause of death	United States of America (1959)	Denmark (1959)	France (1960)	England and Wales (1959)	Israel (1960)	Australia (1960)
Total deaths	100.0	100.0	100.0	100.0	100.0	100.0
Infective and parasitic (B1-B17)	1.4	0.9	2.6	1.2	1.9	1.1
Malignant neoplasms (B18)	15.7	22.8	17.3	18.4	18.6	15.0
Vascular lesions of the central nervous system (B22)	11.6	12.5	12.0	14.2	10.8	13.4
Certain diseases of the circulatory system (B24-B29)	39.5	30.6	19.2	33.2	29.6	37.2
Certain diseases of the respiratory system (B30-B32)	3.6	4.6	5.9	12.0	3.0	5.2

66

Certain diseases of the digestive system (B33-B37)	2.9	2.9	3.9	2.2	3.7	2.5
Certain diseases of early infancy (B42-B44)	4.1	2.3	1.9	1.8	5.8	3.0
Senility, ill-defined, and unknown causes (B45)	1.2	1.5	14.6	1.5	3.3	1.0
All other diseases (B46)	8.1	9.8	11.7	7.6	9.6	8.9

Source: Compiled and computed from data in the United Nations, _Demographic Yearbook, 1961_ (New York: United Nations Statistical Office, 1961).

REFERENCES

ARRIAGA, E.E. and DAVIS, K. (1969) "The Pattern of Mortality Change in Latin America," DEMOGRAPHY 6: 223.

DAVIS, K. (1956) "The Amazing Decline of Mortality in Underdeveloped Areas," AMER. ECON. REV. PAP. AND PROC., 46(Part II): 305.

ERASMUS, C.J. (1952) "Changing Folk Beliefs and the Relativity of Empirical Knowledge," SWEST. JR. ANTHROP. 8: 411.

ERASMUS, C.J. (1954) "An Anthropologist Views Technical Assistance," SCIENT. MON. 78: 147.

FAUST, M. and DOLMAN, A.B. (1958 1965) COMPARABILITY OF MORTALITY STATISTICS FOR THE SIXTH AND SEVENTH REVISIONS: United States Government Printing Office Vital Statist.-Special Rep. 51: 4.

FOSTER, G.M. (1953) "The Use of Anthropological Methods and Data in Planning and Operation," PUBL. HLTH. REP. 68: 841.

FOSTER, G.M. (1962) TRADITIONAL CULTURES: AND THE IMPACT OF TECHNOLOGICAL CHANGE. N.Y.: Harper and Row.

FOSTER, G.M. (1969) APPLIED ANTHROPOLOGY. Boston: Little Brown.

GONZALEZ, N.S. (1966) "Health Behavior in Cross-Cultural Perspective: A Guatemalan Example," HUM. ORG. 25: 122.

POLGAR, S. (1963) "Health Action in Cross-Cultural Perspective," In HANDBOOK OF MEDICAL SOCIOLOGY, edited by Freeman, H.E., Levine, S., and Reeder, L.G.) Englewood Cliffs, N.J.: Prentice-Hall, Inc.

RONEY, J.G. (1954) "The Place of Anthropology in a Technical Assistance Program," SCIENT. MON. 78: 159.

SIMMONS, O.G. (1960) "Popular and Modern Medicine in Mestizo Communities of Coastal Peru and Chile," In SOCIOLOGICAL STUDIES OF HEALTH AND SICKNESS (Edited by Apple, D.) N.Y.: McGraw-Hill Books.

STOLNITZ, G.J. (1955) "A Century of International Mortality Trends: I.," POPUL. STUD. 9: 24.

STOLNITZ, G.J. (1956) "A Century of International Mortality Trends: II," POPUL. STUD. 10: 17.

STOLNITZ, G.J. (1965) "Recent Mortality' Trends in Latin America, Asia, and Africa," POPUL. STUD. 19: 117.

CHAPTER 6

BETWEEN SHAMANS, DOCTORS AND DEMONS:
ILLNESS, CURING AND CULTURAL IDENTITY MIDST CULTURE CHANGE

Libbet Crandon

The simultaneous use of Western scientific medicne and "tradition" (Note 1) medical systems is the subject of a good number of studies (e.g., Kleinman, 1980; Leslie, 1980; Elling, 1981; Gonzales, 1966; Press, 1969; Simmons, 1955; Young, 1976; Young, 1981; Gould, 1957, 1965; Adair, 1963; Alland, Jr., 1964; Horton, 1967, etc.). Many assumed that the Western medical system would replace "traditional" medicine, that doctors and clinics would be recognized as superior to shamans and magic because it is superior (Foster, 1958), and that traditional systems are, therefore, dying out (Woods and Graves, 1973). This view has been replaced itself by more sophisticated analyses that have been more critical of Western medicine and more empirical in the efficacy of "traditional" systems; but more importantly they have recognized that medical efficacy itself is not necessarily the most significant aspect of any medical system. These studies have focused on aspects of medical systems that are economic (e.g., Montalvo, 1967; Wellin, 1955; Cosminsky, 1972), social (e.g., Barber, 1966; Kane and Kane, 1972; Nall and Speilberg,, 1968), legal (Fabrega and Silver, 1973; Selby, 1974), political (Lewis, 1955; Shiloh, 1968; Croizer, 1970; Leslie, 1963, 1968), and psychological (Jahoda, 1961, 1968; Koss, 1967; Kapland and Johnson, 1964; Rolger and Hollingshead, 1961). They argue that these factors inhibit an exclusive acceptance of the Western medical system and perpetuate the value of indigenous systems. They either conclude or imply that, rather than dying out, indigenous medical systems are adapting to change, and that medical pluralism rather than purely Western medicine will replace earlier medical resource use.

Throughout all these studies changing cultural identity persists as the one phenomenon common to situations of multiple medical resource use, or medical pluralism in the third world (Note 2). Only in a few instances has it been discussed directly (Clark, 1959a, 1959b), and only within the limited framework of a basically funcational analysis. These studies imply or state explicitly that traditional medical systems reinforce the traditional social order and its values in the face of neocolonialism, modernization or Anglo-ization. This position, however, contradicts medical pluralism among non-traditional groups such as middle-class Colombians (Taussig, 1980: 105; Press, 1969, 1971), Nigerians (Maclean, 1971), Brazilians (Pujarich, 1976), and even Americans (e.g., Nolan, 1974; Casteneda, 1974!). Nor can it account for the meaning of the content of multiple medical perspectives that are simultaneously held and employed by a single social group without resorting to arguments about complementary functions of the different medical systems, or about which one is more effective:

arguments I would hold, that are distinctly North American.

An alternative position is that elements from different medical systems, discussed or used within specific social contexts, carry information about cultural identify of the speaker, the person addressed, and the patient under discussion. Simultaneous use of several medical traditions permits a dialogue (Note 3) about cultural identity to take place without directly addressing cultural identity itself, which is often too sensitive a topic to be addressed directly. This dialogue in turn affects or even alters the social environment (Note 4). A look from this perspective at multiple medical resource use in a revolutionary setting where some major culture change is taking place, further highlights the specific processes unleashed by the medical doman (Note 5) through such dialogue which affect and are affected by that social change.

The object of this essay is to describe a case of insanity in a mestizo youth as an aspect of a crisis of cultural identity among rural Bolivian mestizos (Note 6) in a small, bi-ethnic agricultural peasant village on the altiplano. The crisis is significant not because it is representative of processes Bolivian (there are few bi-ethnic villages in highland rural Bolivia) but because it identifies aspects of medicine and social change not addressed before, and examplifies a process that may be common worldwide to environments and situations that share certain characteristics: ethnic or class pluralism, scarce resources and radical social change. As cultural identity plays a major role in the direction that national economic, political and developmental processes take at the local level, such crises affect the processes of modernization. More significantly, however, this crisis reveals the dynamic role medical beliefs and medical practices play in culture change, and suggests that multiple medical resource use is a medium by which each individual's identity in a context of radical social change is negotiated and defined.

In 1978, I was carrying out research in a highland village I call Kachitu (Note 7). Its residents are Aymara Indians who are mostly subsistence agriculturalists and mestizos who ruled the countryside around Kachitu and served the interests of the urban elite class by managing, taxing and controlling the Indians until the revolution of 1952 (Note 8) and who now are mostly desperately poor shop keepers and subsistence agriculturalists themselves. During my research a series of events illuminated the role the medical domain plays in the renegotiation of cultural identity between and among mestizos and Aymara in the post-1952 social order in which local Indian political and economic power has increased and mestizo power had radically diminished. **First**, a 22 year old mestizo male named Gonzalo became ill with what he insisted to be an Aymara defined illness: a type of insanity caused by the loss to a demonic being of one of his tree souls. As a mestizo, Gonzalo is a member of the Catholic Church which subscribes to the belief that each individual has one soul. The Aymara, however, though "Catholic," don't subscribe so closely to Church doctrine and hold their own indigenous religious cosmology which, among other beliefs, maintains a belief in three souls. Gonzalo,

70

therefore, claimed an Aymara illness. He rejected the possibility that he was suffering from a Western scientifically defined illness which would carry more prestige among mestizos. Indeed, the mestizos in Kachitu as a general rule, especially older mestizos, usually claim that only Indians suffer from Aymara illnesses (Note 9) if they allow them to be more than superstition at all, implying mestizo superiority over the Aymara and consequent immunity to their supernaturally caused infirmities and mishaps. **Second,** the mestizos in Kachitu differed in their opinion about the specific etiology of Gonzalo's illness, but an underlying grammar of these opinions expresses their consensus that Gonzalo played a critical role in the cultural identity they all share. **Third,** two shamans or **yatiris** attended Gonzalo's bedside but did not complete any cures. And **fourth,** Gonzalo was preceeded by four other recent cases that were similar in social and class position and age of the patient, type of illness, and absense of the shamanistic cure by a yatiri. These four individuals died as a result of their illnesses.

In February of 1978, Gonzalo came home to his village (pop. cerca 1,000) to celebrate the annual village fiesta. He had been working for some years as a cook in Santa Cruz, a city in the lowlands. He returned home with money in his pocket, a skill under his belt, and pride anticipating admiration from his friends and fellow villagers who had never ventured so far afield fromhome. He told wonderful stories of his glorious adventures, of the many women he had endeared to him, and of the luscious gastronomical ecstasies that he now knew how to prepare (e.g., pizza!).

But the mestizos in the village were not impressed with Gonzalo's achievements, adventures and worldly knowledge. To them, Gonzalo was the lazy ignorant son of the town crazy lady, whose worthlessness was blatantly evident in his disreputable behavior of drinking his money away at the fiesta like everyone else, rather than giving it to his mother Hermanea so that she could drink it away herself. In fact, Gonzalo did not drink more than anyone else at the fiesta; and he always bought beer to share with a variety of cohorts whom he wished to impress with his wonderful adventure stores, but to no avail. While it would have been noble for any son to turn over his savings to his mother, such an action for Gonzalo would have been contradictory because Hermanea was the town indigent and alcoholic. Like all the mestizos, Gonzalo did not laive up to the mestizo's image of themselves. While his behavior did not significantly differ from any other young man's at the fiesta, disreputable comportment was attributed to him because he was the son of the town crazy lady.

Just after the fiesta Gonzalo offered to accompany his uncle on a trip over the Andes into the valleys where the uncle would remain for the following months to teach school. The valleys are a magical place for aptiplano folk. Young boys go there with their fathers on commercial trips only when they come of age. The valleys are filled with delicious fruits, warm balmy weather, a different way of life, and magical enchantments that contrast sharply with the cold, barrenness and vast open spaces of the altiplano. To get there one must travel by foot many hours over deserted paths that cross over high mountain passes where the Aymara always leave sacred items to protect themselves from the enchanting but evil beings that haunt such lonely places in search of souls to steal, blood to drink, lives to take, and victims upon which to inflict disease.

Upon returning from the valleys across these deserted roads, Gonzalo saw a demonic old woman, was struck by fright and, he claimed, lost his soul to her thieving and malevolent hunger. That night in the village, Gonzalo rose from his bed and walked through the streets of the town, yelled at the villagers asleep behind their closed doors, broke a few windows and frightened the neighbors. Then he took to bed where he would not respond to questioning except to repeat softly that he had seen an old woman. He passed several days running about hurriedly but directionlessly, talking disjointedly, and behaving in a manner determined by the town to be crazy.

Everyone in town had a different opinion as to what was causing Gonzalo to go crazy. Some held that his craziness resulted from masturbation; others opined it was epilepsy; still others claimed it was laziness or perhaps demonic possession. Three other common explanations begin to shed light on the social role this diagnostic dialogue played within the village. Some individual sagreed that Gonzalo's fate was inevitable because craziness ran in his family. This hypothesis was established on the fact that four other youths related to Gonzalo's family had suffered mental illnesses and died in the process. However, all the mestizos in town are related to Gonzalo's family; and some of the individuals proposing this hypothesis were much more closely related to Gonzalo than these youths had been. Such a statement, therefore, claims either that these diagnosing individuals do not identify themselves as related to Gonzalo, thereby differentiating themselves from him, or that the entire village mestizo population might at any time also go crazy.

Some villagers felt that Gonzalo suffered from **karisiri** which is a condition that results from fat being magically stolen from one's kidneys. Before the revolution of 1952, this fat was stolen by a monk who victimized primarily Aymara, and who then gave the fat to Bishops to make holy oil. Recently this fat began to be stolen by various mestizos who learn the art, put their victims to sleep by blowing ground human bones in their direction, and use special machines which can be bought in pharmacies in La Paz, to extract the fat. Such fat is sold for profit in the city to factories which make expensive perfumed soaps from it to sell to the cosmopolitan elites, and to North American and European tourists. Finally, some villagers agreed with Gonzalo's own diagnosis that he had lost his soul to a demonic and hungry old woman (Note 10).

Mestizos in Bolivia acknowledge soul loss, but the phenomenon only occurs in children and is only fatal among infants. As the child grows, his soul becomes more entrenched in his body, and such soul loss becomes easily curable. It never occurred among adults during my 18 months in the village nor did anyone admit to the possibility of its occurring in mestizo adults as a fatal disease. But the Aymara, on the other hand, believe in three souls. One soul follows the mestizo pattern of growth and development, but a second soul is more crucial, can be lost by an adult, and usually leads to a very rapid death after diagnosis by the yatiri. Mestizos admit that this occurs in Indians, thereby differentiating themselves from that ethnic group.

Gonzalo's family sought help from two yatiris and the town doctor. The first yatiri diagnosed possession by the devil which required killing a red dog, giving the patient the brains and blood to consume, and taking the carcass to the scene at which the soul was stolen by the devil and exchanging it with the devil for Gonzalo's life. Though the family made all the necessary preprarations including finding and preparing a dog, the yatiri never returned to make the exchange.

The second yatiri diagnosed karisiri which required the administration of a special preparation. This particular yatiri was the cousin of a highly respected Aymara who had worked many years in the village clinic and had become thereby financially well off. This yatiri included along with his preparation a prescription for an I.V. solution of sugar water. The doctor took issue with the I.V., refused to sell it, said Gonzalo suffered from Bleuler's disease (schizophrenia), insisted the family keep this diagnosis secret, sequestered Gonzalo in the clinic and prescribed instead three days of sleep under heavy doses of valium and librium. At the end of the three days of sleep, Gonzalo became catatonic and remained that way for several weeks after he was removed by some American interests in the city (stimulated by a meddling, anxious anthropologist) to a hospital there.

The doctors in the city could find nothing wrong with Gonzalo except a metabolic imbalance of the brain, caused by what they did not know, except perhaps heavy doses of valium and librium (Note 11). Throughout this entire affair, which lasted about a month in the village and perhaps four in La Paz, Gonzalo continued to insist that he had seen an old woman and had lost his soul, which by virtue of the fact that he is an adult, would have to be one of these three Aymara souls. That is, throughout his illness, Gonzalo assumed an Indian identity. Furthermore, throughout his illness, the entire village, including Hermanea, assumed that Gonzalo would die.

The socioeconomic history of Gonzalo's family sheds some light on Gonzalo's role in the mestizo crisis in cultural identity in Kachitu because it closely parallels that of the families of the other four victims who died in the midst of illnesses similar to that of Gonzalo (though of different presumed causes). Gonzalo's parents, Don Magno and Dona Hermanea, married in the late 1940's. They were the cream of the prominent members of the local rural mestizo population who served in the countryside the interests of the Bolivian elites, by managing the local Aymara Indian population. But neither absentee landlords nor **patrones** themselves, and socially rejected by the elites they served and aspired to, this mestizo class had access to little cash and played no role in national political or economic processes. They had some privately owned land around the village, presumed Spanish heritage, and political, economic and jural control of the village and the communities around it, and of the Aymara who populated the area, either on haciendas which the mestizos oversaw, or on Aymara community land which the mestizos taxed.

The relationship between the mestizos and Aymara parallelled that of patron to client. The mestizos depended upon virtually free Aymara labor and resources for their subsistence. The mestizos exploited their produce and labor through **compadrazco** or fictive kin ties, and through their socially, economically, and politically superior position. Their superordinate position relative to the Aymara was clearly defined and expressed ritually, and in particular, medically as they looked towards La Paz and the Bolivian elites for both ideology and resources. Though provincial and financially poor, they were **gente decente** or "decent, white people" while the Aymara were **Indios**.

The MNR revolution of 1952 (Note 8) and the subsequent land reform of 1953 gave the Aymara arms, sufferage (Note 12), land, and the right to a minimum wage. Most of the rural mestizo land was reallocated to Aymara. Meanwhile, an evangelical church which had also settled in the village gave the Aymara education and employment. When occupations opened up after the revolution due to changes in the rural economy and the collapse of the hacienda system, the educated evangelical Aymara embarded upon entrepeneurial commercial activity, opening their own **tiendas** or small food stores so that they no longer had to patronize mestizo tiendas, and a variety of other employments that had not existed on the Altiplano before: bakeries, bicycle and radio repair shops, tailoring and shoemaking and other small scale services. One of their specific objectives voiced within the evangelical church was to undermine the Aymara's previous dependence upon the local mestizos. Furthermore, through the encouragement, insistence even, of the revolutionary government, the Aymara also took over the political and administrative positions in the village. Within a few years the evangelical Aymara surpassed the mestizos in education and income, superceded their local political control, and undermined the grounds upon which the mestizo class had expressed their social, even "racial", superiority for the last 400 years.

When the mestizos were confronted with the loss of their domain of power and this complete disruption of their socioeconomic and political universe, there were very few strategies open for them with which to deal with this change, and hopefully for them, reassume a position they could accept as dignified. Confined by their self image as **gente decente** and its corresponding principles of propriety, they could not resort to manual labor. Appropriate professions remained running tiendas, holding local political offices, and teaching school. But now the Aymara tiendas undermined mestizo business, political offices went to Aymara, and teaching positions are both notoriously underpaid as well as held by educated Aymara, further undermining the boundaries of ethnicity that supported the mestizo self image of **gente decente**.

Mestizos saw basically two possible strategies. One was to abandon the village and join the urban sector. But many were uneducated as well as members of the lowest position in the non-Indian Bolivian socioeconomic and political hierarchy; and for them, the prospect of moving to the city was frought with the dangers of urban slum living, poverty and loss of the prestige that had supported a gentlemanly way of life in the countryside. Consequently, some mestizos tried as an alternative strategy to remain in the village in spite of their losses and attempt to maintain their old cultural strategies, even though they no longer had an economic base to do so. And while the educated evangelical Aymara became proud, self-confident leaders, particularly in their chaurch where they gathered to discuss Aymara nationalism and read Paulo Freire's PEDAGOGY OF THE OPPRESSED, the mestizos who stayed on became poor in wealth and land, stripped of the fundamental symbols of their previous ethnic identity and economically, socially and politically impotent.

As the old categories of ethnicity, and appropriate behavior collapsed, the town experienced a crisis, not only in the whole sociopolitical system but in cultural identity as well. Few villagers agreed on exactly who was really a mestizo and who an Aymara, or even on precisely what these categories meant. Mestizos rarely trusted each other, and came to no consensus about appropriate behavior except the certainty that no one followed it. In dress, in conversation and gossip, in decisions, and most particularly in diagnosis (everyone had a diagnosis for everyone else's diseases) the mestizos tried on new identities, old identities, trying in some way to define everyone else's identity, and through this process, find an identity for themselves. The doman of medicine becamse a particularly effective medium through which to negotiate cultural identity. As individuals offered opinions about one another's ailments, conditions and treatments that stemmed from different medical traditions, and cloaked these opinions in social contexts, moods of expression and tones of voice, they also made statements about the identity of the subject, about the identity of themselves, and about the relationship between themselves and the subject.

The 1952 MNR revolution took away most of the land of Gonzalo's father. When Indians refused to work his fields any longer, his own agricultural skills could not compensate for this loss. Having at one time been the town judge, the town president, the **corregidor, preste** and local social elite, the new social order destroyed his prestige by denying him any of these positions. He had seven children to feed, and little means to do so. He became an alcoholic. He became violent, severely abused his wife and children, and drank away what little land they had left. Their tienda on the plaza fell into disrepair. Three children died, two perhaps of abuse. Two sons fled to the lowlands, **and** Hermanea farmed her only surviving daughter out to a family in La Paz where she would be safe from her father's temper and the village's losses, and perhaps learn a trade, in return for servant status throughout her childhood. Within a few years, Don Magno died of alcoholism, leaving Hermanea to survive by begging as the town crazy lady who was always drunk. It is interesting to note that it appeared to be primarily Aymara women who gave alms and alcohol to Hermanea.

The other mestizos in Kachitu abhorred the entire family because they were "filthy," "drunk," and "lazy," and exemplified more blatantly what all the town mestizos were undergoing. For example, while I did not take a survey on alcoholism, its prevailance among older mestizo men is high, and opinion has it that such alcoholism did not exist in Kachitu before the revolution, at least not as a common problem.

Gonzalo was one of the sons that ran away, having been rejected by his father. Unlike his brothers, however, Gonzalo was quite dark. In the Santa Cruz area mestizos are **cruzenos** or **cambas**: light skinned, Spanish emulating and elite aspiring mestizos, not unlike their compatriots from the altiplano, but much more cosmopolitan. They in turn compete against the highland mestizo or **colla**. The more "Indian-like" a colla is, the more the camba discriminates and socially rejects him. Consequently, Gonzalo found himself in hostile territory in Santa Cruz, and was treated as an Indian because he could not pass as a camba mestizo. Though he became a good cook (I assume), his strategies for success were impeded by his physiology and origin. Consequently, he decided to return home once he became skilled and travelled with money in his pocket to set himself up there as a mestizo, rather than as a wealthier "Indian" in Santa Cruz. But his strategy was a gamble. Upon his return, he discovered that there was no place for him at home either. In fact, there was no place at all for a rural mestizo who inherited the ideology of a dead social order and is blocked in all his attempts to fit into a new one.

When Gonzalo got sick several processes were unleashed. First, everyone in town agreed that he was crazy though they differed on how he got that way. At the same time, it had become clear to everyone that Gonzalo had no niche in the community, no social position in which he could exist; just as they themselves no longer had a constructive niche in the new social order. Somewhat worse off than many of the other village mestizos, Gonzalo had no land, and hence in Kachitu where there are no restaurants, he had no means of support and no immediate family to care for him. His situation was an exaggeration of the increasing poverty and powerlessness that all the Kachitu mestizos felt.

Furthermore, while the villagers disagreed on the cause of his craziness, all the etiologies they offered indicated their concurrence that it had been brought on by some shortcoming either of his own or of his family. That is, while they reject him socially, their diagnosis of his illness is an expression of that rejection.

Second, Gonzalo also proposes a diagnosis: he has seen an enchanted old lady and is dying of an Aymara disease which many Aymara no longer have credence in, which he contracted in a magical no-man's-land and from which he could expect to die. He thereby expressed in his self diagnosis his own alienation from his village and his social class.

Third, even the doctor in Kachitu, and later those in the hospital in La Paz provide no social context for Gonzalo's condition. To them, he was either schizophrenic—a disease that was not to be made known socially—or suffering from an inexplicable metabolic imbalance about which they could do nothing. As there is no place anywhere for Gonzalo, he must cease to exist.

Several conclusions concerning the mestizo's attempts to define their own identity through the use of etiological labelling, can be drawn from this case. While everyone agreed Gonzalo was crazy, and that such craziness was his own fault, the nature of that fault differed. Some Kachitunos resorted to scientific ideas (such as epilepsy), others to hispanic and colonial notions (devil possession, masturbation, and laziness), and still others to clearly Aymara ideology (Karisiri, and loss of spirit to a demonic being—or soul theft), and in doing so they expressed their opinion of themselves and of one another and of their relationship to Gonzalo.

Individuals who suggested epilepsy viewed themselves as the town aristocrats, clung on to the pre-1952 image of mestizo culture, and continued to aspire to cosmopolitan ideas. To them, epilepsy is a congenital disease that runs in inferior families and is a disgraceful disease to have within one's lineage. Consequently, the opinion that Gonzalo suffered from epilepsy was to say that one who voices such an opinion is socially upwardly mobile and cosmopolitan in orientation, that Gonzalo himself was inherently (genetically) incapable of becoming a responsible and respectable adult, and that his fate and condition was in no way related to or effected by that of the opinion givers. Likewise the other failures in town, Hermanea and the other four youths who had died, are not a reflection of recent mestizo history but of a family disease.

Individuals who suggested devil possession, masturbation or laziness were older Kachitunos who, like Gonzalo's parents, had lost everything or nearly everything since 1952. Many of the men who offered such opinions were alcoholics. All continued to differentiate themselves in a variety of ways from the Aymara. Their etiological claims do not set them apart from Gonzalo's family but assert instead that Gonzalo's afate is his own fault: the result of his own misbehavior. This blatant individualism does not conflict with the lack of unity and increasing alienation among and between the villagers themselves, and releases them from any responsibility toward Gonzalo. It also implies that those who have such insight into Gonzalo's situation are individuals who are free of demonic influence, do not masturbate (a self destructive and humiliating activity), and exemplify good behavior.

Finally, individuals who expressed Aymara derived etiologies were consistently individuals who had established some sort of egalitarian relations with the Aymara. Such individuals were not limited to the town's most poor though they did tend to be almost exclusively women with three or four children, no land, and husbandswho worked as rural school teachers and were consequently away from home some six or seven months of the year. These women depended primarily on their husbands' income to meet their needs, which husbands frequently did not send home, upon

77

occuasional opportunities to wash sheets from the local six bed clinic that usually had no in-patients, and upon a minimal trade of herbs and magical items they exchanged for grain and potatoes at the local Sunday peasant market. These resources continually proved inadequate. Constantly strapped for resources, such women had established reciprocal exchange relationships and social ties with Aymara women of which their husbands often vociferously disapproved.

For these women, the epxression of Aymara derived etiologies contained multiple statements about their perceptions of changing social relationships within the village. It expressed an acceptance of Aymara beliefs and hence of egalitarian social relations with Aymara individuals. It thereby expressed an acceptance of the end of the old social order that pertained between Aymara and mestizos before 1952 and an acknowledgement of the contemporary inadequacy of the mestizo cultural identity that went with it. It further expressed, therefore, the precariousness of life that can be snatched without warning by a supernaturtal entity and not a natural one, and without moral cause; a precariousness the mestizos had before the revolution been able to shield themselves against when they politically and economically controlled the area. That is, these women expressed in their diagnosis of Gonzalo's illness, the fact that their relationship to economic and political processes that are now controlled by national policies and which exclude active rural mestizo participation, parallels the economic and political relationship that the Aymara had had with the mestizos before 1952.

The very expression within the village of these beliefs further solidifies the various types of social relations each individual was trying to negotiate with one another and with the Aymara. A fusion of interests among the above mentioned women with their Aymara women friends was further demonstrated in their joint contributions to Hermanea's welfare: it was to these women (as well as to Aymara women) that Hermanea could come to beg and receive food and other necessities. Likewise, it was these women who gave Hermanea sympathy in their concurrence with her opinion that Gonzalo was going to die.

The concurrence among all the villagers that Gonzalo would probably die and that the yatiris' refusals to complete Gonzalo's cures point to an evident change in the function of shamanism within the village that also recognizes a shift in cultural identity among mestizos. Yatiris usually rally their talents and paraphernalia to mobilize social support for the ill and reaffirm the patient's rightful position in the society. The dispensation of medical care alone indicates that the community is behind the curer and therefore the individual patient; and care is a symbol of reintegration of the patient into society.

However, for Gonzalo, there is no rightful position so the yatiris do **not** reintegrate him through their cures into village life, but rather reaffirm his alienation by completing nothing. In this way, the yatiris continue to ply their trade, now expressing the socioeconomic and political stress inherent in the village, the impotence and placelessness of all the poor rural mestizos in the town, as well as the entrepeneurial advances of the Aymara through the inclusion of an I.V. prescription in a karisiri treatment. They, like the villagers, use elements from both indigenous and scientific medical system to make statements about social relations as well as to effect those social relations. For them, like the villagers, the simultaneous use of elements from two different medical systems is a tool not only to control illness but to affect social life.

That is, ideology is not a mere reflection of a social environment. It operates instead to change the environment as much as changes in the environment alter it. Through ideology, a dialogue can take place between and among individuals as a continual negotiation process about the moral nature and meaning of a society and what goes on within it. Medical ideology is a particularly powerful instrument through which certain kins of negotiations take place; specifically those pertaining to cultural identity, how people define themselves and others and their own relationships to others.

This suggests that only in an homogenous society in which political and economic resources are distributed to the satisfaction of the entire population, will a single medical system be adhered to, now that multiple systems are nearly universally available. Such an hypothesis might account for such phenomena that is flourishing in our own culture such as health foods, Katheryn Kuhlman, Toni Agpaoa, Norbu Chien, the recent rise in witch ovens, and other alternative healing systems, all of which have more to offer individual subscribers than simply different health measures.

ENDNOTES

1. The term "traditional" as a referrant to a particular type of medical system is highly misleading. It refers to most if not all systems that do not derive from Western science; it implies therefore and quite mistakenly that all such systems are similiar and that Western medicine and its derivitives are universally uniform in value, practice, form and theory. Fred Dunn (1974) has contributed a typology of medical systems, consisting of local, regional, and cosmopolitan systems, which is a small but significant step in addressing this problem and providing a semantic way of handling multiple medical systems.

2. It cannot be said that changing cultural identity is universally common to all instances of medical pluralism, as multiple medical resources use is common among white middle-class Americans. Following my argument in this paper, I might suggest that multiple use in this latter population permits information exchange or a dialogue about the content of class identify.

3. I am using the word "dialogue" in the sense that Michael Foucault uses the term.

4. See, for example, Michael Taussig (1980) who demonstrates the impact of Columbian and Bolivian peasant dialogues upon the encroaching capitalist system. Though his point is different than the medical one I am discussing here, the process is the same. See in particular his discussion of the devil and cosmogenesis of capitalism: 102-109.

5. "Medical doman" refers to all aspects of a medical system and medical beliefs.

6. Mestizos are individuals of presumed Indian and Spanish blood. The actuality of their genetic makeup is less important than the cultural adefinition of their identity. They define themselves as not being Indian, and frequently being hispanic entirely. In fact, they are the population that serves the interests of the elites of the urban centers, in the countryside, which consist primarily of managing and exploiting the Indians. The elites, however, socially reject the mestizos.

7. Kachitu, and the names of the individuals herein are fictitious (See Crankshaw, 1980). The village is composed of approximately 1,000 individuals, about half of which are mestizo, half Aymara. Its population today is somewhat less than it was in 1952.

8. The MNR or **Movimiento nacional revolucionario** was the only real revolution in Bolivian history in that it brought about social change. It destroyed the hacienda system, instituted land reform, and nationalized

the mines which were and remain responsible for some 90% of Bolivia's national income.

9. The mestizos on the altiplano were actually using Aymara, Western, hispanic, and Callaguaya medical systems, a complexity too multifacted to discuss here.

10. Again, the reader is advised to see Taussig (1980) for some interesting parallels and different uses of the image of the devila which emphasize my point that this proces under discussion is a part of the process of modernization.

11. Two possibilities may also have triggered Gonzalo's catatonia. The doctor may in fact have given an intravenous sugar solution and the yatiri may have also provided at least the karisiri potion (but nothing else) which has sugar in it. Excessive sugar after heavy alcohol indulgence can produce catatonia and/or severe convulsions. Gonzalo had been drinking for three weeks as fiesta fell just after Carnaval in 1978.

12. The significance of sufferage was merely symbolic; and today the rural mestizos have no more access to power than the Aymara. Elections in 1978, 1979, and 1980 were overthrown.

REFERENCES

ADAIR, JOHN (1963) "Physicians, Medicine Men and Their Navaho Patients," in I. Galdston, ed. MAN'S IMAGE IN MEDICINE AND ANTHROPOLOGY. N.Y.: International University Press.

ALLAND, ALEXANDER, JR. (1964) "Native Therapists and Western Medical Practitioners Among the Abron of the Ivory Coast," TRANSACTIONS OF THE NEW YORK ACADEMY OF SCIENCES 26: 714-725.

BARBER, C.R. (1966) "An Inquiry into Possible Social Factors Making for Acceptance of Institutional Delivery in a Predominantly Rural Area of Western Nigeria," JOURNAL OF TROPICAL MEDICINE AND HYGIENE 69: 63-65.

BOLTON, RALPH (1980) "On Susto and Hypoglycemia," Paper presented to the 79th Annual Meetings of the American Anthropological Association, Washington, D.C. Accepted for publication by ETHNOLOGY.

CASTANEDA, CARLOS (1974) TALES OF POWER. N.Y.: Touchstone.

CLARK, MARGARET (1959a) "The Social Functions of Mexican-American Medical Beliefs," CALIFORNIA's HEALTH 16: 21: 153-156.

CLARK, MARGARET (1959b) HEALTH IN THE MEXICAN-AMERICAN CULTURE. Berkeley: University of California Press.

COSMINSKY, SHEILA (1972) "Decision-Making and Medical Care in a Guatemalan Indian Community," Ph.D. Dissertation, University Microfilm.

CROIZER, RALPH (1970) "Medicine, Modernization and Culture Crisis in China and India," COMPARATIVE STUDIES IN SOCIOLOGY AND HISTORY 12: 3: 275.

DUNN, FRED (1974) "Traditional Asian Medicine and Cosmopolitan Medicine as Adaptive Systems," In ASIAN MEDICAL SYSTEMS: A COMPARATIVE STUDY. Berkeley: University of California Press.

ELLING, RAY (ed.) (1981) "Traditional and Modern Medical Systems," Special edition of SOCIAL SCIENCE AND MEDICINE 15A: 2.

FABREGA and SILVER (1973) ILLNESS AND SHAMANISTIC CURING IN ZINACANTAN. Stanford: Stanford University Press.

FOSTER, GEORGE (1958) PROBLEMS IN INTERCULTURAL HEALTH PRACTICE. Pamphlet No. 12, N.Y.: Social Science Research Council.

GONZALES, NANCIE (1966) "Health Behavior in Cross Cultural Perspective: A Guatemalan Example," HUMAN ORGANIZATION 25: 122-125.

GUOULD, H.A. "The Implications of technological Change for Folk and Scientific Medicine," AMERICAN ANTHROPOLOGIST 59: 507.

GOULD, H.A. (1965) "Modern Medicine and Folk Cognition in Rural India," HUMAN ORGANIZATION 24: 201.

HORTON, ROBIN (1967) "African Traditional Thought and Western Science," AFRICA 37: 1: 50.

JAHODA, GUSTAV (1961) "Traditional Healers and Other Institutions Concerned with Mental Health in Ghana," INTERNATIONAL JOURNAL OF SOCIAL PSYCHIATRY 7: 245-268.

JAHODA, GUSTAV (1968) "Scientific Training and Persistence of Traditional Beliefs Among West African University Students," NATURE 220: 5174f.

KANE, ROBERT and ROSALIE KANE (1972) FEDERAL HEALTH CARE (WITH RESERVATIONS). N.Y.: Springer.

KAPLAN, BERT and DALE JOHNSON (1964) "The Social Meaning of Navajo Psychopathology and Psychotherapy," in MAGIC, FAITH AND HEALING, Edited by Ari Kiev. N.Y.: The Free Press.

KLEINMAN, ARTHUR (1980) PATIENTS AND HEALERS IN THE CONTEXT OF CULTURE. Berkeley: University of California Press.

KOSS, JOAN (1967) "Therapeutic Aspects of Puerto Rican Cult Practices," Paper presented to the 66th Meeting of the American Anthropological Association, Washington, D.C.

LANDY, DAVID (1974) "Role Adaptation: Traditional Curers Under the Impact of Western Medicine," AMERICAN ETHNOLOGIST 1: 1.

LESLIE, CHARLES (1963) "The Rhetoric of the Ayurvedic Revival in Modern India," MAN 81 and 82 (May), 72-73.

LESLIE, CHARLES (1980) "Medical Pluralism," Special edition of SOCIAL SCIENCE AND MEDICINE 14B: 4.

LESLIE, CHARLES (1968) "The Professionalization of Ayurvedic and Unani Medicine," TRANSACTIONS OF THE NEW YORK ACADEMY OF SEICNE SERIES II.

LEWIS, OSCAR (1955) "Medicine and Politics in a Mexican Village," in Benjamin Paul, ed. HEALTH, CULTURE AND COMMUNITY. N.Y.: Russell Sage.

MACLEAN, UNA (1971) MAGICAL MEDICINE: A NIGERIAN CASE STUDY. Baltimore: Penguin.

MONTALVO, A.S. (1967) "Sociocultural Change and Differentiation in a Rural Peruvian Community: An Analysis in Health Culture," No. 5 dissertation series. Latin American Studies Program. Ithaca, Cornell University.

NALL II, FRANK and Joseph Speilberg (1968) "Social and Cultural Factors in the Responses of Mexican-Americans to Medical Treatment," JOURNAL OF HEALTH AND SOCIAL BEHAVIOR.

NOLEN, M.D., WILLIAM A. (1974) HEALING. N.Y.: Random House.

PRESS, IRWIN (1969) "Urban Illness: Physicians, Curers and Dual Use in Bogota," JOURNAL OF HEALTH AND SOCIAL BEHAVIOR 10: 3: 209-218.

PRESS, IRWIN (1971) "The Urban Curandero," AMERICAN ANTHROPOLO-GIST 73: 741-756.

PUJARICH, ANDREA (1976) SURGEON OF THE RUSTY KNIFE (No publisher).

ROLGER, L.H. and A.B. HOLLINGSHEAD (1961) "The Puerto Rican Spirit-ualist as a Psychiatrist," AMERICAN JOURNAL OF SOCIOLOGY 67: 17-21.

SELBY, HENRY (1974) ZAPOTEC DEVIANCE: THE CONVERGENCE OF FOLK AND MODERN SOCIOLOGY. Austin: University of Texas Press.

SHILOH, AILON (1968) "The Interaction Between Middle Eastern and Western Systems of Medicine," SOCIAL SCIENCE AND MEDICINE 2: 235-248.

SIMMONS, OZZIE (1955) "Popular and Modern Medicine in Mestizo Com-munities of Coastal Peru and Chile," JOURNAL OF AMERICAN FOLK-LORE 68: 57-71.

TAUSSIG, MICHAEL T. (1980) THE DEVIL AND COMMODITY FETISHISM IN SOUTH AMERICA. Chapel Hill: University of North Carolina Press.

WELLIN, EDWARD (1955) "Water Boiling in a Peruvian Town," In Benjamin Paul, ed., HEALTH, CULTURE AND COMMUNITY. N.Y.: Russell Sage.

WOODS, CLYDE M. and T.D. GRAVES (1973) THE PROCESS OF MEDICAL CHANGE IN A HIGHLAND GUATEMALAN TOWN. Los Angeles: Latin American Center, University of California.

YOUNG, ALLAN (1976) "Some Implications of Medical Beliefs and Prac-tices for Social Anthropology," AMERICAN ANTHROPOLOGIST 78.

CHAPTER 7

WOMEN'S HEALTH CARE: A STUDY OF ISLAMIC SOCIETY

Eugene B. Gallagher and C. Maureen Searle

The Islamic Context

Among the ranks of Third World societies, Islamic societies occupy a broad yet distinctive niche. Despite their social and political diversity, their historic shaping by the religio-cultural matrix of Islam gives them a characteristic stance as they attempt to define and maintain Islamic values within the flux of social change.

The quest for modern health services is a high priority on the development agenda of Third World societies. The transition from local, traditional treatment modalities and conceptions of illness to the more cosmopolitan, scientific ways of biomedicine is a dimension of social change that has profound social implications, as profound as those of urbanization and industrialization, which are better-studied dimensions of social change. For those societies within the Islamic matrix, there is a full measure of Quranic prescription concerning health—specific practices enjoined upon the Individual for the preservation of his or her health, and recognition of the importance of healing practices to help ill persons. Because of this traditional orthodoxy, the promulgation and acceptance of modern medical care is a relatively unproblematic dimension of social change in Islamic societies. There is only the practical problem, formidable enough, of how to get enough medical care and how to deploy it most advantageously.

In contrast to the unproblematic nature of the desire for modern medical care, Islamic nations find themselves far less collected and certain concerning the scope and direction of the activities of women in society. Though the weight of tradition in virtually all Third World countries poses obstacles to an expanded role for women, this issue has a special salience in Islamic societies—for in these societies, there is not only the influence of folk practice and tradition but, as a superadded, contemporaneously vital force, the explicit directives of Islam concerning the social role of women, which foster their domestic seclusion and general subordination to male guardians in all extra-domestic, public matters. In relation to health progress, while Islamic societies highly value the health of females, there are thus significant questions of social policy and propriety concerning women as patients and their access to health facilities.

Saudi Arabia: Conservative and Rapidly Developing

This section will explore women's health care in Saudi Arabia in the light of the foregoing considerations. Saudi Arabian society is of current interest to students of social change, for it exemplifies social change on a scale and at a pace rarely if ever matched in human history. Yet Saudi Arabia is also a conservative society, by its own avowal and in the estimation of informed observers. It finds itself caught between contrary goals: wanting to advance technologically and, at the same time, wanting to preserve cultural tradition.

Saudi leaders are aware of the complexities underlying their pursuit of diverging objectives. Bakr Abd Allah Bakr, Rector of the University of Petroleum and Minerals in Dhahran, enunciated the Saudi perception in these words: "Some countries have sacrificed the soul of their culture in order to acquire the tools of Western technology. We want the tools but not at the price of annihilating our religion and our cultural values (Reynolds, 1980)." As it plunges into modernity, Saudi Arabia is using Western technology in its many spheres of development—in housing, in education and mass communications, in the expansion of agriculture, in the establishment of an industrial base, and in the provision of a nation--wide network of health services. However, it is the intention of the Saudi leadership that rapid development in all these spheres be continuously guided and controlled by adherence to tradition.

We can identify an interwoven constellation of tradition, comprised of the following elements: the religion if Islam; the monarchic hegemony of the Al-Saud ruling family; strong kinship loyalty within the nuclear and extended families; and the sequestering of females within domestic space and functions. Of the four elements forming this constellation, Islam is the most basic, giving legitimacy and direction to the others. In point of historical origin, the elements of family loyalty and the seques-tering of females are pre-Islamic and also characteristic of all cultures in the Middle East, whether or not they are Islamic. However, Saudi Arabia has elevated Islam to the level of a comprehensive religious and ideological framework which integrates the entire society and within which other features of the society find their pace and sanction. Thus, the ruling house of Al-Saud bases its claim to authority in large measure upon its promulgation of Islam and its guarantee of pilgrim access to the holy cities of Mecca and Medina. The social homogeneity of the Saudi population greatly buttresses its cultural tradition. The population numbers about 7.5 million persons (there are an additional 1.5 million foreign workers and dependents in the Kingdom). It has an extreme degree of linguistic, ethnic, and religious homogeneity, being virtually 100% Arab and Muslim (Braibanti and Al-Farsy, 1977).

Health Care and Saudi Women: A Non-Traditional Activity

In her account of the "contemporary Saudi woman," Deaver (1980) emphasi-zes the pervasiveness of sexual segregation in modern Saudi society.

Sexual segregation "is ideologically grounded in the Islamic belief system and in basic conceptual categories of the Saudi worldview...This sexual segregation is replicated in the social, economic, and architectural systems of the society. It results in the definition of male and female domains, which...are co-terminous with public and private domains."

The female domain is the home—the sphere of intimate familial relationships, shielded from public concern and view—above all, from contact with "strange men" outside the circle of male guardians in the woman's own family. Traditionally, women lived their lives in domestic privacy and shelter, emerging into public areas only for family business or economic activities. The adult Saudi woman nowadays has fewer responsibilities in household economic production than in earlier times. However, as in the past, her skills are shaped by, and her energies absorbed by, responsibilities ir he immediate and extended family.

With a tremendous expansion of female education, the Saudi girl now emerges from her home for education predominantly secular in content, obtained in an all-female school which is surrounded by high, blank walls. Female education is aimed toward basic literacy and toward domestic vocation. There is virtually no opportunity for women to obtain gainful employment in extra-familial contexts; women are not permitted to work in an environment where men are present. Although there are a few adult unmarried and divorced females who live in the household of their fathers or brothers, virtually all women marry (and remarry if divorced or widowed) and assume an encompassing set of domestic responsibilities. These role-expectations form the aspirations and self-concept of the Saudi female; they also coincide with, and reinforce, behavioral norms concerning the veiling and segregation of females.

Obtaining health care in medical clinics, in dental offices, in health centers, and as a hospitalized patient, is a culturally novelty for Saudi females (and for Saudi males as well).

The foregoing considerations indicate that female patients must cope not only with the newness of professionally-provided, scientifically-based modern health care but also with the fact that it occurs in settings which are discordant with cultural norms for the female role. Modern health care settings are physically public, procedurally bureaucratic, and predominantly male-staffed. Modern health care diagnoses and treats the patient as an isolated "case"—in a cognitive, problem-solving, socially decontextualized mode. In contrast, traditional practitioners as a rule dealt with the patient in recognition and support of her social identity, as part of the treatment relationship. For example, the traditional midwife or "daya," still numerous in some parts of Saudi Arabia but facing an uncertain future, provided prenatal,, natal, and post-natal care in the patient's home. She was known to females of the family and frequently had delivered other babies in the family.

Three aspects of female health care have been selected for attention here: (1) the spatial segregation of female medical care; (2) the situation of male physicians dealing with female patients; and (3) the prospective entry of Saudi female physicians into medical care. Illustrative materials are drawn from the field notes of one (E.B.G.) of the authors during a recent period of ethnographic research in the Kingdom.

Spatial arrangements—Architecture and scheduling

Segregating female from male patients is common in Western countries, e.g., in hospital rooms and wards. In Saudi Arabia this policy has a more explicit rationale and is carried out in a far more thoroughgoing fashion. (It should be noted that Western and Saudi norms for female patient segregation are qualitatively similar, despite the difference in their stringency or threshhold of application).

The norm of segregation is most fully achieved where females have completely separate facilities, analogous to the all-female schools. However, in the massive program of construction of hospitals and health centers which is underway, the architectural pattern designates separate female and male zones within a common building, rather than an entire building for the exclusive use of females. Even with separate-sex wards and waiting rooms, there is usually a common main entrance and there are, usually, elevators used by both sexes, which gives rise to unease and complaint. Shared elevators are particularly upsetting to some females, for they give an uncomfortable sense of close confinement with males.

A customary device to implement segragation are screens or partitions, as the following example shows: The Al-Dunya dental clinic in Dammam has five full-time dentists and two dental hygienists. There is an area in the waiting room which is partitioned off for females by the use of movable wooden panels. The main portion of the waiting room has 20 seats; the partititioned portion has six. The waiting room is usually half occupied. Males constitute about two-thirds of those present, but some are there simply as the auto drivers and chaperones for female patients, not being patients themselves. Of the females in the waiting room, only the veiled Saudi females regularly sit in the partitioned area. The others—foreign females—sit in the common area. They are unveiled but have extremely modest dress by Western standards—their hair is covered, their dresses are long with long sleeves and full covering of neck and shoulders. Obviously the clinic administration is concerned about female segregation. Nevertheless, if it wanted to intensify its practice in this respect, it would seem feasible to establish separate hours for male and female patients. Its failure to do so perhaps reflects a practical reluctance to impose an additional administrative constraint upon the functioning of the clinic.

It is difficult to predict whether female segregation in the Saudi health system will become more pronounced or less so. Although the Kingdom has abundant financial resources, the governmental planning organs do seek to get maximum benefit from the spending of petro-dollars. The building of separate health facilities for each sex on an extensive scale would probably be viewed as wasteful. Consideration has been given to the construction of maternity facilities, in the mode of the lying-in hospitals which are also well-known features of health care in some Western countries. At present, relatively few (probably less than 20%) deliveries occur in hospitals, even in urban areas with easy physical access to hospitals. (The obstetrical services of the new hospitals are, however, almost always full to capacity.)

Given the relatively rapid accommodatin of the population to modern modes of health care, we suppose that within a decade approximately half of all deliveries will be in hospital if there are sufficient physical facilities and professional services to provide for that level of utilization. In view of the high Saudi birth rate, the widespread pronatalist sentiment of the people and the government, and the emphatic celebration of motherhood within the female role, the provision of maternity hospitals seems to be a smooth cultural extrapolation within the development of health services. Separate maternity hospitals would, as well, be an efficient way to deal with large numbers of cases with clinically similar requirements.

Male Physicians and Female Patients

Spatial segregation seeks to prevent or limit the appearance of females in open public space. Whatever the tensions and inconsistencies engendered by the impact of new health services upon the norm of segregation, they are similar in character to those occasioned by the increasing presence of females in other public places—buses, airplanes, food markets, department stores, hotel exhibitions, and restaurants. But health care has the additional unique aspect of "intimate technology"—the subjection of the human body to professional scrutiny and clinical action derived from standards of scientific medicine. The exposure of female bodies to male physicians is an emotionally-charged matter also in Western societies, where women are legally and socially able to hold jobs, drive automobiles, frequent public places unescorted, and interact socially in mixed company. The encounter of female patients with male physicians is, then, doubly sensitive in societies governed by a strict code of female modesty and still more so in Saudi Arabia which, as we have seen, adheres to an especially conservative standard.

In the West, the doctor-patient relationship is a relatively autonomous relationship, insulated on the patient's side from the other collective groupings to which he or she belongs. Such insulation cannot be so easily achieved in Saudi society, where one's family membership exerts an overriding influence in every relationship outside the family. Moreover, every female is under the guardianship and authority of male family members—variously, her husband, father, brother, or son. This basic fact of Saudi social structure reaches into the doctor-patient relationship:

at issue is not only the female patient's own attitude toward the male physician but also the attitude of her male guardian. How far the latter's possessiveness functions to restrict or prevent female access to medical care is thus an important question. It would be easy to assign too great an influence to the restrictive, protective propensities of Saudi males concerning their kinswomen. This is an inherent cultural possibility but balanced against it is a growing awareness of the advantages of medical care and a corresponding desire to have the benefit of such care. Traditional fatalistic attitudes toward illness and health are being rapidly replaced or supplemented by conceptions which readily seek medical attention for illnesses and malaises ignored or dealt with more stoically in earlier days (Nyrop **et al.**, 1977). In other words, considerations of male-female propriety must be weighed against new priorities in health care.

Female Physicians

Within ten years, there will be an appreciable number of Saudi female physicians or "lady doctors." They are being trained currently at the four medical schools in the Kingdom. Although only male students were admitted during the first few years of these recently-opened schools, some currently admitted classes are almost half female. The female students receive their tuition in strict segregation, but its content is the same as that for the males.

The purpose of training female physicians is to provide a cadre of female professionals who can meet the medical needs of the female portion of the Saudi population. By 1990, there will be a pool of approximately 1,000 female medical graduates--enough to make a difference but not nearly enough to deal with the entire female population. At present almost all physicians are male and approximately 91% are foreign (Sebai, 1981). There are very, very few foreign female physicians. The female Saudi physicians will thus offset the current reliance upon foreign male physicians, overcoming both a cultural and gender difference for their patients. Saudi Islamic culture has, as we have seen, created a strong need for female physicians, from the standpoint of compatibility with the female patient. By the same token, it has also made the role of the physician highly attractive and much sought after by young Saudi women.

Medicine is one of the very few lines of education--the others being teaching, social work, and interior design--which can subsequently lead to an extra-domestic vocation for a Saudi girl. The great expansion of opportunities for women in higher education is not matched by employment prospects, despite the facts that oil wealth has spawned a boom economy and that Saudi women, if given greater scope for employment, could quickly reduce the Kingdom's ambivalent dependence upon foreigners for technical, professional and clerical services within the economy (Al--Shami, 1982).

The training of indigenous medical professionals is so new in Saudi culture that the social meaning of "being a doctor" has not yet been established. Its meaning is particularly ambiguous in reference to female doctors. It is expected, however, that medically-qualified females will be viewed as especially desirable wives in the Saudi system of parentally-arranged marriage. The doctor-bride will add to the social prestige of the bridegroom's family. The husband himself will acquire an intelligent wife, as indicated by her completion of medical studies—a wife who will be able to meet, in a competent, resourceful fashion, the all-important obligations of household hospitality. The bride's family will be able to command a high dowry, as determined by negotiations between the fathers of the bridal pair, in exchange for the "loss" of its exceptional daughter.

Another question surrounding the female medical role is that of how steadily and fully the "lady doctors" will want, and be able, to devote themselves to a medical career. Whereas many married female professionals in the West have the difficulty of maintaining career continuity in the face of the demands of household and child care, the total domestic responsibilities (including child care) of the Saudi married woman are appreciably greater, especially the maintaining of contact with a large circle of relatives through a continuous round of birth, marriage, and death ceremonies within the family, as well as religious feats. A countervailing consideration, however, can be found in the strong likelihood that most Saudi doctor-wives will have full-time domestic servants, from abroad, to assist in household and child-care responsibilities. This assistance will free most of their time and energy for those roles which only they can perform, such as serving as family hostess and carrying out medical responsibilities.

Despite their equivalence in training to that of the male medical students, the female doctors will enact a somewhat different brand of medical care. It is anticipated that most of the young Saudi male physicians will proceed to advanced medical training and then move into medical specialty or medical administrative careers. Even if the female medical graduates wee predisposed to seek specialty training, it would be very difficult for them to obtain. Such training programs will be very limited within the Kingdom for the foreseeable future; further, under recent government edict, female citizens are not permitted to travel abroad independently for study.

The medical practice of the female doctors will be directed to a female and child clientele and will emphasize primary care—dealing with uncomplicated pregnancy and childbirth, developmental problems of children, prevalent infectious diseases, and preventive medicine in the clinical context. In stating that their clientele will consist of women and children (under 16) we should note that these two categories cover some 70% of the total Saudi population. Infant and maternal mortality rates, historically high, are rapidly declining and the birth rate remains high (estimated at 50/1,000 population), with a resultant youthful population.

Since female physicians will deal in primary care, those female patients who require specialist treatment will perforce go to male specialist physicians. This may not cut across the cultural grain as much as it appears to at first. Dr. A. K. Chowdhury (1982), a Bangladesh psychiatrist, has suggested that women in Islamic and Middle Eastern culture generally prefer to have the help of other women for "ordinary" health problems and stresses such as pregnancy but that, given prevailing cultural conceptions concerning male expertise and power, many female patients prefer a male doctor to deal with "serious" illness. Precedent for such an arrangement exists in Saudi tradition, by which a woman would have the help of a female midwife for childbirth but a male bonesetter in event of a fracture. In this instance, both types of practitioner are indigenous laypersons, but the bonesetter functions in a more specialized, episodic mode whereas the midwife, in a more diffuse mode, carries out her tasks in a dominant context of emotional support for the patient as well as relating to other females in the family.

The Saudi female physicians are trained in far greater scientific depth and greater clinical breadth than midwives, yet, in a very rapidly changing society, their presence expresses and carries forward the spirit of a separate, distinctive, and largely self-sufficient women's culture, as did that of the midwives. Their actual contribution in medical care will depend not only upon what services they are prepared and trained to offer, but also upon the expectations and needs of their female patients, which are in turn linked to the rapid flux of social and cultural change in the Kingdom.

Social Change and the Role of Women

Veiling and segregation remain, but few women in Saudi Arabia live a daily life similar to that of women two generations ago or even the previous generation. They are less involved in economic production than formerly, and they participate vigorously in an entirely new, urbanized, affluent, consumption-oriented economy that markets many imported goods---foodstuffs, fashionable clothing, stereo and video equipment, household furnishings, children's toys and games---which have drastically altered the role of women in food preparation, child care, family recreation, and household management. Many villagers have migrated to the burgeoning cities, where the ecology of housing and neighborhood, and the rhythms of family life, are quite different from those of the village. There is also the new and broadening availability of medical care, as compared the earlier reliance upon folk medicine and upon a limited number and range of traditional practitioners. Further, popular conceptions of health and disease are coming to embrace scientific knowledge while still retaining the older supernatural beliefs.

Within this current of ideational fluidity and social upheaval, there are numerous perplexities and emotional stresses. In some persons, perhaps those most inwardly vulnerable and outwardly exposed, the stresses of social change can accumulate and precipitate into symptoms or distress which take them to a clinic or doctor's office. This action is in itself a novel event in the cultural repertoire. Rapid social change not only creates stresses but it also produces new strategies and hierarchies of resort in help-seeking, even as it outmodes familiar ones.

Data made available to us for this study included interviews with medical personnel in several practice settings. The following case report shows how within the framework of medical care, the stresses of rapid social change impinge upon women's role contingencies: "Dr. McKenzie is a Canadian internist working in a family clinic on the Prince Abdullah Army Base near Abqaiq in Eastern Province. The family clinic serves Saudi enlisted men and their dependents. Dr. McKenzie reported the case of Fawzia A. as a somewhat unusual but not extreme example of a patient in whom the medical condition is complicated by significant emotional factors.

Fawzia is 17 and has been married eight months. She comes from a large family in Asir Province (southwest Saudi Arabia) and says she is homesick since she has come to live with her husband on the base following their wedding. She has had nine years of education. Ahmed A., her husband and first cousin, is 26 years old. He graduated from high school and serves in the Army as a radio technician, with the rank of corporal. Like most of the enlisted men, he escorts his wife to the clinic but, unlike some others, does not accompany her into the consulting office and examining room.

Fawzia first came to the clinic two months ago with the presenting complaint of nausea. Tests diagnosed her as pregnant. Dr. McKenzie has seen her on the standard clinic protocol for prenatal care. However, she also presents a picture of emotional disruption—hystical outbursts and suicidal threats—occuring at home and sometimes in the medical interview. because of this, Dr. McKenzie has seen her several times on a drop-in basis for counseling.

Dr. McKenzie says the pregnancy is proceeding normally. While it may have exacerbated her outbursts, he feels that the root of her difficulties lies in the social upheaval she has undergone in leaving her family and home community. It is hard for her, he said, to come to live on a military base where she cannot observe usual proprieties of conduct, and where it is difficult to avoid daily contact with strangers. He says that Fawzia complains to him about the apartment which she and her husband have been assigned and about the close proximity of the adjacent apartments. Also, she feels socially inferior to some of the other enlisted men's wives she has met at women's gatherings. Many of them have completed a high school and she has not. This bothers her a great deal.

Dr. McKenzie says that during outburst the patient screams, scratches her face, and pulls at her hair. He feels that she is not mentally ill nor depressed. However, he worries that she will make some kind of suicidal gesture which might be 'accidentally successful'."

Dr. McKenzie felt that the patient had difficulties in adjusting to the social demands of living in the relatively open institutional environment of a military base. For her to undergo a first pregnancy on an army base must have been far different from the more traditional experience of the young wife who comes to her husband's household as a new member of a ready-made, culturally constructed feminine "support group" under the tutelage and authority of her mother-in-law. Although her outlook was quite conservative, she stepped into the role of clinic patient easily and placed upon the physician strong demands for personal attention and support. In her case, the physician and the medical care system were discerning and elastic enough to respond to the patient's needs.

The case of Fawzia suggests the possibility that the emergent Saudi medical care system will be in the position of meeting new forms of expectation from many persons who are caught up in the pressures of social change—even as it organizes itself to provide expertise within the framework of technical medicine. In responding to rising sociomedical needs and expectations, it will be following a pattern in the West, where many individuals also look to the medical establishment for succorance because they are cut off from sources of emotional security and social support. Similar dislocating forces are at work in Saudi Arabia—geographic mobility, individualistic pursuit of career goals, exposure to culturally alien stimuli, new lifestyles, and an almost obsessive sensitivity to the contrast between "modern" and "traditional," all of which challenge the adaptive capacity of Saudis and strike deeply at their collective and individual equipoise.

Summary

Islamic doctrine and practice concerning the social role of women foster a "world of women," within which women look to members of their own sex for personal acceptance and realize their worth through domestic accomplishment (Bourguignon, 1980). This pattern does not yield easily to social change. The strict interpretation and practice of norms pertaining to female segregation and modesty virtually guarantee that Islamic societies will experience severe tensions as they modernize their economic base, establish mass education and communication, and undergo the rural—to-urban and demographic shifts characteristic of developing societies.

We have described the situation of women in Saudi Arabia regarding health care. With its oil-based affluence, Saudi society is undergoing a rapid material and social transformation, yet it is determinedly adhering to Islamic standards. This requires that tradition must be newly defined and implemented in non-traditional contexts, such as in providing modern medical services. Sometimes certain elements of cultural tradition must be sacrificed in order to preserve others, as part of an overall line of advance. For example, there is in traditional Saudi culture no more highly revered and protected role than that of "umm," or mother, but now, for the sake of greater security in child-bearing, women are encour-

94

aged to come forth from their homes for prenatal care and well-baby supervision.

Again, although there is a general cultural and specific legal opposition to the gainful employment of women, some women are being trained as physicians, so that they can minister to the medical needs of other women, as patients. Thus, for the female Saudi, the cultural breach in accepting Western-style medicine and becoming, as patient, a "case," will be cushioned by having "lady doctors." The first generation of Saudi female doctors will function, we suggest, not as midwives in the literal sense, but rather as "cultural midwives" in helping to meet socio-medical expectations, in consonance both with traditional norms and the benefits of modern medicine.

In her study of the social structure of a Saudi village, the Japanese anthropologist Katakura (1977) suggests that "modernization...could draw on tradition to strengthen its own course." Her formulation is apposite to Saudi women's health care, where progress and novelty are being buffered by a selective filtering of tradition.

REFERENCES

AL-SHAMI, IBRAHIM (1982) "Something New, Something Bold—Education in Saudi Arabia," LEARNING TODAY 15 (1): 44-54.

BOURGUIGNON, ERIKA (ed.) (1980) A WORLD OF WOMEN. N.Y.: J.F. Bergin Publs.

GRAIBANTI, RALPH and ABDUL-SALAM AL-FARSY (1977) "Saudi Arabia: A Developmental Perspective," I (1): 3-43.

CHOWDHURY, A.K. (1982) "Psychiatric Programs in Developing Countries: The Bangladesh Example," Public Lecture, University of Kentucky (September 28).

DEAVER, SHERRI, (1980) "The Contemporary Saudi Woman," Chapter 2, pp. 19-42, in E. Bourguignon (ed.) A WORLD OF WOMEN. N.Y.: J.F. Bergin Publs.

KATAKURA, MOTOKO (1977) BEDOUIN VILLAGE. Tokyo: University of Tokyo Press.

NYROP, RICHARD F., BERYL LIEFF BENDERLY, LARAINE NEWHOUSE CARTER, DARREL R. EGLIN, and ROBERT A. KIRCHNER (1977) AREA HANDBOOK FOR SAUDI ARABIA (Third Edition), Washington, D.C.: U.S. Government Printing Office.

REYNOLDS, BARRY (1980) "Their Fathers' Sons," AR:AMCO WORLD MAGAZINE XXXI (1): ppl 2-11.

SEBAI, ZOHAIR (1981) THE HEALTH OF THE FAMILY IN A CHANGING ARABIA. Jeddah, Saudi Arabia: Tihama Publs.

CHAPTER 8

THE PARADIGMS OF HEALTH CARE DELIVERY SYSTEMS: IMPLICATIONS FOR THE THIRD WORLD

Gary G. Grenholm

The poorer and richer nations alike have seen modern scientific medicine as a central part of the answer to the many health problems that beset Third World countries. Resources of people, equipment, and materials from the developed countries have been sought and provided. Sizeable numbers of nationals from the poorer countries have been trained in the health professional schools of the more affluent nations. Training facilities modeled after those of the developed countries have been instituted throughout the Third World, in order to provide local resources for training people in scientific medicine and related health professions. A major programmatic thrust of the World Health Organization during the 1960s and 1970s was designed to increase the capacities of developing countries to train physicians. W.H.O. established regional teacher training centers around the world to upgrade the pedagogical skills of medical school faculties. Scientific medicine and the educational approaches used to prepare its practitioners in the developed countries have been exported on a large scale to help developing countries deal with their health problems.

Along with scientific medicine and its educational substrata, developing countries have also been the recipients of a less concrete aspect of modern medical care. They have received certain principles about the way in which such care is to be made available to people. Modern medical care occurs within an organizational context. Scientific medicine is associated with particular forms of organizational structures within which the medical effort goes forward. In using the methods and approaches of modern medicine, developing countries have necessarily also been exposed to the organizational systems through which modern medicine carries out its functions.

The 'Paradigm' Concept

This discussion takes a step or two away from contemporary medical theory and practice, and from the characteristics of health care delivery systems. It examines instead certain assumptions which underlie scientific medicine and the delivery system. The underlying assumptions will be referred to as 'paradigms.'

A number of scholars in various disciplines have examined the paradigm concept. While it would take us a bit far afield to explore that literature in depth here, it is useful to mention the work of a few representative investigators. The single most influential writer on the topic has been Thomas Kuhn (1970; 1974; Masterman, 1970). Working in the area of the philosophy of science, Kuhn used the term 'paradigm' to describe the shared fundamental assumptions about reality used by a community of scientists to guide their work. Paradigms in Kuhn's sense arise from a particular scientific achievement (e.g., Newton's PRINCIPIA) that for a time establish the type of questions that are to be investigated and the methods that are appropriate for their investigation. Kuhn argues that scientific progress is best understood not as a cumulative evolutionary process, as the traditional philosophy of science would have it. Instead scientific progress is revolutionary. It consists of the overthrow of one dominant, shared paradigm by another. The new paradigm then comes to define the reality with which a scientific community deals. It provides new assumptions, poses new questions, and requires new investigative methods. A new paradigm thus acts to redirect a line of scientific inquiry by providing a new set of fundamental assumptions about reality and about the way that reality is to be comprehended.

In other work dealing with a similar conceptualization, the philosophy Pepper (1942; 1966) suggested 'world hypotheses' and 'root metaphors' as terms for the basic orienting assumtions which underlie philosophical systems. The sociologist Goffman (1974) has dealt with the concept of the "primary framework," acting to provide meaning and interpretability to otherwise confusing and ambiguous experience. The physicist and historian of science Holton (1973) directs attention to preconceptions of an aesthetic nature that are held by scientists. Holton calls such preconceptions "themata;" they serve to mold a particular scientist's research. In each of these instances (and in others; cf., Gomperz, 1957; Nisbet, 1969) emphasis is placed on the importance of pre-existing assumptions or paradigms for constructing the realities with which people and systems deal.

Paradigms in Medicine and in Health Care Delivery Systems

Scientific medicine and health care delivery systems rest on underlying general assumptions about the world. Such paradigms are of central importance in determining what the health care system does and in forming the particular social systems that characterize the health care delivery effort. The form and function of the health care system arises in large part from the paradigms that are embedded in the system. They act to define the reality with which the system deals. They structure the problems the health care system addresses. In addition, such paradigms provide a rationale for the methods used in the system.

When the approaches of contemporary medicine are used in Third World countries, the approaches are necessarily accompanied by their underlying paradigms. It is those paradigms that give medicine its conceptual power and its practical effectiveness in dealing with particular types of problems. Unfortunately, there is no guarantee that the types of problems that scientific medicine can address are the ones that are most pressing in the Third World. Indeed, there is no **a priori** reason to expect that even the reality that is defined by medicine's assumptions necessarily corresponds to the way reality is defined in Third World cultures.

The remainder of this discussion, therefore, explores how well scientific medicine's assumptions about physical and social reality match Third World conditions. The discussion has two parts. **First,** the substance of the underlying assumptions is examined, with respect both to medicine as a profession and with respect to the organizational context used in the health care delivery system. **Second,** the health problems of the Third World are outlined briefly, particularly as reflected in the objectives of the World Health Organization's "Health For All By The Year 2000" initiative. With the medical system's assumptions and Third World circumstances at hand, a few conclusions about the way they mesh will be suggested.

Paradigm Content: Underlying Assumptions in Medicine and Delivery

The paradigmatic assumptions of the health care system will be examined here from the perspective of their socio-historical development through time. Rather than tracing that development in detail here, an overview of its main features will be provided. The Overview deals first with the paradigm used in medicine as a profession and as an intellectual discipline, and then with the paradigm underlying the organizational context through which health care is delivered. While each of these two aspects of the contemporary health care enterprise followed a different developmental course, both rest on fundamentally similar if not identical premises.

MEDICINE AS AN INTELLECTUAL DISCIPLINE AND AS A PROFESSION

Contemporary scientific medicine arose in a long and difficult process of paradigm transformation. The process involved the replacement of a developed medical theory and practice which originated in classical Greece. It dominated medical thought for more than two thousand years. The concept of 'balance' was a central paradigm in classical medicine. All disease was held to be the consequence of imbalance among the humors of the body. Therapy was premised on correcting such imbalances in a variety of ways. But classical medicine was not concerned solely with illness. It dealt as much with the pursuit of higher levels of well-being among the healthy. There too the balance principle was followed, addressing issues of the appropriate relatioships among exercise and rest, diet, and of the person in his interaction with the physical and social environments.

99

The centrality of the 'balance' concept in the conceptual equipment of the classical physician made necessary what in today's terms would be called a holistic and person-centered orientation on the part of the practitioner. The physician's focus of attention was on promoting internal physiologic balance within the person as a complete entity, and on the balance of the person with the environment (Phillips, 1973; Scarborough, 1969; Temkin, 1973). Classical medicine was replaced by a medicine that was based on the new world view that arose in the sixteenth and seventeenth centuries. The new world view envisioned the universe and everything within it as an elaborate mechanism, operating according to mechanical principles in a strictly deterministic manner (Dijksterhuis, 1961; Westfall, 1977; Webster, 1974; Willey, 1953). This 'new philosophy' came from the work of many early scientists, known in their day as natural philosophers. Among the most illustrious of these were Descartes (1596–1650) and Newton (1642-1727).

Descartes established the philosophical foundation of modern science and of modern medicine with his famous enunciation of philosophic dualism. Cartesian dualism divided all realty into two categories—**res cogitan** (things of the mind) and **res extensa** (things of the material world). Descartes held that science must be concerned solely and exclusively with **res extensa.** Newton accepted the Cartesian distinction and added to it the power of quantitative analysis. The joining of the materialistic philosophy with mathematical analytical methods, all within the conception of reality as a complex machine, was the scientific revolution which inaugurated the modern era.

Medicine tried to adopt the Cartesian-Newtonian approach virtually as soon as it began to revolutionize the physical sciences. It seemed reasonable to expect that medicine could share in the dramatic progress taking place in the physical sciences and in the technologies associated with them, if medicine used the world view and the approaches modeled by the physical sciences. Thus the seventeenth and eighteenth centuries saw the rise of **'iatromechanics'** and **'iatrochemistry'** (GK; **iateia**, i.e., the art of healing), attempts to extend the concepts of the physical sciences to medicine in a direct manner (King, 1978).

The early attempts to transform medical theory using an iatroscientif approach were not successful. The Cartesian-Newtonian philosophy required objective, materialistic data free from considerations of mind and of all the human characteristics that **res cogitans** implied—intention, will, intellect, emotion, judgment, choice, affect. Such objective data were alien to the long-standing tradition of classical medicine, concerned as it was with achieving balance within the individual as a holistic entity, and between the individual and the larger environment.

It was not until the end of the eighteenth century and continuing into the nineteenth that medicine achieved its new, objective data base. That was accomplished initially in the hospitals of Paris (Ackerknecht, 1967; Waddington, 1973), and later in the laboratories of France, Germany, and America (Bernard, 1957; Brock, 1975; Bulloch, 1979; Shryock, 1947; Virchow, 1958). It was accomplished by narrowing attention to disordered physiological functioning, to pathophysiology, in order to understand the mechanisms of disease.

Medical attention was progressively narrowed from the sick person to organs, to tissues, to cells, and—today—to intracellular mechanisms and to molecular ones. In that way the tenets of the Cartesian-Newton view of reality slowly came to be realized first in medical theory and then, by the twentieth century, in medical practice. The progressive narrowing of medicine's focus required a new way of perceiving the reality with which medicine dealt. That is true figuratively, in that the physician needed to see the patient as a material **soma** (GK: body) in order to use the Cartesian-Newtonian approach. The view of classical medicine, in which **soma** was integrated with **psyche** (GK: mind), had to be abandoned. At the same time, medicine came to perceive the patient in a different way in a literal sense as well. New imaging technology developed—pulse—taking, the clinical thermometer, the microscope, the stethoscope, x-rays, biochemical analyses, CAT scans—that presented a view of the patient that was altogether free of **res cogitans.** In classical medicine the patient's psychological and social characteristics were unavoidably present in the medical encounter, along with his physical and physiological properties. The new medical technology permitted physicians to see patients as exclusively bio-physical entities (Reiser, 1978).

The Cartesian-Newtonian paradigm has a number of elements, some mentioned above but others not yet outlined. In summary form, the paradigm consists of the following assumptions about understanding natural phenomena: (1) **Mechanistic Explanation:** Nature is viewed as operating like a machine. It is like a complex clockwork, its intricate overall operation the consequence of quite simple physical laws which govern the action of its component parts. The aim of science is to reveal those simple laws, thereby providing an understanding of the machine's operation and making it susceptible to human control. (2) **Materialism:** The issues that are susceptible to scientific investigation deal exclusively with physical entities and to the relationships among them. As such, scientific issues are those that are external to the scientist. The scientist deals with external objects; s(he) is 'objective' and uninvolved with the phenomena themselves, neither influencing nor being influenced by them. (3) **Reductionism:** Understanding is to be pursued by analyzing any given phenomenon in terms of its components. Explanation of a complex entity is carried out by breaking it down into its simpler parts. Any whole is to be understood by study of its parts. (4) **Determinism:** Natural phenomena follow strict causal linkages, in the same manner as the movement of the cogs and wheels in a clockwork. Scientific investigation has the purpose of identifying such linkages, searching for the lawful cause-effect relationships that are presumed to exist. (5) **Quantitative Expression:** The relationships among phenomena are to be expressed in terms of mathematics, based on measurement according to one or another scale. It is expressed in Lord Kelvin's admonition "If you cannot measure, your knowledge is meagre and unsatisfactory" (Kuhn, 1961: 31).

Taken together, these assumptions provided the new machine-inspired framework for the scientific revolution. The mechanistic conception of reality ushered in the modern era, transforming not only science and technology but virtually the entire culture of Western society (Dijksterhuis, 1961). Not until the last half of the nineteenth century was medicine able to reformulate its theoretical base in conformity to the new premises- -those of the scientific revolution in the physical sciences that had taken place two hundred years before. And not until the end of that century and into the present one did medical practice come to incorporate the new premises on a systematic basis. The mechanistic conception of reality that medicine adopted then is still the one it uses today.

THE HEALTH CARE DELIVERY SYSTEM

We turn now to the social system through which health care services are made available to people and to the premises which underlie that system. Attention will focus on just one aspect of that complex system. The focus is on the hospital. The hospital provides a useful analytical focus for two reasons. First, the hospital is the setting in which the most complex and specialized medical services are carried out. Those are the types of services that best express the medical paradigm outlined above. The hospital is the dominant and characteristic context, then, for the services that most typify what the health care system does.

Second, the organizationl structure of the hospital provides a model that is used widely throughout the rest of the system. One reason for that is the hospital's role as a training site for virtually all health workers. The characteristics of the hospital come to be seen as the 'natural' way for organizing collective human effort, during the critical period when neophyte professionals are being socialized into their new roles. The model provided by the hospital serves as a readily-available template for constructing other organizations in the health system. Like medicine, the hospital underwent a massive transformation in taking on the form it has today. The paradigm on which it was based changed dramatically. It came to deal with an altogether different reality than it had dealt with previously. Unlike the situation in medicine, though, the change took place over a relatively short period of time. The transformation in hospitals was form a markedly paternalistic organization to a bureaucratic one. It was a fundamental change in what the organization did as well as in the organizational approach that was used to accomplish its ends.

Before the last quarter of the nineteenth century, hospitals were primarily concerned with providing assistance to the poor. They were a type of social service agency, only incidentally related to health care generally or to scientific medicine specifically. Hospitals in their origins had no relationship at all to health care. They were literally 'places ofhospitality' for those who were without homes for whatever reason. The earliest Greek name for such institutions was **xenodochia,** a house for strangers.

The xenodochia provided accommodation to travellers in the spirit of religious charity during the early Christian era (Gask and Todd, 1953). Over the centuries such **hospitalia** became refuges for the poor and, by the seventeenth and eighteenth centuries, especially for the sick poor. By the late nineteenth century virtually all the residents of hospitals were ill but curable; that is, they suffered from conditions that were self-limiting and from which they would recover. After recovery, the recipients of the hospital's charity were expected to rejoin the labor force and be self-supporting. Others of the poorer classes with less bright prospects—the terminally or chronically ill, the insane, the blind, children, women generally and pregnant women especially—typically were excluded from the hospitals. (The more affluent classes were not eligible for admission—not that anyone who could possibly avoid the social stigma of being a recipient of charity would want to be hospitalized, of course.) (Rosenberg, 1979; Vogel, 1980).

The administration of the hospital was paternalistic, reflecting the social service and charitable objectives of those who supported the institution (Eaton, 1957: 102-112; Rosenberg, 1979: 353-363). Patients were admitted on the basis of social criteria rather than physiological ones. The hospital was essentially undifferentiated internally—all its residents received the same set of supportive services, from a staff that was not specialized into different job classifications.

In changing from refuges for the sick poor to their contemporary role as the dominant organizational type of the health care enterprise, hositals underwent three major changes. They became medicalized, in that hospitals now provide the setting and resources—material and human—for ends determined by scientific medicine. They became, secondly, a facility used by all members of the community, regardless of socio-economic class. Thirdly, they became bureaucratized. They changed from an essentially undifferentiated entity with little task specificity and a loose authority structure to one with a high degree of division of labor and task specification, coordinated and controlled through an elaborate supervisory hierarchy.

It is the third of those changes, the hospital's bureaucratization, that is of particular interest here. The change to bureaucracy established the organizational character of the contemporary hospital. It established as well the organizational approach used very widely throughout modern health care delivery systems.

What is the paradigm on which bureaucracy rests? What are the presuppositions which lead to the pyramid-shaped social structures with a highly rationalized division of labor that are so common in industralized societies? Aspects of the bureaucratic approach can be seen in the theorecracies of ancient Egypt, in the organization of the military from similarly ancient times, and in the hierarchy of the Catholic Church in the Middle Ages and before (Jacoby, 1973). However, full-blown rationalized bureaucracy is best seen as the product of the same 'new philosophy' that we encountered in the emergence of scientific medicine. Bureaucracy is the application to social systems of the mechanistic principles contained in the Cartesian--Newtonian world view. Bureaucracy represents an effort to reduce the variability and unpredictability inherent in human behavior. It uses rules and regulations together with a supervisory control structure for enforcing those rules to bring about organizational performance that is regular and predictable. The goal of bureaucracy is to create a social structure—one composed of people—that functions like a smoothly running machine.

In pursuit of that goal bureaucracies are intentionally depersonalized. For example, organizational charts do not show relationships among particular individuals. They show relationships among offices. Each office is assigned a particular set of concrete, objective functions. Taken together, the functions performed across an entire organization provide a blue-print of the overall operations of that organization, free from any explicit reference to any person. An organizational chart places the **res cogitans** of the people who actually constitute an organization with the **res extensa** of objective, depersonalized offices. Each office is to carry out a defined function in the total organizational machine.

With the machine as its basic model, bureaucracy rests on the same set of Cartesian-Newtonian assumptions summarized earlier. First, a bureaucracy is to be regarded as a social mechanism, operating according to a clearly defined set of logical principles that are like the laws governing physical objects. Second, a bureaucracy is concerned only with **res extensa,** not with **res cogitans.** It is to be see as dealing with material, objective phenomena. Third, bureaucracy uses a reductionistic approach, dividing up the functions to be performed by breaking them down into their simpler components. Fourth, bureaucracy adopts a strictly deterministic orientation. Relationships among its component offices are arranged according to a machine-like causal logic. Finally, bureaucracy places much stress on quantification of all aspects of its operations, ranging from the accounting and bookkeeping functions to quantified performance appraisal of its employees.

Bureaucratization of the hospital transformed it by the second decade of this century into an efficient and dependable social mechanism for pursuing goals that were provided to the hospital by scientific medicine. Scientific medicine and the bureaucratized hospital rest on similar assumptions about reality. Modern medicine applied those premises to health care. The hospital applied them to social organization. When the two came together they matched very well. The combination of scientific medicine and the bureaucratized hospital gave rise to a health care system that is very firmly based in the mechanistic and materialistic world view of the Cartesian-Newtonian 'new philosophy.'

The Cartesian-Newtonian paradigm provides more than a conceptual approach to health care delaivery systems. It also provides a set of valued objectives towards which the system moves. The system is concerned with curing disease by correcting pathophysiology. It is concerned with fixing malfunctioning parts of the human organism viewed as a material mechanism. The paradigm directs attention to the internal operation of the separate components of the body. Value is attached to understanding and repairing those components. The system is strongly biased, that is, towards a reductionistic and specialized approach aimed at cure. The Cartesian-Newtonian paradigm biases the system against prevention, against chronic conditions, and against consideration of the role of psychological and social factors–**res cogitans**––in health.

The Cartesian-Newtonian paradigm is supportive of an increasingly technological approach to dealing with health care issues. That is particuarly true with respect to imaging technology. As we have seen, medicine's paradigm requires a materialistic image of the patient, preferably one that is focused on one or another component part. Technology, typically high technology, is required to provide improved images of that type. In addition, the reductionistic thrust of the Cartesian-Newtonian paradigm requires ever higher levels of technology, both diagnostic and therapeutic, in order to permit the medical effort to go forward at intracellular, molecular, and intra-molecular levels.

Health care systems based on the Cartesian-Newtonian world view have little conceern with the relationship of physical and social environments to health care. That is due in large measure to the importance of the machine metaphor in the paradigm. Machines are self-contained. They are 'closed systems,' operating essentially in independence of their environments. An understanding of a machine requires looking inside it, not in examining the relationships it has with external conditions. That same inward looking orientation characterizes scienfitic medicine and the bureaucratic hospital. Neither one directs much attention to the environments in which the medical effort and the health services delivery effort take place.

The Health Problems of the Third World

One does not need great medical sophistication to characterize the health problems of the Third World. Simply put, such problems are every where the problems brought about by an absence of the minimal requirements needed to sustain life for all the people born there. The problems arise largely from the population outstripping resources. They are the problems of poverty.

An excellent illustration of the nature of Third World health problems is the World Health Organization's "Health For All By The Year 2000" program. The objectives of the program have almost nothing to do with identifying and curing diseases. The emphasis instead is on providing basic survival needs to all the people of the world. Chief among those needs are food, clean water, and adequate shelter.

The World Health Organization's view of global health problems has been well-expressed by its Director-General Halfdan Mahler (1979): "Today nearly one thousand million people, living mainly in rural areas and urban slums...exist in a state of social and economic poverty. This is a pernicious combination of unemployment and underemployment, economic poverty, scarcity of worldly goods, a low level of education, malnutrition, affliction by disease, social apathy, and lack of the will and the initiative to make changes for the better. Taken together these create a vicious circle, and improvement of any one of them could contribute to improvement of all of them."

The problems Dr. Mahler points to are of course not limited to the Third World. They exist in many industrialized nations as well. There is no question, though, that such problems are of much greater magnitude in the Third World.

Implications

The Cartesian-Newtonian premises of scientific medicine and of the bureaucratized hospital have little relevance to the health problems of the Third World. The health care systems of the developed nations focus on pathophysiology. They are intended to rapair ("cure") disordered physiology. Little attention is directed to the psychological or social aspects of health care.

The major health problems faced by the developing nations have little to do with pathophysiology. They concern instead basic survival needs for nutrition, sanitation, and shelter. Their solution requires attention to an interrelated set of environmental variables. As much attention needs to be directed to social, psychological, and economic issues as to physical and biological ones. The approach of the contemporary scientific medicine of developed countries is ill-suited to such problems.

REFERENCES

ACKERKNECHT, ERWIN H. (1973) MEDICINE AT THE PARIS HOSPITAL. Baltimore: Johns Hopkins University Press.

BERNARD, CLAUDE (1957) AN INTRODUCTION TO THE STUDY OF EXPERIMENTAL MEDICINE. N.Y.: Dover.

BROCK, THOMAS D. (ed.) (1975) MILESTONES IN MICROBIOLOGY. Washington, D.C.: American Society for Microbiology.

BULLOCH, WILLIAM (1979) THE HISTORY OF BACTERIOLOGY. N.Y.: Dover.

DIJKSTERHUIS, E.J. (1961) THE MECHANIZATION OF THE WORLD PICTURE. Oxford: Oxford University Press.

EATON, LEONARD K. (1957) NEW ENGLAND HOSPITALS, 1790-1833. Ann Arbor: University of Michigan Press.

GASK, GEORGE E. and JOHN TODD (1952) "The Origins of Hospitals," (pp. 122-130) in E. A. Underwood (ed.), SCIENCE, MEDICINE, AND HISTORY. Vol. I. Oxford: Oxford University Press.

GOFFMAN, ERVING (1974) FRAME ANALYSIS: AN ESSAY ON THE ORGANIZATION OF EXPERIENCE. Cambridge, MA: Harvard University Press.

GOMPERZ, HEINREICH (1957) "Problems and Methods of Early Greek Science," In P. Weiner and A. Noland (eds.), ROOTS OF SCIENTIFIC THOUGHT. N.Y.: Basic Books.

HOLTON, GERALD (1973) THEMATIC ORIGINS OF SCIENTIFIC THOUGHT: KEPLER TO EINSTEIN. Cambridge, MA: Harvard University Press.

JACOBY, HENRY (1973) THE BUREAUCRATIZATION OF THE WORLD. Berkeley: University of California Press.

KING, LESTER S. (1978) THE PHILOSOPHY OF MEDICINE. Cambridge, MA: Harvard University Press.

KUHN, THOMAS S. (1961) "The Function of Measurement in Modern Physical Science," (pp. 31-63) in Harry Woolf (ed.), QUANTIFICATION: A HISTORY OF THE MEANING OF MEASUREMENT IN THE NATURAL AND SOCIAL SCIENCES. Indianapolis: Bobbs-Merrill.

KUHN, THOMAS (1970) THE STRUCTURE OF SCIENTIFIC REVOLUTIONS (2nd ed.) Chicago: University of Chicago Press.

KUHN, THOMAS S. (1974) "Second Thoughts on Paradigms," pp. 459–482 in F. Suppe (ed.), THE STRUCTURE OF SCIENTIFIC THEORIES. Urbana: University of Illinois Press.

MAHLER, HALFDAN (1979) "What is Health for All?" WORLD HEALTH (November): 3–5.

MASTERMAN, MARGARET (1970) "The Nature of a Paradigm," in I. Lakatos and A. Musgrave (eds.). CRITICISM AND THE GROWTH OF KNOWLEDGE. Cambridge: Cambridge University Press.

NISBET, ROBERT A. (1969) SOCIAL CHANGE AND HISTORY: ASPECTS OF THE WESTERN THEORY OF DEVELOPMENT. London: Oxford University Press.

PEPPER, STEPHEN C. (1942) WORLD HYPOTHESES: A STUDY IN EVIDENCE. Berkeley: University of California Press. PEPPER, STEPHEN C. (1966) CONCEPT AND QUALITY: A WORLD HYPOTHESIS. LaSalle, IL: Open Court.

PHILLIPS, EUSTACE DOCKRAY (1973) GREEK MEDICINE. London: Thames and Hudson.

REISER, STANLEY J. (1978) "Inward Vision and Outward Glance: The Shaping of the American Hospital, 1880–1914," BULLETIN OF THE HISTORY OF MEDICINE 53 (Fall): 329–345.

SCARBOROUGH, JOHN (1969) ROMAN MEDICINE. Ithaca, N.Y.: Cornell University Press.

SHRYOCK, RICHARD HARRISON (1947) THE DEVELOPMENT OF MODERN MEDICINE. N.Y.: Knopf.

TEMKIN, OWSEI (1973) GALENISM: RISE AND DECLINE OF A MEDICAL PHILOSOPHY. Ithaca, N.Y.: Cornell University Press.

VIRCHOW, RUDOLPH (1958) DISEASE, LIFE, AND MAN. (trans. by L.J. Rather). Stanford, CA: Stanford University Press.

VOGEL, MORRIS J. (1980) THE INVENTION OF THE MODEREN HOSPITAL: BOSTON, 1870–1930. Chicago: University of Chicago Press.

WADDINGTON, IVAN (1973) "The Role of the Hospital in the Development of Modern Medicine: A Sociological Analysis," SOCIOLOGY 7 (May): 211–224.

WESTFALL, RICHARD S. (1977) THE CONSTRUCTION OF MODERN SCIENCE: MECHANISMS AND MECHANICS. Cambridge: Cambridge University Press.

WILLEY, BASIL (1940) THE EIGHTEENTH CENTURY BACKGROUND: STUDIES IN THE IDEA OF NATURE IN THE THOUGHT OF THE PERIOD. London: Chatto and Windus.

CHAPTER 9

HEALTH CARE IN INDIA: AN ANALYSIS OF THE EXISTING MODELS

Linda L. Lindsey

Introduction

Health care in India is as diverse as the subcontinent on which it is practiced. This diversity is ideologically, politically and socioculturally appropriate in that multiple systems of health care continue to function and thrive even though there are major differences in the medical orientations and philosophies of each. To come to grips with the complexity of this type of health care pluralism, it is necessary to examine the two major Indian medical systems and certain of the components within each. With this as a framework, the objectives of the chapter are to first, demonstrate the historical underpinnings that support this contemporary diversity and secondly, use this evidence in order to predict the future course of health care systems in India.

Ayurvedic Medicine

Of the two major branches of medicine existing in India, one is the indigenous form and the second has been imported from the West. The indigenous form is known as the Ayurvedic medicine and is rooted in the books of the ancient **Vedas,** which are composites of Greek, Muslim, Arab and Persian writings that not only delineate the causes of disease but are also broadly consistent with more general Hindu philosophy. Ayurveda, meaning the "science of life," is based on the theory that health is dependent on the balanced state of all bodily elements, both quantitatively and qualitatively. Through these derivations, Ayurvedic medicine provides the appropriate superstructure that encourages both devout Hindus and Muslims to seek health care from a variety of traditional or so-called "folk" practitioners.

It is important to note here, however, that what is considered Ayurvedic medicine varies greatly. For the sake of simplicity, I have chosen to use the Ayurvedic label as representing the generic, indigenous category and then consider other traditional forms within this. Some writers use a system which divides health care into a modern medicine category which includes scientific, Western or allopathic forms, and an indigenous category which may include Ayurvedic, Unani and Homeopathic forms (defined later). Bhatia (1975) and Banerji (1981) have both made a significant elaboration of this system of classification. Since Ayurvedic medicine is by far the dominant category of India's indigenous health care system,

111

I have elected to use it as the form encompassing the others. Though Ayurvedic medicine per se is tied to Vedic writings, its distinguishing characteristics become blurred when viewing other traditional forms. Also, as we shall see, indigenous practitioners freely borrow both techniques and remedies from other sources than that encompassed in this particular medical category.

Ayurvedic medicine continues to flourish because its practitioners have specialized according to the religious background of their patients. For example, the Muslim form of traditional medicine is known as **Unani,** with its physicians practicing in accordance with the religious and philosophical components of Islam. Ayurvedic Hindu practitioners provide services which are congruent to the lifestyle and culture of their Hindu patients. Thus both groups recognize that medical practices must remain consistent with the belief systems, including dietary habits and daily proscriptions, of their patients and this knowledge is reflected in specific treatment plans and medical regimens. Indeed, it is impossible to consider almost any aspect of Indian culture without focusing to some extent on religion, and Ayurvedic medicine has organized and specialized accordingly. As Rosengren (1980: 229) points out, the very survival of such systems depends on recognition of the prevailing cultural milieu as well as the standards of what the public considers plausible.

Beyond the religious specialization of Ayurvedic medicine, there are numerous compatible subsystems which may be classified as falling within these general boundaries. In this regard, these traditional Indian forms are similar to other "folk" medicial practices existing in cultures, or possibly subcultures, at the same developmental stage. Coe (1978: 135) refers to nonscientific medicine as those traditional beliefs and practices accepted uncritically in part because of their compatible religious and moral structure. This is differentiated from scientific medicine which is based on the rigors of empirical verification and positivistic methodology. The forms described below are essentially nonscientific in orientation and fall under the generic Ayurvedic branch. However, as will be evident, what is perhaps unique about Ayurvedic medicine is that it tends to cross-cut these categories of scientific and nonscientific.

Indigenous medical **practiti**oners (IMPs) with Ayurvedic training may also be treating patients by using a variety of homeopathic techniques in combination with those specific to their training. Homeopathy, a Nineteenth Century European development introduced in India through mainly British influence, is based on the general principle that "like cures like." For instance, small doses of herbal preparations or synthetic drugs which are themselves similar to what is seen as causing the disease may be prescribed. The folk wisdom of treating colds and fevers with methods that would likely produce the same ailments are accepted tenets of homeopathy. What is interesting regarding homeopathy is that though the label of homeopathic medicine was not used until the Nineteenth Century, such procedures have been part of Indian traditional practices for centuries and can also be found in the ancient folk healing customs of numerous other cultures as well. The major difference today is that some IMPs

112

are currently being trained in homeopathic practices in a more rigorous, systematic manner than their ancient counterparts. Educational institutions have been established throughout India specifically for homeopathic training. Vaids and Hakims, Hindu and Unani practitioners respectively, make us of a diverse array of medical procedures, including homepathy, if deemed appropriate.

Naturopathy is a broader orientation that relies on the curative forces of nature to both combat disease and promote health. Perhaps more than other indigenous forms, naturopathy encompasses a greater preventive health care emphasis. The threads of naturopathy are tied to ancient Greece with the conception that the mind, body and spirit are inseparable, a philosophy that is carried through in the Vedic sources concerning health care. The medical procedures and if necessary, drug regimens, that are the least intrusive in upsetting the delicate mind-body-spirit balance are the most popular for naturopathic IMPs. This is consistent with Ayurvedic principales that view humans as conglomerates of five elements or "panchabhutas," air, water, earth, fire and ether, which are subtly combined in each individual. Notice here the connections between this principle and the ancient Greek physician Hippocrates' idea that health is influenced by the totality of environmental factors. Hippocrates saw the body as made up of what he referred to as "humors" which consisted of blood, phlegm, black bile and yellow bile. If environmental and humoral balances were maintained then a person was healthy. Conversely, sickness resulted from any disequilibrium. Leslie (1974) indicates that Ayurvedic theory assumes that the aggregation of panchabhutas along with other bodily substances is a "microcosmic version of the universe," the balance of which is essential to health. Though it is difficult to trace the exact influence from ancient Greek thought concerning health and illness in the Vedas, it is apparent that definite strains exist.

These principles are put into practice in the numerous "nature cure ashrams" (literally translated as "monastic center for retreat") scattered through India. A visit to one such ashram located in Uruli Kanchan near Poona in Southwest India provided an opportunity to witness the operation of Ayurvedic and naturopathic techniques on a daily basis. Though the observations are purely impressionistic the ashram seemed to rigorously uphold the beliefs associated with naturopathy in particular. As the director pointed out to his Western visitors, the ashram translates Ayurvedic theories into medical regimens based on the naturopathic principles of "diet, quiet, merriment and rest." Daily schedules include time for both physical and spiritual exercises, meditation, and group sessions relating to certain therapies. The ashram cultivates its own herbal garden and grows some of the vegetables consumed by patients.

Naturopathy adheres to a rigid dietary system that encourages the consumption of whole grains, unprocessed foodstuffs and a general vegetarianism. These regimens appear to be particularly successful for those patients suffering from stress related diseases such as ulcers, hypertension and gastro-intestinal problems. Such ashrams are attractive mainly to certain of India's middle-class citizens from urban areas. The cost, while very inexpensive by Western standards, would be prohibitive for the vast majority of India's poor. It would also be unrealistic since the poor are more likely to be afflicted with any number of acute diseases. Ashrams are geared more to the chronically ill as well as to those interested in preventive health care measures.

As would be expected, Ayurvedic practitioners make extensive use of herbal and mineral preparations and prescribe remedies which can be more readily adhered to as indicated by the lifestyle and religious customs of the patients they serve. Some IMPs have been trained in the South Indian "Siddha" system of medicine, originated in the pre-Aryan period, which uses pulverized herbs in various combinations. In ash form, these herbs are used to treat a whole range of bodily complaints (Takulia, et al., 1977: 251). Nonetheless, such **formal** training in herbal remedies is rare, with many practitioners relying on apprenticeships to relatives in order to gain their knowledge. Caste ties make the Vaid, Hakim, and even the local midwife or "Dai" as she would be called, hereditary positions despite government efforts to minimize such practices, especially in the villages.

Taken together these indigenous medical forms tend to focus on the entire lifespace of the individual patient and provide for a kind of holistic health care perspective that is compatible to the religious and cultural beliefs of both India's Hindu and Muslim populations. Notwithstanding long term stays in nature cure ashrams, since Ayurvedic medicine does not rely heavily on expensive equipment and synthetic drugs, it remains an attractive alternative to India's poorer citizens. Beyond the political consequences, this factor of cost may be at least part of the rationale for governmental encouragement of Ayurvedic training. In addition, IMPs are the dominant health care force in the villages and rural areas where 80% of India's 680 million people live, partly because practitioners trained in Western medicine are difficult to recruit into these locales. As suggested below, however, the IMPs may be the key for bringing about more of a convergence of Ayurvedic and Western, or allopathic medicine.

ALLOPATHIC MEDICINE

Western medicine in India is known as allopathy and was ushered in during the long era of British colonialism. In most contemporary Western cultures allopathic medicine is regarded as the legitimate form, with others representing either marginal or unscientific systems. The label of "allopathic" to the word medicine is redundant by Western standards since it is assumed to be the type of scientific medicine recognized as basically the only credible form. Medical techniques that do not readily fit into this allopathic mold are seen as suspicious by practitioners and this attitude carries over to the lay public's general acceptance of such techniques. In the United States, for example, chiropractic has worked to overcome the opposition of the American Medical Association and establish itself as a viable, accepted part of health care. At this point, however, it is still

114

viewed by many M.D.s as "cultlike" and consisting of unproven techniques.

It is perhaps ironic that the use of the term allopathy is credited to Samuel Hahnemann, the German founder of homeopathy, who challenged the hegemony of allopathy by creating an alternative system (Frankenberg, 1981: 116). Allopathic medicine is indeed much more instrusive than most Ayurvedic techniques in that it is rooted in the belief that to return the individual to a healthy state, incursions into the body are likely to be necessary, whether it be through surgery, physical manipulation, or the use of patent, synthetic drugs (Rosengren, 1980: 206). It is interesting that allopathy also encountered a credibility gap with the public by these very intrusive methods because at one time it was thought bodily purges were necessary, with bloodletting and the use of diuretics being so common that the "cure" was often worse than the disease itself. Whereas Ayurvedic medicine is rooted in ancient philosophy, the efficacy of allopathic techniques is scientifically based, hence re-evaluation of pre-existing theories are continually being made.

Since allopathy was established primarily for those people involved in the British colonial bureaucracy and military forces, few Indians wee originally able to take advantage of the techniques it offered (Deodhar, 1982: 77). It cannot be said that Ayurvedic and allopathic medicine competed during those colonial years because each system was designed to serve specific populations. It is partly due to this fact that Ayurveda continued to flourish at the same time allopathy grew and expanded in India. However, Banerji (1981) incorporated a distinctly Marxian perspective in suggesting that by denying Indians access to Western medicine, this was a colonialist political strategy designed to weaken the oppressed classes and contribute to the decay of traditional, indigenous systems. Though it may be correct to assess the colonial government's policy in this regard, I think there is ample evidence to suggest that whatever the intentions may have been, Ayurvedic medicine and other indigenous forms were actually strengthened in the long run.

After India achieved its independence in 1947 the fledgling government recognized that health was of the highest priority, with the new constitution stating that the government "shall regard the raising of the level of nutrition and the standard of living ofits people and the improvement of public health as among its primary duties." In order to achieve this, the central government has worked with the states to establish a system of health care education, including colleges, hospitals, clinics, and research facilities, throughout India. What is remarkable about this kind of health care program is that it has helped to institutionalize in India a dual system of medicine, one indigenous and the other Western. And Western medicine brings with it the stigma of the rememberances of colonialism. The question then becomes which system is to be officially sanctioned if one is viewed as alien and associated with feelings of resentment by some, but also possibly more efficacious than the other? As stated above, the question has been answered in such a way that both systems have developed and been nurtured in part with the blessings of the government.

SEPARATE BUT EQUAL?

Both Ayurvedic and allopathic medicine in contemporary India have evolved an elaborate system of educational institutions, hospitals and clinics which puts them on basically equal footing. As we have seen, their philosophies differ considerably, but extensive formal training in essentially the same subject areas (though with different emphases) provides them with similar credentials, at least as far as the lay public is concerned. Unlike many other cultures wherre indigenous medical practictioners continue to learn their trade by informal instruction or thorugh claims of possessing special powers, often magical or supernatural in substance, Ayurvedic practitioners are now being educated in programs that offer a medical degree. As Banerji (1981: 111) points out, there is historical evidence to demonstrate that Indian medicine had begun to sever its ties to "magico-religious therapies" centuries before Christ and began the gradual development of rational therapeutics on which to base its practices. Though this rational basis is not necessarily a scientific framework per se, Ayurveda is currently conducting experiments to determine more precisely the effects of accepted herbal preparations on the body. This is another instance where the categories of scientific versus non-- scientific medicine are crosscut by an indigenous form of health care.

As early as the beginning of the Twentieth Century a number of institutions were designed to educate practitioners in traditional medicine, including both Unani and Ayurvedic forms. These centers were not only to aid in institutionalizing training in indigenous health care, but also to gradually replace the ancient caste orientation that tied practitioners to certain families generation after generation (Takulia, et al., 1977: 252). As a result of formalizing Ayurvedic education, other developments followed. Most states established boards of indigenous medicine to regular, review when necessary, and license practitioners. Also, dispensaries were created that were specifically designed to insure that patients received appropriate Ayurvedic preparations.

However, the number and quality of these dispensaries vary among the states and in many areas the majority of patients still prefer obtaining medicines directly from their Ayurvedic practitioners or from local herbalists. This has led to a trend to practice indigenous medicine but now with all the bureaucratic trappings involved. Though it appears contradictory, it may be that this very bureaucracy is indicative of the upgrading of Ayurvedia as a profession. Thus, even with governmental regulation Ayurvedic practitioners enjoy the autonomy granted by professional status that allows them freedom to practice essentially unhampered by whatever may be occurring in allopathic medicine. Though there are variations, in most Indian states today both Ayurvedic and allopathic physicians must complete, at a minimum, a postsecondary five-year baccalaureate program which allows them to practice. The M.D. degree for both is usually an advanced specialty degree involving three additional years of training. A similar, but not as extensive, system of academics exists for homeopathy and Unani medicine. It is interesting that the

116

term "physician" is commonly applied to many kinds of practitioners, which again points to their parallel positions.

Through the efforts of the British colonial government Indian physicians have been trained in allopathy as early as the 1830s. Jeffery (1977: 562) notes that most of these doctors entered the elite Indian Medical Service (IMS) upon finishing their training. By World War Two approximately 40,00 allopathic physicians practiced in India of which only about 750 were European, which helped provide the structure for Western medicine to continue to expand after independence. With expansion a number of support services developed which are similar to those existing in Western cultures. For example, allopathic physicians depend on the services of qualified pharmacists and compounders to make certain patients receive exact dosages of prescribed drugs, the majority of which are synthetic. As allopathic medicine becomes firmly entrenched in India, the call for health support personnel will increase as well. The steady growth of the health care industry in general, and allopathy in particular, is indicated by the number of people clamoring for admittance into educational institutions. The fact that a college of pharmacy recently opened in Bombay to offer a four year program leading to a Bachelor of Pharmacy degree had over 1,500 applications for the 100 places in the freshman class is demonstrable of this trend. In this regard, India is certainly no different from what is happening with the health care industry in the West.

As would be predicted, allopaths tend to be urban practitioners whose practices often depend on a middle-class clientele. This situation further separates them from their Ayurvedic counterparts who also practice in the cities but provide the bulk of health care services to village and rural populations. Even in light of the fact that the IMPs continue to see the vast majority of the population, Frankenberg (1981: 115) states that "the professional ideology of allopathic medicine with its urban, male, hospital-based, cosmopolitan, curative, and above all individualistic emphasis (gives) a considerable advantage over its fragmented rivals with their lack of a broad social base." In this sense, it is implied that despite governmental intentions of bringing indigenous and allopathic systems on par with one another, practitioners of Western medicine will likely have, at minimum, a financial advantage in that a generally wealthier clientele is served. The consequences of this for the further development of both Ayurvedic and allopathic medicine remain to be seen.

At this point, therefore, India remains pluralistic in terms of health care with a network of practitioners who would appear to have competing medical ideologies but who continue to serve distinct segments of an incredibly diverse population. What has been implied throughout this paper is that in those areas where patients have a choice among a number of health care alternatives they will choose according to their individual needs, finances, religious values and cultural beliefs. Furthermore, it is assumed that one form of health care exists parallel to, but for the most part separated from, other forms because allopathy and Ayurveda appear to be philosophically distant in terms of overall medical orientation.

I would like now to challenge this latter assumption by demonstrating that even if the two are separated by theory and types of medical institutions that have been created, there is still a great deal of interchange between them. And this has occurred despite unsuccessful attempts at formally integrating the two systems.

In 1946 it was proposed that Ayurvedic practitioners could be trained in Western techniques, but difficulties arose due to Ayurveda's lack of a scientific orientation so that by 1961 the few integrated educational institutions that existed were abolished (Health Survey, 1961). However, this did not mean an end to interchange. In a revealing study by Bhatia et al. (1975), interviews with 93 IMPs who worked principally in rural areas demonstrated that approximately 90% used allpathic drugs in their practices. What is most interesting is that many expressed a preference in practicing traditional medicine but found that to do so would have meant losing patients. Apparently they were practicing medicine using certain allopathic drugs and procedures because this is what the villagers demanded (Bhatia et al., 1975: 19).

The widespread use of allopathic drugs and instruments by IMPs has been documented in a number of studies (Kakar, 1972; Singh et al., 1974; Taylor, 1976). Minocha (1980: 22), somewhat critical of this trend, states that "In my own research I have observed many a patient visiting the general hospital to obtain a 'free diagnosis' from the practitioners of modern medicine. The diagnosis is then told to a local 'practitioner' at home, who simply matches a medication with the diagnosis on the basis of information derived from reading pharmaceutical literature or from talking to local pharmacists. The indigenous practitioner in this manner incorporates drugs from modern medicine and uses them indiscriminately on the gullible layman." Her belief is that since patients are increasingly evaluating practitioners on the basis of their efficacy, traditional medicine cannot help but lose ground to allopathy.

This trend is certainly away from the idea that Western medicine could not take hold in villages because it is viewed as alien in terms of beliefs and practices. An older study by Marriott (1955) suggests that the role for allopathy in the villages would be a weak one unless it is defined according to village concepts, since it would be bringing with it Western ideas that are incompatible to village social organization, among other things. In his research on a conservative and very traditional north Indian village, he found major cultural obstacles which effectively blocked the introduction of Western medicine to the villagers. Yet, considering that the study was conducted almost thirty years ago, villagers still requested allopathic drugs which they appeared to view as legitimate curative measures for a number of maladies. It is becoming increasingly evident that Indian villagers, though perhaps suspicious of intrusions from what they perceive as alien way so of thinking, no longer totally reject allopathic medicine. The eradication of smallpox thorugh vaccination helped provide the impetus for this. And the following insight by Minocha (1980: 221) tempers the claim that the two systems are incompati-

118

ble with traditional practitioners being preferred by rural populations. "People," says Minocha, "may rely on traditional practitioners when modern medicine is **not** available to them...This does not warrant the conclusion that they **prefer** traditional to modern medicine, as some scholars and politicians claim. Studies of choice of medical system must take this into account."

Finally, though it may be said that IMPs are now utilizing more Western procedures, instruments and drugs, the reverse cannot be said for the allopaths. Until a sound scientific basis for Ayurveda is discovered, allopaths will likely remain reluctant to utilize indigenous techniques. This does not mean, however, that allopaths will isolate themselves from the villagers. Government incentives have encouraged village practices, with their success not seen in terms of how they can entice villagers to accept Western medicine, but how well they can deal with the local culture. Certainly Indian practitioners would have greater success than similarly trained Westerners on which earlier studies of village acceptance of allopathy were based, such as that described by Marriott (1955).

PREDICTIONS

Given this discussion, I think certain trends are clear. India will remain medically pluralistic and her citizens will have a choice among a number of existing health care systems. It is evident that the government will continue to support allopathic research and development as well as aid in upgrading Ayurvedic and other indigenous subsystems. For political as well as pragmatic reasons research will persist in terms of finding a scientific approach to Ayurveda in order to encourage more fruitful interchange between the two medical forms. As more villagers are introduced to allopathy, often as a result of contacting IMPs who are also knowledgeable of local customs and beliefs, resistance to these techniques will gradually diminish. Though **formal** education will continue to separate allopathy and Ayurveda, government efforts at stimulating research' into a scientific rationale for Ayurveda should produce a more cooperation.

Pharmacokinetics is a discipline that concerns the study and characterization of the course of the drug once it is taken into the body. Studies of drug absorption, distribution, metabolism, and excretion are involved here. The pharmacokinetics of herbal remedies commonly used by IMPs are currently being tested in order to determine specific therapeutic properties. One development coming out of this type of research has produced the drug Serpasil, an antihypertensive that was the result of collaborative efforts of by Ayurvedic and allopathic physicians. Also, allopaths are taking a closer look at the success of Ayurvedic medicine in dealing with certain categories of chronically ill patients, such as those afflicted with arthritis and hypertension. This is significant particularly because Western medicine in India may be re-discovering holistic health care principles that have existed for centuries and that this is paralleling similar developments occurring thorughout cultures that routinely practice allopathy. Perhaps India will be able to implement holistic health care practices with an allopathic system less resistant to such approaches.

Overall, however, I think that cooperative energies between the two systems will in the long run benefit allopathy more than Ayurveda. As Ayurveda continues its trend toward professionalization it may lose some of its unique qualities that separates it from allopathy, regardless of the Vedic philosophy on which it is based. Ayurvedic medicine may thus take the route that osteopathy paved in the United States. With osteopaths now enjoying the same practice rights as allopathic physicians it is often difficult to distinguish between the two. The dilemma that will likely be faced by Ayurveda is one that will perhaps force a confrontation between the attainment of full professionalism at the risk of giving up its uniqueness. Thus to define what "benefit" actually means, one has to consider it in terms of the context of the particular system in question.

It is exceedingly difficult to make any generalizations about India when considering its diversity. India's pluralistic health care policies reflect, and to some extent, encourage and strengthen this diversity. Regardless of the professional stature of either system, the bottom line is how best to serve the needs of a nation that continues to be plagued with high rates of death due to tuberculosis, cholera and maleria, as well as a high infant mortality rate. It is estimated that in 1980 the infant mortality rate was approximately 120 per 1,000 live births, with almost one half of these deaths occurring within a month after birth (Deodhar, 1982: 80). In some areas the rates remain so high that parents will have a naming ceremony for the child only after it has reached one year of age.

With these kinds of sobering statistics, dedication to common goals help to reduce the negative effects of two potentially competing forms of medicine. As I have pointed out in another paper, the reality of India is that of illiteracy, poverty, and disease are embedded in a country whose population will exceed one billion by the turn of the Twenty-First Century. The reality is also that education is spreading to the villages, smallpox has been eradicated, tuberculosis is on the decline, and the first positive signs of public health measures have become manifest (Lindsey, 1982: 17). Certainly the problems facing India's medical practitioners are tremendous. Yet I believe that the very pluralism that some may view as inefficient make these problems a bit more surmountable. Different segments of medicine serve different patient needs. In those areas where several alternatives exist, patients have a choice among a range of legitimized health care practitioners, something that has not been duplicated in the more competitive West, especially with allopathy in the position of controlling medicine as a whole. If cooperation is to be realistic, however, IMPs need to have a greater understanding of the allopathic techniques and procedures they are using.

In the United States medical practitioners are now recognizing that a health care **team** approach is perhaps the most logical method of assuring optimal patient care, particularly given the fragmentation of health care services that currently exists. The notion of a team approach appears to have already taken root in India's health care system and the commitment of its personnel is visible throughout the country—from the urban allopathic physician, to a pharmacist in a regional health center or the IMP making rounds in a number of villages. This is not to minimize the problems that come with such pluralism, but it does suggest that when considering India's diversity, the system that has ultimately developed is conceivably the most appropriate, and perhaps the most functional, terms of her culture.

REFERENCES

BANERJI, D. (1981) "The Place of Indigenous and Western systems of Medicine in the health services of India," SOCIAL SCIENCE AND MEDICINE 15A: 109-114.

BHATIA, J.C. et al. (1975) "Traditional Healers and Modern Medicine," SOCIAL SCIENCE AND MEDICINE 9: 15-21.

COE, RODNEY M. (1978) SOCIOLOGY OF MEDICINE. N.Y.: McGraw-Hill.

DEODHAR, D.S. (1982) "Primary Health Care in India," JOURNAL OF PUBLIC HEALTH POLICY 3: 76-99.

FRANKENBERG, RONALD (1981) "Allopathic Medicine, Profession and Capitalist Ideology in India," SOCIAL SCIENCE AND MEDICINE 15A: 115-125.

HEALTH SERVEY AND PLANNING COMMITTEE (1961) Vol. I. Delhi, India: Publications Division, Government of India.

JEFFERY, R. (1977) "Allopathic Medicine in India: A Case of Deprofessionalization," SOCIAL SCIENCE AND MEDICINE 11: 561-573.

KAKAR, D.N. et. al. (1972) "People's Perceptiion of Illness and Their Use of Medical Care Services in Punjab," INDIAN JOURNAL OF MEDICAL EDUCATION 11: 283-287.

LESLIE, CHARLES (1974) "The Modernization of Asian Medical Systems," in J. Poggie and R. Lynch (eds.), RETHINKING MODERNIZATION. Westport, CT: Greenwood Press.

LINDSEY, LINDA L. (1982) "Pharmacy and Health Care in India," AMERICAN PHARMACY NS22: 14-17.

MARRIOTT, McKIM (1955) "Western Medicine in a Village of Northern India," pp. 239-368 in Benjamin Paul (ed.), HEALTH, CULTURE AND COMMUNITY. N.Y.: Russell Sage Foundation.

MINOCHA, ANEETA A. (1980) "Medical Pluralism and Health Services in India," SOCIAL SCIENCE AND MEDICINE 14B: 217-223.

ROSENGREN, WILLIAM R. (1980) SOCIOLOGY OF MEDICINE: DIVERSITY, CONFLICT AND CHANGE. N.Y.: Harper and Row.

SINGH, S. et. al. (1974) "Assessing the Knowledge and Practice of Rural Medical Practitioners," NIHAE BULLETIN 7. New Delhi.

TAKULIA, H.S. et. al. (1977) "Orienting Physicians to Working with Rural Medical Practitioners," SOCIAL SCIENCE AND MEDICINE 11: 251-56.

TAYLOR, C.E. (1976) "The Place of Indigenous Medical Practitioners in the Modernization of Health Services," in Charles Leslie (ed.) ASIAN MEDICAL SYSTEMS. Berkeley: University of California Press.

CHAPTER 10

PATIENT SATISFACTION IN COSTA RICA:
A COMPARATIVE STUDY OF DIFFERENT LEVELS OF HEALTH CARE

Setha M. Low

INTRODUCTION

Medicine in the Third World is undergoing rapid change because of the increasing impact of urbanization, secularization and modernization on the organization and structure of traditional health culture. The medicalization of society, so accurately recorded for the United States and Europe, also has influenced the health behavior and practices in most developing countries creating a mosaic of diverse beliefs and medical institutions which sometimes enhances but often undermines the perceived quality of available health care. The examination of patient satisfaction provides a window on this medical change process by analyzing the response of the patient to medical treatment in relation to variables of patient beliefs, health practices and health care behavior.

This paper reviews a health care study of Costa Rica funded by the National Institute of Mental Health for fieldwork carried out between 1972 to 1974, with follow-up research completed during the summers of 1976 and 1979. The paper begins with a description of Costa Rica followed by an introduction to the general methodology. The discussion of findings is organized by the methods that produced each interpretation of patient satisfaction and which are presented as a multilevel model. Findings on individual patients are based on interviews that were held in clinics focused on expectations of patients as they enter the medical consultation. At the family level, the findings are based on interviews in the home and tend to focus on health sector utilization models. At the institutional level, in hospitals and the clinics, the findings are based on observation of doctor-patient interactions, interviews with staff and their patients, and statistical documents. The ideology of those institutions and the impact of that ideology on doctor-patient interaction is included as part of the institutional context. Finally, at the cultural level, findings are based on participant observation of sociocultural patterns and focus on expectations of role and social style when entering the medical context. These four different data sets are analyzed to provide theoretical interpretations of how each of these levels influence patient satisfaction and present a complex description of the patient's response to rapidly changing medical practice.

SETTING

Costa Rica is a special Third World country in which to conduct fieldwork due to the fact that it has a successful health care system and health status statistics which reflect a high level of literacy and public health. The Costa Rican population tends to be homogenous culturally, biologically and in terms of language and religion. It is one of the few Central American countries that has a large middle-class population. The pluralistic health care system offers the population a broad spectrum of health care services as well as social security and work disability programs.

When I started my fieldwork, I was particularly interested in urban environments because within the urban environment you have a centralizatin of health services. In order to learn something about services and satisfaction, I felt it was necessary to look at where services were in contact with the largest number of people and therefore with the largest patient load. Within the urban context there is a diversity of users as well as a diversity of services available. Further, the urban environment is where most of the problems in dveloping countries are focused. Because of rapidly expanding services and large numbers of individuals immmigrating into cities from the rural countryside, one tends to see overloaded services and a concern on the part of those governments of using these services in the best way possible. In order to study the importance of patient satisfaction and its relation to health policy, it was essential to evaluate the environment where there is the greatest need for resources and some degree of resource availability so that choices can be made.

Costa Rica is one of the smallest of the Central American countries, with two million, two hundred and twenty thousand individuals in 1980. The small number of indigenous people populating Costa Rica when the Spanish arrived resulted in a population that is basically of European or Spanish origin. The state religion is Catholicism with a patron saint, the Virgin of Los Angeles, who is important in healing and personal religious practices. About 36% of the population currently work in agriculture,, producing coffee, bananas, sugar and cattle while the remainder of the employed population work mainly in service and unskilled labor occupations.

According to recent accounts, Costa Rica is currently in economic straits with a high foreign debt which is difficult to pay, a situation which many other Latin American countries share. This situation in Costa Rica seems to be attributed to their highly developed welfare state based on universal education, pension benefits and extensive health care services.

Historically, Costa Rica was a country of small landowners working on their own land. At least this was true until the 1840's at which time land began to be amassed by those individuals who owned the factories that roasted and cleaned the coffee after it was picked. As individual farmers could not afford this equipment, the land was bought up by the large landowners, and classes which had existed before based on traditions of surname and privilege were reinforced by the differences in resources and land. Today, the gross national product per capita is about $1,500.00, certainly the highest in Central America and one of the highest in Latin America. However, there is an inflation rate that is approaching 100% and may be going higher. The only reason that food is within the reach of poor individuals is that there is state pricing of food.

Health in Costa Rica is a very important concept and the basis of a medicalized, health-centered culture (Low, 1982). More is spent on health than on defense or any other sector in the government structure. Health for Costa Rica is **bien estar** which means well-being, or **estar sano**, to be sane, clean and whole. The goal of life for any Costa Rican is to live tranquilly. Illness represents anything out of balance which disturbs living calmly, and any disturbance of this system will break the balance and harmony one has established.

Costa Rica has a pluralistic health care system which can best be described by dividing it into three sectors. There is a professional medicine sector, which is made up of the Social Security hospital system, the Public Health hospital system, the private hospital and clinic system, social workers, nurses and an entire medical school and other professional schools that produce these professionals.

The second health care sector is what has been described as the popular sector. By popular sector I mean those kind of health care services that are home based and that are available through an individual's actions in his own home economy which includes the use of herbs in home, home remedies, religious behavior, and petitioning to the Virgin of Los Angeles for good health. It includes the use of a folk saint, Dr. Moreno Canas and includes such services as Alcoholics Anonymous, the Family Planning Clinic, and any behavior that the patient initiates based on home health maintenance and family ideas of health.

The third sector, not treated in this study, is the folk medical tradition which has been consistently important in terms of the health concepts and beliefs of Costa Ricans. The Costa Rican hierarchy or resort, the order in which the Costa Ricans visit different medical practitioners, usually begins at home. If the problem is not resolved, then the patient might visit a pharmacy, go to a medical clinic, and finally visit a folk curer. This sequence of health care utilization is similar to the pattern reported for Mexico and other parts of Latin America (Young, 1981; Heller, 1981; Low, 1981b).

Costa Rica can be described as a family culture in the sense that health care does begin in the home, and that the family tends to be the source both of good health and often the instigator or the basis of bad health. If one is rejcted by one's family, and separated, that tends to increase one's poor health and encourage the problems that show up in the form of the symptom **nervios** and other kinds of mental illness (Low, 1981a). San Jose, capital of Costa Rica, was the city in which I did most of my research. It is located in the Meseta Central and is made up of about 500,000 individuals. San Jose is the center of all medical institutions in the country and can be considered a primate urban center in that it is larger than any other combined urban area in the entire country.

The medical institutions that one finds in Costa Rica developed within San Jose. The public health system began in the 1840's at the instigation of the Catholic Church. It was originally charity run, and in the 1890's was secularized when the national government wanted to strip the Catholic Church of some of its control in the welfare services in the country. This also coincided with the expansion of the coffee industry and the accumulation of wealth by the elite, upper class.

The social security system was begun in the 1940's as part of a compromise legislative assembly in which the upper class and conservative dominated assembly formed an alliance with the socialist labor party. This temporary alliance resulted in a law which would include labor restrictions, limit the number of work days, and create a social security system that would guarantee both health care rights and disability pension rights to all workers. For much of the period of time following the formation of the Social Security hospital, large numbers of the population were not covered in that most of the country was self-employed. As more individuals moved into the city and a small amount of light industry developed, more workers became employees until at the time of my study (1974) about 60% of all Costa Ricans were covered by the Social Security system. By 1981, 75% of all workers and their families were covered. In 1973, a law was passed that the Public Health Hospitals would be taken over by the Social Security hospitals and the whole system would be nationalized by 1983. This "translation of services" has in fact been occurring to the somewhat detriment of the economic well-being of Costa Rica.

In terms of health status, however, the outcome of the Social Security system has been truly impressive. Costa Rica has one of the lowest mortality rates in the world, 4.3 per thousand in 1978 (Harrison, 1981). The infant mortality rate is down to 22 per 1,000 which is equal to eastern Europe, and life expectancy is 72.3 years (Harrison, 1981). Population growth, which was at 40 per 1,000 in 1950, was reduced to 28 per 1,000 by 1970 and currently is 32 births per thousand. There has been complete eradication of malaria through a comprehensive immunization program. Malnutrition is so rare that my colleagues who want to study malnutrition had to go to Guatamala and El Salvador to find cases.

The problems that have emerged from this health care system is that it is very expensive to support all the services. Yet there is still a need to bring health care to all the provinces, not just the city, and there still is an imbalanced urban-rural doctor distribution.

METHODOLOGY

The major portion of the research was undertaken in San Jose outpatient clinics in four hospitals within the two principal Costa Rican health care delivery systems, Hosital Claderon Guardia and Hospital Mexico of the Social Security system and Hospital San Juan de Dios and Psychiatric Hospital Manuel Chapui of the Ministry of Public Health. The Social Security system is a semi-autonomous national health, disability and retirement program which at the time of the study enrolled salaried employees and their families from 60% of the total population. The Ministry of Public Health is part of the Executive Branch of the Central Government and operates a lottery run system providing free or low cost inpatient and outpatient care to those not covered by Social Security. Additional fieldwork was conducted with herbalists in the central market, pharmacists in their **boticas,** and with a range of paramedical practitioners in their offices and homes. Extensive ethnographic data were collected while living as a participant observer in a traditional neighborhood in San Jose where I had informal contacts in everyday situations and personal interaction.

The methods employed varied according to the setting and the sequence within the overall research design. Participant observation was part of the overall field experience. I learned what it was to be a Costa Rican and used these insights to understand the cultural aspects of daily life. The initial phase of research was focused on the medical administration and included interviews and observation of doctor-patient interaction in the consultation office. Between consultations, doctors and anurses and social workers and other auxiliary clinical personnel were interviewed with reference to the perceptions of patient behavior in the clinic function.

The second stage began after having estblished the pattern of consultation interaction. A structured interview covering patient perception of their illness and treatment was administered by research assistants in the waiting room before and after the observed medical consultation. Finally, a sample of the interview patients was selected for a home visit during which the researcher and an assistant conducted an open-ended family interview which emphasized personal and family health histories, genealogical and family network material, health utilization patterns, and general questions of values, preferences and health beliefs.

Observation of doctor-patient interaction was chosen as the means of most economically describing Costa Rican disease types, the variety of symptoms and their cultural expression, and doctor-patient interaction in terms of function and outcome. Consultations were recorded and notes taken in diary from which included relevant material on the situational context. The two major hospital outpatient clinics of both the Public Health hospital and the Social Security Hospital were selcted to represent general medicine services in San Jose. Two psychiatric clinics and one psychosomatic clinic were added to gain greater breadth of information of the systems description. The observed patient sample of 457 persons distributed into seven clinics was obtained by working alternate hours and days of the week with as many different doctors as possible. In this manner, an attempt was made to randomize patient attendance patterns.

Approximately 12 to 20 patients were observed with each doctor depending on his case load. Outpatients who entered the office during the observation period were recorded to minimize selection bias. The observation thus described yielded quantitative and qualitative data without intervention but excluded the patient perspective and comparison. Therefore, in the second phase of the research project, the observed patients were also interviewed before and after the consultation. A structured questionnaire elicited open ended responses of patient expectations, concepts of disease causation and treatment satisfaction of the therapeutic encounter. One hundred and seventeen before and after consultation interviews were collected by consecutively interviewing and observing consultations in each clinic setting.

The family sample is made up of nine interviewed patients who agreed to a home visit by the research team and for whom there was also a consultation visit. The intensive home interviews provided intricate data on self-concept, culture beliefs, attitudes, medical system utilization and family organization. The use of hypothetical illness stituations tested the ideal health behavior and lay referral systems. Subjects which were introduced by the patient from the interviews and suggestive of the impor- tance of popular and folk medicine in the urban health system were empha- sized and followed up with detailed questioning. Participant observation in the community where the researcher lived, in pharmacies, paramedical and folk practitioners offices and homes and in the herbal section of the central market provided contextual background for the operating social and medical system.

The research project presented here was a stepwise process. Because of the variety of kinds of methods used, there was some conflict in the data collected. These conflicts will be discussed through the summary of the findings.

FINDINGS

The findings at the level of the individual are the least surprising in that they are most like responses to studies that have been done in the United States (Garrity, 1981; Fox and Storms, 1981; Weinberger et al., 1981). The basis of the individual findings is on the questions to patients before and after consultations. These questions were: the kind of problem they had, where did it come from, the remedy or treatment previously used, asking the patient what the doctor could do for the patient, and then after the consultation, asking the patient how did it go and why, did the doctor explain what you have, did the doctor explain the kind of treatment, and now what are you going to do. The responses were that the patients were basically satisfied. Most patients expected medicine and lab exams; and based on the national statistical average, most Costa Ricans do receive at an average of two prescriptions per consultation, at least one fifth of all patients receive x-rays and over half, clinical exams. **Table I** summarizes individual expectations and requests. From the table it appears that over half of the patients received what they were asking for and therefore individual expectations of actual perform-ance and behaviior by the doctor were acceptable. Most patients at the individual level stated that they wre satisfied with the attention that they had received.

The family as second level of analysis is more difficult to analyze and requires a very different approach. By comparing the data from the before-and-after interview and from their interaction with the doctor with the contextual family interviews, patterns of satisfaction can be outlined. It is more of a glimpse at a hypothesis generating method rather than findings that are replicable and necessarily predictable. On the other hand, they introduce a new perspective into patient satisfaction that has not been presented in the literature.

In **Table II,** the relationship of family context to patient satisfaction is reflected in the nine cases based on three variables: patient expecta-tions, patient explanation of his or her own etiology, and health care sector utilization. By health care sector, I am referring back to the professional, folk and popular health sectors described in the setting section. These three variables emerge as important in distinguishing patients, one, three, four and seven who expressed some form of dissatis-faction from patients two, five, six, eight and nine who reported greater satisfaction with their medical encounter.

The satisfied patients haveexpectationssuch as pills and injections, physical exams and x-rays, which the doctor does and can fulfill. Some patients want to know what their illness is or to be asked questions or given advice, but these requests for an information exchange do not seem to indicate an underlying desire for a life change or psychological readjustment, which is expressed in the expectations of the dissatisfied patient.

Most satisfied patients directly articulate their expectations without recourse to alternating physical and psycholgoical expectations based on differential self diagnosis. In all cases, the expectations of satisfied patients are met during the consultation. The dissatisfied patient expecta-tions, however, are not fulfilled. Their requests tend to be more psycho-logical, requiring greater explanation and longer term solutions not provid-ed by the physician in a single consultation.

There is a good discussion (Young, 1976) of patient expections and satisfac-tions in terms of the practical, social, and symbolic meaning of the healing interaction of relevance here. The practical level of medical evaluation is determined by whether the treatment works, i.e., works in the sense that the patient expectations are met. The social level refers to the quality of the interaction between the healer and the patient, and the symbolic level acknowledges the ontological importance of health and healing in the definition of human action and experience. The expectation data from family cases can be understood in terms of these levels. Satisfaction is recorded when the consultation works by fulfilling the patient's practical expectations, when the physician confirms a social relationship by performing expected medical ritual, and when the physician affirms the patient's existence by resolving the health crisis by proper treatment. The patients who expressed psychological expectations do not experience healing at these three levels. The patient who wants a deep analysis, such as in case four, does not get one in a five minute consultation nor does the physician confirm or resolve her discomfort because his treatment options are limited.

Patient explanations of illness further differentiate the psychological and emotional ideologies of dissatisfied patients from the biophysical and environmental etiologies of satisfied patients. Patient expectations of illness etiology and treatment expectations overlap to form patient explanatory models of specific illness events. These models, when complete, include explanations of etiology, time and onset of symptoms, and course of illness and treatment. Practitioner explanatory models often conflict with those of the patient and their family. When this occurs, the patient may feel dissatisfied and frustrated that the physician doesn't understand his or her case. In the families' cases, it appears that the explanatory models of the dissatisfied patients report a psychological etiology for their illnesses and expect some kind of an emotional or analytic response to their problems. The physician's treatment in these cases was to give medicine based on his own explanatory model and interpretation of the situation. The treatment is incongruent with the patient's explanatory model and therefore the patient feels dissatisfied.

The third variable, family health care utilization, ties the family pattern of health care seeking behavior to the individual outcome of patient satisfaction. Families of satisfied patients use all three health care sectors, professional, popular, and folk for medical treatment and consultation. Families of dissatisfied patients, however, use only the professional sector, usually a private doctor or the clinics of major medical institutions. In two cases, families three and seven, the patients used the professional sector but report having used another sector in the past. Both patients state that they no longer believe in or use the previous modes of health care. The two patients also report dissatisfaction in a milder verbal form than patients one and four. Their responses conform on the first two variables, patient satisfaction and explanation with the other dissatisfied patients, but on the utilization variables, they are in an intermediate position. Their degree of dissatisfaction appears less defined than the other patient's, possibly because of their change in use of health care.

The health care utilization variable also is explained by family socioeconomic status. The family cases suggest that increased education and income restricts rather than expands health care options. That is not

to say that the wealthier patients do not see a large number of practitioners. Kleinman (1980) has confirmed the well documented cross-cultural
pattern in which greater utilization of health care service correlates
with higher socioeconomic status when such services operate on a fee
for service basis. However, the lower socioeconomic status patients
in the family sample utilize a greater number of health care sectors.
Differences in family life style and medical beliefs correspond to the
differences in health behavior. The dissatisfied patients, one, three
and four are all professionals with varying degrees of family mobility
and economic support. Their degree of education is reflected in a medical
orientation that narrowly defines health care in terms of the professional
sector and Western biomedicine. Their complaints, however, are generaliz-
ed and expressed in non-biomedical terms. Their restricted health care
options do not correspond to their psychological and emotional definition
of illness. The patient-physician encounter is limited in time and interview
content, and therefore is perceived as unsatisfactory.

The families of lower socioecnomic status utilize a broader range of
health care practitioners including spiritualists, homeopaths, pharmacists,
herbalists and curers. Their understanding of 'cure' and reported satisfaction relies less on the limited psychological ability of the medical practitioner because they have a larger repertoire of available health behavior.
The dissatisfied patient of family one wanted to make a confession and
have confidence in her doctor, expectations which could have been
fulfilled more easily in a religious healing context. However, her expressed
modern and affluent attitudes are not compatible with religious healing
as a health care alternative.

The dissatisfied patients in families three and four reflect a similar conflict. Both patients wanted an explanation of why a set of disturbing
symptoms had occurred. Their expectations are a mix of moral, metaphysi-
cal and practical requests, and the treatment of symptoms is inadequate
to satisfy the nonclinical needs. These expectations, however, could
have been fulfilled by a folk healer or spiritualist, also available in the
Costa Rican health care system and might have provided the answer
to "why" their illnesses had occurred. The use of multiple therapies
as a means to health care satisfaction is an important variable to consider
in evaluating the family strategies of health care seeking behavior.

The third and institutional level of patient satisfaction is based on my
observation of the 457 doctor-patient interactions. My observations
occurred within seven clinics in the Social Security and Public Health
systems. The Public Health hospital is low cost, public health care service
where the physicians are working under an ideological concern of charity.
The Social Security is a hospital system which was set up based on the
ideology of the socialist members of the legislative assembly and has
an ideology of social equality. The nature of the consultation in these
two clinics is very different. In the Public Health hospital, particularly
in the Hospital San Juan de Dios, the doctor tends to be very authoritarian.
The patient comes in very humbly and says, "I have some sort of hurt

here, and it hits me in the neck, it hits me in the shoulder." The doctor responds, "Oh, my child, or oh, my grandchild, or ho, my dear. I will help you. Tell me more about it." The interaction can be characterized by a kind of authoritian, paternalistic behavior on the part of the doctor and very submissive, passive attitude on the part of the patient. They perform the traditional roles of the patron-client relationship which you find throughout colonial Latin America.

In the Social Security hospital, the interaction style tends to be quite a bit different. The doctor is more solicitous, almost overly solicitious, and asks for constant interpretation while the patient is much more demanding. In this case, the doctor will ask the patient how he is, and the patient will say, "Well, let me tell you what's wrong with me." He will in fact instruct the doctor on how he or she wants to be taken care of and the doctor will often ask about family problems. The consultation will last in most cases close to 15 minutes, much longer than the six minutes that it will last in the Public Health hospital.

What is really interesting, therefore, is that you have this long, interpretive conversation with a rather active patient in the Social Security setting and a shorter, more authoritarian, bureaucratic kind of interaction in the Public Health hsopital; yet, in terms of patient satisfaction, more patients are dissatisfied with the Social Security situation. In consultation, interviews and conversations Social Security patients complained that the wait for services is extremely long, that the medicine is not good, and that the doctors are inattentive.

The Public Health patients by comparison have fewer complaints. The Social Security patient also expresses displeasure during the consultation. Seven patients directly criticized the doctors, nine commented on the long wait, and fifteen said that the medication prescribed was worthless. These complaints by Social Security patients are certainly valid. There should be changes in scheduling of appointments and the comfort of the waiting area, but comparing research observation by hospital system, these complaints don't differentiate clinic function. The wait is long at all clinics. The doctors in the Public Health hospital have even less time to give attention to patients and do so in a brusque manner. The same medicines are used in both institutions and both pharmacies dispense drugs in unmarked metal and plastic containers or brown glass bottles which are relatively inexpensive and encourage the doctor to give dosage instructions. The comparative cost of medicine is also nominal. Higher in the Social Security, if calculated as part of the total deducation, and usually according to the patient's ability to pay in the Public Health facility.

The complaints about the Social Security medicine may well be a response to a consultation interaction perceived as difficult and frustrating. The Social Security patients are in a relationship with a doctor who is suppose to consider the patient his or her social equal, treat the patient with respect, and satisfy the patient's demands. This attitude comes out of the ideological framework of how the Social Security hospital was created. Both the patient and the doctor are aware through, that the sociocultural reality is that they almost always occupy different social and economic statuses.

The few upper-class patients use private practitioners or travel to the United States for treatment and are not found in these clinics. The consultation therefore becomes a conflicted interaction of compromise and negotiation of the social reality. The actual situation and the expectations of social equality complicates the physician's ability to fulfill his or her culturally proscribed doctoring role and alienates the patient by the absence of expected behavior in role performance. The patient does not directly attack the doctor because of his dependence on the medical services, but instead invents dissatisfaction and alienation directly through blaming an ineffective prescribed medication.

Mechanic (1976) suggests that even in the United States patients tend to have ambivalent attitudes about physicians. They feel extremely dependent on physicians when they anticipate or have serious illness. They also feel some resentment about their dependence and the authority of the physician. This is perhaps exemplified by the tendency to speak favorably about one's personal physician but to be critical of physicians in general. Underlying this ambivalence are often very high and somewhat unrealistic expectations of the physician and excessive criticism of any failures to live up to this ideal image.

In the Social Security clinic, patients' expectations are further complicated by the conflicting social ideology and the social reality of the institution. It's not just the social ideology of the institution here I think that is influencing the degree of dissatisfaction with the Social Security physician's performance, but the breakdown in patient satisfaction has to do with institutionalized conflicts between lay and practitioner views of clinical reality and therapeutic success. Culturally and historically patients expect doctors to behave in a particular way. The explanatory models of patients and practitioners are created by these cultural and historical realities. The differences in the explanatory models then of patients and practitioners create obstacles to effective health care. If patients expect doctors to behave in the traditional doctor role, the interpretive style of Social Security doctors negatively influences patient satisfaction.

These two medical institutions no longer exist in the form that they have been studied. In 1973 the health laws transferred all medical assistance responsibilities to the Social security institutions and recreated a Ministry of Health which would coordinate health services and focus on developing a preventive health program. As the Social Security institution takes over the Public Health Clinics and hospitals, the structural influences on consultation will change. In terms of health policy, it will be important to document if in fact patient dissatisfaction and problems with patient compliance do increase with the transfer of administrative authority and medical responsibility. The Social Security system provides excellent medical services, but encourages what are considered culturally disturbing social relationships. It is difficult to judge what satisfaction should be in this context. Medical change which enhances health status statistics in a Third World country may at the same time decrease patient satisfaction in terms of the social and cultural context of interaction.

CONCLUSION

The importance of multi-method research and the multi-level model that I have described for patient satisfaction in Costa Rica is that they provide a broader perspective on the impact of medical and social change. By integrating the individual, family, institutional and cultural levels of the illness seeking experience, we begin to have a more complex and detailed explanation of what the patient is responding to in the medical context. Patient expectations that are complied with increase the amount of patient satisfaction while at the same time the number of health care sectors that a patient visits for health care problems also enhances satisfaction.

These two findings are somewhat in conflict, but yet they realistically reflect a more comprehensive understanding of patient perceptions. The cultural expectations of patients when they enter the medical institution will change what happens and the actual doctor-patient interaction is further influenced by institutional constraints. Ultimately one must understand the entire cultural context and the nature of social relations both in the present and historically in order to interpret the meaning of the breakdown of social interactions in the medical consultation and before one can understand what patient satisfaction means in a change medical context.

TABLE I

PATIENTS EXPECTATIONS AND REQUESTS

EXPECTATIONS	N	% OF ALL EXPECTATIONS
Medicine	62	36.3
Physical or Laboratory Examination	39	22.8
Explanation of Illness	19	11.1
Tranquilizers	18	10.5
Referral	8	4.7
Injection	8	4.7
Incapacidad (Incapacity Petition)	6	3.5
Hospitalization	2	1.2
Other--Don't Know	9	5.3
TOTAL	171	100.0

REQUESTS		
Medicine	48	29.3
Examinations	38	23.2
Explanations	24	14.6
Referral	23	14.0
Hospitalization	10	6.1
Incapacidad	9	5.5
Other	12	7.3
TOTAL	164	100.0

137

TABLE II
FAMILY VARIABLES AND PATIENT SATISFACTION

FAMILY/PATIENT	EXPECTATION	VARIABLES EXPLANATION OF ILLNESS	HEALTH SECTOR UTILIZATION	PATIENT SATISFIED	DISSATISFIED
1	confession confidence	dissatisfaction with job and life, problem is external	professional		X
2	x-rays, examination	from television school, growing	professional, popular & folk	X	
3	results of x-rays, where attack from & why	psychological, nerves	professional (in past used other sectors)		X "relatively well"*
4	deep analysis advice, a cleaning out of the brain, study my case	nerves frigidity	professional		X
5	injection, x-ray, to know what it is	hurt as a result of fall	professional, popular & folk	X	
6	examination, medication	debility from not eating, lack of alimento	professional, popular & folk	X	
7	pills, explanation of illness	from boyfriend, family worries	professional, (in past used other sector)		X "rather not return"*
8	sympathy, treatment, pills	from family, heredity & environment	professional, popular & folk	X	
9	asked questions, given advice & capsules	lack of alimento	professional, popular & folk	X	

* The exact phrase has been included to indicate that in these two cases the dissatisfaction was not as strong as in cases 1 and 4.

REFERENCES

FOX, J.G. and P.M. STORMS (1981) "A Different Approach to Sociodemographic Predictors of Satisfaction with Health Care," SOCIAL SCIENCE AND MEDICINE 15A: 557-64.

GARRITY, T.F. (1981) "Medical Compliance and the Clinician-Patient Relationship: A Review," SOCIAL SCIENCE AND MEDICINE 15E: 215-22.

HARRISON, P. (1981) "Success Story," WORLD HEALTH Feb/Mch: 14-19.

HELLER, P.L. et al. (1981) "Class, Familism and Utilization of Health services in Durango, Mexico: A Replication," SOCIAL SCIENCE AND MEDICINE 15A: 539-41.

KLEINMAN, A. (1980) PATIENTS AND HEALERS IN THE CONTEXT OF CULTURE. Berkeley: University of California Press.

LOW, S.M. (1981a) "The Meaning of **Nervios**," CULTURE, MEDICINE AND PSYCHIATRY 5: 24-48.

LOW, S.M. (1981b) "The Urban Patient: Health-Seeking Behavior in the Health Care System of San Jose, Costa Rica," URBAN ANTHROPOLOGY 10: 27-52.

LOW, S.M. (1982) "Dr. Moreno Canas: A Symbolic Bridge to the Demedicalization of Healing," SOCIAL SCIENCE AND MEDICINE 16: 527-31.

MECHANIC, D. (1976) THE GROWTH OF BUREAUCRATIC MEDICINE: AN INQUIRY INTO THE DYNAMICS OF PATIENT BEHAVIOR AND THE ORGANIZATION OF MEDICAL CARE. N.Y.: John Wiley.

WEINBERGER, M., J.Y. GREENE and J.J. HAMLIN (1981) "The Impact of Clinical Encounter Events on Patient and Physician Satisfaction," SOCIAL SCIENCE AND MEDICINE 15E: 239-44.

YOUNG, A. (1976) "Some Implications of Medical Beliefs and Practice for Social Anthropology," AMERICAN ANTHROPOLGIST 78: 5-24.

YOUNG, J.C. (1981) MEDICAL CHOICE IN A MEXICAN VILLAGE. New Brunswick: Rutgers University Press.

CHAPTER 11

INDOCHINESE REFUGES AND AMERICAN HEALTH CARE: ADAPTIVE COMPARISON OF CAMBODIANS AND HMONG

Robert J. Moser

Introduction

The recent immigration to the United States of over 600,000 Indochinese refugees provides the opportunity to observe how the traditional health care beliefs and practices of these transplated third-world peoples affect and are affected by the health care system of a technological society. Typically, West has met East within the social milieu of the so-called "under-developed" nation, but the cultural exchange in this case takes place in a different setting. Problems associated with promoting family planning, preventive medicine and public health are not confined to health educators in some remote village in Asia, but are experienced daily by clinical staffs at urban medical centers throughout America (Friedman, 1982). The purpose of this essay is to describe the interaction of one such institution with two separate Southeast Asian communities in San Diego, California (Cambodian and Hmong) as an illustration of their different adaptation to medical care in Ameria.

General Background

The war in Southeast Asia and the communist victories have caused massive migrations of refugees from Vietnam, Laos and Cambodia. At least 1.5 million people have fled these countries since 1975 (DeVecchi, 1982). Thailand continues to be the country of first asylum and the United States remains the site of final resettlement for most Indochinese refugees. Between 1975 and 1981, nearly 50 per cent of all Southeast Asian regufees who were resetled came to the United States (U.S. Committee for Refugees, 1982). For FY83, the U.S. Congress has approved an additional 64,000 Indochinese for immigration (Refugee Reports, 1982b: 4).

Two-thirds of America's Indochinese immigrants are Vietnames (67%) with the remaining on-third almost equally divided among Lao (12%), Hmong (11%) and Cambodians (10%) (Office of Refugee Resettlement, 1982: 15). As of November 1, 1982, one-third of all these refugees are located in California and 15 per cent of these reside in San Diego County. This county ranks 14th in the country among impacted areas as measured by the ratio of refugees to native population. The figure for San Diego is 1:159 (Refugee Reports, 1982a: 8). However, one community within the City of San Diego, known as Linda Vista, has been cited as having the highest density of Southeast Asian refugees of any community in the United States (Swanbrow, 1981: 118).

The influx of Indochinese refugees has occurred in two stages, 1975-78 and 1980-present. The first wave resulted immediately after the fall of Saigon, Vientiane and Phnom Penh. These people included the upper strata of these societies and were those who had some familiarity with Western culture. Occupationally, educationally and linguistically many of these individuals were able to adjust to life in America, though many did experience expected difficulties. Some had been able to escape with some resources, and most were able to obtain private sponsors (e.g., Churches, civic groups and families) who assisted them to acquire housing and secure employment. Most spent little if any time in refugee camps in Asia, though the names of Camp Pendleton, Fort Chaffee and Indiantown Gap will remain strong in the memories of this newest immigrant population as Ellis Island did for earlier generations. For these reaons, few of this refugee group had major health problems. Medical studies conducted during this time concluded that the Indochinese posed no significant threat to public health (Barrett-Connor, 1978; CDC, 1979a; Jones, 1980).

For those who arrived after 1980, however, the situation was and is different. These people spent several years living in a communist social order, endured severe hardships and trauma during their escape, and waited years in crowded camps uncertain of their future. Most of these refugees were ill-prepared for life outside their native countries. As farmers, fishermen and soldiers, their rural origins and education backgrounds provided them poor preparation for assimilation into an urban, technological society such as the United States. This problem is particularly poignant in the area of health care since the many have had limited prior exposure to Western medical and surgical practices, yet often they arrive acutely in need of this system.

Reports of health screening programs attest to the high levels of disease, illness and disability in this refugee population (Wallace, 1982). Data from the Centers for Disease Control (CDC) indicate that the prevalence of active TB among arrriving refugees in 1,137/100,000 (CDC, 1981b). This rate is 100 times greater than the prevalence among native Americans. More than half (55%) of all refugees have a positive reaction to a tuberculin skin test. This indicates that they have at some time been infected with **mycobacterium tuberculosis.** In San Diego, the following health problems were also found: intestinal parasites (61%), microcytic anemia (42%), hepatitis B (14%), treponemal or veneral infections (12%), otitis media (15%), dental caries (75%), hematuria (6%), G6PD deficiency, skin lesions, malaria, scoliosis, poor vision, orthopedic problems, malnutrition, congenital heart defects and war injuries (Catanzaro and Moser, 1982; Pickwell, 1982). Significant differences between ethnic groups in the prevalency of most of these conditions were also noted.

Long-term health problems of the refugees can only be anticipated (De Lay, 1982). For those who did not receive INH prophylaxis, there should be some reactivation of tuberculosis. Approximately five per cent of those refugees with interestinal parasites have Strongyloides. Since this organism has the potential for auto-infection, there may be increasing

142

cases of disseminated Strongyloidiasis among those patients who are immuno-compromised. There may also appear increased perinatal complications secondary to hemoglobinopathies and Hepatitis B transmission at birth. Rates of lung cancer and other chronic pulmonary diseases should increase in this population since many Southeast Asian males are heavy smokers. Hypertension can also be expected because the diet of the Indochinese is high in salt content. Finally, Southeast Asian women have much higher fertility rates than American women, therefore, family planning, pre-natal, obstetric, post-partum and new-born care will continue as frequent health needs.

These conditions help bring member of this population into continued contact with the American health care system, and the mutual impact is substantial. The inability to communicate and to understand each other's perspective of the etiology and preferred treatment for an illness can create confusion and conflict between patient and provider. How these outcomes have been avoided with Cambodians but accentuated for Hmong at one hospital shall now be described.

The Medical Center

The medical institution involved in this report is a university-affiliated, teaching hospital. It has 439 in-patient, acute care beds as well as a primary care center (Pediatrics, OB-GYN and Family Medicine) and a specialty care, out-patient center.

This hospital, though not centrally located within any one Indochinese community, is a major provider of health care for all refugee groups. Only one community clinic and the eight Vietnamese and one Lao primary care physicians within San Diego may treat more Southeast Asian patients than this medical facility. The daily Indochinese in-patient census averages 12 ±5, and the mean number of scheduled out-patient appointments per day is 36 ±10. These figures represent 4.8% and 5.2% respectively of the hospital's total in-patient and out-patient population. The ethnic composition of the Indochinese out-patient segment is: Vietnamese, 15; Cambodina, 12; Lao, 6, and Hmong, 3. As can be seen, the Cambodian patient load is one-third of the total, and four times as many as the Hmong. This is interesting since the Khmer comprise only 10% of the city's refugee population and are equal in size to the Hmong community.

Since October of 1980, the medical center has been the site of a special program funded under the Refugee Act of 1980 to provide services to help refugees access health care. These services include health screening, appointment-making, medical translation, health education and follow-up. Since its beginning this program has helped screen over 3,000 newly-arrived refugees and has performed over 15,000 translation episodes. The full-time staff of this program includes three Vietnamese, two Cambodian, one Lao and one Hmong translator. The Cambodian staff includes the current and past presidents of the Cambodian Mutual Assistance Association

143

of San Diego. The author of this essay is the manager of this program and has been a participant observer of various cases that exemplify each ethnic group's experience with and reaction to modern medical care.

In the remainder of this essay, several selected cases of Hmong and Cambodian patients shll be reviewed briefly to demonstrate how different their respective responses are. These two groups were chosen for several reasons. First, the socioeconomic background of many of these refugees is similar. Second, the size of each community within San Diego is approximately 4,000. Third, the need for medical care among each population has been demonstrated to be high. Fourth, the traditional health care beliefs and practices of each ethnic group includes a "spiritual" dimension that utilizes the intervention of shamans. Finally, each community is well-organized and represented by a single mutual assistance association headed by recognized leaders.

The Hmong

Of all the ethnic groups that are called "Indochinese," none is more culturally different from Americans than the Hmong. Called by others the "Meo" or "Miao," which means "barbarians," Hmong is the self-nomenclature of these people and it means "free people." Originally refugees from China, the Hmong had lived for over a century and a half in the mountainous regiions of northern Laos. Though their nationality is Laotian, the language, customs and social systems of the Hmong are different from the lowlander ethnic Lao.

There are other hill tribes people among the refugees, notably the Yao, Mein and Black Thai, but the Hmong are the largest in number and the most well-known. Anthropologists have studied the richness of Hmong culture in their native habitat for years (Lemoine, 1979), but Americans first became aware of these people during the Vietnam War era when it was learned that the Central Intelligence Agency had recruited these people, respected for their military skill and courage, to serve as America's secret army in Laos. Even then, the disruptive effect of this conflict on their society could be discerned (Garrett, 1974).

The Hmong are increasingly becoming more popularly known throughout the United States. There are large Hmong communities in St. Paul, Minneapolis, Providence, Portland, Seattle, Orange County and Fresno, California; Lincoln, Nebraska; Montana and Iowa. Several research programs at American universities, like the University of Minnesota, have focused on the Hmong. Their language system is unique and until recently it did not have a written form.

Two recent programs on public broadcasting have documented the Hmong's process of adaptation to American life (BECOMING AMERICAN and AMERICAN DREAN, AMERICAN REALITY).The Hmong are also well-know for their attractive and intricate needlework, called "pa dau." Finally, the Hmong have become the center of attention regarding a sudden death syndrome that seems to strike their population more than any others (Marshall, 1981; CDC, 1981a; Munger, 1982).

The social organization of Hmong society centers around a patrilineal clan system. There are twenty clans, each with its own characteristic name. The influence of each clan's leadership is substantial. Many major decisions that affect the well-being of the clan members, like migratory relocation (Thao, 1982) and marital conflict resolution, are made by these leaders. Their role in giving consent for major medical and surgical procedures will also be demonstrated.

The traditional Hmong perspective on health is based on a belief system in spirits or "tlan." Those who are animists believe that all things possess a spirit, and if angered or invoked, such supernatural entities can enter a person causing illness. The lowlander Lao call these spirits "phi" and their role in the etiology of disease, both physical and psychological, is believed to be great (Halpern, 1963; Westermeyer, 1979). Similarly, each individual person has several souls called "txim." Illness can be the result of any one of these souls leaving the body.

The responsibility for diagnosing and treating these problems of spirit intrusion and/or soul loss rests with the Hmong shaman known as "txi neng." Such an individual may be male or female and is one who has the power and ability to communicate with the spirit world while in a trance. The language used by the shaman is an ancient Chinese dialect, and the words of magic are called "khawv koob." The "txi neng" interprets the precise cause of the illness using such techniques as reading the yolk of an egg or leg bones of a chicken. The shaman then prescribes and performs the necessary ritual to appease the offended spirit or recapture the wandering soul. This ceremony often involves a sacrifice, usually of a chicken or pig.

The most common ceremony performed to prevent illness or harm is that of a "baci." This entails the offering of prayers and gifts to the spirits and to one's ancestors, and the tieing of white cotton strings around the wrist of those to be protected. Such strings symbolize protection against evil spirits and preservation of one's own soul. The "baci" is still commonly practiced here in the United States and there are several Hmong "spirit doctors" who are called upon by the people to help them with their physical and mental problems. The practice of sacrificing live animals, however, has been curtailed in urban areas, and the offering to the shaman of a pre-slaughtered, pre-packaged, whole "fryer" is itself an interesting example of cultural adaptation at work.

Case 1

The first case occurred in the summer of 1978 and has become almost a legend within the Hmong community. The patient was a 25 year-old male who presented himself to the hosital two months after arrival in the United States with weakness, jaundice and abdominal pain. A physical exam revealed massive heaptosplenomegaly and he was admitted for further studies. Tests showed focal intrahepatic defects, multiple stones and choledocholithiasis. Four days after admission he underwent surgery that involved a cholecystectomy and a choledochoduodenostomy. A series of post-operative complications required three additional operations and several blood transfusions. Six and a half weeks after admission the patient expired. The final diagnosis was oriental cholangiohepatitis.

This individual had no immediate family in San Diego. A distant cousin, a caseworker at a local service agency, assisted in the translation and in the optaining of consent for surgery. Within a week of gaining such consent, this man unexpectedly died in his sleep and became San Diego's first case of unexplained nocturnal sudden death syndrome. The death of the cousin was perceived by the Hmong community as a spiritual sanction against violating a tradition of getting communal consent. The following remarks by one Hmong leader amplifies this community's reaction (Norcross, 1981).

The Hmong community is very angry with the way in which this patient was cared for--"We do not understand English very well, much less medical terminology, but we are aware of what happened. In our country we do not know about infectious disease, but we do understand the spiritual nature of health and illness. Our physicians and shamans prescribe medications for illness; they do not take blood, x-rays, and perform surgery. Blood is precious to the Hmong people, and it is a grave matter to take it from them. This patient was admitted to the hospital at the first visit, during which time he underwent four operations and died. We believe that no one, especially a sick person, can survive four operations in one month. We believe that the physicians caring for this patient should have spoken with representatives from our community before performing these procedures. As is the custom in your culture, permission is obtained from the patient, and from his closest relative. This is not acceptable to our culture."

Case 2

The second case involved a 22 year-old Hmong female who was referred to the hospital from a community clinic after a routine pre-natal visit discovered dangerously high blood pressure. She was diagnosed as being severely pre-eclampsic and an immediate caesarian section was recommended. She was approximately thirty-two weeks pregnant and the prognosis for mother and child was good. She and her husband, however, both refused permission for this procedure. She claimed to feel fine, and since this was their first child, he expressed fear to take responsibility for anything that might jeopardize his wife or child and expose him to the displeasure of his in-laws and clan.

Having learned from the experience explained in **Case 1**, and having some success in a similar situation that involved another Hmong woman, this author contacted the president of the Hmong community and requested his intercession. He spoke with the husband and then explained that permission would have to come from the woman's parents and her clan leader. These individuals were summoned and came to the hospital. The severity of the situation was explained. They listened, and they declined. First, they did not believe that she was ill. Second, they did not trust the hospital. The cited previous examples of conflict situations between the Hmong and the hospital. Third, they felt they had their own ways to take care of her. Finally, it was also learned that a month before another member of this same clan had lost a child during a c-section at this hospital.

The outcome of this case was that she left the hospital against medical advice. One week later she was rushed to the emergency room of another hospital in shock with an initial diagnosis of fetal death. Fortunately, both mother and child were saved.

The Cambodians

The majority of the more than 60,000 refugees from Cambodia (Kampuchea) have settled in Southern California (Long Beach, Santa Anna and San Diego). During 1981, the U.S. State Department sponsored a cluster--site resettlement project in cooperation with the Cambodian Association of America that distributed nearly ten thousand Khmer refugees to twelve selected cities. Despite this, the Khmer have at times been overlooked and underserved by some domestic resettlement programs. Though fewer than the other refugee groups, in many ways they are the most in need.

No refugee group has suffered more than the Cambodians. Their population has been decimated by years of auto-genocide, famine and war. The magnitude of thier tragedy and its devastating effect on their society has recently been illustrated (Allman, 1982; White, 1982).

Part of the damage done during the Pol Pot regime was the near total destruction of Cambodia's medical system. For example, only 10 per cent of Cambodian physicians (53/500) survived the Khmer Rouge's attempt to rid Kampuchea of all traces of Western influence (Levy, 1981: 1442). That fact plus the extreme hardships faced by this population resulted in extensive levels of physical and psychological illness among those who escaped and survived this present-day holocaust. Numerous reports from medical relief workers in the various camps have documented the extent of this harm and have described efforts to reestablish the health of these refugees (CDC, 1979b; CDC, 1979c; CDC, 1980;   Dhalberg, 1980; Leverty, 1980; Smilkstein, 1981).

Even though the medical services in the camps were successful in stemming this tide of human misery, the Cambodian refugees arriving in the United States still possess high levels of pathology. In San Diego screening tests indicate the folowing figures for Cambodians: positive tuberculin reaction, 57%; intestinal parasites, 67%; microcyptic anemia, 57%; and positive serology, 19% (Catanzaro and Moser, 1982). In a needs assessment survey conducted in the same city (SSRL, 1982), only 13% of the Khmer respondents described their health as excellent compared to 23% for Hmong, 31% for Vietnames and 39% for Lao. Thirty-four per cent of the Cambodian respondents reported being under medical care at the time of the interview and everyone had accessed health care at least once. This is in contrast to the Hmong who had 20% who had never seen a doctor.

Given the lack of modern medical care available to most Khmer before their resettlement, therre has been a resurgence of and an increased reliance on traditional folk-healing methods. Whether and how these practices survive in the United States is yet to be learned, but they appear to be flourishing in the refugee camps (Martin, 1978a and 1978b; Champassak, 1982).

If nothing is truly "Indochinese," then the art and science of Cambodian medicine comes close. The influence of Indian and Chinese cultures on Khmer health care is apparent. Superimpose these on their native folk traditions and the result is a rich, diverse and complex system (Huard, 1963). From China comes certain methods and medications, including ointments and herbs, that reflect the Taoist belief in the balance of hot and cold body humors. Few Cambodina homes are without tiger balm, the Asian equivalent of Vicks vapo-rub and many women will drink a fermented concoction called "thnam chheam" during menstruation.

Popular among the Cambodians is the practice called "kosh kchall" or rubbing out the wind. Among the Vietnamese this is called "cao gio" and the hazards of misdiagnosing this practice as abuse have been noted (Yeatman, et al., 1976; gellis and Feingold, 1976; Golden and Duster, 1977). This practice entails massaging the treated area (usually the chest, back, neck, arms or shoulders) with a mentholated ointment like tiger balm and then rubbing the skin with a metal object (usually a coin or spoon) until ecchymoses is created. This treatment is claimed to be effective for ailments involving nausea, vomiting and coughing.

For headaches, the Khmer use a technique called "chap kchall" which involved the pinching of the skin between the eyebrows until it is reddened. Another method known as "chop kchall" ("ventouse" in French) is also practiced. This is a form of moxibustion, i.e., extracting air from a glass or jar with an open flame and then applying this heated vacuum onto the patient's forehead to suction out the ailment. For stomach problems, including diarrhea, a method of burning the skin called "oich" is common. Small balls of a soft, flammable substance are ignited on the skin and let burn until the desired effect is realized. This practice leaves a characteristic scar and is typically patterned around the navel––– one to the left, one to the right and one above. The purpose of these practices is to create a "hot" condition on the external body to draw out and release the "cold" condition causing the internal illness.

India's influence on Cambodian traditional medicine is marked by the magic and mysticism of shamans called "krou." These individuals are learned and skilled in a wide variety of prayers and spells that are chanted in pali and sanskrit. One probable origin of these incantations lies in the ancient vedic literary work know as the **Artharvaveda** or "the Knowledge of Magic Formulas" (Winternitz, 1972: 119).

The activity of the "krou" can be directed at doing good or evil, at causing a curse to be imposed or a malevolent spirit to be exorcised. Many Khmer believe that spirits ("neakta") are the cause of disease and harm. Such misfortune may be prevented by the wearing of amulets and charms that are blessed by the "krou." A magic handkerchief or scarf called a "kanseing yon" or a magic belt called "ksea kiethaa" are inscribed with phrases and apictures designed to protect the wearer from injury. Finally, tattoos ("sak") are a common instrument of magical protection. They often graphically illustrate the cultural combination that underlies Cambodian medicine. One can observe on a man's chest or back a drawing of a Brahman god with a Khmer power object (e.g., lion) surrounded by symbols and words honoring and beseeching the Buddha. These tattoos are frequent among those who were soldiers, and many of these will report stories of how their lives were spared by this magic. Few, however, believe the power of the tattoos is still effective in America, and this practice may soon disappear in America, ironically itself a casuality of cultural adaptation.

Case 3

This case involves a 61 year-old female Cambodian who was screened by the hospital's Indochinese program three months after her immigration. At that visit she complained of headache, insomnia, dizziness and coughing. The results of her complete blood count (CBC) which were received on the same day indicated a severely low hemoglobin level of 5.1. She was immediately contacted, transported to the hospital and admitted through the emergency room. She received a blood transfusion and medications which did not improve her condition. She then developed respiratory complications and was moved from the ward to the intensive care unit. Various studies indicated several systemic problems--hypertension, hookworm infestation, abnormal liver function and respiratory insufficiency. Diagnoses of acute cholangitis, hepatic encephalopathy and plasma cell myeloma were made. Two weeks after admission she expired from brain stem herniation. Since the next of kin refused permission for an autopsy, the origin of her illness can never be known.

The immediate family felt the medical staff did everything they could to save her, but were understandably upset with the rapid course of her decline. Some community members believed that if she did not go to the hospital then she would still be alive. A conference with the family was held and as much detail as was available was shared with them. This author was granted permission to attend a memorial service for the deceased at the family's home, and at that time the same explanation was shared with members of the community. This family continues to come to the hospital for their medical care.

Case 4

The last case deals with a 54 year-old Cambodian female who was referred by the public health department for evaluation of an abnormal chest x-ray. The woman had no pulmonary complaints and was completely asymptomatic. Upon further examination, including a CAT scan and bronchoscopy, a diagnosis of a cystic teratoma was made. All who were involved in this case were amazed at the woman's apparent good health in light of the size of this mediastinal mass, 15.5 x 8.5 cm. Immediate surgery to excise this mass was indicated, but the woman refused. The staff of the Indochinese Center were consulted, and after a careful explanation, including showing her the x-rays, she consented. The surgery was successfully performed, and she was discharged a week later.

Analysis

The reviewed cases all involved life-threatening illnesses. All required consent for invasive procedures that are generally disliked and distrusted by Southeast Asians (Tung, 1980). All included explanations of the risks and benefits of the treatment. Given some of the similarities between the Hmong and the Cambodians, notably their rural origins, their need for health care and their lack of exposure to Western medicine, one might expect similar responses to the medical treatment that was proposed or received. Yet the outcomes were different. Fundamentally, the Cambodians have a positive perspective and the Hmong a negative view. The former has shown acceptance while the latter has expressed rejection. The khmer see it as a place of "new life" and the Hmong as a place to die. Why?

One possible explanation may be rooted in the religious belief systems of each ethnic group. The animism of the Hmong fosters a pragmatic view of life. What is immediate is real; what is precedent causes what is resultant; what is certain outweights what is probably. A venapuncture to remove 10cc of blood to test for anemia is seen as the cause of one's "tired or low blood." The fear of certain pain from a surgical incision supercedes the understanding that death is probable without such intervention.

Most Cambodians, on the other hand, are Buddhists with a world view that is more ascetic than pragmatic. Life is suffering, and detachment from this world is valued. This perspective promoties a more passive approach to medical problems, like disease, than the occidental orientation of trying to overcome these conditions.

A second possible factor is the role played by the leadership of each community. The Hmong look toward their representatives for advice and permission before they decide on something so major such as consent for surgery. In **Case 1** the clan leaders were excluded; in **Case 2** they were consulted but refused cooperation. The Cambodians function more independendtly, though they are often open to being persuaded to comply if the information is interpreted by someone they trust. In **Cases 3** and **4** the Cambodian leaders were directly involved as the translators for the hospital.

I suspect that the success this one hospital has had with the Cambodian community is influenced in large part by its integration of their leadership into its own institutiion. As an insider to both their community and the health system, these individuals identify with an intermediate between each. Their connection promotes cooperation between participants of these two social systems, and the absence of this link with the Hmong may contribute to the conflict that exists with them. This problem is not unique to San Diego and has been reported elsewhere (Holtan, 1979).

A third factor may be each community's general desire for and experience with their assimilation process. Differences have been noted in the number who apply for citizenship (Refugee Reports, 1982: 1) and in their satisfaction with social services directed at assisting them to assimilate (SSRL, 1981: Chp. 12). For example, 84% of the Hmong surveyed in San Diego reported that difficulty in dealing with American agencies was a "very serious" problem. This is compared to 44% of Cambodians who responded similarly. Even more divergent is the percentage of each group identifying prejudice by Americans to be very serious. The respective figures are 82% for the Hmong but only 2% for the Cambodians. In essence, their adaptation to health care may simply reflect patterns of cooperation and conflict in all areas of each ethnic group's contact with American society.

The fourth and final factor is simply luck. One of Murphy's Laws, namely, "if things can go wrong, they will go wrong," can be appended in this case to read "and when they do, they will involve the Hmong." This statement is not intended to be stereotypical, but rather to emphasize the point that despite all efforts, certain circumstances will remain beyond control. Having well-trained medical translators or culturally-sensitive medical staff doesn't help the patient who arrives in the emergency room at one A.M. when these individuals are off duty. Similarly, I suspect that if the patient in **Case 1** had survived then the reputation of the hospital among the Hmong would be radically different, and possibly the patient in **Case 2** would have given consent.

Conclusion

Based on the experiences at this hospital, the following recommendations are made to medical providers to faclitate the adaptation of refugees to the American health care system.

1) recognize that the Indochinese are not a homogeneous group and that substantial cultural differences exist between and within each ethnic group.

2) learn about these differences, especially the variety of health care beliefs and practices (Olness, 1979; Tung, 1980; Hoang and Erickson, 1982); be wary, however, of over-simplifications; as specialized as modern medical practice is, traditional folk healing is also complex;

3) respect these traditions and explore who they may be integrated into the treatment plan;

4) identify the communities' leaders and involve them as leaders in the promotion of health among their people;

5) hope for good luck.

REFERENCES

ALLMAN, T.D. (1982) "Cambodia: Nightmare Journey to a Doubtful Dawn," ASIA March/April: 8-15, 52-54.

BARRETT-CONNOR, ELIZABETH (1978) "Latent and Chronic Infections Imported from Southeast Asia," JOURNAL OF THE AMERICAN MEDICAL ASSOCIATION 239: 1901-1906.

CATANZARO, ANTONINO and ROBERT J. MOSER (1982) "Health Status of Refugees from Vietnam, Laos and Cambodia," JOURNAL OF THE AMERICAN MEDICAL ASSOCIATION 247: 1303-1308.

CENTERS FOR DISEASE CONTROL (1979a) "Health Status of Indochinese Refugees," MORBIDITY AND MORTALITY WEEKLY REPORT 28: 385-390, 395-398.

_____(1979b) "Health Status of Kampuchean Refugees—Sakeo, Thailand," MORBIDITY AND MORTALITY WEEKLY REPORT 28: 545-546.

_____(1979c) "Health Status of Kampuchean Refugees—Khao I-Dang," MORBIDITY AND MORTALITY WEEKLY REPORT 28: 569-570.

_____(1980) "Follow-up on the Health Status of Kampuchean Refugees—Thailand, Nov. 1979-Feb. 1980," MORBIDITY AND MORTALITY WEEKLY REPORT 29: 218-225.

_____(1981a) "Sudden, Unexpected, Nocturnal Deaths Among Southeast Asian Refugees," MOBIDITY AND MORTALITY WEEKLY REPORT 30: 581-584, 589-592.

_____(1981b) "Tuberculosis Among Indochinese Refugees—An Update," MORBIDITY AND MORTALITY WEEKLY REPORT 30: 603-606.

CHAMPASSAK, NANDA NA (1982) "Traditional Medicine in Khmer Camps," REFUGEES 5: 6.

DHALBERG, KEITH (1980) "Medical Care of Cambodian Refugees," JOURNAL OF THE AMERICAN MEDICAL ASSOCIATION 243: 1062-1065.

DE LAY, PAUL (1982) "Anticipated Health Problems for Refugee Populations in the United States," paper presented at the California Refugee Preventive Health Services Conference, San Jose, California, Sept. 10.

DeVECCHI, ROBERT P. (1982) "Politics and Policies of 'First Asylum' in Thailand," in WORLD REFUGEES SURVEY 1982. N.Y.: U.S. Committee for Refugees.

FRIEDMAN, EMILY (1982) "Health Care on the Immigrant trail," HOSPITALS 56: 82-93.

GARRETT, WILBUR E. (1974) "No Place to Run: The Hmong of Laos," NATIONAL GEOGRAPHIC 145: 78-111.

GELLIS, S.S. and M. FEINGOLD (1976) "Pseudobattering in Vietnames Children," AMERICAN JOURNAL OF DISEASES OF CHILDREN 130: 857.

GOLDEN, STEPHEN M. and MARK C. DUSTER 91977) "Hazards of Misdiagnosis due to Vietnamese Folk Medicine," CLINICAL PEDIATRICS 16: 949-950.

HALPERN, JOEL M. 91963) "Traditional Medicine and the Role of the Phi in Laos," THE EASTERN ANTHROPOLOGIST 16: 191-200.

HOANG, GIAO N. and ROY V. ERICKSON (1982) "Guidelines for Providing Medical Care to Southeast Asian Refugees," JOURNAL OF THE AMERICAN MEDICAL ASSOCAITION 248: 710-714.

HOLTAN, NEAL R. (1979) "Health Care Problems Among theSoutheast Asian Refugees," MINNESOTA MEDICINE, 633-634.

HUARD, PIERRE (1963) "La Medicine Cambodgienne Traditionnelle," FRANCE-ASIA 18: 676-686.

JONES, MILES, JOHN H. THOMPSON and NELSON S. BREWER (1980) "Infectious Diseases of Indochinese Refugees," MAYO CLINIC PROCEEDINGS 55: 482-488.

LEMOINE, JACQUES (1979) "La Mort et ses Rites chez les Hmong," OBJETS ET MONDES 19: 196-207.

LEVERTY, DON (1980) "Cambodia--Pharmacy and the Refugees," AMERICAN PHARMACY 20: 125-128.

LEVY, BARRY S. (1981) "Working in a Camp for Cambodian Refugees," THE NEW ENGLAND JOURNAL OF MEDICINE 304: 1440-1444.

MARSHALL, E. (1981) "The Hmong: Dying of Culture Shock?" SCIENCE 212: 1008.

MARTIN, MARIE A. (1978a) "Les Vegetaux dans l'alimentation et la Medicine dans le Cambodge d'apres 1975," ASIE DU SUD-EST ET MONDE INSULINDIEN 9: 209-218.

_____(1978b) "Les Plantes Utilisees dans les Camps de Refugies Cambodgiens de Thailande," ASIE DU SUD-EST ET MONDE INSULINDIEN 9: 219-230.

MUNGER, RONALD G. (1982) "Sudden Adult Death in Asian Populations: The Case of the Hmong," in THE HMONG IN THE WEST: OBSERVATIONS AND REPORTS, ed. Bruce T. Downing and D. P. Olney. University of Minnesota: Center for Urban and Regional Affairs, 307-319.

NORCROSS, WILLIAM et al. (1981) "Fatal Oriental Cholangiohepatitis in a Member of the Hmong Community," THE JOURNAL OF FAMILY PRACTICE 12: 909-911.

_____(1982) Office of Refugee Resettlement, REPORT TO THE CONGRESS: REFUGEE RESETTLEMENT PROGRAM, Washington, D.C.: U.S. Dept. of Health and Human Services, January 31.

OLNESS, KAREN (1979) "Cultural Aspects in Working with Lao Refugees," MINNESOTA MEDICINE 62: 871-874.

PICKWELL, SHEILA M. (1982) "Primary Health Care for Indochinese Refugee Children," PEDIATRIC NURSING 8: 104-107.

REFUGEE REPORTS (1982a) "Statistics," 3(5): 8.

_____(1982b) "Admissions Consultations Held," 3(23): 4.

_____(1982c) "Refugee Citizenship--Coming, But Slowly," 3(24): 1.

SOCIAL SCIENCE RESEARCH LABORATORY (SSRL) (1981) FINAL REPORT: CHARACTERISTICS AND NEEDS OF INDOCHINESE REFUGEES IN SAN DIEGO COUNTY. San Diego: San Diego State University.

SMILKSTEIN, GABRIEL (1981) "The Quiet Americans," CALIFORNIA October, 114-120, 177-183.

THAO, CHEU (1982) "Hmong Migration and Leadership in Laos and the United States," in Downing and Olney, pp. 99-121.

TUNG, TRAN M. (1980) INDOCHINESE PATIENTS: CULTURAL ASPECTS OF THE MEDICAL AND PSYCHIATRIC CARE OF INDOChinese refugees. Washington, D.C.: Action for Southeast Asians.

U.S. COMMITTEE FOR REFUGEES (1982) CAMBODIAN REFUGEES IN THAILAND: THE LIMITS OF ASYLUM. Washington, D.C.: American Council for Nationalities Services.

WALLACE, HAZEL (1982) "Laboratory Findings and Patterns of Disease in Southeast Asian Refugees," paper preented at the California Refugee Preventive Health Services Conference, San Jose, CA, Sept. 10.

WESTERMEYER, JOSEPH and RONALD WINTROB (1979) "'Folk' Explanations of Mental Illness in Rural Laos," AMERICAN JOURNAL OF PSYCHI-

ATRY 136: 901-905.

WHITE, PETER T. (1982) "Kampuchea Wakens for a Nightmare," NATIONAL GEOGRAPHIC 161: 590-623.

WINTNERNITZ, MAURICE (1972) HISTORY OF INDIAN LITERATURE. New Dehli, Munshiram Manoharlal.

YEATMAN, GENTRY W. and VIET VAN DANG (1980) "Cao Gio (Coin Rubbing): Vietnamese Attitudes Toward Health Care," JOURNAL OF THE AMERICAN MEDICAL ASSOCIATION 244: 2748-2749.

CHAPTER 12

THE HEALTH CARE SYSTEM IN KUWAIT:
A SOCIAL WELFARE PERSPECTIVE

Mostafa H. Nagi

Introduction

The health care sector has reached impressive growth and size in most countries. Already among the largest employers of labor, the health industry consumes a great percentage of national resources. And it plays an important role in the political, economic and social life of our societies. Because of these developments the need for comparative studies of the health care systems in different countries was stressed. In 1973 Hollingshead wrote, "Medical sociology is in sore need of research on different approaches to health care prevalent in different cultures and societies. Before the universality of propositions enunciated as theory can be accepted without qualification, cross-societal studies of health care are indicated (Hollingshead, 1972: 540)."

In recent years there has been a great upsurge of interest in describing and comparing health services in different countries (de Miguel, 1975; Djukonovic and Mach, 1975; Kept, 1976; Elling, 1979 and 1980; Wood and Rue, 1980). Whether done by economists, sociologists, political scientists, or others, most of this work has an underlying theme the search for a better way to run a medical care system. In this essay, the health care system in Kuwait has been selected for analysis and comparison.

What lessons can we learn from the experience of Kuwait that may be useful to other countries? Before an answer can be formulated, we must first recognize that a particular health care operation must be examined in the main contours of the political, economic, social, and ideological structures. Thus, in this essay, we assume that the health care is a subsystem of the larger social system. We also realize that health priorities and their rationale are being influenced by different political and economic ideologies.

Despite varying political and sociological interpretations, a growing and converging socialization of the medical care system has been noted in modern nations. This convergence may be the results of the advance of modern technology and the rising expectations of populations for accessible and comprehensive care, or it may be interpreted as an attempted solution to the crisis of contemporary capitalism (Navarro, 1978). In Third World countries, the translation of ideals into action in medicine and public

157

health is being primarily the responsibility of the state, and is increasingly carried out by a centralized administrative apparatus (Bryant, 1969; Elling, 1978). In almost all developing countries, rich or poor, this tendency seems to be the rule. The implication that can be drawn is that health care policies constitute basic elements in the broader social welfare policy of any government.

The concept of welfare state is vague enough to allow one's own definition of it, but all—conservatives, liberals, and socialists alike—seem to agree that western capitalism has already moved into this orbit. The view that welfare states were to be found in all industrial, urbanized societies claimed that welfare capitalism developed inevitably as a part of the logic of industrialism (Kerr, 1962; Wilensky, 1975; Martin and Zald, 1981). That is, less developed nations will become increasingly like the presently developed nations as they approach that level of development. To raise its citizen's standard of living Kuwait created the first welfare state in the Middle East where medical care, education, housing, clean water, telephone, and electric services are free. Every Kuwaiti is guaranteed a job and social security. This in addition to an elaborate system of public assistance and a multitude of social services (Al-Sakawi, 1976).

The country's great wealth, no doubt, produced dramatic socioeconomic changes. In the area of health care the impact of oil income equals or even exceeds its influence on other social services. "The combination of vastly improved preventive public health measures and medical services and facilities for the treatment of disease is the most visible, demanded, and appreciated of social welfare programs (Stone, 1977)." To date, they are probably the most tangible benefits of oil wealth for the population as a whole, with equal access and provision of services according to needs.

The government has accepted full responsibility for the health of every resident and have medical care available to all at no charge to the user. Basic costs are borne by general revenues. Many other governments have enunciated this principle than have been able to bring it to reality. Similar systems of socialized medicine may be found in the Soviet Union and some eastern European and Scandinavian countries, as well as in Cuba, the United Kingdom and New Zealand. Other countries with substantial income from petroleum are also to be found in this category. A distinction must be made however, between one government's policy decision to provide medical care, as a right, to all or part of its population, and the assumption by another government of the burden of medical care for the indigent, looked upon as an assistance or a charity function and often performed with graceless reluctance.

Besides being a part of the overall social welfare services provided by the government, the health care system is closely intertwined with many dimensions of Kuwait's socio-economic development which among themselves are highly interdependent.

Kuwait's development strategies are based on imported labor, imported technology, imported food and consumer items, and imported social and

158

human services. The development process can be best described as a model of imported development. The constraints on the development efforts include: (1) manpower and labor shortages, (2) technology transference problems, (3) the development of consumer-oriented society, (4) a wealth distribution pattern that perpetuates an elitist combination of affluence and poverty, and (5) the creation of an elaborate welfare system (Nagi, 1982).

The reciprocity or mutuality of influences among these aspects of social life renders analysis very complex. However, an understanding of how these development dimensions addressed the health care system, and how the value contexts shaped evolution of policies and programs, can help greatly in understanding the current situation.

Health Services Development

The growth of Kuwaits' health service is perhaps best considered chronologically. "In 1910 Sheikh Mubarak (Kuwait's ruler) sent for Dr. Arthur Bennett, of the Reformed Church in America's Arabian Mission base at Basra, to cure a sick member of the family. During the next twelve months the mission was allowed to build Kuwait's first hospital. It was the first reinforced concrete building in the country and it was put up by two itinerant Americans, Michigan University engineers, called Shaw and Haines. The man in charge of the building operation was Dr. Stanley Mylrea, an Englishman who had studied medicine in America before joining the Arabian mission. Dr. Mylrea, is now something of a legend in Kuwait (where he died in 1952 at the age of 76). The hospital was open for all diseases, but a puzzle which still remains unsolved is that it did not receive its first case of appendicitis until 1942. From 1911 until 1949 the hospital was the only one in Kuwait (Kuwait Ministry of Guidance and Information, 1966: 41).

The now Ministry of Health (the Department of Health) was founded in 1936 and the opening of a free clinic with one doctor and one pharmacist in the year marked the start of its activities. The need for a big hospital was soon realized. Work began on the construction of the (Emiri) hospital, as the project was postponed until the war's end and was finally completed in 1949. In the same year, a hospital was opened for the mentally sick. In 1952, the first tuberculosis sanatorium was opened. In 1955, services were provided in the first maternity and infant child center.

The climax to Kuwait's health aprogram came on June 20, 1962, when the Al-Sabah hospital was opened. This huge institution, by virtue of its specialized work is one of the biggest and most up to date modern hospitals in the Middle East (Kuwait, Ministry of Health, 1978). Since then, the strides made in the development of the health services in the span of one generation in Kuwait have been really phenomenal.

In the last twenty years or so, Kuwait has expended a considerable proportion of its oil revenues in the health sector. In addition to financing the building of reasonably well equipped hospitals, the money allocated has permitted a heavy current expenditure covering wages and salaries, free medicine, and the major expenses involved in sending some patients abroad for medical treatment. Few states indeed can boast that of Kuwait's budget where the largest current expenditure element is devoted to education followed, except for defense, by health (Kuwait, Ministry of Planning, 1980).

In 1981, there werre 20 modern hospitals and over 500 clinics and other health centers throughout the country. These include dental clinics, mother and child care centers, and preventive health centers. The country had over 1,400 fully qualified medical doctors drawn from many countries, which is one of the highest ratios of doctors to population in the world. In the rare event of specialist treatment not being available in Kuwait, patients are flown to appropriate overseas centers at no cost to themselves. In addition, at this time there was a private medical sector comprising substantial staff, 326 doctors/dentists and several private clinics (MIDDLE EAST REVIEW, 1981).

In summary, the evolution of modern health care in Kuwait can be summarized as follows: The first phase, from 1911 to 1949, consisted of the establishment of the American hospital which was the only one in Kuwait. The population then was much smaller than it is today, and most of them relied on Arabic medicine, a knowledge of which was passed down from father to son. This consisted largely of the use of herbs, and of what are today described as counter-irritants applied externally. The second phase (1949--1962) witnessed the development of several general hospitals. The third phase (1962 to the present) is characterized by the introduction of the medical registration system based on territorial principles and a large expansion in clinics, general and specialized hospitals, and other health care facilites.

Organization of Health Services

Many medical care systems, by definition, are monovalent; that is, they are established for a specific, limited purpose. For example, most developing countries have government programs for the control of diseases. Such a system may be temporary, activated at a special threat, as when a specific disease is reported.

In contrast to the monovalent system, but also government run, is Kuwait's all-inclusive medical care system: To provide for all who want it, a comprehensive service covering every branch of medical and allied activity, from care of minor ailments to major medicine and surgery which include the care of mental as well as physical health, all specialist services, all general services (i.e., by doctor, dentist, optician, midwife, nurse, and health visitor) and all necessary drugs, medicines and a wide range of appliances.

In order to realize one of the major values of the welfare state,a the availability and accessibility of medical care to everyone--the medical networks

160

are closely integrated into a system of first contact care, specialist care for the ambulatory, and in-patient services at hospitals. The efficiency of the network system is enhanced by the smallness of the country and the fact that Kuwait is almost a city-state where more than 90% of the population resides in the city (United Nations, 1980). The country is subdivided into 11 districts, which in turn, are subdivided into microdistricts. Under the microdistrict system, a person is assigned to a health territorial unit on the basis of residence.

First contact care is based on the microdistrict principle. These health units are served by their own physicians: a therapist (internist or general medicine), and pediatrician. A strategically located clinic in each district (health combined centers) provide specialized medical services such as family planning services, dental care, preventative care, and vital registration (birth and death), and have facilities for urgent laboratory tests. Such specialized services are available in addition the regular services administered in any microdistrict clinic. They are available on a 24 hours basis to any resident of the district.

The third level in the primary care system is a more general clinic designed to serve between 50-75 thousand of the population. These clinics provide the medical services of orthopedic, gynecological, and skin disease specialists. Each clinic is equipped with an x-ray unit, a laboratory, and a pharmacy.

In general, Kuwait extends primary care services to its population, often with emphasis on common illnesses, and on the health of mothers and children. Such care is offered to the population at the point of entry into the health system, combining the preventive and curative, personal and community, individual and environmental aspects. Primary care services are provided by health workers alone or in teams, at work places, schools, dispensaries, clinics, or other health facilities. Primary care constitutes the basic level of involvement of the Kuwaiti population with health services. The role of the provider is to prevent illness wherever possible, keep minor health problems from worsening, and refer more serious cases to the proper consultant and facility.

Secondary care comprises the general hospital in-patient services and specialist consultations, often on referral from primary care providers. In general the hospitals in Kuwait provide in-patient care and out-patient services. Hospitals are graded according to the type of facilities provided. The first-level hospitals in all areas are district hospitals. These are general hospitals, which deal with common acute and chronic medical, surgical, gynecological, and obstetric conditions. More specialized units are situated in regional hospitals. Patients are normally referred to them through the district hospitals. At the top of this hierarchy are a few hospitals where highly specialized medicine and some research activities are performed, especially in conjunction with the newly established College of Medicine in Kuwait University.

In addition to the territorial public medical network through which the majority of the population receives its care, there are other much smaller networks of private hospitals and independent practitioners. It's services are closely monitored by health authorities through licensing, quality control, and fee restrictions. In many Third World countries, private fee-- for-service medical practice, when exists, usually cater to the small upper class. The situation in Kuwait in regard to the role played by the private practice, however, is different. Neither in the level of medical technology nor in the quality of services is the private sector a serious competitor to the governmentally run health care system. The role of the private sector in the health care resembles those which exist in some socialist countries such as Czechoslovakia and the Soviet Union (Kaser, 19760 where despite of their well-planned socialization of medicine, legal private practices do exist, although not extensively.

The Quality of Care

The quality of medical care can be evaluated by such measures as availability and accessibility of medical services, the level of medical technology (science of medicine), the therapist-patient relationship (art of medicine), and the outcome of medical practice (Maykovich, 1980). Cross-culture comparison of the quality of medical care is rendered difficult by the inadequacy of published statistics and research data.

Availability and accessibility to medical care is high in Kuwait since everyone is assigned to a clinic where an attending physician is available at all times. In less than one generation, usership of modern health services has been extended from a tiny minority to the great majority of residents in Kuwait. The basic system used has been medicine, generally of a familiar kind.

Per capita medical utilization rates (estimated to be 8 to 9 visits per year) are higher in Kuwait in comparison to the United States for example, where the per capita utilization rate is 4 to 6 visits per year (National Center of Health statistics, 1978; and the Ministry of Health in Kuwait, 1979).

The level of technical proficiency in medicine is difficult to assess. Many foreign visitors are impressed by the totality of the health care system and by the use of the most up to date medical technology. The bulk of the patients are attended by highly selected groups of doctors from all over the world who have been attracted by higher salaries and favorable work arrangements. Unlike China or India, for example, Kuwait has made no effort to integrate its indigenous medical practices with modern medicine. The acceptance of the traditional sector was resisted. Medical care has been organized along strictly scientific lines, although folk medicine has not been totally banned.

Health care seeking behavior is not simply a function of the availability of facilites but is affected by sociocultural values and other factors. At this stage it seems that the peculiarities of the "culture of medicine" and the limitations in the culture of the patient, particularly the generally low level of education among the population, represented major impediments to further greater improvement of health.

As for the art of medicine, the absence of freedom of choice of physicians, the bureaucratization of salaried physicians, and the pressure of the work norm may be considered as obstacles to physician-patient rapport. Also, we wish to draw the attention to the professional and organizational "culture" which leads in some cases, to inadequate clinic operations, particularly the long waits, impersonality, and bureaucratic procedures to which the patient must adapt. Although many patients seem to appreciate the pressures of the work load upon physicians, they also note a large individual variation in physicians' attitudes toward patients.

A well known fact in medical care is the "lifestyle" differences patients bring with them to the therapeutic processes. Despite the many health care systems described above, it is likely that perhaps some people (mostly Bedouin) do not receive modern medical care at all. It seems a safe assumption that among those receiving modern medical care, some also consult traditional healers at times (Al-Rumahi, 1977).

Furthermore, laymen hold certain beliefs about modern medicine and doctor's care that affect the patient satisfaction with the service. For example, among the laymen, injections are believed to be stronger medication than pills, colored solutions are preferred to water-colored medications, and women doctors know less than men doctors. Because of sharp sex role differences, some men refuse to allow their wives and daughters to see men doctors.

Other social customs prevalent in regard to illness, especially among less educated people, interfere with the processes of the delivery of health care. These include frequent visitations to hospital patients by family members, relatives, and friends; congregation and long stays in the patients' rooms, and providing home prepared food as substitutes for hospital food which is believed to be inferior.

Any attempt to assess the overall impact of the health service upon the health status of the Kuwaiti population is necessarily fraught with difficulty. The major improvements in the health status of the Kuwaiti population in the period from the 1940s through the early part of the 1960s were almost certainly the consequence of improved standards of living and improved hygienic conditions stemming from public health measures, including fresh water, rather than the result of improvement in the medical treatment of illness and disease. In more recent years, however, the management and treatment of a whole range of illness and disease conditions have improved dramatically.

In comparison to other countries in the middle eastern region (Israel excluded), Kuwait has at the present, the lowest levels of mortality and the highest expectation of life at birth. In 1981, for example, the infant mortality rate was around 39 per 1,000 and life expectancy at birth was 70 years; in contrast, Yemen has an infant ortality rate of around 162 and a life expectancy of about 41 years (Population Reference Bureau, 1982). The relatively small size of the country and the heavy concentration of the population in urban areas have facilitated the delivery of primary health care to nearly every socioeconomic stratum of the population. In addition, the government operates a special state-financed medical office in London and Cairo for Kuwaitis who need specialized treatment that cannot be provided locally.

While no medical system is without problems and none is completely transferable from one society to another, there are lessons to be learned in considering alternative models to our own. During its twenty-year development, the health care system in Kuwait has managed admirable accomplishments, including: (1) eliminating financial barriers to access, (2) making the system more rational and equitable, (3) providing care on a community level with community-based primary physicians, and (4) maintaining a high level of medical care quality. The Kuwaiti health care system is by no means a medical utopia. As it is a public welfare service, it must compete with other services (e.g., education, housing, income maintenance, etc.) for funding and thus by some accounts is perpetually underfinanced, and while inequities of services have lessened, they have not totally disappeared.

Rather critically, an overall question can be asked: Are the people of Kuwait healthier today because of the socialized health care system? There is the suggestion that major improvements in the health status in Kuwait since 1962 are attributable to developments (e.g., better nutrition, housing, living standards, and technological advances) that would have taken place whatever system had been chosen to administer and finance health services.

Were policy-makers wrong in promoting such an elaborate system of publicly financed health services to begin with? My answer is no, for the following reasons: (1) Given the initially low levels of health and welfare of the population, the government had no choice except to expand services in these areas; (2) only the government can contract, import, and administer such large-scale health service programs with professionals and paraprofessionals, technology and equipment, facilities and organizations; (3) administering these programs free is one way of guaranteeing a bottom line of the much needed services for all citizens, regardless of their socioeconomic status; (4) government investment in these programs, although substantial, in purely economic terms, is one major form of wealth dissemination; and (5) these programs remain a main source of employment.

In a society that builds from scratch, there is no alternative to government intervention, especially in the development of a health care sector which if left totally to the market mechanism, would never receive the serious attention of private investors. The Kuwaiti government's responsibilities for providing such services have been widely accepted. These health service programs have become so entrenched now that it is politically difficult to alter, or to transfer to the private sector should this sector prove capable of doing a better job in the future.

SUMMARY, CONCLUSIONS AND GENERAL OBSERVATIONS

This essay is written in the belief that every society which has developed a network of health care policies faces a common problem. By considering the contrasting or, sometimes, similar ways in which different societies approach the problems, we can hope to sense the major characteristics of their health care policies. There is strong evidence from the experience in Kuwait to suggestthat considering the level of economic development as the key determinant of health care policy is unwarranted. Kuwait is a rich country butnot a developed, industrialized country. The evolution of the health care sector was not a natural accompaniment to industrialism and its demographic outcome as was the case in the west.

Cultural diffusion played a major role in the evolution of Kuwait's system of health care. There, foreign influence is apparent in the adoption of health service programs. Policies, statutes, and programs addressed to health care needs in most societies have evolved in an incremental manner, in response to varied diseases and pressures. A review of the medical care program in Kuwait illustrates this fact. However, the experience of Kuwait shows clearly that in the design of a health care system, it may be advantageous to begin from a zero point. When implementing a new system that starts from scratch, many of the problems usually encountered in fixing and overhauling an existing but an ailing system can be shortcut. The experience of England for example, and the problems encountered (Battistela and Chester, 1973) provide good illustrations of the difficulties that arise when the state intervenes in an already functioning health care system.

The Kuwaiti's experience indicates that the age of the system determines neither the role that the state plays in the health care services, nor the level and sophistication of medical care policy. Although it is relatively new, the Kuwaiti health care system is an advanced and well developed system. It exhibits certain cohesion. Its services are in most part related to the true health needs of the population.

The key to understanding the direct role of government in health care lies in the approach to distributing oil wealth taken by the government. The customary approach to the distribution of oil revenues was to establish the provision of social services including medical care on what is, in Western eyes, a lavish scale. The early provision of unlimited fresh water, electricity, and subsidized housing and the including of medical care and education originally satisfied local demand but also created a greater "consumer interest" (Gallagher, 1973). In fat, the scale of provision, initially seen as fabulous, was gradually perceived as inadequate, and with the justification that the ruler was fabulously wealthy, citizens of Kuwait have progressively demanded more health and social services of an improved quality

(Al-Qudsi, 1981).

From the beginning, the Kuwaiti government took a firm stand in favor of the welfare approach to medical care. The officials did not think of medical care as a sporadic activity to be brought into play only in cases of disease breakdown. It can be said that in some respects, Kuwait's comprehensive approach to health services greatly resemble that of the Soviet Union. Given the ideological basis of the Soviet state, it is hardly necessary to make the point concerning the strength of the public sector in the provision of health services (Ryan, 1978).

Given the structure of development (imported) in Kuwait, it is easy to understand the dominant role that is assumed by the government, and the insignificant role played by the private sector. The role of the state is also augmented by other factors, particularly the state control of the wealth (oil revenue), and extreme citizen's dependency on their government. Kuwait's case clearly demonstrates that an advanced form of socialized medicine (financed and controlled by the government) can survive and thrive within the context of the political economy of a highly capitalist society.

Before any conclusion is reached, however, care must be taken in recognizing the difficulties in cross-national comparison and the relative lack of cross-cultural transferability. The Kuwaiti system is the product of a process of socio-economic development which reflects social change more or less peculiar to the Kuwaiti society and is thus not directly or wholly exportable, except to other oil rich countries in the Gulf region. At the present, the experience of Kuwait is considered a model which other oil rich countries in the region try to emulate. With this in mind, we can summarize briefly the relevance of the experience of Kuwait.

Health is considered important not so much for the necessity to carry out societal goals, particularly those related to work, but for the sake of an individual and family's well-being and happiness. Health care policies are by and large a national monopoly formulated by a paternalistic, centralized form of government. The priority to be placed upon health against other issues such as education, defense, housing, etc. is a decision declared by the government. The financial constraints that normally surround such decisions in other countries is minimal considering Kuwait's unlimited supply of capital. Although the redistribution of wealth is not the primary motivation behind national health care, the general welfare of the people is. The interface between health services and other social services in the areas of needs, such as housing, nutrition, income maintenance, clean water, etc., illustrates how a health care system can be successfully integrated as one component of a comprehensive social services program.

Ideally, Kuwait presents an integrated medical system, although in practice the system exhibits several built-in conflicts. The fact that the system is totally imported in terms of manpower and technology highlights the total dependency of the people on foreign doctors. (The percentage of

Kuwaiti doctors in the total number in the country is less than 5%). The failure of the educational system so far to train the much needed manpower in the health fields on all levels is now recognized as serious indeed (Al-Essa, 1981). This situation represents an example par excellence of a cultural lag between, on the one hand, modern medical science and technology, and on the other, traditional values that still govern the educational process. Other problems that exist are not as much a rejection of modern medicine as such, but rather a reflection of a conservative attitude toward other aspects of modernization. We referred before to some elements in the culture of the patients that interfere with the delivery of the health care. Perhaps more serious are some values in the general Islamic culture prevalent in Kuwait, especially those specifying the role of women in work and society. Because women are not expected to work outside their homes except in all female work environments, the role of women as health care promotors and providers is limited. Very few Kuwaiti girls, for example, choose nursing as a career. There is generally a stigma attached to nursing because in her work, the nurse comes in contact with the naked human body. In this conservative climate, the treatment of women is preferred to be rendered by female doctors. This explains, for example, the relatively high percentage of women among foreign doctors who work in Kuwait.

The fact that there is an overwhelming representation of foreign doctors and other health care providers in Kuwait creates an anomaly in the power structure between the expatriots and the indigenous population; a situation where the first group holds much of the power. In the public sector, the largest groups of physicians are from Egypt, Palestine, India, and England in that order. In the private sector the largest group is composed of Palestinian doctors. There is some evidence to indicate that ethnic loyalty is a factor when a choice becomes possible for the selection of one's doctor. This tendency is to be expected in a society that is so heterogeneous as Kuwait.

There are two approaches frequently mentioned which represent different, although related perspectives on the problems of, and the solutions to current medical care in Third World countries. John Ehrenreich (1978) terms these perspectives the "political economic" and the "cultural." The **first** approach, the "political economic," "challenges the poor distribution of an otherwise admirable service" and generates efforts to extend existing medical services to particular under-served polulations, such as the poor. The **second** approach challenges the idea that Western-style medical care is the humane, effective, and desirable solution to health problems that its supporters and even some of its critics believe it to be. Those community projects which adopt this "cultural" perspective seek to develop truly alternative organizations and approaches to health care, such as, for example, a women's self-help clinics. Kuwait's success story can be said to depend wholly on (1) the widespread application of Western-style medical care, and (2) the extension of medical services to all segments of the population.

An important lesson we learned from studying the health care system in China (Heller, 1973; New and New, 1975; Sidel and Sidel, 1973) was that large amounts of money or medical research are not necessary requirements, and that the lack of either should not be accepted as justification for official inaction. Perhaps the most important lessons to be learned from Kuwait is that a large amount of money coupled with an enlightened official action can produce swift and remarkable achievements in the application of modern medicine, even in a traditional socio-cultural environment that is not very hospitalbe to modernization. Thus, the case of Kuwait presents an overwhelming evidence to support Foster's (1978) contention that "in countries where traditional peoples have had acccess to modern medicine for a generation or longer, and where this medicine has been of reasonably good quality, the battle has been won, and scientific medicine is the victor."

The frequently exaggerated ideas emphasizing cultural impediments to the introduction of modern medicine as the primary reason for the current unsatisfactory situation in many Third world countries seem to lack objective assessment. Kuwait presents a clear evidence that when virgorously adopted, aggregatively introduced, and properly administered, modern medicine can be quickly accepted. That is to say, whatever cultural impediments to modern medicine are believed to exist, those can be overlooked once the "demonstration effects" are brought forefully to witness.

Finally, there seems to be a common misconception in the west that most developing countries either have no medical care systems at all, or are incapable of developing one. Kuwait's experience may be relevant to other highly developed countries, both as a field of laboratory for the elucidation of alternatives and as a study of the complexities inherent in any attempt to implement large-scale organizational structures. The country represents the most ambitious attempt to institute comprehensive health services planning and integrated delivery among non-Western capitalist countries.

REFERENCES

AL-ESSA, S. (1981) MANPOWER IN KUWAIT. London: Rutledge Kegan Paul.

Al-QUDSI, SULAYMANS (1981) "Pre and Post-Fiscal Distributional Patterns in Kuwait," MIDDLE EASTERN STUDIES 17: 393-407.

AL-RUMAHI, MAHAMED (1977) CHALLENGES TO SOCIAL AND ECONOMIC DEVELOPMENT IN CONTEMPORARY SOCIETIES IN THE ARABISN GULD. Kuwait: El Safa, Publ.

AL-SAKAWI, ABDEL AZIZ (1976) KUWAITH: A COUNTRY OF SOCIAL SERVICES. Kuwait: Kuwait Sociological Society Ninth Cultural Season.

BATTISTELLA, ROGER M. and THEODORE E. CHESTER (1973) "Reorganization of the National Health Service: Background and Issues in England's Quest for a Comprehensive-Integrated Planning and Delivery System," THE MILBANK MEMORIAL FUND QUARTERLY 51: 489-530.

BRYANT, JOHN (1969) HEALTH AND THE DEVELOPING WORLD. Ithaca, N.Y.: Cornell University Press.

DeMIGUEL, J.M. (1975) "A Framework for the Study of National Health Systems," INQUIRY 12 (2 Suppl.): 10-24.

DJUKANOVIC, V. and E.P. MACH (eds.) (1975) ALTERNATIVE APPROACHES TO MEETING BASIC HEALTH NEEDS IN DEVELOPING COUNTRIES. Geneva: World Health Organization.

EHRENREICH, JOHN (1978) "Introduction: The Cultural Crisis of Modern Medicine," pp. 1-35 in John Ehrenreich (ed.), THE CULTURAL CRISIS OF MODERN MEDICINE. N.Y.: Monthly Review Press.

ELLING, RAY H. (1977) SOCIO-CULTURAL INFLUENCES ON HEALTH AND HEALTH CARE. N.Y.: Springer Publ. Co.

ELLING, RAY H. (1978) "Medical Systems as Changing Social Systems," in Charles Leslie (ed.), THEORETICAL FOUNDATIONS FOR THE COMPARATIVE STUDY OF MEDICAL SYSTEMS, pp. 107-115. Special issue of Social Science and Medicine, 12: No. 2B.

ELLING, RAY H. (1980) CROSS-NATIONAL STUDY OF HEALTH SYSTEMS. New Brunswick, N.J.: Transaction Books.

FOSTER, GEORGE M. (1978) "Medical Anthropology and International Health Planning," pp. 301-313, in M.H. Logan and E.F. Hunt (eds.), HEALTH AND THE HUMAN CONDITION. North Scituate, MA.: Duxburg Press.

GALLAGHER, E.B. (n.d.) "Consumerism and Health Care," pp. 363-379 in Magdelena Sokolowska et.al. (eds.) HEALTH, MEDICINE, SOCIETY. Boston: A. Reidel Publ. Co.

HELLER, PETER (1973) "The Strategy of Health-Sector Planning," in Myron Wegman et al. (ed.) PUBLIC HEALTH IN THE PEOPLE'S REPUBLIC OF CHINA. N.Y.: Josiah Macy, Jr. Fndtn.

HOLLINGSHEAD, AUGUST B. (1973) "Medical Sociology: A brief Review," THE MILBANK MEMORIAL FUND QUARTERLY 51: 531-544.

KASER, MICHAEL (1976) HEALTH CARE IN THE SOVIET UNION AND EASTERN EUROPE. Boulder, CO.: Westview Press.

KENT, P.W. (ed.) (1976) INTERNATIONAL ASPECTS OF THE PROVISION OF MEDICAL CARE. Stocksfield: Oriel Press Ltd.

KERR, CLARK et. al. (1962) INDUSTRIALISM AND INDUSTRIAL MAN. London: Heinemann.

KUWAIT, MINISTRY OF PLANNING, CENTRAL STATISTICAL OFFICE (1977) ANNUAL STATISTICAL ABSTRACT.

KUWAIT, MINISTRY OF GUIDANCE AND INFORMATION (1966) KUWAIT TODAY: A WELFARE STATE. Nairobi: Quality Publs., Ltd.

KUWAIT, MINISTRY OF HEALTH (1978) THE EVOLUTION OF THE MEDICAL CARE SERVICE IN KUWAIT.

KUWAIT, MINISTRY OF HEALTH (1979) ANNUAL REPORT.

MARTIN, GEORGE T. and MYERN ZALD (eds.) (1981) SOCIAL WELFARE IN SOCIETY. N.Y.: Columbia University Press.

MAYKOVICH, MINAKO K. (1980) MEDICAL SOCIOLOGY. Shermanoaks: CA: Alfred PUblishing Co.

MIDDLE EAST REVIEW (1981) KUWAIT.

NAGI,A MOSTAFA H. (1982) "Development with Unlimited Supplies of Capital: The Case of OPEC," THE DEVELOPING ECONOMICS 20: 3-20).

NAVARRO, VICENTE (1978) "The Crisis of the Western System of Medicine in Contemporary Capitalism," INTERNATIONAL JOURNAL OF HEALTH SERVICES 8: 179-212.

NEW, PETER KONG-MING and MARY LOUIE NEW (1975) "The Links Between Health and Political Structure in New China," HUMAN ORGANIZATIONS 34: 237-251.

POPULATION REFERENCE BUREAU (1982) WORLD'S CHILDREN DATA SHEET. Washington, D.C.: Population Reference Bureau, Inc.

RYAN, MICHAEL (1978) THE ORGANIZATION OF SOVIET MEDICAL CARE. London: Basil Blackwell and Mott Ltd., Oxford and Martin Robertson and Co.

SIDEL, VICTOR W. and RUTH SIDEL (1973) SERVE THE PEOPLE. N.Y.: Josiah Macy, Jr., Fndtn.

STONE, RUSSELL A. (ed.) (1977) OPEC AND THE MIDDLE EAST: THE IMPACT OF OIL ON SOCIETAL DEVELOPMENT. N.Y.: Praeger Publ.

UNITED NATIONS (1980) THE POPULATIONI SITUATION IN THE ECWA REGION: KUWAIT. Beirut: United Nations Economic Commission for Western Asia.

U.S. NATIONAL CENTER FOR HEALTH STATISTICS (1974) Physician visits: VOLUME AND INTERVAL SINCE LAST VISIT, UNITED STATES, 197. VITAL AND HEALTH STATISTICS (DHEW PUBLC. NO. (HRA) 75--1524). Washington, D.C.: U.S. Government Printing Office.

WILENSKY, HAROLD (1975) THE WELFARE STATE AND EQUALITY. Berkeley, CA.: University of California Press.

WOOD, CLIVE and YVONNE RUE (eds.) (1980) HEALTH POLICIES IN DEVELOPING COUNTRIES. London: Royal Society of Medicine and Academic Pres Ltd.

CHAPTER 13

THE PEOPLE'S REPUBLIC OF CHINA:
A SOCIO-HISTORICAL EXAMINATION OF ITS HEALTH CARE DELIVERY

Peter Kong-ming New and Yuet-Wah Cheung

Introduction

In the years since the death of Chairman Mao, the Government of the People's Republic of China has been gradually shifting its policies in a number of areas. At the Party Congress which just concluded, in September, 1982, there is now an overt rejection of the "cult of personality," signifying a downgrading of Chairman Mao. Since some of the most radical changes in health care delivery in China were instituted during the height of Chairman Mao's influence, does this also mean that these changes would be nullified? (New, 1982)

Ever since streams of visitors began to go to China to examine various social and welfare programs in 1972, laudatory reports in various sectors began appearing in scholarly journals and the popular presses. In the area of health, there were unanimous praises that health care delivery, public health and preventive measures, and the like had improved immensely, and that these improvements were made since 1949 (Sidel and Sidel, 1973; New and New, 1975b; Lampton, 1977; Chen, 1976).

Were all these achievements accomplished just since 1949? Or, were some of these innovative practices basically continuations of Western health care measures which were introduced since the 1830's when Western physicians, most of whom were medical missionaries, gradually made their way to China? In other words, what were some of the historical antecedents?

In this paper, we have two purposes in mind. First, we will examine a few of the Western health care measures which were introduced into China before 1949. To be sure, in a brief paper, we could not dwell on any of them at length; however, we bring some of them to the reader's attention, as they illustrate some of the possible continuities of health care before and since 1949. Second, we will examine the implications of the shifts in the current policies in China, since the death of Chairman Mao, and speculate on what these shifts means to the general health care of China's multitudes.

Brief Background Sketch

The progress of health delivery since 1949, as a political structure, may even be traced back to 1911 when China broke away from the bonds of early feudal rule. Presumably, modern China began under the leadership of Sun Yat-sen, a modern-day physician who chose a more significant career (Young, 1975). Of course, health care in China followed centuries of traditional and complex philosophies of health and illness in the total cosmology (Risse, 1973; Croizier, 1973; Agren, 1975; Unschuld, 1982).

As Croizier (1968) has discussed, before 1949, there was continuous tension between those who espoused a more "national" medicine (i.e., traditional medicine, or **Chung-i**) and the proponents of Western medicine. When the Western trained physicians had seemed to gain the upper hand in the modern health care movement, an attempt was made in 1929 to outlaw Chinese medicine. As Wu (1959: 566) has noted, on February 23-26, 1929, the newly established National Ministry of Health in Nanjing was asked by a committee of eighteen to abolish the "native practice" of Chinese medicine.

These decisions were immediately met by stiff resistances from the practitioners of **Chung-i** who, until this threat was imminent, had not organized themselves as a pressure group. On March 17, 1929, more than five hundred representatives from over two hundred and sixty **Chung-i** associations in seventeen provinces gathered in Shanghai to condemn the resolutions put forth by the newly formed Ministry of Health in Nanjing. These representatives elected a six-man delegation who went to Nanjing to present their arguments and they succeeded in obtaining a guarantee from the Central Government that the resolution would not be implemented. In commemoration of this "victory," March 17th was designated as the **Kuo-i chieh,** or the Chinese Doctors' Day (Ch'en, 1963: Chu, 1939).

The opposition to these resolutions were not expresse doslely by the **Chung-i** practitioners, as the general public also was not in sympathy with these resolutions. Debates on these issues were reported in many newspapers (Ch'en, 1963: 7-13). Some of the opposition could be attributed to the economic aspects, since any prohibition of the sale and use of traditional Chinese medicine (herbs and the like) would mean a great monetary loss to the traditional practitioners and their related business associates (Ch'en, 1963: 6).

Although the March 17th incident stimulated the establishment of **Chung—yang kuo-i kuan,** the first national **Chung-i** association, as an organized group they never exerted much more influence in health care policies in the Central Government before 1949. The influence which they wanted gradually receeded until Chairman Mao came forth with the proposal that traditional medicine should go hand in hand with Western medicine in treating the patients (New and New, 1975a).

The resolutions which were introduced in 1929 to abolish "native practice" demonstrates the far-reaching influence which Western medicine had gained in China. In this paper, we will briefly follow the threat of how Western medicine gained a foothold in a previously traditional health system and how it was accepted. Through some of these events, we will show that the groundwork for many of the current health care measures were already carried out by the early Western-trained physicians. The current Government possibly had the advantage of a more unified and centralized country to implement public health efforts on a broad front.

The Structure of Health Care Before 1949

Even though the Republic of China was established in 1911, China did not come into a total being until some eighteen years later when Chian Kai-shek made a major push to suppress various warlords. A National Ministry of Health was orgbanized on November 1, 1928, in Nanjing (Wu, 1959: 368), although rural areas often remained outside the Ministry's jurisdiction. Thus, much of the organized, governmentally coordinated, work in health care delivery did not come about until recently. However, this does not mean that health care was left in a void. Briefly, we will review some of the other movements.

MEDICAL MISSIONARIES

The appearance of Western medicine is often credited to Peter Parker, M.D., D.D., an American missionary who went to China in 1834 (Wong and Wu, 1936; Gulick, 1973. For more details on the part that Canadian medical missionaries played in China, see Yuet-Wah Cheung, THE SOCIAL ORGANIZATION OF MISSINARY MEDICINE: A STUDY OF TWO CANADI-AN PROTESTANT MISSIONS IN CHINA BEFORE 1937, unpublished Ph.D. Dissertation, University of Toronto [Sociology], 1982). Along with trying to convert Chinese to Christianity, many medical missionaries also tried to offer health care, no matter how crude (Young, 1973). Their medical work represented the only source of Western medicine for a large population in the rural areas as well (mcClure, 1979). Of course, many more traditional Chinese physicians rendered care to most of the Chinese (Wu, 1959). By and large, the medical missionaries brought with them the armamentaria they were used to: Western style hospitals and out-patient departments staffed basically by professionals trained in their own countries.

However, due to necessity, some medical missionaries began to innovate. For instance, Sturton spoke of various rural clinics which had been establish-ed under his aegis, but these efforts gained momentum only just before 1937 and the mission hospitals which extended their work into the rural clinics did so often without consultation with each other. Sturton described another effort: "...We began with what was termed the 'medical raid,' which means that a party of medical workers, usually comprising at least one doctor, nurse, and dispenser, visited some place for, say, half a day and did as much as possible for the patients who presented themselves. While this makes a good introduction, it is not as satisfactory as regular service, and inevitably leads either to 'medical circus' (I have borrowed the terms from Dr. Bob McClure of Honan) in which a similar team goes around to various places in rotation, or to the establishment of some form of out-station, with a resident doctor or nurse (Sturton, n.d.: 50)."

Indeed, McClure was also carrying out these "medical raids," as Sturton had implied. However, in McClure's case, he was more systematic, as he would have placed certain of his trained health workers in various locales. For certain types of diseases, such as trachoma, McClure would have his health workers identify as many patients as they could and be brought into these clinics so that in one afternoon or even in a few hours they would all be treated (McClure, 1979). After a few years of moving out to establish clinics in the surrounding areas, the out-patient department of McClure's mission hospital was practically phased out. Acute cases were directly referred from clinics to the in-patient part of the hospital. McClure and Sturton were the exceptions as most of their colleagues continued to treat patients within the confines of the hospitals (Scott, 1977).

MEDICAL EDUCATION

Missionaries had already established middle schools and undergraduate colleges in China (Wong and Wu, 1936; Lutz, 1971). With the establishment of hospitals in various parts of China, a natural next step was the planning of medical education in China. In their plans for the establishment of such schools, again the Western model was used. Further, there was the implicit assumption that the administrators and the senior staffs would be non-Chinese, for very good reasons, since so few Chinese were trained in Western medicine in the early 1900's. For those Chinese who were trained, most of them were quite jealous in their desire to propagate Western ideas. In fact, the urban youths of China after 1917 were steadily rejecting traditional ideas, culminating in the May 4th (1919) Movement when there was a broad scale attack on various old ideas (Hsu, 1975).

By 1905, medical colleges, nursing schools, and other health schools (such as pharmacy) were opening in various parts of China almost yearly. Some continued as they were on solid footing, but others closed in a few years. Harvard Medical School, for instance, began training physicians in 1912 in Shanghai, collaborating with St. John's University, but four years later that Medical School closed its doors (Wong and Wu, 1936: 847-849; New and Cheung, 1982a). During this flourish of activities in opening various health training facilities, two questions arose time and again: First, who would be trained, and second, who would be in control? For the leaders of the Rockefeller Foundation who assumed control of the Peking Union Medical College, such questions were answered quite clearly: it would turn out physicians who were going to be equal to the best throughout the world, the "elite corps" who would lead China's destiny in health affairs. This philosophy certainly seemed reasonable. The leaders of the Rockefeller Foundation felt that unless the graduates could compete with other leaders of the world, their effectiveness would not be as great (Ferguson, 1970; Bowers, 1971; Brown, 1979; Bullock, 1980).

As to who would be in control, in the beginning Rockefeller would have its own trusted administrators in control. Gradually, this control would shift to the Chinese. It was hoped that funds to maintain P.U.M.C. would be shifted to donations from influential Chinese citizens. That hope was never realized (Bullock, 1973, 1980). Thus, from the beginning, P.U.M.C. was a first class establishment: the grounds, the beautiful and spacious buildings, the staff, and all that was associated with it. The Rockefellers spared no expense in developing and maintaining this "show piece" of medical training and research (Ferguson, 1970). The early graduates, such as Yao Hsun-yuan and Ch'en Chi-ch'ien, went on to establish experimental health stations in rural areas, and other alumni are even now leaders in their fields of research and practice (Bowers, 1971; Bullock, 1980). The faculty was also drawn from some of the most distinguished clinicians and scientists, including John B. Grant, M.D., who would shape the future development of public health in China (Seipp, 1966).

Yale University, on the other hand, also established a medical college, in Changsha, in the central part of China, but with quite a different goal in mind. Edward H. Hume, M.D., a third generation medical missionary, who family was long associated with missionary work in India, was asked to go to China to develop health work in 1905, specifically to establish a medical school. Yale already had a middle school and an undergraduate college in Changsha. After many years of planning, Hume was able to interest a fellow-Yale alumnus, Edward Harkness, in building a modern hosital, and this became the site of the new medical school as well. However, right from the beginning in 1913, Hume worked with F.C. Yen, one of the few Chinese physicians trained in Western medicine and in public health, to place the control of this school with the Henan provincial authorities (Forde, 1977). Considering that China had barely emerged from the dynastic period into a yet unstable republican government, Hume's philosophy was certainly a bold step (Reeves, 1966).

The impression should not be given that only schools such as the P.U.M.C. and Yale or Harvard-in-China were being established. Other missiongroups were also establishing health training schools. As well, the Chinese Government and provincial governments were also beginning to expand their educational endeavors in Western medicine (Wong and Wu, 1936). There were also some propriety colleges and medical schools. Standards and quality varied greatly; however, even in North America, it took the Flexner Report (1910) to bring about some major changes. This report undoubtedly had a great deal of influence on medical education in China as well (New and Cheung, 1982).

TRAINING OF AUXILIARY HEALTH WORKERS

The lack of support staff in the hospitals was constantly stressed by the physicians such as McClure, Sturton, and others (Scott, 1977; Hume, 1946; Sturton, n.d.). Their missions "at home" tried to interest nurses and others to go out to these remote areas. However, in China very few institutions were established to train nurses and other health workers in any systematic way. as more hospitals were built, they became training facilities as well. Almost all of the missionary clinics and hospitals trained their own middle level health workers—orderlies of sorts to carry out necessary responsibilities within the hospitals.

By now, almost everyone has heard of the role played by Norman Bethune, M.D., in the Eighteen Route Army of the Chinese Communists in training health workers who became models for the latter day barefoot doctors (Allen and Gordon, 1952; Shephard and Levesque, 1982). In the short period that Dr. bethune was in China, he initiated hospitals and training institutions for health personnel in a systematic fashion. After his death in 1939, these efforts were continued on a larger scale through the Bethune Hospital and Bethune Medical Colleges (Minden, 1979). His influence was certainly enormous, but then he was truly a physician with a "broader view," even in his early days in Montreal (MacLeod, Park, and Ryerson, 1978).

However, fewer persons may have heard about the equally significant pioneer work of Robert McClure (Scott, 1977), a physician who is the son of William McClure, M.D., a pioneer medical missionary from Canada who went to China at the turn of the century (New and Cheung, 1982b). McClure, the son, received his M.D. degree from the University of Toronto in 1922, after which he returned to China. Wherever he went in China, he noticed that former health assistants who were displeased with their hospitals would set up practices just across the hospitals. Dr. McClure decided that he would train his own assistants systematically to be stationed in rural areas to practice. He reasoned that if various parts of China finally became staffed with graduate physcians, these assistants would have another occupation to fall back on. McClure's colleagues did not react too kindly to this plan: "They rather scowled on. I was young. I had a great advantage because I had been China-raised. I could speak the language better. I had my written language, so that I could mimeograph my notes in Chinese....P.U.M.C. was utterly disinterested in my scheme....I believe it was the P.U.M.C. who gave me the name "quack doctors." They told me, 'You're introducing quack doctors to China'." (McClure, 1978)

It was McClure's plan to have a "quack in each county and around the quack there would be another satellite group" who could carry out "simpler" duties, such as changing dressings. P.U.M.C., according to McClure, again coined a term for these assistants, "crooks." McClure eventually did not achieve his goal of having a "quack in each county surrounded by seven or eight crooks in the district." By 1932, he did train eight such assistants, spread throughout the southern part of Henan Province (McClure, 1978). By 1937, there were 20-24 "crooks" working with these eight assistants. Regretably, all eight assistants became war casualties (McClure, 1979).

Thus, persons such as McClure and Hume, even though they were not Chinese, were able to adapt Western modes of medicine to the Chinese context. Of those Chinese persons who were trained in P.U.M.C., Yao and Ch'en, under the influence of Grant, also introduced innovative measures in public health.

178

PUBLIC HEALTH AND RURAL HEALTH EFFORTS

One of the most distinguished and far-reaching experiments in rural health care in China began as an urban effort. John B. Grant, M.D., was teaching in P.U.M.C., attached to the Medical School by the International Health section of the Rockefeller Foundation (Bullock, 1980; For a detailed account of public health work in China, see Ka-che Yip [1982].) He was insistent that his students should "get out" and understand the local situation. To accomplish this, he established an urban Health Demonstration Center in Deijing, in 1925, where students could provide health care in a city ward and gain experiences in dealing with every day practicalities of health work. The Center also became a demonstration for city officials of how public health activities could be centralized (Bullock, 1980).

During that same period, Grant becamse acquainted with the work of Y.C. Yen, the director of the Mass Education Movement, which had its base in Ting Hsien, a county with a population of 400,000, about 170 miles from Beijing (Yao, 1931; Gamble, 1954). Through efforts by various Rockefeller Foundation personnel, the Milbank Memorial Fund gave the first of a series of grants, from 1929 to 1937, to assist in some of the major public health demonstrations (Editorial, 1930). Grant was instrumental in having Yao appointed as its first director, followed by Ch'en, who was the Director from 1931 to 1937 (Bullock, 1980). In February, 1981, Ch'en and Yen met in the Phillipines, where Yen founded the International Institute of Rural Reconstruction. Much of the program at the I.I.R.C. was first tried in Ting Hsien (I.I.R.C. Report, 1981: 1-3).

During the Ting Hsien health experiment, numerous accomplishments were achieved: (1) the establishment of three "tiers" of organization, at the village station, sub-district, and district levels (Ch'en, 1936a); (2) the introduction of the village health worker (Ch'en, 1936b); (3) the gradual registration and accurate accounting of vital statistics (Ch'en, 1937); and (4) the training of other health professional workers, such as medical students from P.U.M.C. and recent medical graduates (Ch'en, 1937). Just when all these efforts were beginning to jell, the Sino-Japanese War of 1937 began. The impact of the Center's activities, however, went far beyond Ting Hsien. In 1936, there was already a plan to replicate the experiment in Hengshan, another city in Henan Province, and in Chengdu and Xindu Xian, Sichuan Province (Ch'en, 1937).

PUBLIC HEALTH MEASURES INTRODUCED BY WARLORDS

Although medical missionaries and the Chinese Government began public health efforts, some were carried out by warlords as well. Feng Yu-hsiang was one such warlord who instituted a number of social reforms, including public health projects, when he was the Defense Commissioner in Changde, Henan. Soon after his arrival in that City, this "Christian General" embarked on an anti-vice program to eradicate narcotics, gambling, and prostitution. He banned the sale of opium, arrested its traders, and confiscated whatever drugs he found (Sheridan, 1966: 91-92). He also established a sanitarium to rehabilitate addicts and then sent them to vocational schools to learn a trade. Commendable as it seemed, Feng's various anti-opium campaigns never succeeded because of the lack of cooperation and support from the prosperous landowners, officials, and mechants (Sheridan, 1966: 92).

In 1923, Feng moved to Nanyuan, near Beijing. He again instituted various public health campaigns, such as killing flies and pests, and he organized a clinic which was operated by his "medical corps." He actively sought the help of Charles Lewis, M.D., an American medical missionary, to establish and maintain a civilian hospital which Feng financed. However, these campaigns came to an early end when Feng started fighting against other warlords in 1925 (Sheridan, 1966: 159).

These public health reforms illustrate the fact that Feng's good intentions were constantly being thwarted by the lack of organizational and technical skills, by inadequate financing, the absence of support by the community, and by the vicissitudes of warlord politics. Consequently, they were short--lived and superficial.

SUMMARY

In summary, as one review's China's early efforts to move in the path of modernization in health care, one could not help but notice that the elite among the Chinese were influenced, possibly unduly, by the West and they accepted all that the West has to offer as "good" while rejecting the traditional therapies. The February, 1929, attempt to eliminate traditional medicine and its practitioners was certainly the most blatant example.

At the same time, what we have shown is that before 1949, there were already some attempts made to institute Western forms of health care to the masses. They were offered, however, in limited ways. After the Communists came into power, many of these tentative ideas were translated into bold and successful ventures (Lampton, 1977).

Discussion

From 1949 to 1976, students of health care have marvelled at the massive and almost revolutionary efforts which the Communists took to deliver health care to the citizens. The most significant changes were these: (1) Expanded health care in rural areas; (2) the introduction of barefoot doctors and other health workers at a massive scale; (3) the "leveling" of status between the physician and other health workers; (4) the incorporation of Chinese medicine with Western medicine; (5) the combining of practical work with medical education; and (6) the increase of "generalists" in health work. All these steps were in consonance with the prevailing ideology of that time, "Serve the People." It was no secret that Chairman Mao, himself, pushed for many of these changes (New and New, 1977).

Thus, it was not surprising that after his death, some of Chairman Mao's health policies would be altered or neglected. Of course, the leaders of 1982 had ready answers to account for these changes. For instance, it is now explained that barefoot doctors have served their needs as the number of physicians are rapidly increasing. Also, the barefoot doctors must increase their skills—hence, in recent years, they are all required to pass a series of examinations.

Similarly, medical education which had been shortened soon after schools resumed after the Cultural Revolution is again lengthened to five or six years after high school. Competitive examinations which had been abolished are now again given to all aspiring entrants. Thus,, only the "best" can now enter. This favors the urban-raised youngster rather than the rural youth or the factory worker. There is also the stress on specialty training, with all the attendant "high technology" instruments and equipment, which are eagerly transported to China.

These steps are all taken in the name of "modernization" on various fronts, such as agriculture, science, industry, and defense (Rozman, 1981). Within the context of the socio-historical development of health care, what we are witnessing now, in 1982, can be interpreted as a "cycling back" to the old days. As we have shown, beginning with the late 1800's and early 1900's, Western medicine made steady incursions into China, and the medical missionaries were the chief "agents' for these changes. Even though their numbers were never large at any time (Cheung, 1982), they seemed to have been stationed in strategic places. By sheer patience and, in no small measure, a fair amount of courage, these "foreign devils" did make extensive impacts on certain segments of the Chinese population. They were also able to interest a growing number of Chinese, mainly from the upper-middle class, to enter into the health profession, thus ensuring the perpetuation of the health profession.

The Sino-Japanese War of 1937 halted the spread of Western health care efforts; however, some of these efforts continued in unoccupied China. When the Communists came into power, all the missionary efforts stopped permanently. Instead of uncoordinated, separate, attempts by various missionary, governmental, and private groups to deliver health care, the Chinese were able to coordinate through centralized government. Instead of endless interruptions, from 1911-1937, by various internal and external wars, at least the Communist Government was able to marshall some sense of stability. Thus, the small experiments of Ting Hsien, for instance, could now be expanded to the entire nation, and over amuch longer period of time.

In the last few years, it seems the leaders are now opting for the "high technology," specialized skills, "model." They are quite reminescent of the philosophy which was expounded by Rockefeller Foundation when it built P.U.M.C. To be sure, now these institutions are controlled by the Chinese. Possibly, China has achieved an earlier goal: elimination of communicable disease and health care delivery to all of its people. Now, it must "move on" to catch up with what has been neglected all these years: modern medicine (Lee, 1982; Lampton, 1981; Hinman et al., 1982).

It is much too early for anyone to speculate whether this current shift in health policy will ultimately be of benefit to the masses. One can only hope the leaders will now allow the extraordinary achievements to languish and pass away.

REFERENCES

AGREN, H. (1975) "Patterns of Tradition and Modernization in Contemporary Chinese Medicine," in A.M. Kleinman et al. (eds.) MEDICINE IN CHINESE CULTURES: COMPARATIVE STUDIES IN HEALTH CARE IN CHINESE AND OTHER SOCIETIES. Washington, D.C.: Fogarty International Center for advanced Studies in Health Sciences, pp. 37-59.

BOWERS, J.Z. (1971) WESTERN MEDICINE IN A CHINESE PALACE: PEKING UNION MEDICAL COLLEGE 1917-1951. N.Y.: Josiah Macy, Jr., Foundation.

BROWN, E.R. (1979) ROCKEFELLER MEDICINE MEN: MEDICINE AND CAPITALISM IN AMERICA. Berkeley: University of California Press.

BULLOCK, M.B. (1973) "The Rockefeller Foundation in China: Philanthropy, Peking Union Medical College and Public Health," unpublished Ph.D. Dissertation, Stanford University.

BULLOCK, M.B. (1980) AN AMERICAN TRANSPLANT: THE ROCKEFELLER FOUNDATIN AND THE PEKING UNION MEDICAL COLLEGE. Berkeley: University of California Press.

CH'EN, C.C. (1936a) "The Rural Health Experiment in Ting Hsien, China," MILBANK MEMORIAL FUND QUARTERLY BULLETIN 14: 66-80.

CH'EN, C.C. (1936b) "The Development of Systematic Training in Rural Public Health Work in China," MILBANK MEMORIAL FUND QUARTERLY BULLETIN 14: 370-387.

CH'EN, C.C. (1937) "Ting Hsien and the Public Health Movement in China," MILBANK MEMORIAL FUND QUARTERLY BULLETIN 15: 380-390.

CHEN, P.C. (1976) POPULATION AND HEALTH POLICY IN THE PEOPLE'S REPUBLIC OF CHINA. Washington, D.C.: Interdisciplinary Communication Program, Smithsonian Institution, Occasional Monograph Series No. 9.

CH'EN, T.J. (1963) SAN-I-CH'I KUO-I CHIEH SHIH-CHIEN HUI-I LU (MEMOIR OF THE MARCH 17 CHINESE DOCTORS' DAY), N.P.

CHEUNG, Y.W. (1982) "The Social Organization of Missionary Medicine: A Study of Two Canadian Protestant Missions in China Before 1937," unpublished Ph.D. dissertation, Department of Sociology, University of Toronto.

CROIZIER, R.C. (1968) TRADITIONAL MEDICINE IN MODERN CHINA: SCIENCE, NATIONALISM AND THE TENSION OF CULTURAL CHANGE. Cambridge: Harvard University Press.

CROIZIER, R.C. (1973) "Traditional Medicine as a Basis for Chinese Medical Practices," in J.R. Quinn (ed) MEDICINE AND PUBLIC HEALTH IN THE PEOPLE'S REPUBLIC OF CHINA. Washington, D.C.: Fogarty International Center for the advanced Study in Health Sciences, pp. 3-21.

CHU, H.N. (1939) NIEN PA-NIEN TI SAN-I-CH'I (REMEMBERING MARCH 17 EIGHT YEARS AGO), HSIN CHUNG-I K'AN (NEW TRADITIONAL MEDICINE MAGAZINE), VOl. I, No. 8, March 16, pp. 1-4.

EDITORIAL (MILBANK MEMORIAL FUND QUARTERLY BULLETIN) (1930) "A Rural Health experiment in China: Milbank Memorial Fund Aids the Development of the Public Health Program in Ting Hsien," MILBANK MEMORIAL FUND QUARTERLY BULLETIN 8: 97-107 (Oct.).

FERGUSON, M.E. (1970) CHINA MEDICAL BOARD AND THE PEKING UNION MEDICAL COLLEGE: A CHRONICLE OF FRUITFUL COLLABORATION, 1914-1951. N.Y.: China Medical Board of New York, Inc.

FLEXNER, A. (1910) MEDICAL EDUCATION IN THE UNITED STATES AND CANADA. N.Y.: Charnegie Foundation for the Advancement of teaching, BULLETIN No. 4; reprinted, Washington, D.C.: Science and Health Publications, 1979.

FORDE, R.J. (1977) "The Hsian-Ya Agreements: The Yale Foreign Missionary Society Tries to Cooperate with the Hunan Gentry in Medical Education," unpublished M.D. dissertation, Yale University.

GAMBLE, S.D. (1954) TING HSIEN: A NORTH CHINA RURAL COMMUNITY. Stanford: Stanford University Press.

GULICK, E.V. (1973) PETER PARKER AND THE OPENING OF CHINA. Cambridge: Harvard University Press.

HINMAN, A.R. et. al. (1982) HEALTH SERVICES IN SHANGHAI COUNTY," AMERICAN JOURNAL OF PUBLIC HEALTH, 72, No. 9, September, special supplement.

HSU, I.C.Y. (1975) THE RISE OF CHINA. Oxford: Oxford University Press, pp. 595-618.

HUME, E.H. (1964) DOCTORS EAST AND DOCTORS WEST: AN AMERICAN PHYSICIAN'S LIFE IN CHINA. N.Y.: W.W. Norton.

INTERNATIONAL INSTITUTE OF RURAL RECONSTRUCTION (1981) "Linking Past and Present: Dr. Chen of China," I.I.R.R. REPORT 14: 1-3, Spring.

LAMPTON, D.M. (1977) THE POLITICS OF MEDICINE IN CHINA: THE POLICY PROCESS, 1949-1977. Boulder: Westview Press.

LAMPTON, D.M. (1981) "Changing Health Policy Under the Post-Mao Era," YALE JOURNAL OF BIOLOGY AND MEDICINE 54: 21-26 (Jan.-Feb.).

LEE, R.P.L. (1982) "Comparative Studies of Health Care Systems," SOCIAL SCIENCE AND MEDICINE 16: 629-642.

LUTZ, J.G. (1971) CHINA AND THE CHRISTIAN COLLEGES, 1850-1950. Ithaca: Cornell University Press.

MACLEOD, W., L. PARK, and S. RYERSON. (1978) BETHUNE, THE MONTREAL YEARS: AN INFORMAL PORTRAIT. Toronto: James Lorimer and Co.

MCCLURE, R.B. (1978) Personal Interview with R.B. McClure by P.K. New, December 1st.

MCCLURE, R.B. (1979) "Training of Middle Level Health Workers in China," unpublished comments presented in an Alternate Health Care Meeting, Faculty of Medicine, University of Toronto, February 28.

MINDEN, K. (1979) "The Development of Early Chinese Communist Health Policy: Health Care in the Border Region, 1936-1949," AMERICAN JOURNAL OF CHINESE MEDICINE 8: 299-315, No. 4.

NEW, P.K. (1982) "Changing Health Policies in the P.R.C.: Another Perspective," MEDICAL ANTHROPOLOGY NEWSLETTER 15: 1-2 (Feb.).

NEW, P.K. and Y.W. CHEUNG (1982a) "Harvard Medical School of China, 1911-1916: An Expanded Footnote in the History of Western Medical Education in China," SOCIAL SCIENCE AND MEDICINE 16: 1207-1215.

NEW, P.K. and Y.W. CHEUNG (1982b) "Early Years of Medical Missionary Work in the Canadian Presbyterian Mission in North Honan, China, 1887-1900: Healing the Heathens and the Missionaries," unpublished paper presented in the Department of Sociology, University of Oklahoma, Norman, April 19.

NEW, P.K. and M.L. NEW (1975a) "The Links Between Health and Political Structure in New China," HUMAN ORGANIZATION 34: 237-251, Fall.

NEW, P.K. and M.L. NEW (1975b) "Health Care in the People's Republic of China," INQUIRY 12: 103-113, June, Supplement.

NEW, P.K. and M.L. NEW (1977) "The Barefoot Doctors of China: Healers for All Seasons," in D. Landy (ed.) CULTURE, DISEASE AND HEALING: STUDIES IN MEDICAL ANTHROPOLOGY. N.Y.: Macmillan Publ., pp. 503-510.

REEVES, W., Jr. (1966) "Sino-American Cooperation in Medicine: The Origins of Hsiang-Ya, 1902-1914," in K.C. Liu (ed.) AMERICAN MISSIONARIES IN CHINA. Cambridge: Harvard University Press,

185

NEW, P.K. and Y.W. CHEUNG (1982a) "Harvard Medical School of China, 1911-1916: An Expanded Footnote in the History of Western Medical Education in China," SOCIAL SCIENCE AND MEDICINE 16: 1207-1215.

NEW, P.K. and Y.W. CHEUNG (1982b) "Early Years of Medical Missionary Work in the Canadian Presbyterian Mission in North Honan, China, 1887-1900: Healing the Heathens and the Missionaries," unpublished paper presented in the Department of Sociology, University of Oklahoma, Norman, April 19.

NEW, P.K. and M.L. NEW (1975a) "The Links Between Health and Political Structure in New China," HUMAN ORGANIZATION 34: 237-251, Fall.

NEW, P.K. and M.L. NEW (1975b) "Health Care in the People's Republic of China," INQUIRY 12: 103-113, June, Supplement.

NEW, P.K. and M.L. NEW (1977) "The Barefoot Doctors of China: Healers for All Seasons," in D. Landy (ed.) CULTURE, DISEASE AND HEALING: STUDIES IN MEDICAL ANTHROPOLOGY. N.Y.: Macmillan Publ., pp. 503-510.

REEVES, W., Jr. (1966) "Sino-American Cooperation in Medicine: The Origins of Hsiang-Ya, 1902-1914," in K.C. Liu (ed.) AMERICAN MISSIONARIES IN CHINA. Cambridge: Harvard University Press, pp. 129-182.

RISSE, G.B. (ed.) (1973) MODERN CHINA AND TRADITIONAL CHINESE MEDICINE. Springfield, IL: Charles C. Thomas.

ROZMAN, G. (ed.) (1981) THE MODERNIZATION OF CHINA. N.Y.: The Free Press.

SCOTT, M. (1977) MCCLURE: THE CHINA YEARS. Toronto: Canec Publ.

SEIPP, C. (ed.) (1966) HEALTH CARE FOR THE COMMUNITY: SELECTED PAPERS OF DR. JOHN B. GRANT. Baltimore: Johns Hopkins Press.

SHEPHARD, D.A.E. and A. LEVESQUE (eds.) (1982) NORMAN BETHUNE: HIS TIMES AND HIS LEGACY. Ottawa: Canadian Public Health Association.

SHERIDAN, J.E. (1966) CHINESE WARLORD: THE CAREER OF FENG YU-HSIANG. Stanford: Stanford University Press.

SIDEL, V.W. and R. SIDEL (1973) SERVE THE PEOPLE: OBSERVATIONS ON MEDICINE IN THE PEOPLE'S REPUBLIC OF CHINA. N.Y.: Josiah Macy, Jr., Fndtn.

STURTON, S.D. (n.d.) FROM MISSION HOSPITAL TO CONCENTRATION CAMP. London: Marshall, Morgan, and Scott, Ltd.

UNSCHULD, P.U. (1982) MEDICINE IN CHINA, Vol. 1: A HISTORY OF IDEAS; VOL. II: A HISTORY OF PHARMACEUTICS, unublished mss.

WONG, K.C. and L.T. Wu (1936) HISTORY OF CHINESE MEDICINE (2nd ed.) SHANGHAI: National Quarantine Service; reprinted by A.M.S. Press, N.Y., 1973.

WU, L.T. (1959) PLAGUE FIGHTERS: THE AUTOBIOGRAPHY OF A MODERN CHINESE PHYSICIAN. Cambridge: W. Heffner and Sons.

YAO, H.Y. (1931) "The First Year of the Rural Health experiment in Ting Hsien, China," MILBANK MEMORIAL FUND QUARTERLY BULLETIN 9: 61-77, July.

YIP, K.C. (1982) "Health and Society in China: Public Health Education for the Community," SOCIAL SCIENCE AND MEDICINE 16: 1197-1205.

YOUNG, T.K. (1973) "A Conflict of Professions: The Medical Missionary in China, 1835-1890," BULLETIN OF THE HISTORY OF MEDICINE 47: 250-272.

YOUNG, T.K. (1975) "Sun Yat-Sen: From Medicine to Revolution," CANADIAN MEDICAL ASSOCIATION JOURNAL 112: 614-616, March 8.

CHAPTER 14

INSTITUTIONALIZATION OF FOLK MEDICINE:
THE MENTAL HEALTH PROFESSION AND CURANDERISMO

Mary Romero

Introduction

Pluralist ideology appeared in the U.S. health care system in the 1960's and was manifested in attempts to incorporate lower-class and ethnic culture into special programs and existing services. This paper investigates a specific example of how and why the mental health system incorporated Chicano folk medicine and health pracatices into existing programs. Two major sources of material were used to study how and why Chicano health practices were transformed from Chicano-dominated folk medicine settings to a setting dominated by mental health professionals. One source is the professional mental health literature that has recorded arguments for incorporating Chicano culture, especially Chicano health practices and practitioners. The body of literature also identifies Chicano mental health problems, documents the underutilization of mental health services in Chicano communities, and attempts to explain the discrepancy between need and underutilization of mental health services in Chicano communities, and attempts to explain the discrepancy between need and underutilization of services. The second source is a transcript produced from a tape recording of a mental health workshop on Mexican folk medicine, or **curanderismo**, held in northern Colorado (Endnote 1).

Before discussing how and why mental health professionals plan to incorporate Chicano culture into psychiatry and its therapeutic setting, a description of **curanderismo**, Chicano folk medicine, and **curanderos**, folk healers, is necessary to provide a basis for comparisons. The major aim of this section is to show how broad Chicano folk medicine and health practices are and how many different types of treatment, illnesses, and practitioners **curanderismo** includes.

CURANDERISMO IN THE COMMUNITY

Description of Curanderismo

Like other indigenous folk medicine, **curanderismo** defines health and illness, as well as diagnoses and treat illnesses, within a framework that focuses on the relationship between the spiritual, physical, and mental existence of the client. **Curanderismo** is a holistic approach to health care. As Welclew (1975: 146-147) pointed out: "Diagnosis is a dynamic

189

formulation of all the relevant information and observations derived from the client, his family and if necessary the supernatural. The diagnosis takes into account the client's history, social life, occupational experiences, appetite, sleep pattern, fatigue, facial expressions, body movements, coloring and other factors."

Folk healers, or **curanderos,** may specialize in particular treatments, but the approach to defining health and illness remains holistic. **Curanderos** range from herbalist to spiritualist healers. Their clients may be limited to family members or they may have hundreds of believers revering them as healing saints. The **curandero** may use a variety of treatments: messages, diets, rest, magic, supernatural rituals, consultation, prayers, and herbs.

Folk illness, as well as other recognized illnesses, was traditionally treated by the **curandero.** Descriptions of several folk illnesses found in the Southwest illustrate the broad range of etiology, symptoms, and treatment. **Mal ojo** resulted from a child's expressed or unexpressed admiration of an adult. The child experiences a radical physical or temperamental change. **Mal ojo** is treated by transferring water or salvia from the mouth of the admired adult to the child's mouth. **Mal de empacho** (emphacharse) is the bloating, loss of appetite, and abdominal pain found among young children resulting from complications in digesting bread and tortilla. It is treated by massaging the abdomen and the back with a raw egg. Fright or emotional shock may cause susto. The symptoms are insomnia, nightmares, depression, or general malaise. **Susto** is treated by administering various **remedios** and massages.

Utilization of Curanderismo

Traditional use of **curanderos** in Chicano communities varies through the Southwest. C. Martinez and Martin (1966) claimed about one-fifth of the Chicano population used **curanderismo** services. later Ayala (1972) estimated that sixty to eighty percent of the Chicano population utilized the services of a **curandero.** Studies conducted in Tucson (Rosenthal, Henderson, et al., 1969) and in Los Angeles (Edgerton, Karno, et al., 1970) found a decrease in the use of **curanderismo** services in Chicano communities. Discrepancies are difficult to resolve because of the "underground" nature of the **curandero's** services due to fear of harassment from police, tax agents, and the medical profession. Three accounts given by Chicano mental health directors, during the mental health worshop in Colorado, illustrate how **curanderos** were traditionally used in Southwestern barrios.

One presenter explained how his siter was treated by a **curandera** when he was young. After having gone to three physicians, his sister still was ill. She heard about a curandera from the "grapevine" and requested her services. The curandera cured the sister by administering a cleansing and a sweeping of **piedra de lumbre.**

190

A former clergyman gave two accounts of parishioners' use of curanderos. One parishioner had been suffering from a "very bad skin disorder" and "had to be bedridden at lengths of time." After the last rites were administered, a curandera was called to cure the woman. Several weeks later, the parishioner suffered from a bump on his neck which he claimed was caused from being **embrujado** (bewitched). He went to a curandera and asked for a **remedio.** The curandera placed herbs into boiling water and then soaked towels in the solution which were then placed on the man's back. He was cured in about four weeks.

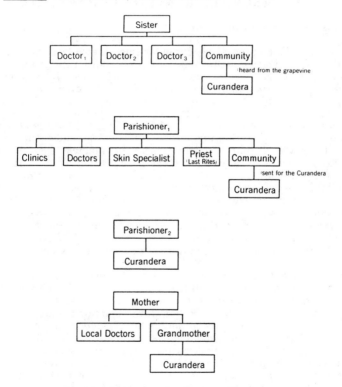

Community—local community sanctions the curandera.

Figure 1.   Accounts of Curanderismo in the Community

Figure 1 illustrates how curanderismo services were used in the Chicano community, as revealed in the above accounts. In three accounts (the Sister, Mother, and Parishioner) medical physicians were consulted first but failed to cure the individual. Members of the family or community recommended a curandera who later cured the person. Parishioner[2] appeared to have gone directly to the curandera. The curandera gained her sanction from the community in which she lived. Community control over the curandera was appropriate since community members received the services. The community did not have any more knowledge about how and why the curandera's rituals worked, but they vouched for her lifetime training, and offered proof of her powers. Frequently, community members did not pay for the services.

CURANDERISMO IN THE MENTAL HEALTH SYSTEM

Arguments for Incorporating Curanderismo

In order to justify incorporating curanderismo, the mental health professionals needed to address arguments against its institutionalization. One argument against the use of curanderismo was that it was practiced among first generation Mexican immigrants and therefore was not important to the larger Chicano population. Torrey (1969) argued that curanderos' techniques were crude and often harmful, yet they had to be left in their natural state to be effective. Willard (1980: 6) outlined the following reasons for leaving "contemporary Chicano/Mexicano folk medicine to contemporary Chicano/Mexicano folk": the medical system does not regard curanderismo as a real medical practice; curanderismo may be unsuccessful outside its settings; and indigenous practitioners would be submitted to bureaucratic administrative controls. Meyer, Quesada, et al. (1971) noted similar arguments based on the following differences between curanderos and psychiatrists: curanderos were more accessible and available (in terms of time and money); curanderos believed they had a supernatural gift; and curanderos had relatively few ethical problems because clients expected to be treated but not necessarily cured.

Numerous arguments for utilizing curandero's services in mental health clinics have appeared in the literature. First of all, curanderismo is defined as an essential part of the Chicano belief system and utilized by some members (Kiev, 1968; Rubel, 1964; Martinez and Martin, 1966). Therefore, the incorporation of curanderismo services can increase mental health consumers in Chicano communities (Endnote 2). Studies documenting the fact that Chicanos underutilize psychiatric services and utilize curanderos' services point out that the mental health system is competing with curanderos (Endnote 3). Therefore, it is in the mental health system's interest to monopolize mental health services by incorporating small businesses engaged in mental health services as special programs. Furthermore, mental health professionals have observed curanderos cure cases that had not responded to therapy or medication. thus, inclusion of a curandero might decrease the mental health professional's failure rate.

Another argument made for institutionalizing curanderismo was the curanderos and psychiatrists share similar professional characteristics. Both occupations represented training which placed the "healer" in an authoritarian position to his or her clients. Clients expected to be helped and believed in the power of the curer, and the believers were healed more frequently than non-believers. Curanderos and psychiatrists alike claim to know better than their clients what ails them and their affairs. In general, the treatment model used by curanderos and psychiatrists is the same: both view society as healthy and the client as in need of adjustment. Neither practitioner seeks to change the world. The possibility of an increase in state and federal funding provided an additional incentive to adopt the program. Kreisman (1975: 83) summarized the advantages of soliciting the curander's services in the mental health system as "positive effect on the treatment," "the increase in rapport and trust within a therapeutic alliance," and "the enlistment of family involvement and support." Positive research results on studies on utilization of curanderos in mental health programs (Nelson, 1971; Aguilar, 1972; Hamburger, 1978) has also provided support for incorporation of curanderismo services.

Institutionalizing Curanderismo

Two major strategies for incorporating curanderismo services were: (1) contracting for services of a curandera or curandero; and (2) bringing the concept within the mental health system. Mental health directors in Colorado advocated the second strategy, which consisted of incorporating curanderismo into the services offered by the mental health clinics.

Strategy #1 consisted of finding curanderos in the neighborhood and contracting out or referring to them. This involved hiring curanderos as consultants or contracting for services. A workshop presenter described an existing program, located in a state hospital, that utilized the contract system: "The curandero arrived early Wednesday afternoon and does his cures there and he doesn't charge anything but he comes in and does his cures and comes back a week later. He is not part of the regular staff." The staff at the hospital were dissatisfied with this method and wanted the curandero hired as a staff member. Another problem with contracting out for services had to do with the mental health professionals' resposibility for determining the credibility among curanderos. Torrey (1969: 370) noted the problem of selecting a curandero out of "many quacks, charlatans, hysterical personalities, schizophrenics, abortionists, and generally unstable personalities." The vital issue against strategy #1 appeared to be control over the curandero. This became clearer from the way stretegy #2 was implemented.

Stretegy #2 was defined by one presenter as "we bring the curanderismo concept into the Mental Health system and monitor that and have it be an important part of the system." This involved hiring a curandero as a staff member. Arguments for hiring a curandero were: (1) curanderos would be legally protected; (2) the curandero would be provided with clinical training; (3) the curandero would have a medical background; (4) clients would be protected from shysters; and (5) clients would be protected from wrong diagnoses and mishandled cures. The two positions proposed for the curandero were a clinician two (Endnote 4) and an "additional outreach worker." A clinician two position was regarded as beneficial because it minimized the cost, since the classification allowed the curander's labor to be used in a regular mental health clinic's functions. the curandero would work under the doctor's supervision, thereby providing medical coverage, and clinical training for the curandero as for any other clinician. This covered legal constraints involved in implementation. The curandero no longer independently worked as an expert on curanderismo, but only with permission and clearance from the physician.

A regular intake and treatment procedure would be utilized: after an evaluation by a clinician the client would see the regular therapist. Then the client would see a curandero if the case was defined as: (1) safe, (2) in the realm of curanderismo, and (3) only if the clinician's attempts were ineffective. The clinician remained above the curandero and in control. The cliniciam decided whether the curandero was capable of working with the client and whether the symptoms were under the curandero's specialty of curanderismo (Endnote 5). Curanderismo was only resorted to when drugs and psychotherapy had failed. One problem with this approach was that medical practitioners seldom admit to failure. Another problem with admitting cases was the general notion that: "there are people in the community that think they need a curandera but they might need psychotherapy or another type of therapy."

Figure 2 illustrates the intake and treatment procedure. The client did not go directly to the curandero for services. He was first evaluated by the clinician who then prescribed the kind of treatment. If the treatment failed, the doctor was called upon to identify the case as "curanderismo-related" and the doctor granted or denied permission to see the curandero.

The steps to the curandero within the mental health system are outlined by one of mental health directors curanderismo account. **Figure 3** illustrates the persons and agencies involved before a curandera's services were sought. The director encountered a boy while working at a psychiatric institute. The boy had lived off and on with his grandparents between his father's marriages; during the stay with his father the boy was abused. A social worker removed the boy from his grantparents' care based on the premise they were too old to care for the child. He was placed in a foster home where he deteriorated mentally and had to be placed in the state hospital. Later he was transferred to a detention home and then to the psychiatric institute where the director had worked. The boy's case history was found to be incorrectly documented. The director also discovered that the grandmother believed strongly in curanderismo. A curandera was called and worked with the boy for two weeks. The boy improved and was placed in a halfway house.

194

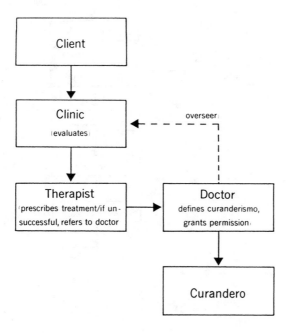

Figure 2. Procedure for Using a <u>Curandero</u>

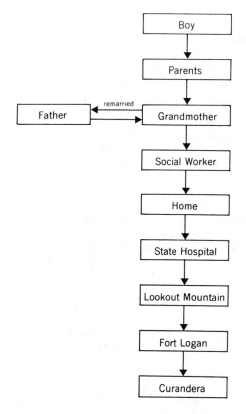

Figure 3. Account of Using the Curandera in
the Mental Health System

Consequences of Incorporating Curanderismo

What happened to curanderismo when taken out of its traditional setting into the mental health system's program? First of all curanderismo did not separate the spiritual, physicial, and mental parts of man. Curanderismo's framework addressed man as a whole person, while the scientific framework divided the three areas and dealt with each as an entity. The mental health system incorpated curanderismo in terms of its application to the minds of Chicanos. However, accounts of curanderismo were not restricted to mental health problems or a hex; the sister, mother, and one of the parishioners were suffering from physical ailments.

Prior to the redefining of curanderismo, the curandero attends to all spiritual, physical, and mental problems. Incorporation of curanderismo into the mental health system denied the use of a holistic approach because modern medical practitioners had already divided the territory into specialties. Hence the mental health staff became engaged in classifying "curanderismo-related things." These things seem to have been symptoms, but they were never really identified. Rather, a dichotomy was proposed between all the "things" cured by drugs and psychotherapy and all those that were not. "Curanderismo-related things" became a residue category for dumping the mental health system's failures.

In dealing with an indigenous psychology, the mental health system's conceptual machinery was adapted to accept only one legitimate reality. Therefore, the indigenous psychology was defined as illegitimate or redefined to fit into the mental health system's conceptual framework. Eventually, the distinctions were blurred and the indigeous psychology was defined as operating with the same conceptual machinery. The indigenous psychology did not gain credibility for having its own conceptual machinery. Translation from one reality to the other resulted in the addition, elimination, or modification of the indigenous psychology where the two conceptual frameworks were incompatible. Under the mental health setting, curanderismo became defined as presiding over a realm of symptoms that were untouched by other psychological treatments. It was also defined as incompetent in treating all other spiritual, physical, and mental problems.

There were differences between using the curandero in a mental health setting (as illustrated in **Figure 2**) and in the community (illustrated in **Figure 1**). In the community, the curandera maintained her autonomy and was the expert on curanderismo. In contrast, the procedure for using a curandera in the mental health system's setting denied the curandera professional authority. Her specialty was redefined and narrowed in order not to infringe upon traditional mental health services. Her duties and responsibilities were broadened to include a traditional mental health worker job description. Her authority in the field of curanderismo was questioned by the therapists' evaluations and the physician's prior approval of her cases. By assigning the curandera other mental health workers' tasks, her function was diffused. Therefore, in order to deny the curandera professional authoritya, curanderismo was not recognized as a legitimate field of knowledge and skill and the curandera's role was diffused.

There was also a difference for the client receiving the curandera's services in a mental health clinic. To acquire the services of a curandera in the community, the potential client negotiated directly with the curandera. The client defined his needs or problems. His symptoms were identified by the curandera and then treated. For instance, in the accounts of curanderismo, the mother, sister, and two parishioners were not labeled schizophrenic, paranoid, psychotic, neurotic, etc. Even when the patient's problems were not strictly physical ailments, the curandero approached them as real symptoms. The patient was provided the means to get well and to redeem himself without having to condemn his actions. The patient did not have to descend into his unconscious self and redefine his past as repressive and sick. Blame and shame were removed by giving the patient a clean slate; and after a cleansing had been performed, he accepted full responsibility for all that followed. The client did not undergo a labeling process or acquire a mental health record, nor was the client charged money by the curandera.

The client had to undergo several steps before reaching the curandera in the mental health clinic. First of all, the therapist evaluated where the client fell in the traditional mental health model. The patient was labeled in terms of a particular personality or psychological disorder. A mental health chart was begun. The therapists determined the required treatment, basing their decision on the "scientific" mental health understanding of how life operates. Therefore, patients using curanderismo services within the mental health system had several labels attached to them by the time they reached a curandero. Rituals became an extension of playing out the patient's "abnormal reality." The patient's symptoms were no longer respected or validated. If the patient believed that only curanderismo would cure him, curanderismo was all that would work. Curanderismo's practicality and workability were therefore based totally on belief by others.

Another important issue in the "double bind" situation created for Chicanos by the intake and treatment procedure for obtaining a curandero's services. The double bind exists when no matter what a person does, "he or she can't win," and it resulted from the contradictions embedded in deception (Bateson, Jackson, et al., 1956). The mental health staff was preparing to create a setting for a particualr type of client. If person X is found, he or she would be looking for a curandero and suffering from malojo, susto, or guilt.

At this point, the mental health staff would decide what is "really" the problem and provide the necessary treatment. If the traditional mental health treatment fails, the client can be treated by the curandero. This step was defined as successful because the client believed in it, not because this type of treatment was "really" needed. Throughout the entire process, the mental health staff controlled reality. They decided what existed and in doing so they also decided what was imagined, simply a belief, or mental illness.

The mental health staff's power was maintained through its prerogative to decide when to accept a particular phenomenon. The client assumed the mental health system's acceptance of curanderismo by housing a curandero. Hence the client revealed symptoms to the therapists during the evaluation and was subjected to the labeling process. Had the client known the modern medical paradigm was being used, appropriate terms would have been selected and certain descriptions would have been withheld. The client responded correctly to the setting presented, but another set of norms was used for evaluation.

Summary

In summary, the consequences or effects appeared to be the following: Chicanos had to be labeled by the dominant group as mentally ill in order to gain access to the curandero; the community no longer sanctioned the curandero; the curandero lost autonomy and expertise on curanderismo; the mental health profession redefined curanderismo; and false impressions about the domain were created to bring the Chicano community to the institution.

ENDNOTES

1. Presenters at the workshop consisted of four mental health disorders and a curandera. One of the directors had been a former mental health worker. All of the directors had served as mental health team leaders in Colorado. One director was a former priest. The curandera was a secretary at a mental health clinic. All of the presenters were Chicanos, and the curanderea, a Chicana.

2. A major argument for incorporating Chicano culture into mental health services is based on the need to consider the patient's cultural frame of reference (Gaitz and Scott, 1974; Kreisman, 1975; Ramirez-Margado, 1975; M. Martinez, 1979). C. Martinez and Martin (1966) noted that patients' folk beliefs about etiology, symptomatology, and modes of treatment affect their expectations and coopeation in therapy. Secondly, studies have consistently shown that an increase in bilingual and bicultural staff in mental health programs leads to an increase in Chicano clients (Karno and Morales, 1971; Phillipus, 1971; Padilla and Ruiz, 1973; Padilla, Ruiz, et al., 1975; Bloom, 1975; Flores, 1978; Acosta, 1979).

3. Common explanations for the discrepancy between Chicano mental health problems and the underutilization of mental health centers include the following: (1) Chicano disorders are less visible because they are expressed in criminal behavior, narcotics addiction, and alcoholism; (2) Chicanos are more tolerant of deviant behavior and hence less likely to seek professional help; (3) Chicanos are too proud to seek assistance; (4) clinics and hospitals do not operate to fulfill Chicano needs; (5) other services in the community are utilized, such as family, priests, family physicians; (6) Chicanos frequently return to Mexico; (7) "they are afraid to get help because the 'establishment' threatens the security of their presence in the United States" (Karno, 1966: 234); (8) a majority speak Spanish; and (9) "their culture provides an etiology, diagnosis preventive measures, and regimen of healing" (Rubel, 1964: 268).

4. The mental health classification of clinician workers referred to here was based on the allocation of responsibility. A clinician three works independently and was not under supervision. The job description included on-call duty. A clinician worked in co-therapy and was under supervision. No on-call duty was required. A clinician one position had the most supervision. These persons did not handle individual cases.

5. It was interesting to notice that the administrators were not identifying symptoms, but rather were defining all those cases not successfully treated by modern medicine as curanderismo-related.

REFERENCES

ACOSTA, FRANK X. (1979) "Barriers Between Mental Health Services and Mexican American Examination of a Paradox," AMERICAN JOURNAL OF COMMUNITY PSYCHOLOGY 7(5): 503-520.

AGUILAR, IGNACIO (1972) "Initial Contacts with Mexican American Families," SOCIAL WORK 17: 66-70.

AYALA, P. (1972) "Curanderismo," Paper presented to the staff of the Pelsin Mental Health Center, Chicago.

BATESON, GREGORY et al. (1956) "Toward a Theory of Schizophrenia," BEHAVIORAL SCIENCE 1: 251-264.

BLOOM, B.L. (1975) CHANGING PATTERNS OF PSYCHIATRIC CARE. N.Y.: Human Sciences Press.

EDGARTON, B.B., KARNO, M., and FERNANDEZ, I. (1970) "Curanderismo in the Metropolis," AMERICAN JOURNAL OF PSYCHOTHERAPY 24: 124-134.

FLORES, JOSE LUIS (1978) "The Utilization of a Community Mental Health Service by Mexican Americans," INTERNATIONAL JOURNAL SOCIAL PSYCHIATRY 24: 271-275.

GAITZ, CHARLES M., and JUDITH SCOTT (1974) "Mental Health of Mexican-Americans: Do Ethnic Factors Make a Difference?" GERIATRICS 29(11): 103.

HAMBURGER, SONIA (1978) "Profile of Curanderos: A Study of Mexican Folk Practitioners," INTERNATIONAL JOURNAL OF SOCIAL PSYCHIATRY 24: 19-25.

KARNO, M. (1966) "The Enigma of Ethnicity in a Psychiatric Clinic," ARCHIVES OF GENERAL PSYCHIATRY 14: 516-520.

KARNO, M., and A. MORALES (1971) "A Community Mental Health Service for Mexican-Americans in a Metropolis," pp. 281-285 in N.N. Wagner and M.J. Haug (eds.), CHICANOS. St. Louis: The C.V. Mosby Co.

KIEV, ARI (1968) CURANDERISMO: MEXICAN AMERICAN FOLK PSYCHIATRY. N.Y.: Free Press.

KREISMAN, JEROLD J. (1975) "The Curandero's Apprentice: A Therapeutic Integration of Folk and Medical Healing," AMERICAN JOURNAL OF PSYCHIATRY 132(1): 81-83.

MARTINEZ, C., and H.W. Martin (1966) "Folk Diseases Among Urban Mexican Americans," JOURNAL OF AMERICAN MEDICAL ASSOCIATION 194: 161-164.

MARTINEZ, MARIA Z. (1979) "Family Policy for Mexican Americans and Their Aged," URBAN SOCIAL CHANGE REVIEW 12(2): 16-19.

MEYER, GEORGE G. et al. (1971) "Curanderos and Psychiatrists and Professional Healers," Paper presented in Mexico City at the Fifth World Congress of Psychiatry.

NELSON, HARRY (1971) "Curandero: Bridge Across a Culture Gap," LOS ANGELES TIMES, April 16, p. 3.

PADILLA, A.M., and R.A. Ruiz (1973) "Latino Mental Health," A Review of Literature. Washington, D.C.: U.S. Government Printing Office.

PADILLA, A.M., R.A. RUIZ, and R. ALVAREZ. (1975) "Community Mental Health Services for the Spanish-Speaking/Surnamed Population," AMERICAN PSYCHOLOGIST 30: 892-905.

PHILLIPUS, M.J. (1971) "Successful and Unsuccessful Approaches to Mental Health Services for an Urban Hispano-American Population," JOURNAL OF PUBLIC HEALTH 61: 820-830.

ROSENTHAL, T.L. et al. (1969) "Social Strata and Perception of Magical and Folk-Medical Child Care," JOURNAL OF SOCIAL PSYCHOLOGY 77: 3-13.

WELCLEW, ROBERT V. (1975) "Nature, Prevalence, and Level of Awareness of Curanderismo and Some of Its Implications for Community Health," COMMUNITY MENTAL HEALTH JOURNAL 11(2): 145-154.

WILLARD, WILLIAM (1980) "Indigenous Practitioner," Paper presented at the 1980 Annual Western Social Science Conference.

CHAPTER 15

DE-WESTERNIZING HEALTH PLANNING AND DELIVERY
THROUGH CONSUMER PARTICIPATION:
Some Lessons From Chile and Tanzania

Claudio Schuftan

"We are in the society of the teacher-judge, the doctor-judge, the educa-tor-judge, the 'social worker'-judge; it is on them that the universal reign of the normative is based; and each individual wherever he may find himself, subjects to it his body, his gestures, his behaviour, his aptitudes, his achievements."

Michel Foucault

When talking about de-Westernization from the political point of view, as we intend to do here, we will be actually talking about Democratization and Decentralization movements in the health sector. To understand why this de-Westernization process seems to be urgently needed in our Western societies, we have to begin by looking back into the history of recent so-called Western medicine.

Understanding the Roots of the Problem

The Western approach to health maintenance and delivery departs from the one-sided and elitest assumption that "Doctors know best"; either as individuals or as leaders or members of a health team. One can, there-fore, certainly expect some of the physicians' ideological biases to be mirrored in the health related policies of a country (**Endnote I**).

It is to no surprise, then, that Western health planning is based on a top-to--bottom decision-making process in which the "experts'" interpretation of the surrounding reality prevails, although they themselves are outsiders to the problems considered. All this situation has created an unhealthy dependence of the health sector on the professionals and the health estab-lishment has definitively had a role in generating this dependence (**Refer-ence 1**).

For one of the authors that has explored this topic deeply, the above dependence is created by the capitalist mode of production and consump-tion: "Medical bureaucracies are not the generators, but the administrators of these dependencies. Social relations determine the type of organization of medicine to be chosen and the type of technology to be used. Technology reinforces the already existing division of labor. In the health team the hierarchy observed is the following: (a) physicians (upper-middle class extraction); (b) nurses (lower middle class); and (c) attendants, auxiliaries and service-workers (working class extraction). Responsibilities in the team are primarily due to the class background and sex roles of the members and only secondarily to their technological knowledge. Education and training is the mere legitimation of that class and sex hierarchical distribution of power and responsibilities. This class structure and hierarchy militates against the provision of comprehensive medical care. A strategy for better care requires, not the authoritarian (vertical), but the collaborative (horizontal) distribution of responsibilities, including the patient. Further, it should be pointed out that since the health industry is administered but not controlled by the medical profession, the main conflict in the health sector is nothing but replicating the conflict in the overall social system, and that conflict is not primarily between the providers and the consumers. Therefore, the deprofessionalization of medicine and its democratization are not possible within our class-structured society" (**Reference 2**).

From this perspective, one can accurately say that in modern times the types of health services have continuously changed and been redefined according to the needs of the capitalist mode of production. The medical profession is a guardian of the definition of these bourgeois values, but not its ultimate definer (**Reference 2**).

We will now consider the case of Chile. Unless otherwise stated, data for the Chilean case are from my own experience there and from References 9 and 10. Data for the Tanzania case are from Reference 11. A separate Appendix that reviews, both, the Tanzanian and Chilean case studies in depth is available from the author on request. Chile is no exception to the history of a hierarchical organization of the health system overall although as early as 1952 a National health Service was created that intended and pretty much succeeded to cover up to 70% of the population. Nevertheless, the priorities in the health sector very closely followed the priorities of health services in the developed countries with an emphasis in specialized, hospital-based, urban, technologically-- intensive, curative and personal health services. National health expenditures, despite the creation of the NHS, continued to be biased towards the upper classes that consumed a fee-for-service medicine. This maldistribution clearly followed the distribution of economic and political power.

In Tanzania, services were provided first by the German (1891) and then by the British (1923) colonial governments. These services were almost exclusively urban and also followed classical western patterns with an urban hospital-based medicine. This trend was not changed in the first years of independence. The majority of the population was, therefore, **not** covered by Western medicine and continued to make use of traditional medicine.

Now, looking at the situation from the consumers' side, it is interesting to note that societies most often complacently accept this medically proposed resource allocation mix for health services. While this may provide a steady-state, it also represents a set of implicit priorities which, while lending stability, may well be blinding to the potential benefits of resource allocation to other more pressing needs. Without explicit popular pressures to alter confortable implicit priorities, resource reallocation in the production of health will occur slowly if at all (**Reference 3**).

In Chile, these pressures came in 1970 when Salvador Allende took the presidency with only 35% of the votes of the electorate. The United Popular parties had come to power with a basic plan of government that included important socializing elements in the health front and that called for restructuring priorities towards democratization and decentralization of the NHS and the consolidation of all government health plans under a new roof, the Servicio Unico. Concientization of the consumers along these lines had already occurred since the beginning of the presidential campaign in 1969 and continued throughout 1973.

In Tanzania, it was not until 1967 (The Arusha Declaration) that health was declared a priority area in the overall rural development programs. Preventive, as well as, primary curative health programs were incorporated to annual development plans. It was only by actively involving the community in these pgorams that the authorities were able to maximize the effects of meager health resources. (It is expected that the community gets involved in projects as early as the planning stages and then very heavily in the implementation of programs).

The question that inevitably comes to our minds following this brief analysis is whether all what we have said so far means that the socialist countries solved the problems we described for Western medicine. The answer is a partial **no**. Socialist societies also have full fledged bureaucracies as the controllers of social activities. These bureaucracies---including the medical bureaucracies---are not the primary controllers and planners of this social activity, but are subservient to a larger authority, the political party. When the accumulation of capital became a primary goal in those socialist countries they used their political control not to decentralize and democratize services but to optimize control by increasing centralization and hierarchisation. The party and its bureaucracies determined the replication of similar, although not identical, class relations to those in Western societies. Although there is a considerable overlapping of membership among party and bureaucracy, still the bureaucrat and technocrat are both dependent on the political party. The democratization of the former would require the democratization of the latter. In summary, one might say that the socialization of the means of production is a necessary but not sufficient condition for its democratization. The political centralization of power can bring about a reappearance of class relations (**Reference 2; Endnote II**).

Let us now explore the two basic components of de-Westernization and the experiences Chile and Tanzania had in implementing them.

The Participation Issue

Participation is not immediately and automatically exercised by people when the opportunity is offered to them, especially in rural areas. Peoples' expectations to fulfill their felt needs have to rise objectively in order for them to participate and offer their collaboration.

The example of Chile's attempt to democratize the health structure during the Frei government is illustrative to this point. Already during his administration (1964-1970), Community Health Councils had been created as advisory bodies to the direction of health institutioins. Most probably because of their limited potential impact, in an advisory capacity, these Councils never became very successful. They were perceived by the working class as coopting mechanisms that gave them a "feeling of participation," but no power of decision.

The question of how to create viable alternatives for peoples' expectations, that suit both, national leaders and villagers, remains probably the most important issue for future development in this area (**Reference 4; Endnote III**).

The first principle of community organization and participation is to start with people as they are and where they are. If one wishes to help a community improve its health, one must learn to think like the people of that community and understand their habits. Questions like: How does a human community accomplish its; business? What keeps it in its course? Howe does it see and solve its problems? How does it perceive and receive efforts from the outside or the inside to improve its health? must be addressed. Vast stores of information about measures useful in solving health problems are actually found within the community. It is in the public part of public health that we are the weakest (**Reference 5; Endnote IV**).

The question, then, arises: can government schemes alone do anything to help villagers to fulfill their own health care requirements? The planners' skills and wisdom are most often not very relevant to local village--level problems: "What is required are people in each village who know something about the environmental health care needs of their fellow villagers: such people would come from the village and remain part of its day to day functioning. There is no way to put the large number of people needed for such work on ministerial payrolls; therefore, they must continue to make their livelihood from within the village itself. Most ministries are not only incapable of giving the kind of support needed at the village level, but are themselves actually destructive of the possibilities of self-reliant village development" (**Reference 4**).

In rural Tanzania, most of the population has been relocated into Ujamaa Villages, which group 100-500 families working on a communal basis. In this context, mass mobilization is used as a deliberate political tool to raise social conciousness of health as the people's responsibility. The aim is to develop people's projects rather than impose projects on the people. Most development projects in Tanzania include an element of self-help. Thus, for instance, it is expected that the construction of health centers is done on a self-help basis. Also, in the last few years, impetus for improved environmental health services in the rural areas has probably been developed through government-encouraged community self-help schemes. So far, people have been more willing to participate in the implementation of projects than they have helped to plan.

Allende committed himself to real democratization not only of the health sector, but also of other areas of the economy. Democratization was then a result of popular and community pressures plus the commitment of the ruling political parties to implement it. The government encouraged worker and consumer control over health policy in neighborhood health centers and hospitals (in which the author participated), but avoided compulsory measures to implement this action. A first important setp was to work to institutionalize the principle of free medical care in all hospitals and emergency services. The government tried to increase inpatient and ambulatory services in rural provinces and even sponsored a "health train" (in which I also served) that toured the southern provinces, treating over 30,000 people.

Decentralization

Better coverage of the population with basic health services needs to be achieved through a set of deliberate policies that place value on the health of all citizens. In countries with limited resources, this will necessarily mean a redistribution of emphasis towards the traditionally more deprived areas, often those that do not get any health coverage at all. The latter, definitively means more emphasis on the provision of decentralized primary health care services. It also means getting **away** from medical specialization, closed urban hospital-care, and intensive and curative, highly personal, health services.

This is bound to hurt the feelings of a number of the involved professionals, and therefore, calls for the training of new intermediate health personnel, strongly attached to the areas where they are going to be working. Of

207

course, one important added requirement for this new decentralized approach to work more efficiently, is the delegation of authority to more local decision-making bodies.

The Tanzanian Ujamaa Village Policy, indirectly contributed to the decentralization efforts in health since development of health services was incorporated into overall rural development strategies. The expansion of village health posts, rural dispensaries and rural health centers have received clear priority over the expansion of hospitals, as well as, the training of village medical helpers, MCH aides, health auxiliaries, rural medical aides and medical assistants.

In Chile, after 1970, the delivery of ambulatory health care and preventive services to marginal urban and rural areas also became a higher priority over hospital-centered activities. More resources and more physicians' hours were allocated to these activities. Physicians entering their NHS career were supposed to serve a three year rural service term. The milk distribution program was also significantly expanded to cover the needs of the more peripheral beneficiaries. New support staff was also actively trained and a new decentralized regionalization of the NHS structure was enforced.

Steps Towards De-Westernization

Solving the existing health problems is not primarily a technological task or challenge. It is importantly an ideological problem in which the challange is to offer the services objectively needed. But the latter depend on a number of different perceptions of reality about the most pressing health problems in a given community. To provide the needed health services, this incongruency and the contradictions it creates have to be resolved. Since the process of de-Westernization of health planning and delivery is necessarily political, de-Westernization efforts have to create instances that allow the beneficiaries of health services to give their inputs and views of reality, from their perspective, before decisions are made. In this context, de-Westernization is nothing but the more logic reaction to reverting alienation in the health sector.

In order to attain health, the people must change their way of living, not just "buy more medicine"; but lifestyles are deeply rooted in the way in which society operates economically, politically and culturally. Therefore, a change in lifestyle means profound changes in all three of these parameters (**Reference 1**).

The greatest potential, then, for improving the health of the majorities, is **not** primarily through changes in the behavior of individuals, but primarily through changes in the patterns of control, structures and behavior of the economic and political system of a country. The latter could lead to the former, but the reverse is not possible (**Reference 2**). Popular participation, it seems, can become real only in nations that have organized themselves in keeping with the needs of the whole of the population (**Reference 4**). This is probably demonstrated by the fact that the countries that started the process of national change (in health) by a political process have so far shown a clear advantage in speed and enhance (**Reference 6**). Both countries here considered were (or are) deeply involved, at the time, in building a socialist society. Macroeconomic changes were, or have been, in the forefront of their strategies. The new health strategies were, therefore, only part of a mosaic of profound changes in the patterns of social and political control in the country as a whole.

De-Westernization efforts, to be successful, have to simultaneously attack two fronts. One has to do with (A): enhancing all positive trends and currents that lead to a more participatory health planning and delivery system, and the other calls for, (B) decisively acting on the factors that oppose or put brakes on such an effort. An example of the risks of **not** attacking both fronts was seen in Chile, where the Unidad Popular was successful in mobilizing the poor to identify their own health needs, but was much less successful in compelling the medical profession to serve basic rather than profitable needs.

In the end, the positive trends will, most probably, only be actively persued by governments politically committed to overcome the inequalities of capitalism.

A. Several of the areas that need to be attacked simultaneously in this "positive trends" front are: **Community organization and participation in overall local improvements:** This participation, in the case of health, has to be at several levels.

(1) Grass roots (the community itself)---Here is where the major emphasis is needed. Work should be channelled through the local natural leaders, creating awareness and raising conciousness to stimulate real involvement of the people. Also, at this level, the training of local health promoters can be a positive step. The same is true for popularizing health education, in order to elicit participation and responsibility in health related matters; conventional and non-conventional educational means should be used to this end. The challenge is to bring people from a state of self-interest to the crystallization of self-help initiatives.

An interesting experience was seen in Chile during the Allende Government; a series of specially prepared educational comic-books and cartoons were distributed widely, many of them created around important health messages, although often used as vehicles for political education of the masses. The language was kept very simple and the popular acceptance was great.

In terms of health education, Tanzanians use a "campaign" approach to insure that villagers are continually supplied with reading material so they do not relapse into illiteracy. Villagers get information on the symptoms and prevention of common diseases. Radio broadcasts, magazines, newspapers, booklets and posters are used to effectively disseminate health information.

Active participation of peasants in agrarian reform activities and institutions, and participation of urban workers in neighborhood councils, in Chile and the participation of of peasants in the running of the Ujaama villages in Tanzania are other examples of new active participation opportunities created by the political processes in both countries.

(2) Other local levels: Local organized labor and local units of political parties and, in general, any other living organizations of the community should also have a mechanism to express themselves in terms of their reactions and priorities towards health programs.

It was a standard procedure, in Chile, to have labor representatives in the newly created local health councils discussing local health priorities and problems; local school representatives, as well as, representatives of womens' groups also participated representing the beneficiaries.

On the other hand, health issues very often came up in party discussions (be it the Unidad Popular parties in Chilea or TANU in Tanzania) and general policies were explored. Since there is frequently a cross-participation of members in the community and political organizations these policies often found their way to final implementation when concensus was reached.

(3) Regional and provincial Health councils: This level definitely requires greater political awareness and education of its active members, given the executive power these councils should have. Their main task is to bring to the central levels the feelings and demands of the beneficiaries of the health services and on the other hand, they discuss and pass down to the implementation levels and supervise new policies.

These higher level councils were also created and functioned in the Chilean case. They actually became the cornerstone of decentralized decision--making at the NHS. Frictions were frequent at this level since the physicians represented in these councils often vehemently objected to community perceived priorities. Many good initiatives were filibustered and delayed in this final process. No clear guidelines existed to overcome these kinds of impasses, this being one of the unforeseen weaknesses of the democratization process in Chile.

In principle, this structure also exists in Tanzania. One of its peculiarities is that it is deeply interwoven with the party decision-making structure, but it still is strictly regional at this stage. Potential conflicts are probably more easily resolved, given the clear authority of TANU over policy issues. This political clout was never achieved in the Chilean context.

Overall Democratization and Decentralization of the Health Bureaucracy is a must, so that the organized community and the health service workers can really participate in the planning of new policies and have some kind of control over the process. An advisory role alone is not enough as should be clear from the Chilean experience cited earlier. Since for most of the underdeveloped countries it will be impossible to train enough physicians in the decades to come, to cope with the present and future health delivery needs, one of the highest priorities in the democratization process is a decisive move towards the training of intermediate health personnel in order to be able to staff new health care facilities in deprived areas. The Tanzanian experience reviewed is illustrative in this respect.

Changes Towards a more Equitable Distribution of Income and Health Services in the Country—these changes are also a must. Participation alone will **not** solve the health problems of the poor. In general terms, income redistribution could be achieved through one or several of the following deliberate mechanisms (**Reference 7**).

a. Differential salary adjustments following inflation (proportionately higher raises for lower income groups).
b. Progressive taxation system on income and properly.
c. Land reform.
d. Transfer of technology and credit discrimination towards small enter-prises.
e. Other (vocational and technical education, nationalization of natural resources and financial institutioins, etc.).

In terms of more equitable distribution of health services, four interconnected interventions should be considered (**Reference 6**).

a. More equitable reallocation of health resources between all segments of population.
b. Introduction of programs of self-reliance and self-help (urban and rural).
c. Allocation of a larger percentage of the health budget to the development of peripheral primary health care services.
d. Redesigning of the overall health services to support primary health care as a priority in rural and periurban areas (**Endnote V**).

These overall and specific measures, here listed, were almost all implemented both in Chile and in Tanzania.

A new Doctor-Patient Relations (Reference 8)—Although this is difficult to impose by decree, some efforts towards this end have to be made. A change of attitudes towards patients should occur, both, at an individual and a collective level. At the individual level, reducing the "distance" between doctor (or health provider) and patient is the final goal; also, the patients should be encouraged to gain more "control" over their own bodies as part of this process. At the collective level, the whole health team needs to become more involved in community affairs and problems to, hopefully, share health priorities and felt needs with the community that can be translated into specific effective demands. Only if this process is successful, and it will take quite revolutionary changes to get there, will "the" local doctor or clinic become "our" doctor or clinic.

Efforts in this direction were only sporadically visible in Chile given the opposition of most physicians to the whole concept of democratization of the NHS and given the short time span into which the Chilean experience was telescoped (1970-1973). At the collective level, perhaps more was achieved with the incorporation of beneficiaries into health team activities through their participation in the local councils.

The Tranzanian health delivery system has been much more responsive to this issue of creating new relations with the patients at a more egalitarian level. This primarily because the health providers are usually chosen from the community itself, therefore, having more "in common" with the beneficiaries they serve. Not infrequently do the health team members also participate in other community and/or political activities in the village.

(B). As for the factors that oppose a more participatory health planning and delivery system, important sources of conflict can be expected in the de-Westernization process in any country. Often it is professional organizations that respond resisting the changes; in our case, mainly the medical establishment. The Chilean experience is particularly illustrative of this potentially very powerful burden to the implementation of needed reforms.

In 1972, the Chilean Medical Associatioan began a vigorous campaign against the Unidad Popular Government. Only 30% of the profession continued to support Allende's goals. In October, 1972, and August, 1973, doctors' strikes were organized by the Medical Association. Other health workers did not support the stoppage. Health services continued to function through the combined efforts of community residents, non- and paraprofessionals and a minority of pro-government physicians (myself included). At this time physicians not only revolted because they had allegedly technical objections to the democratization process in the health sector, but because the whole national process towards socialism threatened their interests. Their action certainly helped lay the ground work for military dictatorship.

Tanzania, with a proportionately much smaller number of physicians (around 500 compared to more or less 5,000 in Chile, in 1973) did not have this particualr problem, although some open objections to the new policies were voiced by hospital-based physicians.

But there are also other forces opposed to the de-Westernization process of medicine, if sometimes acting indirectly. Without going into any detail, I want, even at least to mention one, briefly. That is the expanding trend in the use of Western-type medications and medical technology around the world. This trend is mainly the result of the aggressive marketing attitudes of transnational pharmaceutical houses and other medical technology corporations in the Third World. Perhaps the most dramatic example of this is the Westernizing trend in infant feeding that is being observed in Africa, Asia, and Latin America as a result of aggressive promotion of infant formulas and bottle feeding done by these companies. The whole system is often built on heavily influencing physicians and other health personnel through the use of general advertising, the handing out of free samples and generous gifts and through the use of other "incentives."

As I said earlier, if de-Westernization is to succeed, **active** and decisive measure have to be taken to counter the internal opposing forces as they arise. Political steps will almost always be needed to do this successfully. In terms of effectively opposing organized resistance from within the country, I tend to agree with what Waitzkin said in his paper (**Reference 9**). The whole de-Westernization process has to be implemented quickly, letting the community representatives take **early control** of the democratization process and of the newly created structures. The pressures from without, that stand in the way of de-Westernization will also need to be neutralized early and decisively, i.e., letting the government take into its hands the purchase and distribution of drugs and baby foods (**Endnote VI**).

Finally, let me emphasize that it is difficult to generalize about measures or steps towards de-Westernization from the political point of view. Each country is different and each country can only go so fast as its political conjuncture will allow at the time the decisions are made to democratize and decentralize their health services. No imported "prescriptions" will be valid or applicable to the local reality. Overall health cannot improve as an "island" without an overall improvement in the socioeconomic conditions of the poor majority.

213

ENDNOTES

1. "Industrailization of medicine has actually lead to the creation of a corps of engineers, the medical profession. Because of their technical expertise, physicians have come to believe that professional dominance over health policies is justified. The medical profession has, therefore, a monopolistic power of definition of what is health and what method of care may be publically funded. This fact is bound to create conflict between the medical profession, the medical care system and the consumers." (Illich, I., "Medical Nemesis: The Expropriation of Health," Caller and Boyars, London, 1975). Carrying the latter to an extreme, for example, some authors contend that in Western medicine the physicians' skills are often put to non-medical purposes. In such specialties as, say, plastic surgery, practices aim not at the patients' health but rather at satisfying his, albeit in some cases reasonnable, wishes. These are acts not of medicine but of gratification: for consumers, not patients. (Leon Kass, as cited by George Will, WASHINGTON POST, July 9, 1978).

Illich's whole thesis of de-Westernizing medicine seems to "leak" because he does not spell out his thoughts causally and he refuses to discuss real remedies. (Joseph Lella, see Reference 1). Therefore, no more attention is given to his approach to de-Westernization in this paper.

2. The experience of Cuba, at present, is interesting to note at this point. After their initial phase of de-Westernizing medicine infectious diseases became a secondary problem in Cuba, in terms of patient consultations. Now, more grass-root desires have arisen for higher technology medicine. Therefore, a shift in policy towards the more traditional practice of doctor-centered responsibility for individual patients has occurred. (For more details see Guttmacher, S. and Danielson, R. "Changes in Cuban Health Care: An Argument Against Technological Pessimism," INTERNATIONAL JOURNAL OF HEALTH SERVICES, 7(3), 1977).

3. "The relationship between rural hopelessness and health is a complex one. Ill health adds to hopelessness, but its removal does not mean there is hope...The problem and the priority have to be the total rural hopelessness complex and not just ill health. We are only slowly beginning to understand that people themselves are aware that health may have a low ranking among the starting points for change." (See K. Newell, Reference 5).

4. People basically "do for themselves" with regard to their own health requirements, this meaning a departure from the accepted technological approach to health. Villagers have at least the potential, if not the capacity, for organizing their own lives to produce sufficient skills to do most of what is required to create a healthy environment. (O. Gish, see Reference 4).

5. These components represent possible different levels or approaches to de-Westernization in the health sector. Each country should choose its priorities starting, whenever possible, from the people's felt needs, trying to compatibilize them with the technical measures that make best sense in each case.

6. Algeria, Guinea and New Guinea, for instance, have drastically reduced their imports of infant formulas and have made these products available only by prescription.

REFERENCES

1. LELLA, J. (1977) "Critical Analysis of Illich's Impact Upon the Medical Profession," ABSAME NEWSLETTER, Association of Behavioral Science and Medical Education. VII(4), September.

2. NAVARRO, V. (1975) "The Industrailization of Fetishism or the Fetishism of Industrialization: A Critique of Ivan Illich," SOCIAL SCIENCE AND MEDICINE. IX: 351-363.

3. DUNLOP, D. and CALDWELL, H. (1977) "Priority of Determination for the Provision of Health Services: An Economic and Social Analysis," SOCIAL SCIENCE AND MEDICINE. XI: 471-475.

4. GISH, O. (1975) "Planning the Health Sector: The Tanzanian Experience." N.Y.: Holmes and Meier Publ.

5. PAUL, B. (ed.) (1955) "Health, Culture and Community: Case Studies of Public Reactions to Health Programs." N.Y.: Russell Sage Foundation.

6. NEWELL, K. (ed.) (1975) "Health by the People," W.H.O.: Geneva.

7. SCHUFTAN, C. (1978) "Household Purchasing-Power Deficit: A More Operational Indicator to Express Malnutrition," accepted for publication in ECOLOGY OF FOOD AND NUTRITION.

8. For an excellent review of this topic, see FANON, F. "Medicine and Colonialism," Chapter 4 in "Studies in a Dying Colonialism," MONTHLY REVIEW PRESS, N.Y., 1965.

9. WAITZKIN, H. and MODELL, H. (1974) "Medicine, Socialism and Totalitarianism: Lessons from Chile," THE NEW ENGLAND JOURNAL OF MEDICINE. VOl. 291 (4): 171-177.

10. NAVARRO, V. (1974) "What Does Chile Mean?: An Analysis of Events in the Health sector, Before, During and After Allende's Administration," MILBANK MEMORIAL FUND QUARTERLY.

11. CHAGULA, W.K. and TARIMO, E. "Meeting Basic Health Needs in Tanzania," published in Reference 6.

CHAPTER 16

NATIONAL HEALTH SYSTEM AND POPULAR MEDICINE:
THE CASE OF COSTA RICA

Sharleen H. Simpson

Located in Southern Central America, Costa Rica with a population of slightly over 2 million people has one of the most effective and aggressive health systems in Latin America, encompassing both curative and preventive medicine. An infant mortality rate in 1980 of 19.1 per 1,000 population and a life expectancy at birth of 73.4 years (Ministerio de Salud, 1982) reflect the general health status of the population.

The health system as it is currently organized dates from the early 1970's when the National Plan of Economic and Social Development was implemented. This plan has as its goal the improvement of the quantity and quality of basic services available to Costa Rican citizens and was begun in rural areas in 1973 and in urban areas in 1974. In relation to health care, these basic services involve the cooperation of the Ministry of Health, the Costa Rican Social Security Administration, the Costa Rican Institute of Aqueducts and Sewers and the National Insurance Institute.

The goals of the program are as follows: (1) To extend basic health services to poor rural and urban communities using health auxiliary workers. (2) To control and reduce infectious diseases through immunizatin programs. (3) Referral of patients to either preventive or curative facilities, depending on medical diagnosis. (4) Daily planned visits to homes and businesses to evaluate health needs. (5) Emphasis on environmental health, health education and community organization (Freer Miranda, 1980).

Sixty-five percent of the community health program's activities have to do with maternal/child health. This program operates in both rural and urban areas and has had a great success. As an example, in the area assigned to the Hatillo Health Center, which is one of the largest in the urban San Jose area, about 56% of the 80,000 inhabitants have been surveyed and are covered by a health auxiliary worker who makes daily home visits (Alvarez Elizondo de Quiros et al., 1982). Interviews with the Director of Nursing for the Health Center and the Director of Community Health Nursing, however indicate that about 80 percent or more of the population comes to the health center for services even though they are not included in the areas organized for home visits (Jaensthke Maglakin, 1982). At any rate, if children's immunizations are used as indicators, the program is certainly successful. As part of an investigation in infant nutrition, 107 children born in 1980 were selected at random using birth registers from low income areas all over the city of San Jose. All of these children were between the ages of 1 and 2 years. It was found that all had some immunizations and more than 90 percent had all their immunizations up-to-date. Thus, in contrast to behavior reported elsewhere (Solien Gonzalez, 1966), in Costa Rica the population in general has widely accepted preventive medicine in the form of the services rendered through the community health programs.

As part of the National Plan of Economic and Social Development, in 1973-74 nearly all public curative health facilities, including clinics and hospitals, were combined under the Costa Rican Social Security Administration. Before that time hospitals like the San Juan de Dios in Metropolitan San Jose had been run by non-profit groups such as the Junta de Proteccion Social. These institutions provided care to private citizens and also to the poor. The Social Security hospitals such as the Hospital Mexico in San Jose and the outlying clinics were available to workers insured through the Social Security Administration. When all hospital facilities were combined under the Social Security Administration, the indigent population theoretically, at least, was supposed to be able to use these same facilities after having a social worker approve their application.

It is fair to say that care is now available for these people, however, the largeness of the Social Security System since the merger has tended to increase the patient load, requiring doctors to see large numbers of patients in a relatively short time. Rarely does the same doctor in a Social Security hospital see the same patient each time that patient attends. The result is a very impersonal doctor/patient relationship. In addition, the long waits to be seen and the expense of going to the hospital or clinic have had negative effects on the way people relate to the health system.

In contrast to the Social Security program which has moved toward centralizatin in curative medicine (probably because of the cost of hospital supplies and equipment), the aim of preventive medicine has been to decentralize services and put them on a personal basis through a system of outreach clinics in poor rural and urban communities. The key to this program has been the use of health auxiliary workers who are trained to give primary health care in the home. These people have a secondary education and are given 4-6 months of training in community health. They then work under the supervision of a registered nurse who is a specialist in community health or maternal/child health. These health auxiliary workers are each assigned an area which has had a census and a health evaluation done on every household.

These workers are in daily contact with the people of their areas (usually about 500 families) both in the homes and in community organization work. They work with groups of community members on committees to deal with community health problems as well as carrying out their respective programs of home visits. After a year or two they are well known and are familiar with the people they work with by face and even by name in many cases. The relationship is in large part very personal. The result is that preventive medicine has become an integral part of

Costa Rican life. As Vargas Gonzalez (1977: 363) notes, describing the rural health program, the myth of the inaccessable population has been destroyed. As noted earlier, this situation is quite different from the usual picture which has emerged with respect to the acceptance of preventive medicine in developing countries.

POPULAR MEDICINE

In the past it was frequently assumed that folk medicine existed only among the uneducated and traditional segment of the population and that if people utilized folk medicine they did not utilize scientific medicine or they tended to underutilize it. This, of course, has been amply demonstrated to be a false assumption by many researchers, including Solien de Gonzalez (1965) in Guatemala, Scott (1975) in Miami and Press (1969; 1978) in Bogota. They present a picture of dual or multiple use, especially in more cosmopolitan urban areas with hetergeneous, multi-ethnic populations. Press (1978) also notes that folk medicine is resilient and may survive long after concepts of folk illness have disappeared. I would agree and add that the practice of folk medicine is a reaction or adaptation by society to a specific set of health problems which may be called folk illnesses.

As long as the society exists, therefore, the reaction of adaptation continues. What changes are the specific problems or illnesses, and the way they are viewed or defined by the population involved. Twenty-five years ago Gould (1957) made a similar observation based on his work in India when he noted that folk medicine or its functional equivalent would never wholly disappear from the Indian scene. It seems logical, therefore as Spicer (1977) suggests, that the term "popular medicine" is preferable to "folk medicine" because it is less ambiguous and doesn't imply a dying tradition. With respect to Costa Rica, Ma. Eugenia Bozzoli de Wille (1971b: 76) has observed, "It is has been said many times that medico-magic practices are the product of ignorance and that they disappear with greater education. It is obvious that with greater education certain forms disappear but others appear" (Translation mine).

Certainly it is true that in spite of a well developed formal health system popular medicine is still alive and well in Costa Rica. In fact, more than simply existing, it is thriving. Richardson and Bode (1971: 251) based on their work in Putarenas, Costa Rica (a pacific seaport town) defined popular medicine as the medicine of the populace, particularly the part that belongs to the lower economic segment. Included in their definition were the medical facialites available to the populace, healer-patient relationships and the concepts of illness and health. They also divided the system into empirical elements (i.e., physicians, midwives, homeopaths) and non-empirical elements (spirits, God, etc.).

For the purposes of this paper, however, popular medicine is considered to be basically separate from orthodox scientific medicine with overlaps in certain specific areas involving some practitioners and illnesses (See **Illustration I**). In general licensed practitioners of orthodox scientific medicine do not participate in the system of popular medicine although some peripheral workers, e.g., pharmacists, nurse aids, may do so.

The system of popular medicine includes a variety of practices, practitioners and philosophies. The illustration shows a sketch of the relationship of the two systems and their practitioners as I view them. Bozzoli de Wille (1971b) notes that in Costa Rica attitudes toward scientific medicine have been favorable and that usually popular medicine is complementary, only acquiring importance when a medical treatment has not been successful, when the cost of treatment is high from the point of view of the patient and his family or when treatment is not available for a specific condition.

FOLK ILLNESS AND PRACTICES

Included among the illnesses currently treated by practitioners within the system of popular medicine are **quebranto, aire, pegas, nervios**, and various chronic type illnesses also recognized by orthodox scientific medicine. In addition to actual folk illnesses the phenomenon of self-medication with both patent medicines and herbal remedies for all types of illnesses is included among the practices which are encompassed by popular medicine. Illnesses caused by witchcraft (**brujeria**) also exist but are not as common. Bozzoli de Wille (197a; 1971b), in a study on witchcraft and medico-religious practices interviewed practitioners, clients and other residents of a small town which is now like a suburb of San Jose. She concluded that people continue to believe in this phenomenon and that the clientele came from all socioeconomic strata and educational levels.

Nervios

The most extensive study done on this particular complaint was Low's (1976) work on the meaning of nervios. Symptoms include general malaise, a feeling of detachment or somehow being "out-of-control," and in my experience, a whole range of rather vague psychosomatic complaints. According to Low (1976: 173-174) nervios appears as a symptom of family interaction discord, family structure disruption and past family disturbance. People suffering from nervios were more often single, separated or widowed and related family or spouse abandonment and death or abuse to their symptoms. I consider nervios as being one of the overlapping areas between the world of orthodox scientific medicine and popular medicine, since it seems to be a folk diagnosis that is also accepted by physicians.

Self-Medication

Self-medication is a phenomenon which, like nervios seems to have a foot in both medical systems. Certainly there has long been a tradition of self-medication in Costa Rica; the difference is that in the past homeremedies based on herbs and other vegetable materials were used while today both herbal remedies and patent medicines are used, depending upon what type illness or ailment is being treated. Pardo Angulo (1981) feels that capitalists are taking advantage of the custom of using herbal medicines to introduce new and more costly pharmaceutical products for popular consumption. Melesio Nolasco (1981) did a study on advertising commercials for patent medicines in Costa Rica and concluded that one of the effects of advertising was to make people think that only brand-name products are effective, causing loss of confidence in both traditional herbal remedies and the generic name medicines provided by the Seguro Social. The present economic crisis, however, which has made imported medicines so expensive, has caused many people to turn again to traditional herbal remedies and has also tended to reinforce the practice of self-medication.

People also self-medicate with medicines perscribed by doctors for friends or for prior illness. Although narcotics have long been available in Costa Rica only with a doctor's prescription, until recently such drugs as amphetamines for weight loss, antibiotics and anti-histamines were available without a prescription. One could consult with the friendly pharmacist and on his suggestion buy the appropriate drugs to treat one's illness. Or one could by the medicine that had worked for Uncle Jorge when he had the same thing. The Ministry of Health is now in the process of instituting stricter controls on the sale of prescription drugs but has as yet succeeded only partially.

Aire and Quebranto

Aire and quebranto are folk illnesses which are residuals from earlier times. Although some people still believe in their existence, particularly rural people, they are not as common as they evidently were 50 or 100 years ago. They seem to have been affected more than other folk illnesses by the introduction of scientific medicine. Aire occurs when someone becomes chilled or a cold draft touches their body. The person may develop aches and pains in the area affected, e.g., chest, leg, and may have a slight fever. This is generally treated by a **sobada** or rubbing with vegetable shortening or some other greasy substance. Quebranto usually occurs only in babies under 6 or 7 months of age. If the baby is handled roughly its hips and legs are believed to be damaged. The symptoms of quebranto include irritability and crying and having one leg shorter than the other when the baby is placed on its stomach and the legs measured against each other. The treatment for this in the past and at present was a sobada or rubbing of the hips and legs with vegetable shortening or grease and then binding up the hips and legs.

221

It may be that this illness is not as common because at least some of the cases diagnosed as quebranto probably involved congenitally dislocated hips, which are now found very early, either in the hospital after birth or in the well-baby clinic at the health center.

Pega

Of all the folk illnesses encountered within the Costa Rican system of popular medicine, pega is the one which, in my opinion, most demonstrates the effects of the various changes in the National Health System. Pega is used to describe an illness which occurs when a food becomes "stuck" in the stomach, causing such symptoms as loss of appetite, sunken eyes, sometimes vomiting and/or diarrhea and sometimes fever. The glands behind the ears may also be swollen. My informants told me that when these cases are taken to the hospital they are most commonly diagnosed as **gastro** (gastroenteritis). Pega occurs most frequently in children, but adults may also be affected. There does not seem to be any specific food involved, rather a pega can be caused by almost any food, depending upon the circumstances. The conditions surrounding ingestion of the food are more important than the food itself. For example, eating too much or eating something which is not liked (as frequently happens when one is visiting since in Costa Rica it is almost obligatory to offer guests food and when this happens it is an insult not to eat what is offered).

The treatment for pega is a sobada or rubbing with vegetable shortening or some other greasy substance by a person who knows how to do this. In general the illness is diagnosed by the sobadora by feeling the anticubital space for a small lump or ball, feeling behind the ears for lumps and thumping on the stomach and listening to the sounds. If the stomach and abdomen should full it is a sign that pega is present. Proper diagnosis is considered very important. The eight sobadores interviewed were very specific about symptoms and indicated that if they didn't really think the patient had pega he/she was sent to the hospital and no attempt was made to sobar. Mothers interviewed concurred with this, many having taken children to the sobador and been sent to the hospital or health center instead.

Once it has been determined that a pega is present, the sobada or rubbing is begun. The usual order is to first rub the anticubital space and down toward the hand, then between the thumb and forefinger, behind the ears, the back of the neck and in some cases the back, and then behind the knees. After this rubbing has been carried out the patient is given a gentle purgative such as milk of magnesia, **manzanilla** mixed with lemon juice and baking soda or **dulce** (cane syrup) with salt and told to refrain from eating anything for a day. Sometimes, if the case is difficult, for example if it has gone on a long time before the sobador was consulted, the procedure may have to be repeated two or three times before he/she is recovered.

The people who practice as neighborhood sobadores do not usually charge

222

anything. When their work has been successful,however, people tend to give them gifts in kind such as fruits and vegetables. Most sobadores also insist that the patient be fasting for a day before beginning the treatment.

The majority of the sobadores are women but some men do sobando also. There are also some people, mostly men who do sobando for athletes and other people with pulled muscles and sprains. I should note here that I have translated sobar as "to rub" rather than "to massage" because there is another word in Spanish—**masaje**— used to describe what goes on in a massage parlor or a gymnasium, while sobar and sobada always refer to rubbing or touching with the hands with the intent to heal.

Pega is an example of a folk illness that has changed with the times. Sicne Costa Rica is a country with a high rate of literacy, the people are more informed consumers of health services than would be found in most developing countries. This extends to popular medicine as well as scientific medicine. The sobardores I interviewed are educated and are good examples of healers who have adopted many relatively sophisticated practices in their work. For example, one of the symptoms mentioned was a full sounding stomach and abdomen. I have seen several of these sobadores percuss the stomach and palpate the abdomen with the same techniques the physician would use. Also, I have frequently told that in earlier times sobadores would massage the stomach as part of the treatment but that this practice is known now to be dangerous. All but one of the practitioners interviewed did not massage the stomach and abdomen as part of the treatment. Indeed, if pega is usually diagnosed by physicians as gastroenteritis as my informants indicated, then the elimination of foods for a time as part of the treatment should be medically acceptable.

During the course of gathering data for a study on child malnutrition, I became aware of pega as a widespread phenomenon. To discover how prevalent this illness was, I began to systematically interview the families of the 44 children (all from low income areas) we were following. In about 90 percent of the families either the child being followed and/or another child or adult in the same family had had a pega one or more times and been treated by a sobador. In trying to discover the reasons behind this aparent resurgence of a traditional folk illness, I was told that although the condition called pega had existed for years, at one point a few years ago it was very difficult to find anyone who knew about sobando and these were mostly older women. Now, however, many informants noted that there are many people.

Many people told stories of themselves or their family and friends nearly losing children or other family members because they had been taken to the hospital and given **suero** (glucose water) when what they had was a pega which the doctors don't know how to recognize or treat. I was cited examples where, after being several days in the hospital, the child was no better so the mother took him/her to a sobador who was able to successfully treat the illness. Most people, however, when the child had the symptoms mentioned earlier went to the sobador first. Althugh people who consult the sobador really do seem to believe in both the illness and the treatment, many also cited long bus rides, long waits for appointments, and doctors who really don't look at them or listen to what they say as reaons for preferring to use the sobador when possible.

CONCLUSIONS

The relationship between popular medicine and orthodox scientific medicine in Costa Rica presents contradictions. On the one hand, preventive medicine has been embraced wholeheartedly through the community health program, while on the other, there seems to be an increase in the use of folk practitioners, particularly on the curative side of medicine, as has been particularly demonstrated by the widespread prevalence in the urban area of pega and the sobadores who treat it. This is an inconsistency since usually when any aspect of orthodox medicine is accepted it is the curative part rather than the preventive part.

It seems to me that several factors are functioning here. First, there is the size and resultant unresponsiveness of the Social Security System since taking over almost all other curative facilities; then there is the very personal patient/health worker relationship maintained by the community health program. Personal relationships are basic to Costa Rican society, especially when anything so intimate as the health of one's own body is concerned. The Costa Rican may go through formal channels to obtain something but always feels more at ease if there is an acquaintance or friend within the institution from whom assistance can be sought. Thus the mother of a small child with gastrointestinal symptoms weighs the alternatives——the hospital, the health center or the sobador. At the hospital she can expect at best a lukewarm reception and at worst a scolding for whatever it is that she supposedly has not done. At the health center she has a more personal relationship but with symptoms like those of pega she will probably be sent to a hospital anyway.

Going to the hospital involves taking a bus and waiting, many times without eating because there is no money to buy food. Also if a mother needs to take one child to the hospital, she will probably have to bring two or three others as well because there is no one to take care of them while she is gone. They cannot be left by themselves or with anyone but relatively good friends or family because a visit to the hospital or clinic usually takes the better part of a day. Considering these disadvantages as well as the fact that the sobada has been part of Costa Rican tradition, it is not surprising that many mothers are opting to utilize these practitioners rather than the hospitals and clinics of the Social Security Administration.

While the increasing use of sobadores seems to be a response to the inability of the Social Security System to meet the needs of the poor; in terms of the structure of the health system itself this phenomenon takes on another significance. Because of rising inflation and problems with the balance of payments Costa Rica has been passing thorugh an economic crisis. The Social Security Administration has been especially affected because many of the medicines and hospital supplies and equipment which are used have to be imported. The resulting economic crisis has also made many people of higher socioeconomic classes who normally utilized private physicians, turn to the Social Security system for care because of the cheaper cost. Both of these factors have combined to put a strain on the ability of this institution to provide care to all who are entitled to receive it. This has caused a subtle change in the relationship of the system of popular medicine and the orthodox medical establishment.

Instead of being complementary to the orthodox system as it seems to have been in the past, popular medicine is now becoming more and more necessary as an escape valve serving people of low socioeconomic status. If the random sample of children I observed is any indicator of conditions among the urban poor, elimination of the neighborhood sobador would literally inundate the clinics andhospitals with children suffering from some kind of gastrointestinal complaint. Not only would it be difficult for Social Security to provide care to all who demanded it but it certainly would be impossible for them to do so at the current cost, since most of the population who would be involved are not insured or insured at very low rates of income. Thus the system of popular medicine may very well be subsidizing the orthodox scientific medical system and in effect ensuring its ability to provide care for the middle class. I have discussed this relationship only with regard to pega and the sobadores who treat it since that is the aspect I have investigated most closely. It is quite likely, however, that the same thing is occurring in relation to illnesses treated by other practitioners of popular medicine in Costa Rica.

IMPLICATIONS AND RECOMMENDATIONS

One of the implications of these conclusions is that something needs to be done soon to improve the ability of the Social Security Administration to respond to the needs of the poor. This might be accomplished without incurring the costs that higher doctor/patient ratios would entail by adopting the same philosophy as the community health program and using more paramedical personnel in the hospital and clinic setting for delivery of primary health care. The greater use of nurse practitioenrs, for example, could permit a more acceptable patient/practitioner relationship. Physicians would then be free to see more complicated cases while each nurse practitioner could be assigned to cover routine visits for patients coming from a specific area, allowing development of more rapport and trust.

Another recommendation would be to scientifically investigate some of the practices of popular medicine, particularly those involving locally available herbal remedies as Pardo (1981) and others have suggested. Many of these remedies are effective as well as being cheaper. The work of Sarkis and Campos (1981) in compiling some of these remedies is a first step.

The treatment and diagnosis of pega, at least as practiced by the sobadores interviewed does not appear to be particularly harmful. Both mothers and sobadores interviewed felt that there was a high rate of success. Probably this is in part due to the ability of the practitioner to correctly diagnose an illness which should be seen by a physician. Given the experimental work on Therapeutic Touch and the phenomenon of healing by the laying on of hands,however, it would seem that some scientific research into the physiological effects of the sobada are warranted before it is condemned. Grad, a biochemist at McGill University, was able to demonstrate significantly increased healing of wounds in mice subjected to the touch of a well-known healer (Grad et al., 1961). Krieger, in strictly controlled experiments which were successfully repeated several times, was able to demonstrate significant changes in mean hemoglobin in patients subjects to therapeutic touch by nurses trained in these techniques (Krieger, 1972; 1975; and Krieger et al., 1979). It may be that the sobada represents an as yet untapped resource for health care.

In summary, the Costa Rican Health System is something the country can be justly proud of because, even with its problems, it has more effectively dealt with the health problems of the population it serves than most developing countries and perhaps even some so-called "developed" countries. The preceeding analysis and its implications and recommendations are offered constructively with the hope that some of the ideas may be useful in explaining the changes which are occurring thus serving to suggest ways the system can come to grips with its problems.

REFERENCES

ALVAREZ ELIZONDO DE QUIROS, J., E. JAENSTHKE MAGLAKIN, and C. CASTRO RIVERA (1982) "Salud Comunitaria en al Distrito de Hatillo," MINISTERIO DE SALUD. San Jose, Costa Rica.

BOZZOLI DE WILLE, MA. E. (1971a) "No Creer ni Dejar de Creer," REVISTA DE COSTA RICA 1: 35-56.

BOZZOLI DE WILLE, MA. E. (1971b) "No Creer ni Dejar de Creer," REVISTA DE COSTA RICA 2: 67-84.

FREER MIRANDA, E. (1980) "Extension de los servicios de salud en Costa Rica," ESCUELA DE MEDICINA, CATEDRA MEDICINA PREVENTIVA, UNIVERSIDAD DE COSTA RICA.

GOULD, H.A. (1957) "The Implications of Technological Change for Folk and Scientific Medicine," AMERICAN ANTHROPLOGIST 59: 507-516.

GRAD, B. et al. (1961) "The Influence of an Unorthodox Method of Treatment on Wound Healing in Mice," INTERNATIONAL JOURNAL OF PARAPSYCHOLOGY 3: 5-24.

JAENSTHKE MAGLAKIN, E. (1982) Recorded interview, Centro de Salud de Hatillo (Sept.).

KRIEGER, D. (1972) "The Response of In-Vivo Human Hemoglobin to an Active Healing Therapy by Direct Laying-On of Hands," HUMAN DIMENSIONS 1: 12-15.

KRIEGER, D. (1975) "Therapeutic Touch: The Imprimatur of Nursing," AMERICAN JOURNAL OF NURSING 75(5): 784-787.

LOW, S.M. (1976) "The Meaning of Nervios: Social Organization of Urban Health Care in San Jose, Costa Rica," Ph.D. dissertation, University of California, Berkeley.

MELESIO NOLASCO, MA. S. (1981) "La propaganda comercial de medicinas," REVISTA CENTROAMERICANA DE CIENCIAS DE LA SALUD 7(18): 93-102.

PARDO ANGULO, M.E. (1981) "Patrones de automedicacion," REVISTA CENTROAMERICANA DE CIENCIAS DE LA SALUD. 7(19): 57-62

PRESS, I. (1969) "Urban Illness: Physicians, Curers and Dual Use in Bogota," JOURNAL OF HEALTH AND SOCIAL BEHAVIOR 10(3): 209-218.

PRESS, I. (1978) "Urban Folk Medicine: A Functional Overview," AMERICAN ANTHROPOLOGIST 80(1): 71-84.

RICHARDSON, M. and B. Bode (1971) "Popular Medicine in Puntarenas, Costa Rica: Urban and Societal Features," MIDDLE AMERICAN RESEARCH INSTITUTE. Tulane University: New Orleans, No. 24.

SARKIS, A. and V. CAMPOS (1981) CURANDERISMO TRADICIONAL DEL COSTARRICENSE. San Jose: Editorial Costa Rica.

SCOTT, C.S. (1975) "Competing Health Care Systems in an Inner City Area," HUMAN ORGANIZATION 34(1): 108-110.

SOLIEN DE GONZALEZ, N.L. (1965) "Medical Beliefs of the Urban Folk in Guatemala," AMERICAN INDIGENA 25(3): 324-328.

SOLIEN DE GONZALEZ, N.L. (1966) "Health Behavior in Cross-Cultural Perspective: A Guatemalan Example," HUMAN ORGANIZATION 25(2): 122-125.

SPICER, E.H. (ed.) (1977) ETHNIC MEDICINE IN THE SOUTHWEST. Tucson: University of Arizona Press.

VARGAS GONZALEZ, W. 91977) "El programa de salud rural de Costa Rica: un modelo para las poblaciones marginadas," AMERICA INDIGENA 37(2): 353-365.

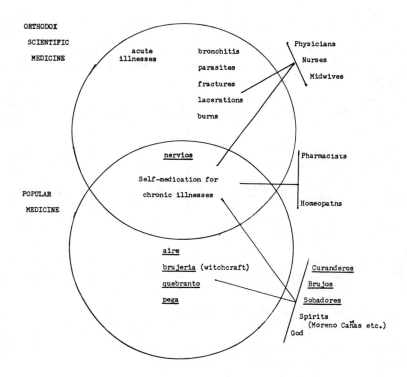

Illustration No. 1: The Relationship of Popular Medicine to Orthodox Scientific Medicine in Costa Rica.

CHAPTER 17

NONPROFESSIONAL PRIMARY HEALTH CARE WORKERS:
SOCIOPOLITICAL ISSUES IN UTILIZATION

Ruth Stark

"Ernesto was a primary school teacher working in a remote village when he came to our health promoter course. He was a Cachiquel Indian, about 25 years old, one of the first from his village to go to secondary school. He said he wanted to study health care because there was no one with any (medical) training in his village, and people already brought their sick children to him because he was a teacher. He did very well in the course, and he also met Clara, a young Cachiquel woman from a different town whom he eventually married. When he returned to his village he organized a local water system for the village. He made contacts with another Private Voluntary Organization that works on water projects and the system was eventually completed. When the army came to his town, Ernesto was a recognized leader of his community....He was abducted from his house at night, tortured for two days and eventually killed. His body was thrown out on the road in front of his house. Clara buried him and then she and her two small children went into hiding..."[1]

This incident is an example of what is becoming an increasing concern to professionals involved in the training of indigenous primary health care workers who will serve the Third World. While primary health care workers are not identified as such in the notices of their deaths, they are increasingly swelling the lists of the disappeared, kidnapped and murdered.[2]

In this paper, such sanctions will be examined as evidence of the multiple latent and manifest functions to be found in the role of the primary health care worker. Using data from the literature, from international health professionals, and from the author's experience in Latin America, the paper argues that the delivery of primary health care is a complex, political act which may involve an unavoidable risk to the provider.

Background

The World Health Organization sponsored an International Conference on Primary Health Care in 1978. The result of that conference was the Declaration of Alma-Alta which concluded that the existing gross inequality in the health status between the haves and have-nots was socially, politically, and economically unacceptable, and therefore, of common concern to all countries. Governments and international organizations were encouraged to work toward the attainment by all peoples of the world by the year 2000 of a level of health that would permit them to lead a socially and economically productive life. Primary Health Care was identified as the key to attaining this goal. As the first level of contact with the national health system, primary health care identifies the main health problems in the community, providing promotive, preventive, curative and rehabilitative service accordingly. It includes at least: education concerning prevailing health problems and the methods of preventing and controlling them; promotion of food supply and proper nutrition; an adequate supply of safe water and basic sanitation; maternal and child health, including family planning; immunization against major infectious diseases; prevention and control of locally endemic diseases; appropriate treatment of common diseases and injuries; and provision of essential drugs. Primary health care involves all related sectors and aspects of national and community development and requires and promotes maximum community and individual self-reliance and participation in the spirit of social justice. Finally, the Declaration of Alma-Alta asserts that primary health care, is most effectively delivered by community health workers who have the confidence of the people, who understand the health needs of the community, and who can be trained in a short time to perform specific tasks.[3]

Non-professional Primary Health Care Workers (PHCW's) are the key agents in almost all primary health care programs in the Third World. It has been stated that they are the most "talked about, worshipped, and conferenced group of health workers" in the world.[4] As referred to in this paper, the PHCW is an individual with minimal prior education who has received a relatively short course of training in some essential aspects of primary health care. They come in a confusing array of titles (village health workers, health promoters, auxiliaries, etc.) and types (sanitarians, midwives, generalists,, etc.). Typically, PHCW's are respected men and women from rural communities who continue to work the land while providing health care on a volunteer or part-time basis to their neighbors. Traditionally trained over the past several decades by missions and other non-governmental organizations, PHCW's have demonstrated their ability to provide quality health care which is both affordable and appropriate.[5]

It is now accepted throughout the International Health Community that, given adequate training and support, PHCW's could effectively relate to the needs of the four-fifths of the world's population, a population that is without access to any permanent form of health care. Therefore, the World Health Organization, along with other international health and development agencies, has used its influence and funds to encourage member nations to train and utilize PHCW's as an immediate strategy in the implementation of the Primary Health Care Model. Thus the traditional programs have been supplemented by governmental programs for the training and deployment of PHCW's.[6]

The political implications of Primary Health Care are not debated. In a study by the UNICEF/WHO Join Committee on Health Policy, it was concluded that the Primary Health Care approach implies a major social transformation. "In most countries the poor are not poor mainly because of an absolute scarcity of resources, but because of the socioeconomic structures which prevent them from working productively, reaping the benefits of their labor, and raising their living standards. In so far as ill health is related to poverty, attention needs to focus not so much on poverty as such, but on what has made and keeps the poor poor. Health improvement in developing countries has to relate to the political economy of health and the Primary Health Care approach cannot make significant progress unless these fundamental sociopolitical issues are acted upon."[7]

Political Functions of the Primary Health Care Worker

If we accept that primary health care is rooted in the socio-political milieu, then we may also acknowledge the role of a PHCW as a political agent. In China, barefoot doctors were a tool to break the power of the medical professions, to give the people a part in providing their own health care, and to distribute the health resources more equitably.[8] In Mozambique during the 1970's, PHCW's were medics in the armed struggle for political liberation, providing health care for the population in the liberated zones as well as to the guerilla army. They were one manifestation of the developing revolutionary line within the independence front, FRELIMO, to create a just society involving popular participation in social affairs.[9, 10] In Democratic Yemen, the revolutionary wing of the National Front, upon coming into power in 1969, responded to the immediate needs and demands of the population by training PHCW's and encouraging community organization around the issues of health.[10] And in the United Republic of Tanzania, the PHCW provides health care as part of his or her contribution to the communal effort in the village. The health care they provide in the villages is part of a structured national plan to provide health coverage for the entire population.[11]

In each of the aforementioned examples, the provision of primary health care has been an outcome of political ideology and an integral aspect of a program for social development. In this situation, the PHCW's functions are to deliver quality, low cost health care and to serve as a manifestation of the new government's commitment to a fundamental shift of wealth and power to those who previously had neither.[12] These functions of the PHCW role are compatible with the goals and perceived needs of the population as well as with the priorities of the professional health bureaucracy and the government in power. Accordingly, the effective PHCW may receive personal benefits in the form of increased social status and, in certain instances, financial security as a government employee.

However, in countries where the wealth is in the hands of the few, the PHCW, working with an impoverished population, is in a far more complex and potentially dangerous situation. For the role of the PHCW, trained by the Government's Ministry of Health or an International Agency supportive of the Government, may include functions intended to maintain the existing social institutions. And these functions are in conflict with the PHCW's manifest function; that is, to improve the health status of the community.

Primary Health Care Workers as "Spies"

That PHCW's have been used by governments in power to gather intelligence data on the identity and movements of insurgents is difficult to document but is common knowledge in the community of international health professionals. Labeling their function that of "medical police," Jaime Breilh writes that "the medical bureaucratic apparatus, when penetrating into the poor urban district or rural village is tantamount to an invisible surveillance network that penetrates the daily lives and families and has a triple function: to assert the present and hierarchial role of state representatives among the poor population; to feed back to the state's information system relevant social data by formal or informal channels; and to achieve adequate conduct of the people by means of a subtle disciplinary apparatus that operates through a reward-punishment method, sanctioning 'normal conduct' that conforms to the dominant ideology."[13]

Primary Health care Workers as "Cooling" Agents

In countries where life conditions are worsening for the masses of the population, the utilization of PHCW's may become a strategy to "take over" struggling liberation groups and to 'cool out' potentially explosive situations.[14] The United States government has been accused of sponsoring Primary Health Programs in areas of Latin America where social conflicts were most overt and violent with the intent of weaking the community's demand for better conditions of living and health.[15] Because PHCW's in these programs spend a significant amount of their time collecting census data and health statistics, it is often difficult to separate out the "cooling" functions from the "spy" functions. However, it is clear that the very presence of PHCW's assocated with the Ministry of Health is designed to serve as a manifestation of the government's "commitment" to improve the well being of the poor. Of course, this demonstration of the government's "good faith" is more often than not bolstered with foreign aide and prodding and may be abandoned in favor of sheer force should the civil strife escalate or the foreign dollars for the project become unavailable. The empty cement block health posts that dot the landscape in some rural areas of Latin America give evidence of this phenomenon.

Finally, evidence of the importance of the "cooling-out" function of PHCW's following his study of programs in Latin America which make significant use of PHCW's concluded the following about the large regional or national programmers: "As for the large regional or national programs----for all their international funding, top-ranking foreign consultants, and glossy bilingual brochures portraying community participation---we found that when it came down to the nitty gritty of what we ging on in the field, there was usually a minimum of effective community involvement and a maximum of dependency creating hand-outs, paternalism, and superimposed, initiative-destroying norms. In certain programs, a different breed of village health worker is being molded; one who is taught a pathetically limited range of skills, who is trained not to think but to follow a list of very specific instructions or "norms," who has a neat uniform and a handsome diploma, who works in a standarized cement block health post, and who is subject to restrictive supervision and rigidly defined limitations. Such a health worker has a limited impact on the health and even less impact on the growth of the community. He, or more usually she, spends a great deal of time filling out forms."[16]

Since their latent "cooling out" or "spy" function is their primary function, it is not essential that PHCW's be competent health providers. It is only necessary that they be present and appear to be competent.

"Cooling-out" functions may be seen as a strategy for defusing politically explosive areas or as a preventive measure to keep an area from becoming politically problematic to the government. In the latter case, the provision of health care may be seen as a carrot with the threat of its withdrawal being one form of social control. Primary health care can provide important linkages between the central government and the periphery. The following excerpt from a report about a project in Thailand funded by the Asia Foundation is illustrative.

"Nonghkai is a province in northeastern Thailand that borders on Laos. The villagers are very poor and have few services. This is a province that is plagued with border squabbles and the villagers are subject to frequent raids by "guerillas" and deaths of villagers are not uncommon. The village medical assistant program was started under the interest and perserverance of the wife of the governor of this province. It was intended by the governor and his wife in collaboration with the district health centers and provincial hospital, to bridge a gap in medical care which, because of limited population, did not permit the establishment of public health centers for rural inhabitants of the province. Training carefully selected persons from the surrounding villages as volunteer medical assistants would be able to provide basic and intermediate medical care on behalf of the more remote villages and determine which cases to refer to the district health centers or the provincial hospital. In addition, the project was to provide the villagers in these "sensitive" areas with an on-going link with the Thai government. The hope was that through the program, the remote villages would feel support as a group, and be able to resist some of the border movements. A total of 64 village medical assistants were to be trained under this project, with the Asia Foundation providing training materials, transportation, and medical kits for the students. The provincial medical and public health authorities would provide the professional and technical staff for training the medical assistants and developing the linkages under which they would operate.

233

Responsibility for selection of the trainees was done by the villages. The student must be less than 25 years of age, be in good health, have the support of their village and an interest in health matters. In addition, they must have leadership potential and have demonstrated commitment and interest in promoting good relations between the village and the Thai Government."[17]

The Primary Health Care Worker and the Community

As the newly trained PHCW's return to the community, a number of things may happen. They may function as extensions of the professional medical bureaucracy, assisting the physicians and filling out the endless forms. Such workers serve only as "lackeys" to the physicians at the health clinics and are incompetent to provide care when the physician is unavailable; that is, the majority of the time. PHCW's also have the option to capitalize upon their access to the power structure and become intermediaries between the community members and those who control the resources. In this role as brokers, PHCW's are able to secure certain benefits for their families and friends, thereby developing their own power base.

Other PHCW's, frustrated by their lack of skills, may seek out alternative sources of education, such as those available from foreign health personnel. Missionary nurses have long provided this type of practical clinical training. In fact, in Latin America, long before the governments got into the business of training non-professional PHCW's, missionary nurses, Catholic sisters in particular, were providing direct care to patients, health education to the community, and clinical training to select individuals. Currently, with government programs in place in some areas, the missionary nurses have served to provide clinical training for primary health care workers in the following ways:

(1) Providing "pre-training" courses to give the "basics" to indigenous people who want to enroll in a government-sponsored primary health course but who have inadequate prior educational background.
(2) Providing "advanced" courses to PHCW's inadequately trained in government programs.
(3) Working in health posts with PHCW's.
(4) Being available to consult with PHCW's on difficult clinical cases; and (5) Sposoring their own training programs where there is no government program, and, less often, as an alternative to government programs.

As the Church has increasingly embraced liberation theology, many Church-sponsored programs have changed from traditional forms of religious education to facilitating a process whereby people, reflecting on their own reality, can analyze the causes of their poverty and illness and develop community strategies for appropriate action.

Similarly, a number of other small, non-governmental programs approach training using Paulo Freire's methods of education through conscientization. These programs, like those based in liberation theology, encourage health workers to participate with the community in a critical analysis of the root causes of their ill health and to participate with the community in the development and implementation of strategies designed to combat the underlying social causes of their problems. For instance, the objectives of a successful program in Honduras which trains housewives to be PHCW's includes the following:

1. To promote and fight for women's dignity.
2. To involve women in a community development.
3. To work with other popular organizations to obtain social justice for the oppressed campesino population.
4. To train the health promoter so that she is able to animate the women of her community, so as to gain their active support for the health programs and consequently other popular organizations.[18]

In contrast to official health programs designed to let the government "off the hook," such efforts by non-governmental organizations, which may be genuinely motivated to help the poor improve their health situation and their socioeconomic position, are faced with considerable obstacles. Lillian Gibbons, as Regional advisor for the Pan American Health Organization's Committee on Primary Health Care, commented that, in Latin America, the issue of community participation has become volatile. The "conscientizing" of local villagers is coming to be perceived by some officials as a tremendous political threat.[19] A study in 1981 sponsored by the UNICEF/WHO Joint Committee on Health confirms that this is the case in countries where the rural poor are made up of small holders of landless workers, while large landowners mobilize the main productive resource as well as the channels of commercialization. If the hostility of the local elite is aroused, it is likely to be backed up by the machinery of the state, and the community-involving activities will be neutralized or proscribed as subversive.[20] One of the ways these community-involving activities are "neutralized" is the elimination of the effective PHCW. Zafrullah Chowdhury, Project Coordinator of the People's Health Center, Savar, Bangladesh, reported the following case of a PHCW in his program: "In our organization, a community development project twenty-two miles from Dacca, our paramedic Nizan did face the established corrupt structure, of the village. In an area where among other similar practices, he began to expose the system. It was a matter of time. He was eventually murdered..."[21]

Other examples include the well known Project Piaxtla, located in the Mexican Sierra, where health workers have been jailed and intimidated for the openness with which they work for social change. And in one Central American Project, six PHCW's were killed between July and December of 1981.[22] A comment of the impact of such an outcome is warranted.

Responding to this critical situation, many of these programs are beginning to assume a low profile. In fact, some programs are becoming almost invisible operating on a **sub rosa** basis. One program, in an effort to avoid being labeled as supportive of the guerilla movement, no longer has courses entitled "first aid." A number of programs no longer teach preventive health and health education as these involve group activities which may become labeled subversive.[23]

The Primary Health Care Worker as a Political Figure

Zafrullah Chowhury has recently stated "....the good health worker will inevitably become a political figure and this, as the situation stands in most countries today, gives him an uncertain future[24] One Way PHCW's may become political targets is that, in the process of providing health care, they learn aboutg the root causes of disease and work to cure them. The following is illustrative.

When Mario was selected by his village to take the primary health care course offered by the government, he was a 37 year old man respected in his community. He farmed a small plot of land and was known to be dedicated to his family and an industrious, honest worker. Mario studied hard in his course and began providing care to his neighbors even before he got his "certificate." Many of the infants and young children brought to him suffered from diarrhea. Over a period of time, Mario learned that these diarrheal problems resulted from malnutrition and lack of an adequate water supply which, in turn, made the youngsters susceptible to infection. He also learned that, in a cyclical manner, the diarrhea contributed to the malnutrition. Accordingly, Mario counseled the mothers to boil the water and to give the children proper food. As he became more intimate with the families of his village and of the surrounding villages, he realized that they simply didn't have enough land on which to grow food sufficient for their families. He finally suggested that the community work together to grow corn on a piece of land that was owned by a man who lived in the capital city. The land had been vacant for many years. The community responded enthusiastically and began to till the land. One late afternoon, Mario and six men were picked up by the local police, tortured and threatened with death if they didn't stay off the land. The community voted to abandon the project.[25]

The risk to PHCW's is not confined to those who are politically aware, or to those working on the social causes of illness. Any health worker who is conscientiously trying to deliver health care in the context of gross socio-economic inequity is at rish. The potential that they will suffer personal harm increases within the context of socio-political change. Not all the PHCW's terrorized recently have been trained in programs which encourage a critical analysis of their reality. And, not all the PHCW's killed recently are involved in community action for social change. Some have been providing only curative care to their neighbors. One possible explanation is that, in their function as a health worker, PHCW's enable people to give up their magical view of health, making it possible for them to discover cause-and-effect relationships.[26] It is perhaps also true that, when people no longer see illness as "God's will" or otherwise inevitable, they will become less fatalistic and more active in shaping their own reality.

It is clear that the PHCW is treating the ills of the social system, and may, in fact represent a latent critic of that system. An effective PHCW in a context of severe economic deprivation does not have to be "politically active" to be a leader. The healing role potentially gives the PHCW intimate access to the community and considerable social status. Thus, it may be that even the PHCW's, trained and working in a government intiated program and sincerely working to effectively fulfill their manifest functions as clinicians, will be perceived as a threat to an oligarchial or neo-colonial government struggling to maintain power. For, in their very effectiveness in delivering primary health care, they may not fulfill their functions as agents to support the existing social structures. And it is for these functions that they have been trained and utilized by the government.

Conclusion

In conclusion, the author concurs with the following warning issued by Werner and Bower in an early draft of their book, HELPING HEALTH WORKERS LEARN: "For health workers to stand up for the interests of the poor and to work toward changing the social causes of poverty, hunger and poor health involves a certain risk. The degree of risk will vary from country to country, and even from village to village.

For this reason, the openness with which health workers work toward social awakening and change, and the methods they use, need to be adapted to each local situation...Unfortunately, countries where the health needs of the poor are greatest are usually the same countries where repression and violation of rights by those in control is most severe. These are the countries where leaders of the poor and those who work for social change are in greatest danger.

We urge planners and instructors of health workers as well as health workers themselves to move forward with their eyes wide open. Evaluate the possible benefits and risks of any approach or activity you consider, especially if it involves confrontation or conflict of interests. The risks of taking any particular step toward change need to be weighed against the risk of not taking that step: 'How many people may suffer from repression if we take a stand on this issue?' How many children will continue to die of hunger-related diseases if we don't".

Before training health workers in a people-centered approach, be sure that both you and they carefully consider the range of possible consequences."[27]

REFERENCES

1. Unpublished letters (1981) to participants at the National Council for International Health 1981 International Health Conference, Washington, D.C., (June).

2. ibid.

3. WHO/UNICEF (1978) ALMA-ALTA 1978 PRIMARY HEALTH CARE, Geneva: World Health Organization, pp. 2-6. 4. Wood, Christopher (1981) "The Selection, Training, and Support of Primary Health Care Workers," PROCEEDINGS 1981 INTERNATIONAL HEALTH CONFERENCE, June 15-18, Washington, D.C.: National Council for International Health.

5. Werner, David (1981) "The Village Health Worker: Lackey or Liberator," WORLD HEALTH FORUM 2(1): 46-48.

6. ibid.

7. UNICEF/WHO (1981) NATIONAL DECISION-MAKING FOR PRIMARY HEALTH CARE, Geneva: World Health Organization, pp. 21-22.

8. Rifkin, S.B. (1978) "Politics of Barefoot Medicine," THE LANCET 7(34).

9. Segall, Malcolm (1977) "Health and National Liberation in the People's Republic of Mozambique," INTERNATIONAL JOURNAL OF HEALTH SERVICES 7(2): 319-325.

10. WHO/UNICEF (1981) NATIONAL DECISION-MAKING FOR PRIMARY HEALTH CARE, Geneva: World Health Organization, pp. 14-15.

11. Bennet, F.J. (1979) "Primary Health Care and Developing Countries," SOCIAL SCIENCE AND MEDICINE 13A: 505-514.

12. ibid.

13. Breilh, Jaime (1979) "Community Medicine Under Imperialism," INTERNATIONAL JOURNAL OF HEALTH SERVICES 9(1): 5-25.

14. Elling, R.H. (1981) "Political Economy, Cultural Hegemony, and Mixes of Traditional and Modern medicine," SOCIAL SCIENCE AND MEDICINE 15A: 88-99.

15. Molina-Guzman, Gustavo (1979) "Third World Experiences in Health Planning," INTERNATIONAL JOURNAL OF HEALTH SERVICES 9(1): 139-150.

16. Werner, op. cit. pp. 47-49.

17. Devereaux, Mary O'Hara and Len Hughes Andres (1977) "Some Approaches to Rural Primary Care in Alaska and Asia," unpublished Report on Projects visited in 1977, pp. 20-23.

18. Byrne, K. (1978) "Programma de Promotores de Salud," Olancho, Honduras, unpublished document, May.

19. Gibbons, Lillian K. (1979) PAHO AND POLITICS, HEALTH FOR HUMANITY: THE PRIVATE SECTOR IN PRIMARY HEALTH CARE, National Council for International Health Proceedings, Washington, D.C., p. 67.

20. UNICEF/WHO (1981) NATIONAL DECISION-MAKING FOR PRIMARY HEALTH CARE, Geneva: World Health Organization, pp. 34-35.

21. Chowdhury, Zafrullah (1981) "The Good Health Worker Will Inevitably Become a Political Figure," WORLD HEALTH FORUM 2: 55-56.

22. Personal interviews with project personnel.

23. Unpublished documents, and letters.

24. Chowdhury, op. cit.

25. A combination of two incidents of which the author has personal knowledge.

26. Emrich, Susan (1981) "Some Thoughts on the Use of Non-Formal Education in the Real World in the Training and Support of Primary Health Care Workers," PROCEEDINGS 1981 INTERNATIONAL HEALTH CONFERENCE, June 15-17, 1981, Washington, D.C.: National Council for International Health, pp. 68-71.

27. Werner, David and Bill Bower (1982) HELPING HEALTH WORKERS LEARN (early draft), Palo Alto: Hesperian Foundation.

CHAPTER 18

THE STUDY OF WOMEN, FOOD AND HEALTH IN AFRICA*

Meredeth Turshen

In this chapter we argue for a radically different approach to the study of women, food and health in Africa. The common approach is to look at women as housewives, usually within the confines of a single discipline. Medical anthropologists, for example,typically study the rituals surrounding marriage, birth and death; they catalogue taboos that influence health, such as prohibitions of certian foods during pregnancy and prescriptions of intercourse after childbirth. We are critical of this approach because it results in a static view of society, one that lacks reference to the historical past or political present, one that isolates the local economy and stereotypes women.

In our view the problems of the health and nutrition of women and their families cannot be understood or solved if they are analyzed at the level of the household economy alone. A multidisciplinary approach is needed, which combines the interests and insights of economics, sociology and political science. Looked at through these lenses, women emerge as farmers and marketers, wives and mothers, members of cooperatives and political activists. Women's contribution to the village economy is linked to national and even international economics, in this analysis. These linkages are made necessary by the fact that some of the fundamental causes of malnutrition and disease are beyond the control of African women; some causes are rooted in the structure of the global economy.

The research methodology and analytical framework of the multidisciplinary approach are described in part one. We begin by laying out schematically the relationships between food production and nutrition, between women and food production, between nutrition and health, and between women and health. An explanation of the theoretical underpinnings of the argument follows. In part two the approach is applied to the current situation in Tanzania, where food shortages threaten to lower the nutritional status of families.

How to Study Women's Health

The study of women's health starts with their nutrition which, together with land tenure, food production, food distribution, processing, preparation

---

* An earlier version was presented at the Conference on Women, Health and International Development, Michigan State University, Oct., 1982.

of meals, preservation, storage, and consumption, must be considered as a system. (Note: The United Nations Research Institute for Social Development is carrying out a research program called "Food Systems and Society" that uses this approach). This is because, in the rural areas of Africa, agricultural productivity---in its broadest sense, from plant seeds to the meal served---determines nutritional status. Unfortunately, it is rarely the case that food production and nutrition are conceived as a system; all too often agricultural planners ignore the problems of food consumption and nutrition, especially in countries where cash crops are grown for export (World Bank, 1981).

If the relationship between food production and nutrition is a conceptual one, that between women and food production is an observed fact in Africa. In many countries the food system centers on women, who perform most of the manual labor at all stages of the production process. (Note: The argument for considering food and nutrition as a system together with women's role in agriculture is made in a report prepared for the United Nations Protein Advisory Group [Eide et al., 1977]). As long ago as 1928 Baumann observed that the field work of subsistence farming in Africa is done exclusively or predominantly by women. Yet planners continue to ignore women in their role as farmers and they treat the food women grow for domestic consumption differently from export crops. Even when the commodity is the same---for example, rice and maize are both food crops consumed domestically and cash crops raised for export---and even when women work on both garden plots and cash plantations, their contribution is disregarded. Despite much rhetoric since International Women's Year about involving women in development, male planners persist in designing improvements in cash crop production for male farmers. Barbara Rogers (1979), in her study of development planning, castigates the policy makers of bilateral and multilateral aid agencies for their discrimination against women.

A concommitant problem with agricultural inputs is that of the very land being farmed. Patterns of communal land tenure, dating back to the pre-colonial era, have changed in this century; under systems of private property now obtaining in many countries, women lose traditional land rights. Where there is land scarcity, as in the coffee farming areas of Mt. Kilimanjaro, male competition for land suitable for cash crops pushes women off their maize shambas and vegetable plots.

The relationship between nutrition and health is one of synergy: nutrition is the basis of good health and the determinant of the outcome of most diseases. Malnutrition both increased susceptibility to infectious disease and influences the course and outcome of illness. (Note: Resistance to infection is determined by a number of host factors, but a significant variable is the adequacy of immune response; available evidence suggests that cellular immune response and antibody synthesis are two mechanisms by which malnutrition can depress host resistance [W.H.O., 1972]). The interaction of nutrition and infection varies with the type of disease. At one end of the spectrum are diseases not dependent on nutritional status, like tetanus of the newborn, smallpox, and most of the vector-borne infections, although nutrition does affect case fatality rates. At the other end are most of the communicable diseases of childhood, diarrheal diseases, and respiratory infections---the incidence and outcome of these are very much conditioned by nutritional status. It is this latter group of diseases that is most common in Africa and claims the most infant lives. Diarrheas and respiratory infections are not preventable by medical means, however, and it is in this context that the special role of women in health arises.

Women are the provideres of informal health care: as wives and mothers they are often called upon to nurse the young and the old, the sick and the disabled. Even as the network of rural health services expands in some parts of Africa, women still undertake the work of primary prevention by preparing meals, drawing water, bathing children, washing clothes, clearing the compound of refuse, and gathering fuel to light fires on cold nights in the mountainous areas of the continent.

This traditional form of informal health care was subject to contradictory pulls in the colonial period. On the one hand, the need for it grew as new types of work gave rise to new health problems and as the public and private sectors of the colonial system failed to provide adequate welfare or social services (Turshen, 1977). The need was especially great in those subsistence areas to which male migrant laborers returned when old, ill or unemployed. On the other hand, women's informal nursing skills were undermined as health care was socialized (in the sense of being performed as a service outside the home) in government and missionary clinics and as traditional medical knowledge was devalued and replaced by western medicine. Demand for home care was rising at the same time as traditional medical knowledge, especially of herbal remedies, was declining.

These, then, are the relationships between women, food and health. Our next task is to make explicit the theoretical underpinnings of the analysis. To build a complex argument such as this, it is necessary to draw upon theory that facilitates the process of relating information from several separate academic disciplines---in this instance, agricultural economics, medicine, public health, and women's studies; in other words, there is a need for theory that encompasses interdisciplinary studies. A second need is for historical method, because there is no adequate explanation of the current development dilemma in Africa without reference to African history. Colonial accounts of the last century are not useful substitutes for the combination of oral history and anthropological field work that gives Africans the central role in their own stories.

Third, one needs theory to make sense of contradictions, which seem to abound in descriptions of Africa. One narrow example from African women's history will serve as an illustration. A number of authors (Boserup, 1970; Robers, 1979) have made convincing, if damning, critiques of the education given African girls by Christian missionaries. The emphasis on home economics (interpreted as cooking and sewing), not only belittled the African woman's understanding of her familial environment, but also taught her to want European manufactured goods that were often inappropriate and beyond her means. Yet if one reads the biographies of today's African women leaders, it is interesting to note how many of them are gradutes of such classes, or are the daughters of women trained in this way.

Finally, one needs theory to explain the social oppression of women, their subordinate political position, and their economic exploitation. To make sense of the realities of women's lives in a sophisticated way requires theory that differentiates the nature of constraints on a woman like Jihan Sadat from the actual existence of a poor village woman living in rural Egypt.

To sum up, the theory employed is interdisciplinary, uses historical method, relies on dialectics to analyze contradictions, and combines feminist theory of women's subordination with Marxist theory of class conflict. Hypotheses based on this body of theory are best tested in participatory research. (Note: Sources of information on participatory research methodology are the International Council for Adult Education in Toronto and the United Nations Reserch Institute for Social development in Geneva). In participatory research, the subjects become the research workers by defining their own problems, gathering empirical data, experimenting with solutions, and using the results to refine the analysis of their problems. This technique is particularly important for women who are too often cast as passive recipients of development programs or, at best, as respondents in surveys. Participatory research empowers women in a way that traditional methods, including participant-observation, can never do. It also has the advantage of speeding up the process of returning research results to the people most directly concerned.

With these research tools it is possible to analyze the international situation in African countries and find out how women, food and health are linked to the economic, social and political system. Internal analysis is insufficient, however, since the national system is subject to international control. One form of international control is neocolonialism, which is continuing economic domination of a former colony by the metropolitan power. Many would say that Gabon is still controlled by France in this way. A more subtle form of control is exerted by international institutions like the World Bank and the International Monetary Fund which dictate the terms on which African nations can borrow money for development projects. Marxist theories of imperialism are useful in understanding international relations, including the role of financial institutions (Brewer, 1980).

Women's Health in Tanzania

There is so little information available on women in general and women's health in particular that it is easier to begin this discussion with a description of the present economic crisis in Tanzania and deduce its impact on women. In terms of levels of analysis, we will be moving from the national up to the international economy and then turning to the village and household economy. This process may be thought of as linking macroanalysis to microanalysis.

The nature of the present economic crisis in Tanzania is described in the following news report. "Tanzania's economic problems...have forced the suspension of development projects in the 1982-83 fiscal year. President Julius Nyerere said the country's small amount of foreign exchange earnings would instead be used to pay for spare parts and other essentials. Observers said that shortages had reduced Tanzania's small manufacturing sector to 30 percent of capacity, and that there were widespread shortages of such essentials as flour, sugar and cooking oil. Inflation is running between 40 and 60 percent annually. Although Nyerere had refused IMF demands to devalue the Tanzanian shilling, the currency was in fact devalued by 10 percent in March, 1982. The IMF had sought a 50 percent devaluation" (AFRICA REPORT, 1982b).

Why does the IMP seek a 50 percent devaluation of the Tanzanian shilling, and why does Nyerere refuse? Tanzania is unable to balance its international income (composed of export earnings and current borrowing) with its international expenses (imports and debt servicing). There are three ways to deal with balance of payment deficits: (1) impose import restrictions or capital controls, (2) deflate the economy by reducing economic activity, or (3) devalue the currency (Block, 1977). The IMP recommends devaluation because it leaves the market open and unimpaired, and the capitalist firms that the IMP serves want to continue selling their manufactured goods to Tanzania unimpeded by import restrictions. The firms are not affected if it costs Tanzania twice as much to buy their products.

Nyerere opposes devaluation because it raises the cost of imports and reduces real wage levels. With dwindling reserves of foreign currency and unable to negotiate a loan from the IMF (with which Tanzania has been bickering for years over terms and conditions), he is forced to cut imports. The effect of the cut is to create a shortage of spare parts, which in turn reduces manufacturing to 30 percent of capacity. With machines turned off, men and women seeking employment in Tanzania's small industrial sector must be turned away those who hold onto their jobs receive wages worth 10 percent less. A new system of financial incentives allows industry to knock an additional 10 to 20 percent off the pay of 'idle'---that is, less productive---workers (Dimsdale, 1982).

What will be the impact on women workers? Women are concentrated in low paying jobs, in Tanzania as elsewhere; their incomes are already inadequate (Shields, 1980). Urban women thrown out of work will spend more time cultivating their small **shambas** (the kitchen gardens found near all residences) and may turn to casual prostitution to supplement their incomes, according to a survey of women workers in Dar es Salaam (Bryceson, 1980).

Meanwhile, inflation is running between 40 and 60 percent a year. In North America and Europe, inflation rates of 10 percent are a cause for alarm and government intervention; the impact of rates that average 50 percent in Third World countries less able to absorb inflation is devastating. Since it falls to women in Africa to purchase the food and clothing they and their children need——and in the cities they must also buy fuel and water——inflation will lower their standard of living, including nutritional standards.

One cannot assume,however, that all essentials are there to be purchased at any price, since the article in Africa Report states that there are widespread shortages of flour, sugar and cooking oil. These commodities are essentials to urban women. Inevitably, a black market has appeared and there are reports of hoarding and corruption. According to NEW AFRICAN magazine, "sugar at the controlled price cost Tshs 8.50 a kilo but during a serious shortage, prices can shoot up to Tshs 30 a kilo" (NEW AFRICAN, 1982a).

In the countryside there is a return to the subsistence economy; surpluses are being bartered rather than sold (Dimsdale, 1982). (Note: Subsistence today should not be imagined as a return to the romantic villages described in anthroplogical accounts of the colonial era. Too much change has occurred——in land tenure and cropping patterns, for example——for that past to be recaptured, if indeed it ever existed). If this means that women are now grinding their own grain, pressing oil seeds, and processing sugar cane, then their work load is increasing. One wonders which of their many other duties will be neglected, and what will be the impact of increased energy expenditures on their own health.

To secure a large loan from the IMF, Tanzania has adopted a program designed to increase the coffee crop by 5 to 6 percent ayear. (Note: Tanzania was unevenly developed in the colonial period, with cash crop areas receiving most of the colony's resources. the coffee areas are on the northeastern and northwestern borders where the climate is favorable. Population density is quite high in these regions). This program will deepen the crisis for women in rural and urban areas, according to our analysis. To understand why we draw this conclusion, it is necessary to read reports on increased coffee production (AFRICAN BUSINESS, 1982) together with earlier notices of expected widespread food shortages and possible famine (AFRICA REPORT, 1982a). In 1981 Tanzanian officials predicted that food stocks would run out within a year. In January, 1982, the Minister for Agriculture announced that Tanzania would need 300,000 tons of food aid . [Three months later Western nations offered 260,000 tons of emergency food aid] (AFRICA REPORT, 1982a).

Food aid, however, is not a long-term answer. Even the official agencies now admit its failure. NEW AFRICA (1982b) reported the findings of a confidential report by the European Court of Auditors, which severely criticizes the European Economic Community's food aid to Third World countries during the last decade. A few years ago such scandals were reported, not by official agencies, but by groups like the Institute for Food and Development Policy (Lappe and Collins, 1977) and individuals like Susan George (1976). Of course the donor countries are not yet ready to abandon food aid altogether; it remains a convenient way to dispose of agricultural surpluses "while profiting from the resultant political and economic influence" (NEW AFRICAN, 1982b).

The connection between famine and increased acreage under cash crops turns on insufficient food production. While the IMF is pushing for more land to be given over to a non-nutritive export crop, the World Bank reports that in Sub-Saharan Africa as a whole, food production per person declined in the 1970s. "Imports of food grains (wheat, rice and maize) soared---by 9 percent per year since the early 1960s---reinforcing food dependency" (World Bank, 1980: 3). To realize what increased coffee production means to rural women in Bukoba or Kilimanjaro where most coffee plantations are located, we must turn to the internal analysis of women, food and health at the microlevel of the household and village economy.

Studies that describe the relationship between women, nutrition and food production in northeastern Tanzania were reviewed by the authors of a report prepared for the United Nations Protein Advisory Group (Eide et al., 1977). These authors conclude that although cash crop areas like Mt. Kilimanjaro are supposedly the prosperous regions of the country, infant mortality is exceptionally high there. (Note: This finding is not reflected in official statistics for Kilimanjaro Region; the discrepancy may be accounted for by the level of aggregation of government data). Infant deaths are more numerous on the mountain than on the poor maize--growing plains to the south. The authors relate this finding to what they term 'culture-specific factors' that help to determine women's position in the family (Eide, 1977: III.85).

Factors such as intrafamilial food distribution appear to be crucial when economic conditions are unfavorable, as they are now (AFRICAN BUSI-NESS, 1982). Coffee growers receive an average price of Tshs 15 per kilo as compared with the 1981 world market price received by the Coffee Authority of Tanzania, which was Tshs 28 per kilo, and growers may have to wait as long as six months to receive payment. As a result, an estimated 30 percent of the crop is reportedly smuggled into Kenya, where the price received is six times the Tanzanian prince (Dimsdale, 1982). The loss of foreign exchange to the Coffee Authority only aggrevates Tanzania's crisis. In these circumstances, the tradition of differentiating between men and women's food and the custom of serving husbands large portions of meat result in nutrition problems for less privileged family members.

Prevailing inequalities in landholdings in this region are accentuated by coffee production. The wives of better-off farmers with more land and cattle are under less strain than women in low income groups. Wealth allows some women to ride to distant farm plots while poorer women

247

walk. Wealthier women can hire workers to help harvest crops and to transport them, while poorer women may spend long periods away from home walking to their fields, working in them, and carrying heavy harvest loads uphill on the return journey. A little wealth also makes it easier to keep cattle and goats since cash buys lorry loads of grass, which has to be brought up from the plains to feed animals kept in stalls or tethered because there is no grazing land available on the mountain, nor is there space to grow fodder.

Cash crops are a source of income to men and, in households where income is pooled----a practice by no means to be taken for granted in Africa (Shields, 1976)----women may profit and use the money to lighten their workload. But studies show that such women are a minority. For the majority of poor women, coffee crops "on nearby land will force them to walk farther to grow maize on distant fields; they will have a heavier work load as food producers, less time for household tasks and a bigger struggle to provide the family with nutritious food" (Eide et al., 1977: II.87).

For solutions we must turn once more to the international level, not because Tanzania bears no responsibility for its internal affairs nor because there are no further improvements to be made in domestic policy, but because the ultimate determinants of solutions are external. Few countries have tried as hard as Tanzania to improve the living standards of their masses, but government plans have often been sabotaged by unfavorable international terms of trade. Yet the IMF and the World Bank do not suggest changes at the international level; indeed the degree to which they shift responsibility for economic crises to national governments is striking. The adjustments recommended by the IMF as conditions of loans are always national policy changes, which have significant social consequences. The lending policy of the IMF encourages 'loan dependency' in the same way it fosters food dependency and leads to what Cheryl Payer (1975) has called the 'dept trap.'

The World Bank's solutions, presented in the report on "Accelerated Development in Sub-Saharan Africa,:" emphasizes production of cash crops for export (World Bank, 1980). The Bank claims that there is an extra-ordinary degree of similarity throughout the region in the nature of the policy problems that have arisen and in the national responses to them. (One wonders what role the IMF has played in its imposition of uniform conditions). Among shortcomings of existing policy cited by the Bank area a bias against exports and a bias against agriculture. In reading the Bank report, one experiences the sensation of **deja vu;** in the nineteenth century, imperialists rationalized their colonial policy with the doctrine of natural advantage. Once again the Bank seems to be advocating that African nations specialize in producing primary commodities for the nothern industrialized nations.

The countries of the Third World oppose that rationale and have submitted a program for change called "The New International Economic Order"

(United Nations,1974). It is not possible here to describe the program in detail; it may suffice to say that implementation of the program of action on trade and development of raw mateials and primary commodities would offer Tanzania more options than that of devaluing its currency or curtailing its development programs. The amelioration of terms of trade would offer Tanzanian coffee farmers better returns on the crop they now produce, obviating the need to expand production at rates of 5 and 6 percent per annum. Improved terms of trade would also alter the economic circumstances of women and offer the possibility of better health and nutrition for themselves and their families. The New International Economic Order holds the promise of a future for Tanzania radically different from the grim one currently predicted.

REFERENCES

AFRICAN BUSINESS (1982) (Sept.): 40.

AFRICA REPORT (1982a) (March/April): 37.

AFRICA REPORT (1982b) (May/June): 30.

BAUMANN,HERMANN (1928) "The Division of Work According to Sex in African Hoe Culture," AFRICA I.

BLOCK, FRED (1977) THE ORIGINS OF INTERNATIONAL ECONOMIC DISORDER. Berkeley: University of California Press.

BOSERUP, ESTER (1970) WOMAN'S ROLE IN ECONOMIC DEVELOPMENT. N.Y.: St. Martin's Press.

BREWER, ANTHONY (1980) MARXIST THEORIES OF IMPERIALISM: A CRITICAL SURVEY. London: Routledge & Kegan Paul.

BRYCESON, DEBORAH (1980) "The Proletarianization of Women in Tanzania,": REVIEW OF AFRICAN POLITICAL ECONOMY 17.

DIMSDALE, JOHN (1982) "Two Roads to Socialism," AFRICA REPORT (Sept/Oct): 14-17.

EIDE, WENCHE BARTH et al. (1977) "Women in Food Production, Food Handling and Nutrition with Special Emphasis on Africa," UNITED NATIONS PROTEIN ADVISORY GROUP.

GEORGE, SUSAN (1976) HOW THE OTHER HALF DIES. Harmondsworth: Penguin Books.

LAPPE, FRANCES MOORE and JOSEPH COLLINS (1977) FOOD FIRST. N.Y.: Ballantine Books.

NEW AFRICAN (1982a) (March): 23.

NEW AFRICAN (1982b) (June): 40.

PAYER, CHERYL (1975) THE DEBT TRAP: THE IMP AND THE THIRD WORLD. N.Y.: Monthly Review Press.

ROGERS, BARBARA (1979) THE DOMESTICATION OF WOMEN. N.Y.: St. Martin's Press.

SHIELDS, NWANGANGA (1976) "The Relevance of Current Models of

Married Women's Labor Force Participation to Africa" Seminar on House-hold Models of Economic Demograhic Decision-Making." Mexico City (Sept.).

SHIELDS, NWANGANGA (1980) "Women in the Urban Labor Markets of Africa: The Case of Tanzania," WORLD BANK STAFF WORKING PAPER No. 380.

TURSHEN, MEREDETH (1977) "The Impact of Colonialism on Health and Health Services in Tanzania," INTERNATIONAL JOURNAL OF HEATLH SERVICES 7: 7-35.

UNITED NATIONS (1974) GENERAL ASSEMBLY RESOLUTIONS 3201 (S-VI) and 3202 (S-VI).

WORLD HEALTH ORGANIZATION (1972) HUMAN DEVELOPMENT AND PUBLIC HEALTH. WHO TECHNICAL REPORT SERIES NO. 485.

WORLD BANK (1981) "Nutritional Consequences of Agricultural Projects: Conceptual Relationships and Assessment Approaches," WORLD BANK STAFF WORKING PAPER NO. 456.

WORLD BANK (1980) ACCELERATED DEVELOPMENT IN SUB-SAHARAN AFRICA. Washington, D.C.

CHAPTER 19

HEALTH CARE AND SOCIAL CHANGE:
THE CASE OF NORTHEASTERN MALAWI

Arnold P. Wendroff

Introduction

Malawi, like many other Third World nations, is in the throes of rapid and accelerating social change, change that extends to the ways in which people perceive illness and attempt to deal with it. This essay examines the changes in Malawi's health-care practices that are part of the broader socio-technological ferment taking place in the country today. The field work on which the essay is based was carried out mostly in the Rumphi and Karonga districts of northeastern Malawi, so that the discussion focuses on that area   but much of what is said applies to the country as a whole.

The indigenous health care practices of northeastern Malawi have been modified by their interaction with a western culture that was first introduced into the area by Christian missionaries towards the end of the nineteenth century. Since that time, the bearers of this essentially alien culture have included the representatives of the British colonial government, European traders, planters, and civil servants, local men returned from working abroad in the more developed nations to the south, and western-trained physicians and nurses (both European and native-born) who staff the country's government and mission hospitals.

In Malawi, as elsewhere in the Third World, Christianity and its attendant culture have been the agents of powerful dislocation in the fabric of traditional culture and society. Prior to European contact, social stratification based on wealth was unknown in the northeastern area except among herders belonging to outlying tribes and those few Swahili Arabs engaged in slaving in the extreme north. The European missionaries introduced literacy and formal education not only as an aid to proselytizing, but to provide useful skills to converts destined for employment in what David Livingstone envisaged as a Christian commerce that would supplant slaving as a source of cash income for the people of the area.

The new relilgious, educational, and economic opportunities that proceded from a Christian reordering of traditional values, created the grounds for a large-scale stratification of society. The revised social order differed from that of the past not just in its level of stratification, but by being based not, as it had been, on ascribed status, but on wealth and achieved status. In this way, the basis was laid for "what Veblen called 'invidious comparison' " (Mitchell, 1970: 307)---what is commonly termed jealousy by Malawians today, who regard such aggravated covetousness as the principal incitement to the practice of witchcraft. The importance of these socio-economic upheavals to an understanding of present-day health care in Malawi becomes more fully apparent once we know that witchcraft is generally believed to be responsible for most serious misfortune and disease, not just in the northeast but throughout Malawi.

The imposition of British rule brought with it the virtues as well as the liabilities of the Pax Britannica, though it isn't always easy to distinguish the one from the other. In the field of health care, the British generally allowed for the unhindered practice of indigenous medicine, but here too there was an attempt to enforce change. The attempt took most notable early form in the Witchcraft Act of 1911, which severely curtailed the ability of traditional practitioners to treat those people believed to be ensorceling their fellows. The Act came just at a time when such practices as socery would have been on the rise. The hut tax that had been imposed in stages during the 1890's had forced many men, when they could not find work in the economically-backward northeast, to seek employment in the south and in the Rhodesias and South Africa. Such absences eventually gave rise to a considerable social disruption, due not only to the loss at home of the absent labor, but to the workers' fears that their wives would be unfaithful during their sojourns abroad, fears which often enough proved justified. It is just such tensions and fears as these that cause men to resort to magic to keep their wives faithful, and to sorcery to punish adulterers.

Witchcraft And Social Change

Although the Witchcraft Act of 1911 specifically prohibited both witch-craft practice and accusation, and institutions such as the Christian missions and the educational and medical establishments have attempted to wean people from a belief in witches, witchcraft continues to be thought of by most Malawians as the single most important cause of death and of serious misfortune and illness. That this is so is hardly surprising. Not only have the western-style laws and institutions of Malawi been largely ineffective in discouraging traditional witchcraft belief, the social stratification that has accompanied the establishment of these same laws and institutions, and the rapid social change of which they are a vehicle, have, ironically, served to foster and intensify the very beliefs they set themselves to combat.

In pre-colonial times, the northeastern area, like the rest of Malawi, was far more socially homogenous than it is now, with most people sharing the same type of subsistence-level existence. With the advent of Christianity, formal education, and a cash economy, differences among people began to appear where before there had been none. As the level of relative deprivation in the society increased under the impact of economic development and social change, so, inevitably, did occasions for envy, jealousy, and resentment. In a society in which hostile feelings of this kind are all but universally held to give rise to the practice of witchcraft, it was equally inevitable that an increase in the occasions for such hostile feelings should bring with it a corresponding increase in general witchcraft belief and in individual accusations of witchcraft. All the more was this so in that, as an explanation of economic deprivation, witchcraft had and continues to have the special merit of accounting for a wide range of cases, and of fastening blame on the witch rather than on acts of omission or commission by the supposed victim.

Witchcraft, or (to use Evans-Pritchard's terminology) sorcery (Evans--Pritchard, 1937: 21), is strongly believed in by Malawians of the northeast not only because "victims" attribute their troubles to it, but because in an area in which the general belief in the efficacy of magic is high, many people actually do practice sorcery. Even more engage in various forms of "white" magic. This is not to say that such practices ever produce their intended results, rather to emphasize that the criteria people use to evaluate the effectiveness of witchcraft practices are pre-scientific, and that, by western standards, the population is credulous. Thus when people openly confess to having ensorceled their neighbors, as they do regularly, they do so not merely because of the social pressure brought to bear on them by a designated witch-finder or by a court, but because, in some cases at least, they have in fact engaged in necromancy.

The Poison Ordeal and the Witchcraft Act

Witchcraft (technically, sorcery) and witchcraft accusation were in pre--colonial days kept in check by means of **mwabvi** or the poison ordeal. This institution used to be widespread through much of east Africa and is still in use today, only on dogs and chickens as surrogates for humans. The ordeal was usually administered under the supervision of the local chief, and consisted of the accused witch---and often his or her accuser as well---being given an infusion of the bark of the mwabvi tree to drink. Those who vomited up the poison were believed to be innocent; those unfortunates who retained it and died were held to have been witches. In theory, mwabvi was impartial and infallible. The administrators of the Nyasaland Proectorate (as Malawi was known under British rule) took a different view, however, and looked upon the ordeal not as a valuable judicial instrument in cases of suspected witchcraft, but as a killer of people who were, by western standards, innocent of any wrongdoing. Having some two centuries earlier themselves outgrown a belief in witchcraft, the British were not inclined to look with favor on a latter-day African variety.

The legislative outcome of these conflicting interpretations of reality was the Witchcraft Ordinance of 1911, later called the Witchcraft Act and still very much on the books. This statute not only outlawed the poison and other witchfinding ordeals, but the very leveling of an accusation of witchcraft against anyone, except before a properly constituted authority such as court officer, chief, or policeman. The solicitation and employment of witchfinders was also forbidden, as was the profession of witchfinding. With its many provisions severely restricting traditional methods of witchfinding, the Witchcraft Act appeared to the public to be heavily biased in favor of the witch. The Act did have a section forbidding persons from representing themselves to be wizards or witches, but this was of small consolation to an alarmed populace aware that most sorcerers practice in secret.

The Witchcraft Act of 1911 thus forbade the use of methods which had long been held to be the most effective in protecting the public from sorcery, and to the outlawed methods offered no viable alternatives. Since the belief in witchcraft as the chief cause of misfortune and disease continued unabated, some new means of dealing with the problem had to be evolved. The new method has turned out to be a species of quasi--judicial divination of ambiguous legality and wide use.

The Expanded Role of the NCHIMI

Even had people continued, clandestinely, to resort to mwabvi, a less draconian way of dealing with sorcery would have had to be found: since it frequently killed its subject, the poison ordeal inevitably attracted the unwelcome attention of the authorities. The **nchimi** or diviner is the latter-day successor to mwabvi. His numbers seem to have proliferated in direct response to the ordeal's legal suppression. Without physically harming the alleged witch, the nchimi, guided by **mizimu** (ancestral spirits) or by God himself, is believed to be unerring in his or her pronouncements of culpability (though not quite as unerring as mwabvi). Although he cannot rid society of the witch's person, he is believed able to render the witch innocuous, and so to effect a long-term cure of the witch's victim.

In his special capacity of diviner, the nchimi relies on purely psychic powers. He or she possesses, in fact, all of the expertise of the **nganga** or herbalist, but has the additional ability to do diviniation, and especially witchfinding, without having to rely on the apparatus used by nganga. Nchimi are able to confront a witch, to cause him (or her) to confess and surrender his evil charms or **nyanga**, and then to administer potent medicines which will prevent him fron engaging in sorcery in the future (Marwick, 1950: 103; Redmayne, 1970: 119).

Prior to the suppression of mwabvi, most specialist health care in Malawi was in fact provided by nganga, who make their diagnosis by questioning the patient and by the use of various forms of divination apparatus. These practitioners attempt to treat all manner of complaints, mainly by the use of herbal medications administered internally and externally in an assortment of ways. Nganga are not adept at witchfinding, however, although they can often ascertain whether or not a person is bewitched. Since most serious misfortune and illness in Malawi is likely to elicit at least a suspicion of witchcraft, some practitioner with more expertise in witchfinding was clearly required once the poison ordeal had been outlawed.

The prestige and dignity that attach to the nchimi's calling by virtue of his divinatory powers, are reflected in the arrangements he makes for seeing his patients. Whereas nganga are outpatient-oriented, nchimi traditionally keep inpatients, some practitioners boasting extensive hospital villages with huts for over a hundred patients. Some of these inpatients may be in treatment for months at a time. A number of nchimi have adopted the symbols and aplicances of western healers in order to enhance their own impressiveness: the wearing of a white coat; the preparation of medicines in pill form; the use of a dummy stethoscope; the sewing of crosses on professional garments in imitation of the clergy. Much of the ritual that accompanies the exercise of an nchimi's divinatory powers involves the singing of hymns, many of which are taken directly from the Christian liturgy. Borrowings such as these testify to the continued potency of western forms in Malawi's poverty-stricken and still largely illiterate society.

A number of traditional healers in the northeast, herbalists and diviners, have joined professional associations based either in southern Malawi or in Zimbabwe. Such bodies seem to be primarily concerned with fulfilling their latent functions—generating income for their organizers by charging entrance and annual membership fees; providing members with impressively-worded certificates designed to legitimate the practitioner in the same way that a medical school diploma serves a western M.D. Healers used to obtain letters from their local District Commissioner attesting to the legitimacy of their practice under the law. But such letters were hard to get, and nowadays anyone can obtain an even more impressive document merely by applying to a herbalists' association, and sending in a few dollars.

The stated aims of these professional associations include: "...the endeavor to follow the most up-to-date methods in the care and treatment of patients....to punish any person who is **not** a member of the Association who is practicing as a herbalist....to ensure that cooperation be maintained without talking ill of fellow members....to cooperate with the Government, the Party, and everything that is under rule....to promote the African Herbalism." (African Herbal Association memberhsip certificate, 1976). Needless to say, the associations have no means and make no attempt to carry out these aims.

Traditional healers are, in fact, basically solo practitioners, and have little professional contact with each other. Nganga and nchimi tend to be secretive about their methods and **materia medica;** they rarely share their knowledge with their fellows or with outsiders. The introduction of literacy to Lamawi has for the first time made it possible to codify traditional remedies; and some healers, as well as laymen, have written down their formulations for their own or their family's use (Young,

257

1932). But such material remains essentially private, and must be regarded as no more than a precursor of an indigenous medical literature.

The Changed Role of the Village Headman in the Healing Process

In pre-colonial times, village headmen and chiefs played an important role as arbiters in cases of suspected witchcraft, and as overseers of the poison ordeal. The legal suppression of mwabvi, and of witchfinding in general, has had the effect of limiting the role these officials play in sorcery cases. It has also subjectedheadmen and chiefs to considerable role strain, since the anti-witchcraft laws they are required by the government to uphold are strongly at odds with their own and their villagers' beliefs (Gluckman, 1949: 93-94). Although the law still specifically allows witchcraft accusations to be made to them, chiefs and headmen are nowadays expected to promote alternative explanations to witchcraft for their villagers' misfortunes, or to refer witchcraft cases to the police or courts. The stiff penalties established by the Witchcraft Act for seeking out the services of a witchfinder are a strong deterrent to the use of such professionals.

Nevertheless, headmen face much the same problems and bear much the same responsibilities today as they did prior to the Witchcraft Act's initial passage in 1911: witchcraft accusations and disputes are regularly brought before them, and have to be resolved. With mwabvi outlawed, the favored instrument for such resolution has become the nchimi. It is to him that the headman now refers complaints of suspected sorcery, in the expectation that his exceptional powers and prestige will compel assent from all the parties involved. Of course such referrals are themselves illegal, but they are usually carried out with what one must assume to be the tacit approval of the local government, or at least the turning of a blind eye: the practice must be common knowledge, yet few offending headmen are prosecuted.

Occasional prosecutions do take place, however, and serve to remind everyone concerned of thr risks they run. One such prosecution occurred in 1973, **Republic vs. Donald Gausi.** Gausi was a headman who summoned a witchfinder to his village to explain the cause of several recent deaths. For his violation of the law's anti-witchfinding provisions, the unfortunate headman was given a six-month suspended sentence as a first offender. The following letter, directed by another village headman to a witchfinder and perhaps reflecting the climate of apprehension brought on by the Gausi prosecution, illustrates the headman's quandary: "(December, 1973) Nchimi __X__ , I am very happy to write you this letter; but people are scaring me. They say I will be arrested because I send people to you. They have gone to lodge a complaint against me. They have gone to chief __Y__ . The complaint is that he says I have pointed out that he is a witch...Yours, Village Headman __Z__ ."

Letters of referral such as that written by Village Headman __Z__ are an obvious instance of western influence on traditional health care in

Malawi, since before the European penetration literacy was more or less unknown in the country. Such letters are commonly directed to nchimi by headmen and chiefs on behalf of villagers who suspect that the misfortune or disease they are suffering is due to sorcery. So much a part of traditional health care have these letters of referral become, that nchimi often require them as a form of quasi-official authorization for them to engage in witchfinding. The letters state, in effect, that the headman accepts responsibility for the consequences of the diviner's findings, consequences which in witchcraft cases may extend to violence between accuser and accused.

In return for committing his reponsibility in a letter of referral, the headman normally asks to be informed of the nchimi's findings in writing, so that he can deal with the case in his village as the findings warrant. Often the nchimi will send for the suspected witch to be "searched"—interrogated concerning his or her alleged evil practices——and it is in such cases the headman's responsibility to induce (in some instances, coerce) the often-unwilling suspect to go to the nchimi and suffer this procedure. If the suspect is indeed found to be a witch, the headman will be informed, and will determine what action, if any, is to be taken. Although there is usually nothing he can do legally, the group social pressure he is able to mobilize will often bring about the desired result. On rare occasions a person may be forced to leave the village.

Thus we see how a basic mechanism of present-day traditional health care in Malawi has been shaped by western influence in two key ways: from reliance on the draconian and outlawed poison ordeal, the parties to a witchcraft dispute have been compelled to rely instead on the special but less deadly powers of the diviner; and in having recourse to this health--care professional, they have developed a system of formal written referral which, in easily recognizable ways, mimics that in use in the developed countries of the west. Finally, we see how these changes in the traditional mechanism afor resolving witchcraft disputes have resulted in a change and a contraction in the role played in such disputes by the village headman, though by no means the elimination of that role.

Christianity's Influence on Traditional Health Care

Before the introduction of Christianity, traditional religion throughout Malawi centered around the mizimu or ancestral spirits, who oversaw men's behavior and acted as intermediaries between man and **Chiuta**, the remote high God (Msiska, 1969). Many of the physical, mental, and social troubles that fell to a person's lot were attributed to acts of commission or omission on his part which, by violating the norms of traditional morality, angered the mizimu and brought down their vengeance on the transgressor or his relations in the form of sickness and misfortune. Acting as intermediaries betweeen man and the mizimu were priests, who conducted the rites deemed necessary to propitiate the restive and angered spirits.

In the northeast, as elsewhere in Malawi, Christianity has made its way at the expense of these traditional beliefs; only vestiges of the belief in spirits as the agents of disease survive in the area today. Yet while Christianity succeeded in undermining the explanatory and coercive foundations of traditional morality and belief, what it offered in their place has for many people failed to prove emotionally or spiritually or even intellectually satisfying. As a consequence of this failure, and of the rapid social and economic changes taking place in secular life (that one can even divide the concerns of present-day life in Malawi into spiritual and secular illustrates just how far contemporary western modes of thought have usurped Malawians' traditional unified world view), a kind of anomic void has been created in the lives of many Malawians. The marked increase over the last century in the belief in sorcery as the cause of misfortune and disease, and in the actual practice of sorcery, may be seen as one of the ways in which people have adjusted to and unconsciously sought to fill this spiritual and emotional void.

Ironically, Christianity, with its biblical codification of a host of supernatural phenomena—familiar spirits, witches, demons, laying on of hands, spirit possess, exorcism, miracles—has served in many ways to reinforce traditional belief in the supernatural etiology and treatment of disease, rather than, as its purveyors intended, lessening such belief. As a result, in Malawi today people in distress seldom resort to the Church for aid, especially if they suspect their trouble to be of supernatural origin. The Church, whether Protestant or Catholic, is seen as having little to offer victims of witchcraft. Most clergymen themselves believe in sorcery, and so refrain from publicly denouncing traditional methods of dealing with it. The Churches have all declared their opposition to the use of nchimi, calling them false prophets, and some sects go so far as to suspend members guilty of patronizing them; but this does not prevent many members from consulting the diviners clandestinely. As one writer on the subject has put it: "Everyone under the cover of darkness treks to them" (Kapapa, 1979: 1).

The loss in stature which the mizimu have suffered under the impact of Christianity has been accompanied by a corresponding rise in the importance of the cult or **vimbuza.** Vimbuza is a type of spirit possession involving not one's own ancestral spirits, but those belonging to other, often remote peoples (Chilivumbo, 1972; de Winter, 1972: 94). Thus the Tumbuka people who predominate in northeastern Malawi are possessed by spirits of the Ngoni, Bemba, Chewa, and other outlying tribes, and even on occasion by British spirits. Such spirit possession is commonly reckoned a disease, one with a host of possible symptoms.

As is the case with suspected sorcery, the inability of western medicine to effect a rapid cure of a given complaint is ordinarily taken as a diagnostic sign that the complaint in question may be due to vimbuza and not to natural causes. Once such a possibility arises, the patient will turn for help to traditional healers. One popular interpretation of vimbuza is that its symptoms are caused by the conflict being waged within the victim between a sorcerer's deadly medicine or nyanga, and the chimbuza or friendly spirit that is attempting to save the person from death. With the mizimu having been discredited by Christianity and with Christianity having shown itself powerless to combat sorcery, the vimbuza spirits may be looked upon as conjured up to fill an emotional and explanatory void---for an afflicted people literally and figuratively a form of spiritual succor. We have seen the same compensatory process at work in the rise of the nchimi to replace the legally-banned poison ordeal, and in the marked increase in sorcery belief to make up for Christianity's relegation of the mizimu.

Education's Impact on Health Care

In Malawi, formal education is neither compulsory nor free. In 1977-78 just over half of school-age children in the northeast were attending school; less than half of those entering standard 1 of the primary school could be expected to complete standard 8. The teaching of primary-school science remains poor. Efforts at implementing an innovative experimentally-oriented science curriculum have been largely frustrated by the painfully inadequate training of teachers (one-third of the primary-school teachers in the northeast in 1977-78 had themselves completed less than ten years of schooling). The teaching of health is, if anything, even worse than that of general science, with very little practical health information assimilated by students. To most young Malawians completing their primary-school science requirement, the "germ theory" is still no more than a theory. Their perception of disease and their practical response to it will be shaped not by such pallid western semi-abstractions (for so these ideas must often appear), but by the much more emotioally and intellectually satisfying belief in witchcraft.

It is by virtue of what it leaves out rather than what it includes that the established school science curriculum helps to determine this choice of disease explanation. The curriculum's only attempt at discrediting traditional concepts of disease causation and treatment occurs in the health-education syllabus for standard 7, where one unit out of thirty-seven is devoted to traditional medicine. The negative aspects of both traditional herbal healing and of contemporary patent medicines are briefly discussed, and children are asked "to realize that sickness cannot be caused by other people's bad thoughts or by 'Spirits' ": "Superstition of this kind causes many deaths and great fear....Pupils (are asked to) discuss the difference between the good herbalist doctor in the village and the doctor who encourages superstition and deals in 'witchcraft'." (Moss, 1971: 128).

But in practice even this material is largely ignored. Like children everywhere, students in Malawi acquire most of their knowledge and their values not in the classroom but from personal experience and by observing the example of their elders. That experience and that example (including the example of their teachers, who patronize both traditional and western healers) powerfully reinforce traditional concepts of disease causation, at the expense of the western concepts taught in the classroom.

Further reinforcement comes through a student's contact with the Bible. All primary school students, beginning in Standard 1, take religious education, familiarly known as "Bible Knowledge." It involves "listen(ing) to the Bible as the Word of God...as they (the children) learn from the Sacred Scriptures of experience similar to their own" (RELIGIOUS EDUCATION, n.d. [c. 1976]: 1). While his interaction with western medicine leaves the student with few experiences comparable to those narrated in the Bible, traditional healing as he has come to know it abounds with parallels, parallels which the child is not likely to ignore. Biblical allusions to supernatural disease causation and to supernatural healing are numerous, and serve to strengthen belief in the traditional supernatural diagnosis and treatment of disease. Bible study, therefore, presented in an uncritical manner tends to create a perceived reality that is congruent with traditional notions of causality.

TRADITIONAL MEDICINE AND THE LAW

Although the Witchcraft Act outlaws those aspects of traditional healing that have to do with witchfinding, and while the government, until very recently, made no effort to promote the use of traditional healers, there are two laws in Malawi that specifically allow for the practice of traditional medicine. These laws recognize, in effect, that western medicine is not able to provide all that is demanded of it, quantitatively or qualitatively: its practice in clinics and hospitals is impaired by an often serious lack of manpower and of money; its western-trained personnel are ill--equipped to deal with patients who firmly believe their physical or emotional disorders are supernaturally caused, some of whose disorders, indeed, are not even officially recognized.

The Medical Practitioners' and Dentists' Registration Act, while requiring that western healers be trained to internationally-recognized standards and forbidding the practice of quack medicine, nevertheless allows "the practice of any African system of therapeutics; by such persons as are recognized in Malawi to be duly trained in such practice." The other legal concession to "African medicine" is in the Pharmacy and Poisons (Control of Patent Medicines) Order. In a section banning the manufacture and sale of any patent medicine intended for the treatment of venereal disease, this law all the same---and, it would seem, with a great deal of inconsistency---permits "the sale to any African of any African medicine, compounded or prepared within Malawi and intended for the prevention, cure or treatment of venereal disease, by an African who is recognized by the community to which he belongs as being competent to treat venereal disease." The Pharmacy and Poisons Order not only exempts traditional healers from its own edict, but from the provisions of the venereal diseases section of the Public Health Act, which limit the diagnosis and treatment of venereal disease to the western medical establishment.

262

While the Medical Practitioners' Act and the Pharmacy and Poisons Order allow, they do not encourage traditional healing. Such official encouragement has over the years been more often hinted at than actually given. On two occasions---a Weekend Seminar of the Malawi Medical Association in 1972, and a National Seminar on Primary Health Care in 1978---the possibility was raised of integrating traditional and western systems of health care. But apart from a (reasonably successful) program to train traditional midwives in the rudiments of western obstetrics, little has been done to make such medical integration a reality.

In 1976 the Regional Office for Africa of the World Health Organization called for "multidisciplinary mechanisms for integrating traditional healers into health teams in order to promote their activities, particularly in rural areas (W.H.O., 1976: 18). The same W.H.O. report noted that, in order to implement such a program, "a political decision at the top is indispensable." Such a decision has yet to be made in Malawi, although the nation's sole political party has given token support to a professional organization of herbalists.

One likely reason why the government is shy of actively encouraging the practice of traditional medicine is that traditional medicine recognizes witchcraft as the primary cause of serious disease, and thus sets itself to find and treat witches as well as victims, in much the way western allopathic medicine seeks to find and treat asymptomatic carriers of contagious diseases like typhoid. Since, so far as official government policy is concerned, belief in witchcraft is harmful and wrong, the government inevitably finds it difficult to effect a meaningful rapprochment between western medicine and a system of traditional health care founded on the very belief government itself condemns. A good illustration of the difficulties which the government's ambivalence places in the way of rapprochment is a recent article on "the Role of the Traditional Healer in Malawi and Zambia" (Kapapa, 1979). Despite his announced subject, the author of this piece, a Malawian psychiatrist, fails to even mention the all-important divinatory and witchfinding roles of traditional healers, having felt constrained from doing so in an official government publication.

The Use of "Alternative" Medicines

The many herbalists andherbalist-diviners practicing in northeastern Malawi as an important part of their therapy prescribe and dispense **mankwala**---medicine in the broadest sense of the term. Besides more conventional herbal preparations, mankwala may take the form of charms, amulets, and philtres. Western medicine is also available to the public, but ethical drugs can be obtained only from government and mission hospitals and health centers, since there are no private western physicians or pharmacies in the northeast (there are a handful in the south in the capital and in the largest city). Alternative sources for western style non-prescription drugs do exist, however, Most shops in the area stock a variety of heavily-advertised brands of aspirin, anti-malarials, and

263

anti-helminthics, as well as fanciful nostrums recommended for coughs, backache, women's complaints, and as potency enhancers. Unfortunately, the labels on most of these drugs are in English, and in a country where most of the population is either totally illiterate or, at best, literate only in their mother-tongue, a great deal of medicine is bought without the purchaser having a clear idea of its properties or intended use. The situation is aggravated by the often extravagant claims made by drug advertisers. The result of all this is that the use of an over-the-counter drug is often the prologue to a visit to a health care professional, either traditional or western.

The postal system makes it possible for residents of the northeast to order traditional medicines through the mail, both from sourses with Malawi and from abroad (South Africa, Nigeria, the United States). Much of this material consists of magical charms, which are promoted with all the shamelessness and guile of practiced quackery: "Good Luck Magnet: Famous for Attracting Good Luck, Fame and Success"; "Protector: You'll be safe from bad people, spirits and medicines wishing to harm you. This is your shield." Such claims are readily believed by most people. One well-educated man, a former member of the Parliarment, ordeed a variety of charms from a firm in Chicago, including a magical hankerchief rendering its owner "unaffected by any so-called unfavorable influence"; a magical key whose "reassuring conformation is said to give new confidence to the mind"; and a "Psyalm" ball-point pen "inscribed with blessings, (and whose) instructions for use included prayers for success in life and love.

Despite the effort made to disseminate western ideas concerning illness and disease, for most Malawians western medicine remains but another form of magic, albeit of a foreign variety. These same people have only the most tenuous grasp of human anatomy and physiology. Medical person-nel make very little effort to add to their understanding, being most of them possessed of only a scant amoung of knowledge and being overworked into the bargain. Most patients in western hospitals are ignorant of their western diagnosis, nor do they know what drugs they are receiving. Pa-tients' grasp of the rationale behind traditional therapy is not much better, and their ignorance is fostered by the traditional healing profes-sion, which is by nature secretive and whose members themselves often have no real idea of what is ailing a patient, or of the effects of the drugs they are administered.

Western Medicine: Agent and Object of Change

Western medicine, in Malawi a major social innovation in its own right, has itself been modified by the social and economic circumstances that prevail in the country today. Government health services are free, but missions---which provide almost half of western-style health care---charge a nominal fee, nominal, that is, by our standards, but often onerous in a country with a per capita income of around $100 a year. Remote and sparsely-populated areas have to be served by mobile clinics that are periodically sent out by government and mission hospitals. Since people cannot uniformly be relied on to seek medical help when they need it, special teams of health workers are sent out to locate cases of eye disease, leprosy, and tuberculosis. Owing to the ever-present constraints imposed by limited funds and limited manpower, a choice has had to be made to concentrate preventive medicine on children under five and on mothers-- to-be. For mothers, nutrition classes are taught and ante- and post-natal clinics held on a regular basis. These efforts at preventing disease deserve much of the credit for the country's substantial improvement in infant and child mortality in recent years.

What we would call informed consent is for most medical procedures in Malawi not possible to obtain. Nevertheless, the country has virtually no medical-malpractice lawsuits, although (again by our standards) there is a great deal of medical malpractice and iatrogenesis on the part of both western and traditional healers. Some traditional healers, and many more persons working at western health care facilities, steal hypo- dermic syringes and (often out-dated) injectables, and administer them on a fee-for-service basis to an eager public. Patients are in fact generally quite keen to receive injections, the indigenous and time-honored practice of rubbing medicine into shallow cuts in the skin no doubt serving to sharpen their alacrity. Even at western facilities injections are often demanded---and given---on a clinically-irrational basis, as when penicillin is injected for lumbago. In their competition for business and prestige, some traditional healers go so far as to attend out-patient or mobile clinics in order to obtain pills and capsules which they can in turn dispense to their own patients. And we have already noted the traditional healer's fondness for borrowing the accoutrements of his western counterpart, usually without paying much attention to practical benefit (as when a "stethoscope" is fashioned out of a conch shell and some string).

Since its introduction at the turn of the century, western medicine in the northeast region has steadily increased in popularity, in part at the expense of traditional practice. In 1977, the Rumphi and Karonga districts that comprise the region had a combined population of 168,000. That same year, the seven major hospitals and health units that lie within the two districts admitted some 14,000 inpatients, who stayed a total of 103,000 inpatient-days; outpatient attendance totaled 400,000. These same seven institutions had 32,000 ante-natal visits, delivered over 5,000 babies, and oversaws almost 90,000 under-fives or well-baby examinations at their clinics.

Such figures testify to the strong acceptance of western medicine in the northeast region. Yet despite their impressiveness, and although no such statistics are compiled for traditional medicine, my own observa- tions and the observations of others leave no doubt that the traditional healer is still a major contributor to the region's health care. the fact that in 1977 there were only 407 deaths at the western medical facilities of Rumphi and Karonga districts, when the region's crude death rate was twenty-eight per thousand, by itself indicates that a sizeable number of sufferers must seek out some other form of treatment than the kind dispensed at these facilities. The conviction of widespread alternative use is further strengthened by the example of one nchimi with a large hospital-village in the area: his record books list visits by 1,700 patients for 1973 alone.

The truth of the matter seems to be that in many cases people use western medicine less as a trusted means of cure than as a diagnostic aid. In cases of gross physical trauma—fractures, wounds, and the like—western medicine is the uncontested therapy of choice. But if an illness proves refractory to western diagnosis or treatment, this circumstance is by itself taken as a sign that the problem in question is probably due to sorcery or to spirit possession, and the sufferer, having reached this conclusion, will turn his back on western means of cure and betake himself to a traditional healer instead. The fact that, in general, people are willing to give traditional treatment more time to effect a cure than western medicine, accounts for the many sad instances in which a patient in the terminal stages of disease will present himself at a western hospital, having come to realize too late that the nganga's or nchimi's promised "cure" was in reality no cure at all.

I wish to thank my brother, Dr. William H. Wendroff, for his valuable editorial assistance.

REFERENCES

CHILIVUMBO, A.B. (1972) "Vimbuza or Mashawe: A Mystic Therapy," AFRICAN MUSIC SOCIETY JOURNAL V(2): 6-9.

DE WINTER, ERIC R. (1972) HEALTH SERVICES OF A DISTRICT HOSPITAL IN MALAWI. Assen, Netherlands: Van Gocum.

EVANS-PRITCHARD, E.E. (1937) WITCHCRAFT, ORACLES AND MAGIC AMONG THE AZANDE. Oxford: Oxford University Press.

GLUCKMAN, MAX (1949) "The Village Headman in British Central Africa," AFRICA XIX(2): 89-94.

KAPAPA, P. (1979) "The Role of the Traditional Healer in Malawi and Zambia," MOYO XI(4):1-4. Lilongwe, Malawi: Health Extension Services, Ministry of Health.

MARWICK, M.G. (1950) "Another Modern Anti-Witchcraft Movement in East Central Africa," AFRICA XX(2): 100-112.

MITCHELL, J.C. (1970) "Race, Class, and Status in South Central Africa," pp. 303-343 in Arthur Tuden and Leonard Plotnicov (eds.), SOCIAL STRATIFICATION IN AFRICA. N.Y.: Free Press.

MOSS, S. (1971) HEALTH EDUCATION MANUAL, STANDARDS 5-8. Blantyre, Malawi: Ministry of Education.

MSISKA, S.K. (1969) "Traditional Religion Among the Tumbuka and Other Tribes in Malawi," MINISTRY IX(1): 3-11.

REDMAYNE, ALISON 91970) "Chikanga: An African Diviner with an International Reputation," pp. 103-128 in Mary Douglas (ed.), WITCHCRAFT CONFESSIONS & ACCUSATIO London: Tavistock.

RELIGIOUS EDUCATION IN PRIMARY SCHOOLS: TEACHERS' GUIDE TO STANDARD ONE (Ex-n.d. perimental). Blantyre, Malawi: Distributed by Malawi Book Service, c. 1976.

WORLD HEALTH ORGANIZTION (1976) TRADITIONAL MEDICINE AND ITS ROLE IN THE DEVELOPMENT OF HEALTH SERVICES IN AFRICA. Brazzaville: World Health Organization, AFR/RC26/TD/1.

YOUNG, T. CULLEN (1932) "Three Medicine-Men in Northern Nyasaland," MAN XXXII: 224-234.

CHAPTER 20

CHICANOS, CURANDERISMO AND MENTAL HEALTH:
CONCLUSIONS AND IMPLICATIONS

William Willard and Silverio Arenas, Jr.

Chicanos represent the second largest non-majority ethnic group in the United States (**Endnote 1**). Like other such groups, they are characterized by various indices of second-class citizenship, including poverty, low educational achievement, poor health, high unemployment rates, and social or political ineffectiveness (Grebler, Moore, and Guzman, 1970). Their psycho-historical and socioeconomic development has been markedly influenced by oppression, subjugation, exploitation, and discrimination (Alvarez, 1973).

Given these conditions and situations, one would surmise that Chicanos experience extremely high levels of stress and that this would lead to high reported incidence rates of emotional and behavioral disorders. Indeed, a number of studies have shown that life conditions and experieces similar to these are highly correlated with high incidence rates of "mental illness," especially psychosis (Hollinghead and Redlich, 1958; Leighton, 1959; Langer and Michael, 1963). Accordingly, the utilization of mental health care facilities by Chicanos would also be expected to be high, or at least consistent with expectations based on population statistics. This, however, is not the case. A wide variety of studies over the past few years have indicated that Chicanos paradoxically underutilize mental health care facilities (Jaco, 1959; Karno and Edgerton, 1969; Kline, 1969; Kruger, 1974; Padilla, Carlos and Keefe, 1976; Padilla and Ruiz, 1973; Padilla, Ruiz and Alvarez, 1974).

Various explanations have been proposed to account for this under utilization paradox. Some investigators claim that Chicanos actually do experience emotional and behavioral problems at a lower rate compared to other populations (Jaco, 1959). The Chicano family, which is strongly-knit and supportive, is said to provide them with viable stress-reducing and problem-solving processes (Jaco, 1959; Medsen, 1964). Another explanation proposes that the Chicano family protects "mentally ill" members by tolerating them instead of referring them to psychiatric facilities (Clark, 1959; Madsen, 1964; Saunders, 1954).

Chicanos are also said to experience significant psychiatric problems but these are less visible because they are "expressed" in such activities as criminal behavior, narcotics addition, and alcoholism (Karno and Edgerton, 1969). Other explanations include: (1) mental health facilities exclude Chicanos from their services through discriminatory or culturally insensitive policies and practices; (2) Chicanos avoid mental health services because they are culturally irrelevant in terms of values, expectations and language; and (3) Chicanos choose to consult with other resources, including relatives, friends, community leaders, priests, and especially physicians (Karno and Edgerton, 1969; Karno and Morales, 1976; Miranda and Kitano, 1976; Morales, 1976; Yamamoto, James and Palley, 1968).

Most of these explanations are quite plausible, and they probably account for underutilization to a substantial extent. Most intriguing, however, is an explanation which proposes that many Chicanos, especially those that are more traditional, utilize an alternative, indigenous folk-medical system known as **curanderismo** for the treatment of emotional and behavior disorders (**Endnote 2**). Several investigators have asserted that this folk--medical system provides these Chicanos with a culturally relevant and quite effective source of mental health care (Clark, 1959; Kiev, 1968; Madsen, 1964, 1966; Rubel, 1960, 1966; Saunders, 1954; Torrey, 1970, 1972).

The term **curanderismo** comes from the Spanish word **curar**, which means "to cure." Individuals who are trained in its concepts and curing techniques, and are sanctioned as practitioners within the traditional Chicano community, are known as **curanderos** (**Endnote 3**). Curanderismo is a comprehensive and viable system of folk medicine with its own theoretical, diagnostic and therapeutic aspects (Kiev, 1968; Trotter and Chavira, 1975). It consists of a large body of folk medical beliefs, materials, rituals, and practices that has evolved over the centuries to meet the physicial, psychological, and social needs of the traditional Chicano people. Curanderismo is conceptually holistic in nature; no separation is made between the body, the mind, the spirit, and the social and physical environment as in the standard health care system **Endnote 4**). In the past, because of the unavailability or inaccessibility of standard medical services, curanderos were relied upon to treat physical as well as psychological and spiritual disorders.

With the increased extension of these services to traditional Chicanos, curanderismo has increasingly become more of a mental health care resource (Kiev, 1968; Trotter and Chavira, 1975). Traditional Chicanos consult with physicians for physical disorders and with curanderos for those that are psychological or spiritual. This does not mean that they do not seek curanderos for physical disorders or standard mental health care professionals for those that are emotional or psychological. Traditional Chicanos flexiby participate in both systems of health care. They will consult with a curandero either before, while, or after being seen by a physician or mental health care professional. The degree to which Chicanos, traditional or otherwise, use curanderismo as a mental health resource is generally unknown. Most of the studies that have documented the existence and use of curanderismo have been carried out in rural or semi-rural areas (Madsen, 1964, 1966; Rubel, 1960, 1966; Saunders, 1954). Those studies investigating curanderismo in urban settings are inconclusive; some studies have indicated that it is not a viable mental health resource (Edgerton, Karno, and Fernandez, 1970; Karno and Edger-

270

ton, 1969) and some studies have indicated otherwise (Kiev, 1968; Torrey, 1972; Weclew, 1975). Generally, it can be safely stated that curanderismo appears to be a viable mental health care resource wherever traditional Chicanos are found in substantial numbers, be it in urban or rural settings.

Chicanos utilize curanderismo as a mental health care resource because it is consistent with and relevant to their world view. The term "world view" is used in the anthropological and pyshcological literature to refer to the manner in which people in a given cultural or social group collectively structure their reality (Torrey, 1972). A world view cam be thought of as a type of cognitive-perceptual process that serves both as a filter and as an organizer for an individual's experiences.

Viewed from another perspective, world views that are quite different might seem foolish, superstitious, bizarre, or abnormally delusional. People from different world views might appear to be living in a "separate reality" with their perplexing system of logic and causality, their bizzare or delusion-like beliefs, and their strange manner of behaving. Traditional Chicano world view includes many ideas and concepts about reality that are radically unique and different, yet are culturally consistent. A review of some of these ideas and concepts highlights this.

In the traditional Chicano world view, the natural and supernatural are not divided into separate compartments. Harmony between these two conceptual realities is considered essential to health and stability; disharmony causes illness and instability (Madsen, 1969). Individuals are said to be composed of a corporal being (**cuerpo**) and an immaterial soul or spirit (**espiritu**) that may wander freely at times, especially during sleep and after death. This soul can be dislodged through physical and supernatural trauma, allowing other spirits to enter the vacant bodies. Some individuals are said to be unusually sensitive or receptive to acquiring alien spirits, either as victims that become possessed by evil entities or as mediums whose bodies serve as "boxes" (**cajitas**) or empty "vessels" through which good spirits can exercise their benevolent missions (Maclin, 1978; Trotter and Chavira, 1975).

Communication with the spirit world is possible; the living can talk with the dead and the dead can influence life on earth (Gonzales, 1976). Parapsycholgical phenomena, in such forms as clairvoyance, precognition, telepathy, and psychokenesis are also part of this world view (Johnson, 1972; Trotter and Chavira, 1975). Magic (**magia**) and witchcraft (**brujeria**) are important concepts in traditional Chicano life. Individuals are said to be able to cause illnesses and misfortune in others (i.e., hex them) as well as help them, through various means. Imitative and contagious magic are used to harm enemies, to control peoples' behavior, or to cure illness and "neutralize" evil forces (Trotter and Chaveria, 1975). Imitative magic involves the use of images or figures that represent the victims (e.g., dolls, molded wax, pictures, etc.) or the manipulation of certain objects or materials (e.g., magical powders, perfumes, amulets, etc.). In contagious magic, objects or things that were once in contact with the victims (e.g., personal belongings, locks of hair, fingernail trimmings, etc.) are used for the same purposes. Bewitchedment (**embrujamiento**) can also be accomplished by introducing or directing various objects and substances into victims' bodies (e.g., powders, potions, negative energy, etc.). Religion, especially Catholicism, also plays an important role in traditional Chicano life. A violation of religious and moral standards is believed to lead to illness or misfortune. God is believed to intervene directly in the affairs of humans. A variety of saints, both formal (e.g., St. Jude, St. Martin, the Virgin Mary, etc.) and folk (e.g., el Nino Fidencio, Don Pedrito Jaramillo, Santa Teresa, etc.) are also believed to cure illnesses and remove obstacles in life (Kiev, 1968; Madsen, 1964; Macklin, 1978; Rubel, 1964; Trotter and Chavira, 1975).

Curanderos share this unique and culturally significant world view with their clients. Their diagnostic and treatment activities reflect this perspective. A review of these activities, as reported in the literature (Gonzales, 1976; Kiev, 1968; Madsen, 1964; Trotter and Chavira, 1975) demonstrates this. For example, illness is believed to result when an imbalance occurs between an individual and his physical, social, spiritual and environmental aspects. This imbalance is said to be caused not only by natural processes like physical trauma, genetic factors, "germs," poor nutrition, bad hygiene, toxic substances, faulty learning and even "psychological" trauma; but also by such supernatural processes as spirit possession, soul loss, imitative and contagious magic, object and substance intrusion into the body, the use of "psychic energy," and the intervention of God, the saints, and especially Satan. Curanderismo relies on both natural and supernatural diagnostic techniques in gathering data for conceptualizing and classifying disorders. The natural techniques include interviewing clients and any potential informants, directly observing the clients' behavior and affect, and obtaining corroborative evidence in the form of magical items, substances, etc. Supernaturally, curanderismo depends on such techniques and processes as reading cards; interpreting the meaning of candle drippings or burn markings on lemons, eggs and other materials; "visualizing" images in water or oil; and directly obtaining information from spiritual sources.

In terms of treatment, curanderismo involves an attempt to re-establish a harmonious balance between an individual and his physical, social, spiritual and environmental aspects. This is accomplished through various methods and techniques, again both natural and supernatural. The natural techniques include information-giving and clarification, advice and reassurance, suggestion and persuasion (including placebo) and the prescribing of over-the-counter patent medication and herbal remedies. Supernatural techniques include the neutralization of magical processes; removal of hexes; counter-hexing; exorcism of evil spirits; recapturing lost souls, spiritual "alignment;" spiritual sweepings or cleansings; the use of talismans and amulates for protection, pwer or knowledge; votive offerings; praying for divine intervention; the facilitation of spiritual intervention; and the use of such parapsychological processes as psychokenesis and telepathy.

A review of how curanderos practice their trade also serves to demonstrate how curanderismo is consistent with and relevnt to traditional Chicano world view. Trotter and Chavira (1975) have identified three technical areas or levels of healing in curanderismo. In the material level (**lo material**), which is the simplest and most common, curanderos are said to work while awake, as opposed to being in a trance state. Those healers working in this level use common objects and simple rituals in their activities. The objects used include herbs, patent medicines, common household items (e.g., eggs, lemons, garlic, ribbons, etc.), and religiously or mystically symbolic materials (e.g., crucifixes, oils, incense, perfumes, etc.). Rituals used include prayers, spiritual "sweepings" (**barridas**) or "cleansings" (**limpias**), and other magico-religious types of ceremonies. The spiritual level (**lo espiritual**), which is less common than the material, involves individuals who enter into trance state in order to perform their healing activities. Curanderos in this level believe that their own souls or spirits are projected out of their bodies, making them "vessels" for other spirits. Benevolent spirits are said to take over or possess the curanderos' bodies and it is these spirits, not them, who heal.

Individuals who work in the spiritual level are also known as **espiritualistas** and **espiritistas** (Macklin, 1978). Espiritualistas organize their activities around a "temple" or "church" and are usually "possessed" by only one formal or folk saint during their trance states. Espiritistas do not function in a church-like setting, and a variety of healing spirits, including formal and folk saints, historical figures, famous folk healers, physicians, relatives, etc., heal through them. The mental level (**lo mental**) is the least common and least researched of the levels and involves various processes and activities that can be referred to as "psychic healing." In this level, it is believed that mental energy can be directly channeled from a curandero's mind to a client. Curanderos employing this level engage in such activities as precognition, clairvoyance, telepathy, psychokenesis, etc.

Traditional Chicano world view and curanderismo recognize and define a number of disorders that can be said to be culture-specific. Culture-specific disorders are illness syndromes that are not recognized by majority culture medicine but which are recognized by non-majority culture peoples and their folk-medical systems. This is not to say that a culture-specific disorder's corresponding symptoms or behavioral patterns are not found in other cultures. Physical illnesses and maladaptive behaviaors have cross-cultural manifestations, but these are perceived, explained, grouped, interpreted, and labeled diffeently in each culture according to their world view. Some examples of culture-specific disorders recognized by curanderos include **susto, mal ojo,** and **mal puesto.**

Susto or "fright" (also known as "soul loss") is a disorder believed to be caused by a sudden and traumatic experience, such as a near miss by a speeding truck. If the traumatic experience involves being frightened by a ghost or spirit, the term used is **espanto.** Individuals suffering from susto become glassy-eyed and appear to be in a "trance-like" state. They seem apathetic and listless, with a restless sleep and occasional

273

night sweating. Other symptoms include anxiety, indigestion, palpitations, depression, withdrawl, irritability, insomnia, loss of appetite and subsequently, loss of weight (Kiev, 1968; Trotter and Chavira, 1975). The underlying theory behind susto is that the soul becomes separated from the body and treatment involves recapturing the soul and returning it (Kiev, 1968).

Mal ojo or "evil eye," is a condition that results when a person with "strong vision" admiringly or enviously looks at a person and doesn't "neutralize" his power by immediately touching them. Some kind of "electrical energy" is said to be transmitted through the eyes. Children are said to be more susceptible than adults, although some adults are considered to be quite weak and more vulnerable than others. A person afflicted with mal ojo experiences headaches, crying spells, irritability, and restlessness. Sometimes these symptoms are accompanied by fever, diarrhea, vomiting, and loss of appetite (Gonzales, 1976; Kiev, 1968; Trotter and Chavira, 1975).

Mal puesto, or "hex," otherwise known as **embrujamiento** (bewitchment), is a catch-all term used for a wide variety of symptoms and behaviors. Some of the symptoms of mal puesto include such things as visual and auditory hallucinations, strange or bizzare behavior, obsessive-compulsive states, anxiety states, disassociative states, conversion reactions, phobias, and delusional states, especially those with grandiose or persecutory features. Most of what would be considered to be psychotic reactions (e.g., manic-depression, schizophrenia, paranoia, etc.) would be included in the category 9Kiev, 1968). The assumed etiological factors in mal puesto, while many and varied, are usually of the supernatural or magical type.

Traditional Chicanos utilize curanderismo for the treatment of emotional and behavioral disorders because it is consistent with and relevant to their world view. Indeed, this consistency and relevancy is what makes curanderismo the most appropriate and successful, as well as ethical, source of mental health care for these traditional people. The importance of taking a person's cognitive framework into account in working with him/her psychotherapeutically has been repeatedly pointed out by numerous clinicians and researchers. Frank (1973) emphasizes the importance of clients' "assumptive worlds" (world view) in shaping their behavior, attitudes, values, self-image and sense of well-being. According to him, the aim of psychotherapy is to help these individuals to feel and function better by enabling them to make appropriate modifications in their "assumptive worlds." Torrey (1972) asserts that the effectiveness of all healers, whether "witchdoctors" or Western psychotherapists, depends to a great extent on the fact that they share a common language and world view with their clients; including common ideas about causation and a common way of classifying disorders. Dominguez-Ybarra and Garrison (1977) affirm that clinicians need to understand and acknowledge their clients' conceptual framework before they can diagnose and treat emotional and behavioral disorders successfully.

Given that the development, expression and maintenance of emotional and behavioral disroders directly involves cognitive-perceptual and verbal--symbolic processes, and given that the understanding, diagnosis and treatment of them is also dependant on these same processes, it is imperative that they be taken into consideration in psychotherapeutic intervention, especially when dealing with people from different world views.

This, however, is not the case. Standard mental health care approaches in the United States are based on the world view or "assumptive" reality of the majority culture (Torrey, 1972). As such, their concepts about etiological processes (causality), their diagnostic and nosological (classification) systems, and their treatment methods are to a great extent culture--specific and culture-bound. That this is so, however, is not fully recognized or acknowledged by standard mental health care agents. These agents are ethnocentrically trained to believe and expect that their ideas of what constitutes mental health are universal and valid for everybody else in the world, regardless of their social or cultural background.

Generally, it is expected that clients whose beliefs and world view are not consistent with the majority culture's will either give these up or change them if they are to benefit from the mental health care system (Bolman, 1968; Bruhn and Fuentes, 1977). Those individuals who fail to do so are differentially treated. Studies have shown that thes clients are referred for individual or group psychotherapy less often, they receive less lengthy or intense treatment (e.g., are terminated sooner or are not recommended for continued sessions), they are assigned to the least experienced therapists, or they are more likely to receive medication, as compared with standard clients (Karno, 1966; Yamamoto, James and Palley, 1968). Standard mental health care agents have a tendency to selectively work with those persons that are more like themselves, that is, white, middle or upper class, educated, English-speaking, and who adhere to standard world view beliefs and values (Lorion, 1973). Those clients who do not meet these criteria are oftentimes overlooked, ignored, or belittled (Helms, 1974; Meyer, 1975; Saunders and Hewes, 1953).

Traditional Chicanos who have expressed a belief in folk-medical or supernatural phenomena have often been described by standard mental health care agents as being foolish, ignorant, superstitious, childish, or psychopathologically deviant (Dominguez-Ybarra and Garrison, 1977; Torrey, 1972). Serious consequences can result when a person believing in one framework is treated by a person who believes in and is trained in another. This has occasionally led Chicanos to be diagnosed as suffering from serious psychological disturbances when actually they are not (Galvin and Ludwig, 1961; Karno, 1966; Trotter and Chavira, 1975).

Traditional Chicanos are not seen at standard mental health care facilities because they continue to rely on curanderismo as a source of treatment for emotional and behavioral disorders. they prefer this folk-medical system because: (1) the standard mental health care system is ethnocentrically based on the world view of the majority culture and thus is irrelevant and inappropriate for them, (2) curanderismo is culturally congruent with and reflective of their traditional world view, and thus is relevant and appropriate for them, and (3) being that psychotherapeutic systems require a congruence in world views in order to be effective, curanderismo is probably more effective for them. Given these assertions, what are the implications for traditional Chicanos, for curanderismo and for the standard mental health care system? Based on the material reviewed and on the field experiences of the authors with numerous curanderos in Arizona, Colorado, Texas and New Mexico, the following discussion is offered.

Traditional Chicanos will probably continue to consult with curanderos as long as their world view remains distinctly different from the majority culture's. Curanderismo exists because traditional Chicano world view creates a need for it. This folk-medical system provides traditional Chicanos with a means of making sense out of non-sense; with a way of understanding what it is they are experiencing when they are uncertain about themselves or others. It serves to clarify, validate or restructure (modify or change) their emotional, cognitive and behavioral responses to their environment---all within their cultural reality or world view. Their own values, beliefs, expectations, symbols and behaviors are employed in helping them restructure their cognitions, control their emotions and change their behavior in accordance with what "mental health" is within their cultural reality.

What this implies in terms of adhering to a traditional world view while having to function and participate in a society or cultural group that adheres to a different one certainly needs to be addressed. While traditional Chicanos might be successfully benefiting from curanderismo clinically, and even socially as far as their cultural group is concerned, what about in terms of their relationship with the majority culture? Is curanderismo reinforcing values, beliefs, expectations, symbols and behaviors that will ill-prepare them to deal with an increasingly scientifically sophisticated society? No matter how much one learns to "compartmentalize" and "divide" their conceptual reality into natural or supernatural and scientific or mystical, there are bound to be problems.

Curanderismo is a folk-medical system that has had to function covertly because the standard health care system and majority culture have vehemently opposed it and made it illegal to practice. Charges are occasionally filed by the authorities against some curanderos for practicing medicine without a license. Although some of these incidents involve questionable motives on the part of the authorities, that is to say that some of these involve territoriality and other such power issues between competing systems, an increasing number of incidents do involve what could be considered to be ethical transgressions against clients. In the past, curanderos were characterized as being highly religious and benevolent members of their communities. They were well known by their clients and had achieved a great degree of respect and reverence due to having practiced in one location for many years. The community provided a screening and sanctioning mechanism whereby unethical and unscrupulous practitioners were censored and not utilized. That situation has changed considerably over the last few years.

The situation now is one where the practice of curanderismo is quite open to individuals who are not as religious, benevolent or ethical. A number of factors are probably responsible for this. Curanderos are no longer as religiously based because of the changes in orientation that curanderismo has experienced in the last twenty years. It used to be that the material level, which relied extensively on religious concepts and practices, was the main orientation used. Practitioners using this level had to be, in principle as well as practice, religious and benevolent. With the acceptance of the spiritual and mental levels, however, a new type of practitioner has emerged. These latter approaches do not espouse as firm of a commitment to religion as the material level. They depend on more secular types of concepts and practices, and even utilize some that would be considered to be unreligious or contrary to the teachings of the Catholic Church. Also, given that people can move about more freely via transportation, curanderos move around more often and clients other than those in their immediate communities consult with them.

Today's curandero is not as religiously bound and is more prone toward less benevolent behavior, tends to use concepts and practices that are more open to misuse and abuse, and does not depend on a clientel who are able to observe his behavior over a long period of time and utilize their screening and sanctioning powers. All of these factors have led to a situation where some people are probably being unethically exploited----psychologically, physically or economically. Not all present day curanderos engage in unethical or unscrupulous practices, of course. There are well intentioned, sincere, benevolent and ethical practitioners around, and probably the majority of them are so. The situation is such, however, that the system is more vulnerable to abuse by those who are knowingly exploitative or those who are pathologically abusive. Given the questionable power of community sanction in adequately "screening out" such individuals, the duty falls on the majority culture and their authorized agents. These agents will not make an effort to distinguish between those curanderos who are "good" and those who are "bad." Consequently, all curanderos suffer the consequences because of a few "bad seeds."

The standard mental health care system is not about to radically change its philosophical, conceptual or procedural foundations in order to accommodate non-majority culture world views, or the people who adhere to them. That system will continue to promote its own position over others, including curanderismo. Why shouldn't it anyway? After all, it does represent the world view of the majority culture, and the majority culture holds the power to dictate the rules. Nevertheless, being that both systems function in a pluralistic society that proclaims equal opportunity for all people, some compromise is indicated. What should be expected is not a blending of the standard mental health care system with curanderismo, or the inclusion of curanderismo in the mental health care system as a "separate but equal" entity. Both of these approaches would lead to a dilution of either system's effectiveness, with curanderismo being affected the most.

Granted, the standard mental health care system can learn a lot from curanderismo and vice-versa. In fact, probably the most feasible option that the standard system can choose is to recognize its limitations and acknolwedge the appropriateness and success of curanderismo with traditional Chicano clients. This would hopefully lead to a situation where there would be open communication and even some interaction between standard mental health care agents and curanderos whenever the need arose with clients. If each system understood each other's strengths and weaknesses in dealing with certain clients, an inter-referral and co-consultationtype of relationship could emerge. It is not inconceivable that a traditional Chicano could be seen at a standard mental health care center for medication or some type of educational-advising service and then also be seen by curandero for culturally relevant "psychotherapeutic" work. The involved agents in both systems could be continuously communicating with each other to avoid giving the client double messages, preclude a competitive situatuion between the agents, and keep from giving the client opposing instructions. In this way, the client would not be caught in the middle and end up confused, frustrated or worse.

A number of researchers have advocated the inclusion of curanderos as members of the staff in standard mental health care facilities (Arrendondo-Holden, 1978; Espinoza, 1977; Hamberger, 1978; Torrey, 1972). Although a large number of problems would result for each system curanderismo would be the one to suffer the most. Taking curanderismo out of its element and imbedding it in a system that is alien to it and even resentful of it would place it in a very precarious position. Observations by one of the authors have led to the conclusion that the type of curandero that would be accepted would not necessarily be one that was appropriate, but one who matches the requirements for social acceptance that the standard system expects. This leaves the door open for individuals who can "play the game" but are not fully qualified or sincerely committed to be selected as the "curandero in residence."

Another problem pertains to status. Being thrust amongst standard mental health care agents with their academic or professional degrees would not exactly make a curandero feel good. The curandero's lower position in the scheme of things would be communicated continuously, both directly and subtly. In trying to "win" acceptance, the curandero would end up "mimicking" his standard colleagues in terms of behavior, speech and even thought. It is indeed sad to see curanderos "parrot" terms that they don't fully understand and to hear them refer to themselves as "having the equivalent of a Ph.D. in curanderismo." Such mimicry indicates that a co-option of the folk system by the much more powerful standard system is in progress. The result is that a poor imitation of curanderismo is then presented and offered to clients as the "real thing."

In closing, three statements will serve to summarize our position regarding traditional Chicanos, curanderismo and standard mental health care:

(1) Traditional Chicanos who adhere to a traditional world view are better off consulting with curanderos;

(2) Curanderismo, while being clinically beneficial, still presents with a number of unanswered questions regarding its present and future role in the lives of traditional Chicanos;

(3) The Standard mental health care system should not seek to include curanderismo as a part of its services because to do so would be problematic for both, especially curanderismo.

ENDNOTES

1. The term Chicano is used to refer to people of Mexican descent who are living in the United States. They can be either native born or naturalized in this country. These people are also known as Mexican Americans, Mexicans, Spanish-Americans and Hispanic Americans.

2. The term traditional, as used in "traditional Chicanos" and "traditional world view," refers to those Chicanos who are less accultured into the majority culture group in the United States. These people usually are recent immigrants, both legal and illegal, from Mexico, or native born Chicanos who have maintained most of the values, beliefs, traditions, customs, and language of the Mexican culture.

3. The term **curandero** will be used to refer to Chicano folk-medical practitioners regardless of gender or healing orientation. The term **curandero** regularly refers to a male practitioner and the term **curandera** refers to a female practitioner. As for healing orientation, a number of other terms are used to refer to folk-practitioners who follow certain orientations.

4. The term "standard" is used to refer to that which is a part of the "majority culture" in the United States.

REFERENCES

ALVAREZ, R. (1973) "The Psycho-Historical and Socioeconomic Development of the Chicano Community in the United States," SOCIAL SCIENCE QUARTERLY, pp. 920-942.

ARREDONDO-HOLDEN, J. (1978) "La Salud Mental de la Raza: Curanderas and Mental Health Centers in Two Mexican-American Comunities," Ph.D. dissertation, University of Denver.

BOLMAN, W.M. (1968) "Cross-Cultural Psychotheraphy," AMERICAN JOURNAL OF PSYCHIATRY 124(9): 123-130.

BRUHN, J.G. and FUENTES, R.G., Jr. (1977) "Cultural Factors Affecting Utilization of Services by Mexican-Americans in Psychiatry and the Hispanic American," PSYCHIATRIC ANNALS 7(12): 20-29.

CLARK, M. (1969) HEALTH IN THE MEXICAN-AMERICAN CULTURE: A COMMUNITY STUDY. Berkeley: University of California Press.

DOMINGUEZ-YBARRA, A. and GARRISON, J. (1977) "Towards Adequate Psychiatric Classification and treatment of Mexican-American Patients," PSYCHIATRIC ANNALS 7(12): 86-96.

EDGERTON, R.B., KARNO,M., and FERNANDEZ, I. (1970) "Curanderismo in the Metropolis: The Diminishing Role of Folk-Psychiatry Among Los Angeles Mexican-Americans," AMERICAN JOURNAL OF PSYCHOTHERAPHY 24(1): 124-134.

ESPINOZA, J.A. "The Underutilization of Mental Health Services by Mexican-American Males," Ph.D. dissertation, United States International University.

FRANK, J.D. (1973) PERSUASION AND HEALING: A COMPARATIVE STUDY OF PSYCHOTHERAPY. Baltimore, MD.: The Johns Hopkins University Press.

GALVIN, J.A.V., and LUDWIG, A.M. (1961) "A Case of Witchcraft," JOURNAL OF NERVOUS AND MENTAL DISEASES 133(2): 161-168.

GONZALES, E. (1976) "The Role of Chicano Folk Beliefs and Practices in Mental Health," in Hernandez, C.A., Haug, M.J., and Wagner, N.N. (eds.) CHICANOS: SOCIAL AND PSYCHOLOGICAL PERSPECTIVES (2nd ed.) St. Louis: The C.V. Mosby Co.

GREBLER, L., MOORE, J.W. and GUZMAN, R.C. (1970) THE MEXICAN--

AMERICAN PEOPLE: THE NATION'S SECOND LARGEST MINORITY. N.Y.: The Free Press.

HAMBERGER, S. (1978) "Profile of Curanderos: A Study of Mexican Folk Practitioners," INTERNATIONAL JOURNAL OF SOCIAL PSYCHIATRY 24: 19-25.

HELMS, L. (1974) "Mexican-Americans," J.A.C.H.A., 22: 269-271.

HOLLINGSHEAD, A. and REDLICH, F. (1958) SOCIAL CLASS AND MENTAL ILLNESS. N.Y.: John Wiley and Sons.

JACO, E.G. (1959) "Mental Health of the Spanish Americans in Texas," in M.K. Opler (ed.) CULTURE AND MENTAL HEALTH: CROSS-CULTURE STUDIES. N.Y.: McMillan Co.

JOHNSON, H.S. (1972) "Mental Health Needs of Mexican Americans," paper prepared for the Region Training Program to Serve the Bilinguial/- Bicultural Exceptional Child, Mental Education Associates, San Fernando, CA, Feb. pp. 1-22.

KARNO, M. "The Enigma of Ethnicity in a Psychiatric Clinic," (1966) ARCHIVES OF GENERAL PSYCHIATRY 20(2): 233, 516-520.

KARNO, M. and MORALES, A. "A Community Mental Health service for Mexican-Americans in a Metropolis," In Hernandez, C.A., Haug, M.J., and Wagner, N.N. (eds.). CHICANOS: SOCIAL AND PSYCHOLOGICAL PERSPECTIVES (2nd ed.) St. Louis: The C.V. Mosby Co.

KIEV, A. (1968) CURANDERISMO: MEXICAN-AMERICAN FOLK PSYCHIATRY. N.Y.: The Free Press.

KLINE, K.Y. (1969) "Some Factors in the Psychiatric Treatment of Spanish- -Americans," AMERICAN JOURNAL OF PSYCHIATRY 125(12): 1674-1681.

KRUGER, D. (1974) "The Relationship of Ethnicity to Utilization of Community Mental Health Centers," Ph.D. dissertation, University of Texas at Austin.

LANGER, T.S. and S.T. MICHAEL (1963) LIFE STRESS AND MENTAL ILLNESS. N.Y.: Free Press of Glencoe.

LEIGHTON, A. (1959) MY NAME IS LEGION. N.Y.: Basic Books.

LORION, R.P. (1973) "Socioeconomic Status and Traditional treatment Approaches Reconsidered," PSYCHOLOGICAL BULLETIN 79: 263-270.

MACKLIN, J. (1978) "Curanderismo and Espiritismo: Complimentary Approaches to Traditional Mental Health Services," in B. Velimirovic (ed.) MODERN MEDICINE AND MEDICAL ANTHROPOLOGY IN THE

282

U.S.-MEXICO BORDER POPULATION. Washington, D.C.: Pan American Health Organization, Scientific Publications, PAHO No. 359.

MADSEN, W. (1964) "Value Conflicts and Folk Psychiatry in South Texas," in A. Kiev (ed.) MAGIC, FAITH AND HEALING. N.Y.: The Free Press., pp. 420-440.

MADSEN, W. (1966) "Anxiety and Witchcraft in Mexican-American Acculturation," ANTHROOLOGY QUARTERLY 39(2): 110-127.

MADSEN, W. (1967) THE MEXICAN-AMERICANS OF SOUTH TEXAS (2nd. ed. N.Y.: Holt, Rinehart and Winston.

MEYER, G.G. (1975) "Folk Medicine in the Southwest," TEXAS MEDICINE 71(Feb.): 96-100.

MIRANDA, M. and KITANO, H.H.L. (1976) "Barriers to Mental Health Services: A Japanese-American and Mexican-American Dilemma," in Hernandez, C.A., Haug, M.J., and Wagner, N.N. (eds.). CHICANOS: SOCIAL AND PSYCHOLOGICAL PERSPECTIVES (2nd ed.) St. Louis: The C.V. Mosby Co.

MORALES, A. (1976) "The Impact of Class Discrimination and white Racism on the Mental Health of Mexican-Americans," in Hernandez, C.A., Haug, M.J., and Wagner, N.N. (eds.) CHICANOS: SOCIAL AND PSYCHOLOGICAL PERSPECTIVES (2nd ed.). St. Louis: The C.V. Mosby Co.

PADILLA, A.M., CARLOS, M.L., and KEEFE, S.E. (1976) "Mental Health Utilization by Mexican-Americans," MONOGRAPH NUMBER THREE OF THE SPANISH-SPEAKING MENTAL HEALTH RESEARCH CENTER, June.

PADILLA, A.M., and RUIZ, R.A. (1973) LATINO MENTAL HEALTH: A REVIEW OF THE LITERATURE (H.E.W. Publication No. HSM 73-9143). Washington, D.C.: U.S. Government Printing Office.

PADILLA, A.M., RUIZ, R.A., and ALVAREZ, R. (1975) "Community Mental Health Services for the Spanish Speaking Surname Population," AMERICAN PSYCHOLOGIST 30:892-905.

RUBEL, A.J. (1960) "Concepts of Disease in Mexican-American Culture," AMERICAN ANTHROPOLOGIST 72(5): 795-814.

RUBEL, A.J. (1966) ACROSS THE TRACKS: MEXICAN-AMERICANS IN A TEXAS CITY. Austin: University of Texas Press.

SAUNDERS, L. (1954) CULTURAL DIFFERENCES AND MEDICAL CARE: THE CASE OF THE SPANISH-SPEAKING PEOPLE OF THE SOUTHWEST. N.Y.: Russell Sage Foundation.

SAUNDERS, L., and HEWES, G.W. (1953) "Folk-Medicine and Medical Practice," JOURNAL OF MEDICAL EDUCATION 28(9): 43-46.

TORREY, E.G. (1970) "The Irrelevancy of Traditional Mental Health Services for Urban Mexican-Americans," paper presented at the meetings of the American Orthopsychiatric Association.

TORREY, E.F. (1972) THE MIND GAME: WITCHDOCTORS AND PSYCHIA-TRISTS. N.Y.: Emerson Hall.

TROTTER, R.I., and CHAVIRA, J.A. (1975) THE GIFT OF HEALING. Edinburg, TX: Pan American University.

WECLEW, R.W. (1975) "The Nature, Prevalence, and Level of Awareness of 'Curanderismo' and Some Implications for Community Mental Health," COMMUNITY MENTAL HEALTH JOURNAL 11: 145-154.

YAMAMOTO, J., JAMES, Q.C., and PALLEY, N. (1968) "Cultural Problems in Psychiatric Therapy," ARCHIVES OF GENERAL PSYCHIATRY 19: 45-49.

CHAPTER 21

ORGANIZATION AND DELIVERY OF HEALTH CARE:
A STUDY OF CHANGE IN NICARAGUA

Harvey Williams

Introduction

Of the many Third World countries which suffer from poorly developed health care systems, only a few have passed recently through a revolution which has brought with it significant and positive changes in the organization and delivery of health care. This chapter describes such changes in Nicaragua as they existed three years after the triumph of the revolution. It discusses the process by which a country moves from defining health care as an economic commodity, subject to the vagaries of the marketplace, to defining it as a right and a social need which should be equally accessible to all citizens.

General Background

The country of Nicaragua straddles the Central American isthmus between Honduras and Costa Rica. Its area of 57,143 square miles and 1981 estimated population of 2.8 million make it comparable with the state of Iowa, which is slightly smaller in size but has about a 20 per cent larger population. A northwest to southeast central mountain region separates the Pacific lowlands from the broad Atlantic plain. Less than 10 per cent of the population lives in this tropical eastern zone, which is largely inaccessible by land transport. About 30 percent of the population lives in the moutainous central region. This is an area of farms, coffee plantations and cattle ranches. The majority of the population lives in the Pacific region. The largest cities (including the capital, Managua, with over 500,000 inhabitants) and the limited industrial production are located here. This area also produces cotton, cattle, sugar cane and coffee.

Although Nicaragua is primarily an agricultural country (approximately two-thirds of its export earnings being derived from coffee, cotton, beef and sugar), approximately one-half of the population is classified as urban. Compared with the other countries of Central America, Nicaragua has a very low population density. It is the lowest in the region, and lower than most agriculturally-based developing countries. It was estimated that it had an annual natural increase rate of 3.4 per cent in 1980, a rate exceeded by only four other countries in the world. And it is one of the few countries in which at least half of the population is either under

15 or over 64 years of age (Haub, 1981).

Nicaragua's history is replete with natural and man-made disasters. Earthquakes, floods, drought and volcanic eruptions are frequent occurences. Managua has been decimated twice this century by earthquakes. The most recent, in December of 1972, killed an estimated 8,000 persons and demolished the central core of the city. Floods from tropical storms cause more widespread demage. In may of 1982 over 60,000 persons were rendered homeless and millions of dollars worth of crops were destroyed by tropical storm Aleta.

Civil wars and North American filibusters were common in the nineteenth century. In the early part of this century, U.S. Marines occupied the country on and off for eighteen years, during which time they unsuccessfully attempted to put down the revolution of Augusto Sandino and his followers. The Marine-trained National Guard later assassinated the rebel leader and initiated forty years of dictatorial rule by the Smoza family. In 1979, after months of fighting and great loss of life and property, the Sandinist revolutionary forces overthrew the Somoza regime and instituted a new government dedicated to building a new Nicaragua.

Prerevolutionary Health Conditions

Prior to the revolution, the health conditions in Nicaragua were among the worst in Latin America. The estimated crude death rate (12 per 1,000) and infant mortality rate (122 per 1,000 live births), were exceeded only by Haiti and Bolivia, and only those countries had a lower life expectancy at birth than Nicaragua's 55 years (Haub, 1981).

The number one cause of death was diarrhea and enteritis. Tetanus, whooping cough and measles, usually rendered insignificant by appropriate vaccination, were also among the top ten causes of death among children. Malaria, tuberculosis and intestinal parasites, rare in countries with well developed public health systems, were endemic in Nicaragua (Halperin and Garfield, 1982). Contributing to the prevalence of these diseases was the poor development of sanitary services, especially in the rural areas. Portable water was available to just 65 per cent of the urban population and only 5 per cent of the rural population. Most residents of the larger cities had access to sewer service but this was rare in the smaller cities and virtually unknown in the rural areas, where many homes did not even have latrines. Malnutrition, estimated to affect two out of three children under five years of age (Bossert, 1982) increased the impact of childhood diseases and contributed to the high infant mortality rate.

The Formal Health Care System

Confronting these problems was a highly inadequate health care system.

Bryant's description of an anonymous Latin American country fitted prerevolution Nicaragua well: "...the system for delivering health care is fragmented and of limited effectiveness, and the system of medical education is antiquated, underfinanced, and out of touch with the needs of the country (1969: 71)."

Under Somoza there existed several divisions of the health care system within the public sector, complemented by others in the private sector. The government's Ministry of Health was responsible for preventive health care. The National Social Assistance board was responsible for national and local social assistance programs for the indigent, particularly the practice of curative medicine. Funding for these programs came from the national lottery. The National Board and the various local boards controlled most of the country's public hospitals and clinics but there was little coordination between their efforts and those of the other parts of the health care system (Rosenberg, 1980).

The National Social Security Institute, established in 1955, provided medical care to less than 10 per cent of the population. These were persons employed in the two principal cities of Managua and Leon who were contributers to the social insurance program. the military and their dependents (about 5 per cent of the population) were covered by their own system of services and facilities. In the private sector, many physicians (including those employed in public programs) maintained treatment clinics for private patients. Severan churches ran hospitals and clinics, some in the more remote areas of the country. And the Red Cross managed a system of emergency centers, ambulance services and the national blood bank.

As Bossert suggests, on the surface the health care system under Somoza appears to have been "...not severely inadequate to the task of caring for the rather small population of 2.3 million. In 1977, there were fifty hospitals and clinics with a total of 4,675 beds, or 2 beds per 1,000 people. In 1975, it was estimated that there were a total of 1,357 doctors in Nicaragua, a fairly high average of 6 per 10,000 people. These figures compare very favorably with Guatemala and Honduras, and not far below those of Costa Rica" (1982: 261-262). And these facilities, especially in the rural areas, were often substandard. A report prepared in 1976 by the USAID mission in Nicaragua "state that 'hospitals are obsolete, dillapidated, dingy, overcrowded, unsanitary and lack many essentials to the physical comfort, safety, and well-being of patients' " (Rosenberg, 1980).

The training, distribution and utilization of professional health workers were also significant problems in Nicaragua. In spite of an increase in medical students in the 1970's, there were less than 6 physicians, 3 nurses, and 13 auxiliary nurses per 10,000 persons. As with facilities, nurses and doctors also were concentrated in the urban areas. Managua, with approximatley 20 percent of the population, had 50 per cent of the physicians and 70 per cent of the nurses. There were only small numbers of students enrolled in professional programs each year: 100 in medicine, 50 in nursing and 100 in auxiliary nursing. Although the need was great, there were no regular training programs for health technicians (Rosenbaum and Hildner, 1979; Escudero, 1981).

The economic and financial factors limiting access to the formal health care system resulted in approximately 75 per cent of the population being excluded (Holland, et al., 1973). And it was estimated "that 90 per cent of the medical services were directed to 10 per cent of the population" (Halperin and Garfield, 1982: 389).

The Informal Health Care System

Although the vast majority of the population was excluded from the formal health care system prior to the revolution, it is important to recognize that these persons did not passively accept illness as a natural condition. Those without access to the formal system, and even many others with limited access, depended upon various aspects of the informal health care system or what has been referred to by others as the indigenous system (Freidson, 1960; Roemer, 1976). The informal system includes folk practitioners who are believed to have the ability to treat specific kinds of ailments, such as the "evil eye," as well as a wide range of other skilled lay persons. While the informal system may seem relatively more important as one moves farther from the formal, urban-centered system, our observations indicate that it was important wherever the people were underserved.

In 1977 we undertook a health needs assessment study (Comite Tecnico de Nutricion, 1977) of a working class neighborhood outside of Managua. The suburb had a population of 25,000, most of the residents having been relocated there following the 1972 earthquake. The families were all low income, living in modest structures that most had built themselves. About 70 per cent had potable water and 25 per cent had electricity. Therer was no sewerage, garbage collection, pavement or sidewalks.

There were no resident professional health workers. The Social Assistance clinic provided one physician and two nurses six days a week for outpatient consultation. The Ministry of Health maintained a local health center which was staffed by two nurses and three auxiliary nurses, who worked five hours per day, six days a week. Two doctors and a dentist were available two hours per day. Despite the limited facilities for such a large population, utilization was reported to be low.

Through interviews of the residents we acquired a more complete under-standing of their illness behavior. We learned that there were four private hysicians and a dentist who came from Managua ι on an irregular basis to provide outpatient consultation. We also located many other persons who were recognized by the residents as part of their informal health care system. Among the persons identified were folk practitioners and herbalists, midwives, and "injectionists," who administered hypodermic medications brought to them by their patients.

Although there was only one pharmacy, served daily by a non-resident pharmacist, drugs were widely available. Nearly all of the many small shops which sold basic foodstuffs and household supplies also sold drugs. These included not only a wide range of non-prescription remedies but also many prescription drugs, especially antibiotic medications. The only medications which were difficult to purchase at these stores were tranquilizers and narcotics, and, because of the limited number of residents who had electricity, medications requiring refrigeration.

When asked about why they did not make more use of the government health facilities, the residents provided several responses. The most frequent reason was lack of accessibility. Neither the Ministry health center nor the Social Assistance clinic provided service evenings or Sundays, and their limited schedules on other days made utilization difficult. For the majority who were employed, going to the clinic meant missing work. Few who were sick enough to miss work were willing to wait until they could be seen during regular hours.

A second frequently voiced complaint was the quality of the service, including the attitude of the health workers. Many residents felt the physicians and nurses, commuting daily from Managua, were not sensitive to the patients' problems. Many also felt that those assigned to the neighborhood clinic and health center were not well trained. And most recognized that the facilities were poorly supplied, having limited diagnostic or treatment equipment, and few medications.

A final frequently mentioned reason was appropriateness of service. The Ministry health center was recognized as providing primarily preventive services: well-baby clinic, immunizations, prenatal care, family planning and health education. The Social Assistance clinic, with its limited staff and facilities, was seen as primarily treating minor illness, particularly in women and children. Neither facility was viewed as an appropriate place for the treatment of folk ailments, for childbirth, for the purchase or injection of medications, for severe or chronic disease which might require sophisticated diagnostic or treatment equipment, hospitalization or even minor surgery.

As a result of one or more of these limiting factors, only one-half of those interviewed said that they had ever used the government facilities in the neighborhood, while about 40 per cent said that they had gone directly to hospitals or clinics in Managua. All residents knew of the informal health care system persons and nearly all reported using their services much more frequently than those of the formal system.

In summary it can be stated that the prerevolutionary formal health care system was poorly developed, poorly organized and inaccessible to the overwhelming majority of the population. It was a system which perceived health care as an economic commodity rather than a right or social need. It encouraged a dependence on untrained participants of the informal health system, and emphasized fragmented organization, curative medicine and crisis response over preventive medicine and integrated health care delivery.

The Postrevolutionary Health Care System

The central role of the health care system in the new Nicaragua was early acknowledged by the revolutionary government, and after three years it continued to be perceived as the most important of the social sector programs. Only two weeks after its establishment, the government decreed the establishment of a National Health System, under the direction of the Ministry of Health. Under the new system all former public programs and facilities were brought together in a centralized, integrated system. Restrictions and distinctions between social security members, social assistance clients and military personnel were eliminated. All citizens were welcome at any public facility. An ambitious plan for the repair of war-damaged facilities and the construction of new hospitals, clinics and health centers was developed. Extension of services into the rural areas and the underserved urban areas was initiated. Coordination was established between the government programs and the many private programs sponsored by churches and international agencies.

The government more than tripled the public expenditures for health in the first three years of its administration (Ministerio de Planificacion, 1981) and public spending for health services rose from 6 to 17 per cent of the national budget. In 1982 four major regional hospitals were being constructed in outlying areas, a pediatric hospital was completed in Managua, and the government projected the completion of 79 new health centers, mostly in rural areas, by the end of the year. These new facilities were organized in a regional network, with a feeder system flowing from the rural health centers through the regional hospitals to the major facilities in Managua (Halperin and Garfield, 1982).

But while the capital expenditures for facilities and equipment may seem impressive, and they certainly were by prerevolutionary standards, they represented less than 20 per cent of the total health budget. The new government was quick to recognize that a devotion to capital intensive high level technology was not a cost effective way of dealing with the major medical problems of Nicaragua, and "would support a vertical medical-surgical superstructure with little popular participation" (Escudero, 1982: 4). Therefore, the principal objectives of the National Health System, referred to as "the linchpin of the social sector programs" were "...to develop a new concept of health, where the people develop by means of their own efforts their capacity to produce basic health, which requires not so much institutions, doctors, medicines, nor huge budget, but rather popular education and community organization to produce maternal infant health; occupational health, improving working conditions; preventive medicine with immunization compaigns against polio, DPT, measles, etc., and environmental health based on creating elementary hygenic conditions in nutrition, in the construction of latrines, the water supply, the control of diarrhea, malaria, etc." (Ministerio de Planificacion, 1981: 107-108, author's translation).

This deemphasis on centralized high technology and corresponding emphasis on the extension of preventive services into underserved areas, using paraprofessional health workers, had previously been proven successful in Chile (Roemer, 1976) and Cuba (Danielson, 1979). And it had been repeatedly recommended to the Somoza regime (Holland, et al., 1973; Heiby, 1981). In the new Nicaragua these efforts are concentrated in four themes: preventive care, popular participation, increased professional and paraprofessional training and integrated planning.

Preventive Care

As noted above, many of the most serious health threats, particularly those affecting children, are relatively easy to prevent. One of the first major efforts of the new government was to institute widespread immunization programs. These were integrated into the highly successful literacy campaign, which recruited and trained young volunteers to go out in literacy brigades. These volunteers not only brought literacy to thousands of adults, reducing the previous illiteracy rate from over 50 per cent to 12 per cent, but they also introduced political awareness and basic education in a variety of subjects. They helped initiate mass immunization programs against polio, measles, tetnaus, and other childhood diseases.

In the first half of 1980 alone there were 1.2 million immunizations administered, a number of two and one-half times greater than the total for the last year of the Somoza regime (Ministerio de Planificacion, 1981). They have also helped to organize and carry out campaigns for the control and treatment of mosquito borne diseases (malaria and dengue fever) and tuberculosis. The results of these efforts were impressive. In the first half of 1982 there was not a single reported case of polio, diphtheria, or dengue fever. Reported cases of measles dropped from 3,784 in 1980 to 121 in the first nine months of 1982, while whopping cough dropped from 2,469 to 265 for the same period. For malaria, which exceeded 25,000 cases in 1980, there were reported only 4,600 cases in the first half of 1982 (Ministerio de Salud, 1982).

In 1979 the government initiated a new program for the emergency treatment of dehydration resulting from acute diarrhea, the most common cause of infant mortality. In less than three years more than 300 oral rehydration centers were established. Nearly 100,000 children were treated for diarrhea in the first two years of the program, and one in five of these suffered from serious dehydration. This timely attention reduced deaths among those treated to nearly zero, and was "likely to have a striking effect in reducing infant mortality" (Halperin and Garfield, 1982: 390).

Programs were initiated for the reduction of environmental health hazards, particularly those related to the previously indiscriminate use of agricultural chemicals and the improper disposal of industrial wastes. A latrine building program, to reduce the spread of intestinal parasites, was providing latrines for 24,000 homes per year. And community-based health education promoted better personal hygiene and nutrition.

Popular Participation

The key to the Nicaraguan health plan was its reliance on popular participation. "...The revolutionary government has chosen a strategy which fuses public health and politics. A health network based on popular participation and control is being formed which should not only decrease the high rates of malnutrition and infectious diseases in a cost-effecient manner, but should increase the strength of the revolution as well" (Escudero, 1981:3). In the cities as well as in the countryside, citizens were involved in the health care process, not only in carrying out government programs, but also in the planning and decision making which took place within the community mass organizations. In every commuity and neighborhood there werre Committees for the Defense of Sandinism (CDS). The CDS were born as community support networks during the revolutionary struggle, and gave the masses a voice in the planning of programs. While their effectiveness varied and some were not as politically oriented as others, they consistently served well as the fundamental units of social programs (Harris, 1981), and they were essential for the accomplishment of most of the preventive programs described above.

Increased Professional and Paraprofessional Training

By 1982 there have been significant increased in the number of professional health workers in training. Yearly enrollment for nurses had increased from 50 to 400, for doctors from 100 to 500, and for auxiliary nurses from 300 to 1,000. A second medical school had been opened in Managua, and medical residency programs had been initiated. For the first time there were regular training classes for health technicians (350 enrolled yearly) and for health outreach workers (600 enrolled yearly). Training programs had been modified to emphasize community and preventive medicine and to reduce the proportion of time spent studying the exotic and less common diseases. The tradition of installing a physician as minister of health was broken with the selection of a woman with administrative experience, and advanced training programs in health administration and epidemiology were initiated.

Steps were undertaken to incorporate elements of the informal system into the formal system. Training in first aid and hygiene was given to many who were self educated injectionists, herbalists or folk practitioners. A nationwide program for the training of midwives was undertaken, giving them not only training but also official recognition and material support.

This program was particularly important given the high incidence of postnatal tetanus and the fact that births attended by midwives still represented nearly 50 per cent of all deliveries in 1981 (Ministerio de Salud, 1982).

Integrated Planning

Throughout the health care system there were examples of the importance of integrated planning. This has been mentioned in education, the integration of the literacy volunteers into the community health programs, and the changes in medical education. The Ministry of Health worked closely with many other ministries and public agencies. In the area of nutrition they coordinated their efforts with, among others, the Ministries of Planning, Social Welfare, Commerce, and Education, with the Agrarian Reform Institute, and with mass organizations such as the Nicaraguan Women's Association.

But the Ministry also had a close cooperative relationship with a wide range of private programs. An example of this cooperation was seen in the local affiliate of the International Planned Parenthood Foundation. "Formerly devoted exclusively to contraception, (the) clinic has now become the health center for the district of Managau in which it is located, providing all types of health care. In addition, it has recently secured large stocks of vitamins from international donations, which were turned over to the health ministry for nationwide distribution" (Escudero, 1981: 14). Many church groups, most notably the Baptists, had continued to carry on their long standing health programs, now coordinating their efforts with the government.

The important role of accurate information in the planning process was recognized early. A national program for the registration of births and deaths was initiated, investigation and data collection increased, and personnel were trained in computer based data management and analysis.

Problems and Prospects

That the Nicaraguan National Health System had made significant progress and that the health of the average Nicaraguan had been much improved in the first three years of the new government were facts which were both obvious and impressive. Nonetheless, significant problems still existed. Most of these could be classified as either economic or sociopolitical in nature.

Economic Problems

The problems of financing the investment in health care are great, particularly for countries with limited resources. Because social investments rarely produce short term economic returns, there is considerable pressure to reduce or delay such expenditures until the economic situation has been improved. This was true of the new Nicaragua, whose government had explicitly declared the economically productive sectors as priority groups. The social sector programs, which include not only health, but also education, social welfare, social security, housing and other programs, received less than 25 per cent of the national budget (Ministeriio de Planificacion, 1981).

The situation was further exacerbated by international complications. While financial assistance came from parts of the world, socialist and capitalist alike, it was not as generous as that which the Somoza regime received following the 1972 earthquake. This was especially true so far as the United States was concerned. Not only had the U.S. government greatly reduced its development efforts in Nicaragua, but it has also promoted and supported destabilization and attempted to use its influence to restrict international financial aid (Dixon and Jonas, 1982; Halperin and Garfield, 1982). The lack of foreign exchange and favorable credit had forced restrictions on the importation of medications, new equipment and supplies, and repair parts for deteriorating older equipment. It was estimated by the Minister of Planning that as much as 90 per cent of the foreign exchange to be generated through 1985 would have to be used for payment of international debts (La Prensa, 1982).

Paradoxically, the very success of the new government's health programs in reducing major barriers to health care---financial cost, time and distance, stigma, and anticipation of unresponsiveness of health personnel (Lewis, et al., 1976: 18)---led to greatly increased demand for services. There were significant rises in hospital admissions, attended births, surgical interventions and outpatient visits (Ministerio de Salud, 1982), all of which increased much more rapidly than did facilities or health care personnel. And the success of the early intervention and prevention programs in lowering the infant mortality rate had contributed to a significant rise in the population growth rate, which was estimated to have reached 4.5 per cent (Halperin and Garfield, 1982). This increase in demand for services was consistent with experiences in other improved health care systems (Woods and Graves, 1973; Roemer, 1976), and had already led to some frustration among those whose expectations had risen faster than the system's ability to respond. Although this did not seem to be a serious problem in Nicaragua at that time, it has been cited as a critical factor in other situations (Lewis, et al., 1976).

Sociopolitical Problems

The new government of Nicaragua was explcitly and unswervingly committed to the creation of an egalitarian social system. While few would argue that the Somoza regime was better, there were some who believed that the creation of a new system must somehow only be accomplished without any reduction of their former power or privilege. Even though an estimated 25 per cent of the physicians emigrated following the revolution, the number of physicians present in late 1982 exceeded the pre-revolutionary figures due to recent graduations, the return of some self-exiled Nicaraguans, and the introduction of physicians of other nationalities (El Nuevo Diario, 1982; Ministerior de Salud, 1982).

Among the original physicians remaining not all have been willing to concede their professional independence and control. Physicians and registered nurses were now outnumbered by auxiliary nurses in the union of health workers, and therefore no longer dominated the policy making process (Escudero, 1981). And as physicians were still given the freedom of maintaining a private practice and setting their own fees, a two-level system continued, offering a different quality of care to those who could pay for it (Halperin and Garfield, 1982).

There was also criticism among those enrolled in the social security system. Previously blessed with a relatively high quality of care, many complained that they had difficulty getting an appointment to be seen. They were particularly irritated because their payroll deducations are being used (in part) to finance the system now used by all (Rosenberg, 1980). Even some individuals of the most humble station rejected the notion that they should have to participate in the creation of their own "basic health." By their definition, the revolution was for the purpose of giving them the things that were previously enjoyed only by the few, not for the purpose of making them produce their own rewards. While the participatory nature of the revolutionary process allowed all of these dissidents a voice, it did not guarantee a mutually satisfactory resolution of differences.

Individuals were not alone in opposing the direction of the revolution. Some organizations likewise resented the government's policy of allowing relative autonomy only to those private groups that will work in a coordinated effort with the National Health System. A few international programs reduced their efforts or withdrew completely rather than give up their independence. One international group gave up its attempt to fund the construction of a new hospital when they were informed that its location and administration would have to be consistent with the government's health plan.

In spite of the problems discussed above, there seemed little reason for pessimism concerning the future of health care in the new Nicaragua. Dedicated and imaginative personnel, Nicaraguan and international, were applying themselves to the creation of a more efficient and more equitable formal health care system. Their progress after only three years was impressive and serves as encouragement and as a model to many other countries with conditions similar to those of Nicaragua before the revolution. It would take considerable time, money and effort before the inheritance of the past could be overcome. Undoubtedly the informal health care system would continue to be relied upon where the formal system was weak. And some form of differential quality of treatment would be likely to persist. But the commitment of the Nicaraguans to the consideration of basic health as a right and a social need had started them advancing in a direction from which they would be unlikely to retreat.

Research for the preparation of this article was supported in part by a grant from the Stanford-Berkely Joint Center for Latin American Studies, and by a professional development grant from the University of the Pacific. The author acknowledges the cordial and extensive cooperation of the people of Nicaragua, and the assistance of the staff of the Nicaraguan Interfaith Committee for Action.

REFERENCES

BOSSERT, THOMAS J. (1982) "Health Care in Revolutionary Nicaragua," pp. 259-272 in Thomas Walker (ed.), REVOLUTION IN NICARAGUA. N.Y.: Praeger Publ.

BRYANT, JOHN (1969) HEALTH AND THE DEVELOPING WORLD. Ithaca: Cornell University Press.

COMITE TECNICO DE NUTRICION (1977) "Enfoque General del Barrio Open #3." Mangua: Ministerio de Salud (mimeographed).

DANIELSON, ROSS (1979) CUBAN MEDICINE. New Brunswick, N.J.: Transaction, Inc.

DIXON, MARLENE and SUSANNE JONAS (1982) "The New Trojan Horse: Transnational Banks and the Sovereignty of Peoples." San Francisco: Institute for the Study of Labor and Economic Crisis (mimeographed).

EL NUEVO DIARIO (1982) "En Nicaragua Ahora Hay Mas Medicos y Medicina." Managua: October 22, 1.

ESCUDERO, JOSE (1981) HEALTH CARE IN THE NEW NICRAGUA. N.Y.: Casa Nicaragua.

FREIDSON, ELIOT (1960) "Client Control and Medical Practice," AMERICAN JOURNAL OF SOCIOLOGY 65(Jan.): 374-382.

HALPERIN, DAVID C. and RICHARD GARFIELD (1982) "Developments in Health Care in Nicaragua," NEW ENGLAND JOURNAL OF MEDICINE 307(6): 388-392.

HARRIS, HERMIONE (1981) "Nicaragua: Two Years of Revolution," RACE AND CLASS 23(1): 1-23.

HAUB, CARL (1981) WORLD POPULATION DATA SHEET. Washington, D.C.: Population Reference Bureau.

HEIBY, JAMES R. (1981) "Low-Cost Health Delivery Systems: Lessons from Nicaragua,," AMERICAN JOURNAL OF PUBLIC HEALTH 71(May): 541-519.

HOLLAND, B., J. DAVIS and L. GANGLOFF (1973) SYNCRISIS: THE DYNAMICS OF HEALTH. VOL. XI: Nicaragua. Washington, D.C.: U.S. Dept. of H.E.W.

LA PRENSA (1982) "Ruiz: Vienen Dos Anos Duros," Managua: November 8, 1.

LEWIS, CHARLES E., RASHI FEIN and DAVID MECHANIC (1976) A RIGHT TO HEALTH: THE PROBLEM OF ACCESS TO PRIMARY CARE. N.Y.: John Wiley and Sons.

MINISTERIO DE PLANFICACION (1981) PROGRAMA ECONOMICO '81. Managua: Secretaria Nacional de Propaganda y Educacion Politica del F.S.L.N.

MINISTERIO DE SALUD (1982) "El Sistema Nacional Unico de Salud: Tres Anos de Revolution 1979-1982," Managua: Ministerio de Salud.

ROEMER, MILTON I. (1976) HEALTH CARE SYSTEMS IN WORLD PER- SPECTIVE. Ann Arbor: Health Administration Press.

ROSENBAUM, HAROLD D. and JACK H. HILDNER (1979) "Radiology in Nicaragua: Lessons from a Radiologic Paramedic Training Effort," AMERICAN JOURNAL OF ROENTGENOLOGY 133(Dec.): 1161-1165.

ROSENBERG, MARK B. (1980) "Social Reform in the New Nicaragua." Miami (mimeographed).

WOODS, CLYDE M. and THEODORE D. GRAVES 91973) THE PROCESS OF MEDICAL CHANGE IN A HIGHLAND GUATEMALAN TOWN. Los Angeles: Latin American Center, U.C.L.A.

CHAPTER 22

COMMUNITY-BASED HEALTH CARE PROGRAMS IN KENYA:
THREE CASE STUDIES IN PLANNING AND IMPLEMENTATION

Dennis G. Willms

Introduction

The planning process for health care programs in Third World countries is currently undergoing significant policy changes (**Endnote 1**). In principle, there is a noticeable shift from a direct emphasis on conventional forms of clinical care to that of a predominant (although supplementary) emphasis on disease prevention, health promotion, and family planning. The conceptual and organizational vehicle for accomplishing this intended change is popularly known as PRIMARY HEALTH CARE (PHC) or COMMUNITY--BASED HEALTH CARE (CBHC).

The World Health Organization (WHO) and the United Nations Children's Fund (UNICEF) are the principle architects and engineers of this international program. They define Primary Health Care as "...essential health care made universally accessible to individuals and families in the community by means acceptable to them, through their full participation and at a cost that the community and country can afford. It forms an integral part both of the country's health system of which it is the nucleus and of the overall social and economic development of the community" (Director-General of the World Health Organization and the Executive Director of the United Nations Children's Fund, 1978: 2-3).

Community-Based Health Care (CBHC) is considered to be the "primary health care" step in the rural community's "health seeking process" (for an explication of this notion, see Chrisman, 1977). In other words, the immediate, most accessible health worker in the community is to be the COMMUNITY HEALTH WORKER (CHW). These Community Health Workers are considered to be part-time employees of the communities they serve and are trained to manage common illness complaints in their village community. For example, they are trained and equipped to treat minor cuts and burns, worm infestations, scabies, and to provide the appropriate treatment regimen for the malarial victim. More importantly, they are trained to screen risk from non-risk illness cases so that those patients they are unable to treat can be referred to the nearest clinical facility---an essential structural component in CBHC is the referral back-up to clinical health care delivery. Nevertheless, the principle function and focus of the Community Health Worker is on disease prevention, health promotion, and family planning. In this capacity, CHWs are usually trained to educate and "motivate" members of their respective communities to boil their drinking water, build drying racks for dishes, build and use pit latrines, consider available methods of family planning, utilize the Maternal Child Health (MCH) clinics, prepare oral rehydration fluids for children who suffer from diarrhea and vomiting, and consider necessary nutritional advise for children who are malnourished (**Endnote 2**).

The stretegy of CBHC is not a recent innovation in the Republic of Kenya. Mission hospitals, research organizations, and, in at least one instance, an independent rural peasant community (**Case 2**) have tried and tested the "community-based health care" (CBHC) approach (**Endnote 3**). What is occurring, however, is the fact that the Ministry of Health (**Case 1**) is responding to the success stories of the non-government organized CBHC programs, and is considering and also "experimenting" with Pilot Projects in CBHC through its Rural Health services Program (see for example Were, 1979). There are obvious reasons for this shift in its rural health care service strategy. The Kenyan Ministry of Health is being encouraged (financially and ideologically) by the World Bank, which together with other donors interested in the Kenya health sector is causing the Ministry to seriously consider CBHC as the organizational vehicle of future health care policy and planning efforts. Not surprisingly, the Ministry of Health is beginning to voice---as yet on paper, or rhetorically (see Mburu, 1979)---a serious interest in the CHBC rural health care model.

With this increasing tendency to "use" the language of "community-based health care" (CBHC), CBHC has emerged as a gloss with varying and sometimes disparate meanings. In Kenyan government, non-government, and traditional health care situations, it is interpreted differently and reflects the epistemological reality dominant in the particular setting. I maintain that potential problems in the development of a government--imposed CBHC program could be attributed to these apparent epistemological considerations, and not, as has so frequently been suggested, to the organizational models employed.

There are numerous models of and for CBHC that have already been tested and reported on in the literature to establish a reasonable organizational guide(see for examples the cases published in CONTACT). In other words, without a knowledge of how peasants in the rural areas construct, experience, and manage "illness" events---and conversely, "health," "health care," and "community-based health care"---it will be inopportune to negotiate appropriate health care strategies in rural situations (**Endnote 4**). It is essential, therefore, to examine the "ethnographic realities" (Foster, 1981) of those rural communities in which CBHC will presumably develop as a health care possibility.

The following three case studies are intended to illustrate the variability in interpretations, approaches, and experiences of the idea of "community--based health care" (CBHC). The first case study outlines the ethnographic reality of the Kenyan Ministry of Health: it will demonstrate the case where CBHC is formulated and constructed in a **technical** epistemological mode. Yet among communities and missions in the Republic of Kenya, existing CBHC programs appear to center on two types of epistemological realities; a **moral** and a **spiritual** health care modality. The Saradidi Rural Health Development Project (a Luo ethnic community in Siaya District) will illustrate the case of the CBHC program that is implemented in essentially moral terms. Lastly, I present the case of the Nangina Community Health Program (an Abasamian ethnic group in Busia District); in this hospital mission-inspired CBHC program, CBHC is experienced in predominantly spiritual terms. Issues of ethnicity and religion underlie the interpretation of CBHC in the last two cases.

CASE 1: The Ministry of Health

The Ministry of Health is the major health care service provider within the Republic of Kenya. Like other bureaucratic organizations in the Third World, it is regarded as being "top heavy" in its administrative and managerial organization. District and provincial level managers are compelled to act on the major policy and planning decisions that are formulated at Ministry of Health headquarters in Nairobi. As such, it exemplifies an administrative situation in which "downward communication is facilitated and expected; lateral communication is forbidden; and upwards communicatione except upon request is not sought" (Moris quoted in Janovsky, 1979: 58).

The upper-level managers who create health care policies, plans, and programs in the Ministry of Health are usually health care professionals (either physicians or nurses) and political appointees (in the top positions, by the President and through **fiat**). Through necessity they are given to propound the political **cum** economic development model as posited by the current government in power, as well as the clinical emphasis of their medical profession.

As far as community-based health care (CBHC) is concerned, these political economic, and professional orientations support the formulation of a national CBHC policy. CBHC is in agreement with the 'self-help' rural development strategy initially created by Kenyatta (his motto was **Haraambee**; in Kiswahili, "let us pull together") and sustained by his successor, President Moi (his motto being **Myayo**; in Kiswahili, "in his footsteps"). CBHC is also welcomed as an economically feasible health care service strategy; in the proposed INTEGRATED RURAL HEALTH AND FAMILY PLANNING (IRH-FP) program, rural communities would be held responsible for the financing of their own health care programs. The health care professionals within the Ministry of Health are also in support of a national CBHC program; through the creation of another cadre of health care workers in the rural communities (that is, the CHWs), their status as clinicians working out of static health care facilities is supported and not undermined. Unfortunately, even though CBHC within the Ministry of Health is considered to be ideologically expedient, it is organizationally and administratively burdened by bureaucratic tactics and technicalities.

The "technical" characteristics of the Ministry of Health's approach in the construction of rural health services is illustrated in the manner in which rural health care services have been evaluated in the past, and consequently conceptualized, organized, and managed in the present (**Endnote 5**). Consider, for example, the following rural health care problem in the Ministry of Health's rural health care program.

Research carried out by the Ministry of Health---as well as by non-government research organizations---indicates that approximately "20-30% of the rural population actually benefit from and utilize rural health services" (Migue and Ndungu, 1979: 22; in reference to earlier research studies). In response to these damaging reports of the rural health care services utilization record, upper-level managers in the Ministry decided to: (i) increase the rate of expansion and construction of rural health facilities---health centers, health sub-centers, and dispensaries (Ministry of Health, 1972); (ii) implement an "integration" of services approach, thereby merging ante-natal, post-natal, maternity, child welfare, family planning, and health education services (Rural Health Development Project, 1979); and (iii) organize a re-training program for existing cadres of health workers in order that they might act as "community animateurs" in the rural communities (Wan'gombe, 1980: 2).

In other words, existing health workers would be taught how to present to and convince rural peasants of the **worthwhileness** of the government's health care programs. Concurrent with the initial structural alterations ("i" above) in the rural health care system, it was mentioned that "...most of the people do not know how to make the most effective use of either preventive or curative medical services, even when they are available" (Ministry of Health, 1972: 2). While the changes that were implemented in the rural health care system were administratively sound, as a bureaucratically structured organization with its own "ethnographic reality," it appears to be uninterested in fully understanding the health care situation and expectations of the communities it purports to serve.

The most recent example of this is evident in the new Integrated rural Health and Family Planning (RH-FP) Program (Ministry of Health, 1981). The same bureaucratic tendencies of centralized control, administrative dominance from headquarters, and the authoritative imposition of health care ideas is reproduced. Rather than critically assessing its previous methods and tactics in the provision of rural health services, it has elaborated even further its bureaucratic infrastructure to accomodate its own interpretation of CBHC. The following organizational framework illustrates again the technical approach to CBHC posited by the Ministry.

At the Central (headquarters) Ministry of Health level, a COMMUNITY--BASED HEALTH CARE DEVELOPMENT UNIT is planned. This unit would "...help to formulate policy, promote community-based health care schemes, review and approve proposals for schemes to be funded from project funds, set guidelines for CHW (Community Health Worker) stipends, train staff of district Rural Health Management Teams in 'community-based health care,' and monitor and evaluate schemes" (Ministry of Health, 1981: 75).

At the District level, a "community-Based Health Care Team"---an organizational arm of the new RURAL HEALTH MANAGEMENT TEAMS---would act as a facilitator for the organization of CBHC programs in rural communities. These Teams would act as a "communication tool" for the construction of CBHC programs. In this capacity, the "Community-Based Health Care Team"---an organization vehicle that has been in the "planning stage" for a number of years---is designed to act as a "community support structure" so as to assist in "(i) the process of **defining** and **delineating** the unit of community---the functional base for community-participatory activities; (ii) the **establishment** of Community Health Committees; (iii) the **establishment** of Community Accounts; and (iv) the **selection** of Community Health Workers" (MINISTRY OF HEALTH AND DEVELOPMENT OF COMMUNITY HEALTH, 1978: 13-14; emphasis added).

In order to construct and "establish" this community-based organization, the District level Team would select pre-formed "target groups" to act as a spring board for the CBHC program; these groups might be church groups, cooperatives, women's groups, schools, or other development groups in the community. The Community Health Workers (CHWs) are to be part-time employees of their communities; in most cases, they are to be women, married, with children, literate in the local language, and respected members of their communities. Their health care duties would involve the following, "...all would be expected to undertake the treatment of common ailments, including oral rehydration, health education, family planning counselling, motivation and client follow-up, the administration of simple vaccines, and to take part in campaigns against communicable diseases" (MINISTRY OF HEALTH, 1981: 74-75).

All in all, CBHC in the hands of the Ministry of Health is an extended "technical" exercise. It is, in actual fact, little more than an **ad hoc** response to an internationally embarrassing rural health care service record; at the same time, it is an attempt to satisfy interested international donors. Unfortunately, in the process of reproducing previous models of service delivery---with an additional CBHC component alteration---it is unable to elicit and appropriate substantive health-related knowledge from the communities it expects to serve. Rather, it persists in formulating health care assumptions based on the above illustrated health care view.

In the following two cases, evidence will be given for an epistemological view of health care that differs from that constructed by the CBHC unit within the Ministry of Health; rather than positing a **disease** model, a **well-being** model for CBHC is implemented. These cases, alternatively, are situations that permit a more authentic expression and construction of CBHC as recommended and internationally agreed upon the World Health Organization (see World Health Organization, 1978).

CASE 2: The Saradidi Rural Health Development Project

The SARADIDI RURAL HEALTH DEVELOPMENT PROJECT is perhaps the only CBHC program in the Republic of Kenya that has been initiated without the external intervention of government, mission hospital, research, or aid organization. As an independent, community-initiated CBHC program, it is characteristically "moral" in its interpretation and experience of "community-based health care" (CBHC). That is, in an effort to ameliorate the agreed upon problems in the community (inadequate water sources, unemployment, lack of clinical facilities, and an inefficient transportation and communication system), the leaders in the community created a program that underscored "community" values and can be considered a revitalization of traditional experiences of "community life."

The Project is situated near the shores of Lake Victoria and in the two sub-locations of Asembo East and Asembo West. The Luo peasants who live in the Project area are mainly subsistence agriculturalists **cum** pastoralists; they grow what they eat (maize, cassava, millet, peas, groundnuts, and potatoes), but in most cases, are unable to store enough to take them from one harvest to the next. The Saradidi peasants are generally very poor. It is estimated that only 11% of the persons in the Saradidi Project area is salaried or receives a regular income through self-employment (Kaseje, 1980: 1).

In addition to the problem of poverty, the experience of illness is an everyday reality. Malaria is probably one of the most serious diseases; it is endemic to the area and affects mainly children under five years of age and women who are pregnant. Undernutrition and malnutrition are also serious problems with 40% of the children under three years of age (5-10% of them severely malnourished) in this category (Kaseje, 1980). Other causes of mortality and morbidity are diarrheal diseases (approximately 80% of children under five years of age have worm infestations) and measles (Kaseje, 1980).

In many respects, the Saradidi community feels that the government has neglected them in the provision of essential services. The nearest hospital, for example, is at Siaya (30 ms. away); there is a dispensary at Ong'ielo (13 kms. away), but it is predictably short of necessary drugs. Given this inadequate system of health care services, the leaders of Saradidi were prompted to construct their own "development" program. As they envisioned it, their program would encompass a "total" development effort: the construction of a self-help dispensary, the establishment of income-generating projects in the smaller village communties, and the formation of a CHW program to address the issues of disease prevention, health promotion, and family planning. Furthermore, in the process of constructing the Saradidi CBHC program, there has been a deliberate and conscious attempt to "break the ties of church and clan"---and presumably any politically induced 'self-help' (**Harambee**) effort of the government---so as to unite the people in a singular development program.

"Community," in the sense that it is experienced here, is a reworking of the Luo **oganda** or "subtribe," which is the larger collective unit that rallied in response to critical life events in traditional times, as for example, in warfare, famine, etc. (**Endnote 6**).

The Sardidi Rural Health development Project was initiated by a self-appointed committee of influential community leaders. This "Interim Committee" was composed of those individuals whose idea it was to construct a CBHC program. After an initial period, during which time they introduced the idea to other prominent village elders or **jodongo**, they called a general meeting of the larger community for purposes of appointing a PROJECT COMMITTEE. At the same time, they decided on an appropriate site on which to build the Saradidi self-help dispensary; later on in the Project's development, this dispensary became the training site for the Community Health Workers.

The Project Committee that was elected at this time was made responsible for the initiation of VILLAGE HEALTH COMMITTEES (VHCs). In Luoland, there is no such thing as a "village" (Southall, 1952: 25). For the purposes of the Project and election, however, groups of contiguous homesteads or **dala** were identified whose occupants have a "feeling of belonging together." The complex of homesteads, or "village," that is situated along the length of a ridge, traces their descent to the same core patrilineage; in this sense, the identified Project "village" can be considered a segmental division, clan or **dhoot**, of the maximal patrilineage. The elders of these traditional clan-based or "village" units, traditionally formed the group of clan elders or **jodongo**; in the Project, these elders met as the Village Health Committee (VHC). Each Village Health Committee in turn is represented on the Project Committee which has elected an EXECUTIVE COMMITTE (EC) to manage the everyday affairs of the Project.

Before the implementation of the Saradidi Rural Health Development Project, members of various clans called on the herbalist **cum** traditional birth attendant or **nyamrerua**, during times of illness or when a woman was about to deliver a child. Since the nyamrerua was an obvious candidate for Community Health Worker (CHW), the leaders on the VHC usually selected this traditionally recognized health care practitioner for training. Renamed VILLAGE HELPERS TOWARDS HEALTH (VHsTH), the nyamrerua is usually a woman with children, married to a resident of the community, between 25 and 35 years of age, and considered to be a compassionate and respecte person.

The nyamrerua is taught by the Project's Kenyan Community Nurse (hired through Project funds) in matters of disease prevention, health promotion, and family planning. Since the nyamrerua is essentially taught how to teach, she must be a gifted communicator and at least in the company of people. The motto "Prevention is Better than Cure" is constantly reiterated by the nyamrerus in her discussions with villagers at the clinic (where she is under the supervison of the Nurse) and in her own community where she spends time visting homes assisting therapeutically when she

305

is called on to do so. She is a part-time worker, and as in the role fulfilled as nyamrerua, not paid for her services; rather, she is paid in kind (eggs, a hen, or some vegetables) and respected as a moral member of the Luo community.

Nevertheless, there are changes in the Saradidi community that result from the obvious influence of Western, modern trends. On the Executive Committee (EC) itself, these tendencies are evident in those leaders whose authority is derived from socio-economic rather than generation/-lineage considerations (Parkin, 1978); for example between headmasters, teachers, and businessmen, and traditional elders and leaders. While these separate leaders are prone to emphasize different aspects of the Project---for example, income-generating projects over those of the health care program---there is a strain towards the "collective good" as opposed to that political or economic benefit. In many respects, this tendency is accomplished through the work of the nyamrerua and the Project Director. As traditionally respected persons in the village community, the nyamrerua bridge and negotiate the dual emphases of health care and income-generating projects in the village; at a larger organization level, the Project Director negotiates within the leadership ranks between "professional" and "traditional" leaders. In this sense, he fulfills to some extent, the position of the charismatic leader or **jabilo** in traditional times; rival groups were made to reconcile their differences so as to organize and unite against a common enemy.

In the Saradidi Rural Health Development Project, every attempt has been made to transcend rival and community group differences by: (i) identifying those elements in community life that everyone can agree on---namely, the shared experiences of disease, poverty, and suffering----and on that basis, (ii) organize with singleness of mind in order to effectively, and in a moral fashion, resolve these problems.

CASE 3: The Nangina Community Health Program

Nangina's CBHC program is unlike other hospital-inspired programs in administration, organization, and management. Although it was initiated (in principle) through the activities of the Medical Mission Sisters at Nangina Hospital---and in its earlier stages was completely controlled by Hospital personnel---full responsibility for the program has been successfully transferred to community members. Much of this success is attributed to the emergence of clan-based CHRISTIAN COMMUNITY GROUPS (CCGs). Those CHWs who represent their respective CCGs, negotiate an interesting and constructive relationship between the rural, clan-based community (where they live), the hospital (where they are trained as CHWs), and the Mission (where they are spiritually directed). The particular ambience created in this communication and interaction of social and cultural groups, has caused the Nangina CBHC program to become a uniquely "spiritual" activity.

306

Nangina Mission and Hospital is located in Busia District, Western Kenya, and is situated on the murrain road that connects the port town of Sio Port (on Lake Victoria) and the market town of Bumala. The Abasamia peasants (a subtribe of the Abaluyia) who live in Samia Location and in the environs of the hospital compound, are dependent on a mixed pattern of subsistence agriculture for their livelihood (cotton, sugar cane, sunflower, simsim, maize, millet, cassava, sorghum, and groundnuts) combined with livestock farming of cattle, goats, poultry, and sheep. It is a heavily populated area in Kenya and is known to have the highest population growth rate in the world (MINISTRY OF HEALTH, 1981). The average household size, for example, is estimated at ten people, made up of a man, his two wives, and their seven to eight children (MINISTRY OF ECONOMIC PLANNING AND DEVELOPMENT, 1980: 4). The most common illness complaints for children are: malaria, respiratory tract infection, gastro-enteritis, scabies, intestinal worms, measles, and diarrhea. In addition, the government reports the prevalence of tuberculosis, leprosy, venereal disease, pneumonia, bilharzia, and cholera; kwashiokor and marasmus is also common.

Since many of the illness complaints were seen to be preventable, the sisters at Nangina Hospital deliberately shifted their health care emphasis to a variety of MATERNAL CHILD HEALTH (MCH) clinical and educative programs in the community. While the PUBLIC HEALTH AIDES, UNDER FIVES CLINIC, and NUTRITION AIDE FIELD WORKER education programs were reasonably successful, these newly formed community health workers were considered to be too dependent (in salary, status, and clinical concerns) on their "professional" association with the Hospital.

Nevertheless, while these community health programs were in the process of developing thorugh the impetus of the Medical Mission Sisters, there were significant changes in the rural communities that were predicated on "spiritual" events at the Mission. The parish priest at Nangina Mission (a Dutch Mill Hill Father), personally experienced a conversion experience that marked the beginning of a spiritual renewal in the clan-based communities. Preaching a message of "reconciliation, unity, **metanoia,** and suffering," CLAN COMMUNITY GROUPS emerged as general community-based care groups; emphasis was placed on building huts for the poor, income-generating activities, communal gardens, other forms of coopeative activity, and praying and reading Scripture together (**Endnote 7**). Since the activities of these groups overrided the specific interests and boundaries of the traditional clan structure, there was a change in name to CHRISTIAN COMMUNITY GROUP so as to emphasize the experience of "togetherness as Christians."

Given the multiplicity of voluntary social programs that developed thorugh these groups, the Medical Mission Sisters felt that this would provide a reasonable support structure for a voluntary CHW program. As a result, community leaders were approached to select CHW representatives from their Christian Community Groups. Rather than depending on the financial and professional support of the nursing sisters, the cadre of voluntary

COMMUITY HEALTH WORKERS (CHWs) that has emerged rely on the spiritual and social supports of other Christian Community Group members.

Generally speaking, those CHWs selected are recognized for their leadership abilities (approachability, trustworthiness, commitment to the job), as well as for their "spirit." these attributes, along with wisdom and the experience of age brings, appear to be more important than their level of education. Most of the CHWs are women who are illiterate and are forty-five years in average age. They are trained in elements of basic midwifery, basic health and nutrition, material child health care, hygiene and sanitation, the simple treatment of common ailments (including first aid), the detection and reporting of some common diseases, and family planning. Since the training session is two weeks in duration, the opportunity is given to impart only basic health education knowledge. The primary aim of the course is really to "create awareness about health" in the Community Health Workers. Additionally, the CHWs are given the opportunity to upgrade the level of their health care knowledge through experience assisting at the mobile clinics in their communities, as well as through the yearly refresher courses given at Nangina Hospital.

The principle mandate of the Nangina CBHC program is "to make every parent a health educator in his/her own family" (Nangina Hospital, 1979: 39). As volunteers, the Community Health Workers (CHWs) are motivated in their attempts to communicate this available health care knowledge because of their respected social position in the Christian Community Group and because of the spiritual "gift" that they feel has been given. When they attend to the needs of a person who is sick, these various aspects merge in the therapeutic event. For example, if Chloroquin tablets are prescribed for a patient with malaria, the tablets are prayed over so as to be made efficacious; similarly, if the CHW is busy organizing transportation to take a sick person to Nangina Hospital, members of the Christian Community Group are called on to pray for the person at the same time.

Conclusion

In the published report of "The Alma-Ata Conference On Primary Health Care," the World Health Organization emphasizes the element of "community participation" in CBHC programs: "...the people have the right and duty to participate individually and collectively in the planning and implementation of their health care. Primary Health Care...requires and promotes maximum community and individual self-reliance and participation in the planning, organization, operation and control of primary health care, making the fullest use of local, nation, and other available health care, making the fullest use of local, national, and other available resources, and to this end develops thorugh appropriate education the ability of the communities to participate" (WORLD HEALTH ORGANIZATION, 1978: 428-429).

Health care planners who have wanted to accomplish effective CBHC, often think of "community participation" and CBHC itself in an organizational, bureaucratic way. They are concerned with the problem of "how to facilitate the process of community participation," or perhaps, "how to convince rural community leaders that the health care measures being suggested are legitimate." This was illustrated in the case of the Ministry of Health who, encouraged by international standards, monies, and ongoing non-government organized programs, have begun to implement CBHC according to a technical, "disease" model of health care delivery. Alternatively, in the traditional world of the Luo ethnic community, CBHC has been implemented in a moral fashion, and in accordance with a model that continues to sustain the "well-being" of community members. The mission-inspired CBHC program has also acted on the CBHC rhetoric; rather than actualizing CBHC in a strictly moral way, the "caring" concerns of CHWs are accomplished for spiritual reasons.

In conclusion, this paper has demonstrated the **sui generis** nature of CBHC ethnographic realities. By indicating that CBHC is often interpreted and experienced in moral, spiritual and technical modes, it raises altenative planning and policy considerations: (i) How is CBHC a possibility in rural peasant communities?, and (ii) How may it be possible for there to be an articulation and negotiation of mutually supportive systems (i.e., between the clinical health care infrastructure and the CBHC programs)?

ENDNOTES

1. I would like to thank Professors Ken Burridge and Nancy Waxler for valuable suggestions on problems related to the subject of CBHC. Professor Carole Farber provided an inciteful critique on an earlier draft of this paper and Deborah Nelligan typed under difficult time constraints; I thank them both. In addition, I acknowledge the financial support of the Office of the Dean, Faculty of Social Science, University of Western Ontario, for funds made available in the preparation of this paper.

2. Many of the non-government organized CBHC programs train their CHWs in the "psycho-social method" (see Freire, 1970). In Kenya, the best example of this method in a CBHC program is the Machakos Village Health Workers Program (see Huising, 1981).

3. The Kenya Catholic Secretariat has implemented a number of CBHC programs throughout Kenya: the most successful of them being the Kisii Public Health Aides Program in Kisii District, the Nangina Community Health Program in Busia District (**Case 3**), and the Machakos Village Health Workers Program in Machakos District. Among the Protestant mission hospital organizations, the Church of Scotland Mission have organized a CBHC program at Chogoria Hospital in Meru District, and the Methodists have a CBHC program at Maua Methodist Hospital, also in Meru District. Besides managing a CBHC program at Kibwezi in Kitui District, the African Medical and Research Foundation (AMREF, incorporating the 'Flying Doctor Service') has created a "Community Health Worker Support Unit" to assist in the organization of CBHC programs and to assist in the training of Community health Workers (CHWs) in their own villages. In total there are approximately twelve ongoing CBHC programs in the Republic of Kenya.

4. Recent work by Kleinman, Eisenberg, and Good (1978) provides a useful distinction between illness (the patient's cultural experience of sickness) and disease (the analytical construction of the physician); concomitantly, it is possible to explicate how expectations for healing (the illness) and curing (the disease) differ as separate symbolic realities.

5. The Rural Health Services branch of the Ministry of Health is responsible for providing essential health care services to approximately 14 million people who live in the rural areas of the Republic of Kenya (Integrated Rural Health and Family Planning Program, 1981).

6. All **bold** foreign words are from the Luo language.

7. Metanoia, in theological terminology, refers to a conversion ("turning around and back") experience.

REFERENCES

CHRISMAN, NOEL (1977) "The Health Seeking Process: An Approach to the Natural History of Illness." CULTURE, MEDICINE, AND PSYCHIATRY 1: 351-377.

DIRECTOR-GENERAL OF THE WORLD HEALTH ORGANIZATION AND THE EXECUTIVE DIRECTOR OF THE UNITED NATIONS CHILDREN'S FUND (1978) PRIMARY HEALTH CARE: REPORT OF THE INTERNATIONAL CONFERENCE ON PRIMARY HEALTH CARE. Geneva and New York: World Health Organization.

FOSTER, GEORGE M. (1981) "Primary Health Care: Its Conceptual Ties to Commuity Development." SYMPOSIUM ON ANTHROPOLOGY AND PRIMARY HEALTH CARE, INTERNATIONAL UNION OF ETHNOLOGICAL AND ANTHROPOLOGICAL SCIENCES (IUAES) INTER-CONGRESS, Amsterdam, The Netherlands.

FREIRE, PAULO (1970) PEDAGOGY OF THE OPPRESSED. N.Y.: The Seabury Press.

HUISING, GERARDA (1981) "Planning as Organizational Transaction and Bargaining: The Case of Health in Kenya." Ph.D. dissertation, Harvard University.

KASEJE, DAN C.O. (1980) A COMMUNITY-BASED HEALTH CARE PROGRAM: SARADIDI HEALTH PROJECT. Nairobi: Department of Community Health, Faculty of Medicine, University of Nairobi.

KLEINMAN, ARTHUR, LEON EISENBERG, and BYRON GOOD (1978) "Culture, Illness, and Care: Clinical Lessons from Anthropologic and Cross-Cultural Research." ANNALS OF INTERNAL MEDICINE 88: 251-258.

MBURU, F.M. (1979) "Rhetoric-Implementation Gap in Health Policy and Health Services Delivery for a Rural Population in a Developing Country." SOCIAL SCIENCE AND MEDICINE 13A: 577-583.

MIGUE, M., and L.K. NDUNGU (1979) RURAL HEALTH MANAGEMENT: THE KENYAN EXPERIENCE. Nairobi: Ministry of Health.

MINISTRY OF ECONOMIC PLANNING AND DEVELOPMENT (1980) BUSIA: DISTRICT DEVELOPMENT PLAN 1979-1983. Nairobi: Republic of Kenya.

MINISTRY OF HEALTH (1972) PROPOSAL FOR THE IMPROVEMENT OF RURAL HEALTH SERVICES AND THE DEVELOPMENT OF RURAL HEALTH TRAINING CENTRES IN KENYA. Nairobi: Ministry of Health, Republic of Kenya.

MINISTRY OF HEALTH (1981) THE INTEGRATED RURAL HEALTH AND FAMILY PLANNING PROGRAM, APPRAISAL REPORT. Nairobi: Republic of Kenya.

MINISTRY OF HEALTH AND DEPARTMENT OF COMMUNITY HEALTH (1978) PRIMARY HEALTH CARE: KENYA EXPERIENCE. Nairobi: Ministry of Health and Faculty of Medicine, University of Nairobi.

NANGINA HOSPITAL (1979) NANGINA HOSPITAL AND PUBLIC HEALTH REPORT. P.O. BOX 57, Funyula, via Kisumu: Republic of Kenya.

PARKIN, DAVID (1978) THE CULTURAL DEFINITION OF POLITICAL RESPONSE: LINEAL DESTINY AMONG THE LUO. London: Academic Press.

RURAL HEALTH DEVELOPMENT PROJECT (1979) LINEAGE FORMATION AMONG THE LUO. International Africa Institute, Memorandum 26. London, N.Y., and Toronto: Oxford University Press.

WAN'GOMBE, JOSEPH K. (1980) ECONOMIC STUDY OF THE COMMUNITY-BASED HEALTH CARE PILOT PROJECT IN WESTERN KENYA. Nairobi: Institute of Development Studies, University of Nairobi.

WERE, MIRIAM K. (1979) PEOPLE'S PARTICIPATION IN THEIR HEALTH CARE: A PRELIMINARY REPORT ON THE NATIONAL PILOT PROJECT IN COMMUNITY-BASED HEALTH CARE—A KENYAN EXPERIENCE. Nairobi: Ministry of Health and the Department of Community Health, Faculty of Medicine, University of Nairobi.

WORLD HEALTH ORGANIZATION (1978) "The Alma-Ata Conference on Primary Health Care." WHO CHRONICLE 32: 409–430.

THE EDITOR

John H. Morgan, B.A.Hon.(Berk.), M.A., Ph.D.(Htfd.), D.D.(Unit.Inst.) is an Anglican Priest and Director and Senior Fellow of the Library Research Council in the Social Sciences at Notre Dame and currently Visiting Professor of Sociology and Anthropology at Saint Mary's College (Notre Dame). Trained at Hartford Seminary Foundation, Princeton, and Yale, Father Morgan was formerly National Science Foundation Fellow in the Center for the Study of Man (Notre Dame) and Research Associate in the History and Philosophy of Science. The author/editor of twenty books, his most recent publications include a research bibliography series including SOCIOBIOLOGY, BEHAVIOR AND GENETICS, and SOCIO-PHARMACOLOGY, and a forthcoming work entitled HEALTH CARE IN DEVELOPING SOCIETIES: ESSAYS IN SOCIAL SCIENCE AND MEDICINE. Father Morgan lives with his wife and three daughters on their farm in Bristol, Indiana, where they raise horses, pigs, chickens, turkeys, rabbits, and cows and where he is parish priest in the village Church of Saint John of the Cross. A native of Texas born in 1945, he has held faculty appointments at the University of Connecticut and the University of Texas and visiting research appointments at the University of Chicago, Hebrew Union College, Princeton, and Yale University.

CONTRIBUTORS

(NOTE: Contributors are listed in alphabetical order. When a chapter is co-authored, the first author is listed alphabetically and the co-authors are listed alphabetically immediately under the first author.)

JAMES G. ANDERSON is Professor of Sociology at Purdue University and Visiting Research Professor of Medical Sociology in the Division of Academic Affairs at the Methodist Hospital of Indiana. He holds the Ph.D. from The Johns Hopkins University.

STEPHEN J. JAY is Vice President of Academic Affairs at the Methodist Hospital of Indiana and Professor of Medicine at the Indiana University School of Medicine. He holds the M.D. from the Indiana University Medical School, having done his residency at the Parkland Memorial Hospital in Dallas, TX.

PAMELA ANN GRAY-TOFT is Vice President of Human Resources and Organization Development at the Methodist Hospital of Indiana and holds the Ph.D. for Purdue University. Her B.A. is from the University of Sydney.

Dr. F. P. Lloyd is President and Chief Executive Officer of the Methodist Hospital of Indiana and holds the M.D. from Howard University School of Medicine, having previously been Director of Medical Research at the Methodist Hospital of Indiana.

ROBERT T. ANDERSON, Professor of Anthropology at Mills College, earned his doctorate (Dr.U.P.) in sociology at the University of Paris (Sorbonne) after having earlier been granted the Ph.D. in anthropology at the University of California, Berkeley. He has completed the four-year course of training at Life Chiropractic College-West, where he practices spinal manipulative therapy and serves as Director of Research.

DEBORAH E. BENDER is Assistant Professor in the Department of Community and Family Medicine at the Duke University Medical Center and Associate Director of the Andean Rural Health Project. She holds the Ph.D. in anthropology from American University and the M.P.H. in Health Policy and Administration from the School of Public Health, University of North Carolina at Chapel Hill.

CAROLYN R. CANTLAY is Assistant to the Associate Director of the Andean Rural Health Project at the Duke University Medical Center and candidate for the M.S.Ph.H. from the School of Public Health at the University of North Carolina, Chapel Hill.

GENE E. CARNICOM is Director of Mental Health and Social service

314

at the Mescalero Indian Health Service Hospital on the Mescalero Apache Indian Reservation in New Mexico and holds the Ph.D. in anthropology from Southeastern University and has taught at the University of Maryland and Baylor University.

CHARLES EDWIN CIPOLLA is Associate Professor of Sociology at Salisbury State College and holds the Ph.D. in sociology from the University of Georgia and is presently Chairperson of the Maryland Consortium for Gerontology in Higher Education (1982-1984).

LIBBET CRANDON is Assistant Professor at the University of Connecticut joint position with the Department of Anthropology and the Department of Community Medicine as well as being a faculty member of the Latin American Studies Program and the Center for International Community Health. Her Ph.D. is from the University of Massachusetts.

EUGENE B. GALLAGHER is Professor in the Department of Behavioral Science at the University of Kentucky Medical Center and holds the Ph.D. from Harvard University's Department of Social Relations. His most recent book is INFANTS, MOTHERS, AND DOCTORS (Lexington Books, 1977).

MAUREEN SEARLE is a Postdoctoral Fellow at Duke University and holds the Ph.D. from Yale University.

GARY G. GRENHOLM is Assistant Professor of Health Professions Education at the Center for Educational Development in the Health Services Center of the University of Illinois at Chicago. He holds the Ph.D. in sociology and history of health care systems from the Union Graduate School.

LINDA L. LINDSEY is Assistant Professor of Medical Sociology at the St. Louis College of Pharmacy and holds the Ph.D. from The Case Western Reserve University. She is the co-author of a forthcoming book entitled PHARMACY AND HEALTH CARE SYSTEMS.

SETHA M. LOW is Assistant Professor at the University of Pensylvania and hold the Ph.D. from the University of California, Berkeley, and has recently published with Regrave Publishing of New York CULTURE, POLITICS AND MEDICINE: A MEDICAL ANTHROPOLOGICAL STUDY OF COSTA RICA.

ROBERT J. MOSER is Program Supervisor of the Center for Indochinese Health Education in the Department of medicine at the University of California Medical Center at San Diego. He holds the Ph.D. from Syracuse University.

MOSTAFA H. NAGI is Professor of Sociology at Bowling Green State University and holds the Ph.D. from the University of Connecticut and is the author of a Praeger Publication entitled LABOR FORCE AND EMPLOYMENT IN EGYPT. He spent two years in Kuwait as a Visiting Professor with Kuwait University.

PETER KONG-MING NEW is Professor of Sociology at Florida State University and formerly Professor in the Department of Behavioural Science in the FAculty of Medicine at the University of Toronto. He holds the Ph.D. from the University of Missouri and is past Chair of the Medical Sociology Section of the A.S.A. and President of the Society for Applied Anthropology.

YUET-WAH CHEUNG is Lecturer in Sociology at Lingnan College, Hong-kong and holds the Ph.D. from the University of Toronto. He is a former Managing Editor of the CANADIAN CRIMINOLOGY FORUM.

MARY ROMERO is Assistant Professor at the University of Wisconsin—Parkside. She received her Ph.D. in sociology from the University of Colorado at Boulder.

CLAUDIO SCHUFTAN is Assistant Professor in the Nutrition Department of the School of Public Health and Tropical Medicine at Tulane University and holds the M.D. from the Universidad de Chile.

SHARLEEN HIRSCHI SIMPSON is a Ph.D. candidate in anthropology at the University of Florida and holds the M.S. in community health nursing from the University of California (San Francisco) and a M.A. in anthropology from the University of Arizona.

RUTH D. STARK is Director of the Stanford Women's Health Care Training Project. She is a registered nurse and holds the B.S. from Arizona State University and the M.H.S. from the University of California at Davis.

MEREDETH TURSHEN is Associate Professor in the Public Health Program of the State University of New Jersey Rutgers and holds the Ph.D. from the University of Sussex, England.

ARNOLD P. WENDROFF is a Ph.D. candidate at the City University of New York Graduate Center and holds the M.Phil. from that institution. He is a former member of the Peace Corps serving in Malawi.

WILLIAM WILLARD is Chair of the Department of Comparative American Cultures at Washington State University and holds the Ph.D. in anthropology from the University of Arizona.

SILVERIO ARENAS, JR. is a Graduate Teaching Assistant II in the Department of Comparative American Cultures at Washington State University and holds the M.S. degree. He is a Ph.D. student in clinical psychology at the same institution.

HARVEY WILLIAMS is Associate Professor of Sociology at the University of the Pacific and was a Fulbright Latin American Teaching Fellow at the Universidad Centroamericana in Managua. His B.A. is from Berkeley and the M.A. and Ph.D. in medical sociology from Vanderbilt University.

DENNIS G. WILLMS is a Ph.D. Candidate in anthropology at the University of British Columbia and a Lecturer in the Department of Anthropology at the University of Western Ontario. His fieldwork in anthropology was conducted in the Republic of Kenya, East Africa.